CONVENT OF SOLOVETSK IN THE FROZEN SEA.

RUSSIAN INFANTRY ON EASTERN STEPPE ESCORTED BY KOZAKS AND KIRGHIZ.

FREE RUSSIA.

BY

WILLIAM HEPWORTH DIXON,

AUTHOR OF

"FREE AMERICA," "HER MAJESTY'S TOWER," &c.

NEW YORK:

HARPER & BROTHERS, PUBLISHERS,

FRANKLIN SQUARE.

1870.

PREFACE.

Svobodnaya Rossia—*Free* Russia—is a word on every lip in that great country; at once the Name and Hope of the new empire born of the Crimean war. In past times Russia was free, even as Germany and France were free. She fell before Asiatic hordes; and the Tartar system lasted, in spirit, if not in form, until the war; but since that conflict ended, the old Russia has been born again. This new country—hoping to be pacific, meaning to be Free—is what I have tried to paint.

My journeys, just completed, carried me from the Polar Sea to the Ural Mountains, from the mouth of the Vistula to the Straits of Yeni Kale, including visits to the four holy shrines of Solovetsk, Pechersk, St. George, and Troitsa. My object being to paint the Living People, I have much to say about pilgrims, monks, and parish priests; about village justice, and patriarchal life; about beggars, tramps, and sectaries; about Kozaks, Kalmuks, and Kirghiz; about workmen's artels, burgher rights, and the division of land; about students' revolts and soldiers' grievances; in short, about the Human Forces which underlie and shape the external politics of our time.

Two journeys made in previous years have helped me to judge the reforms which are opening out the Japan-like empire of Nicolas into the Free Russia of the reigning prince.

February, 1870.
6 *St. James's Terrace.*

CONTENTS.

CHAP.		PAGE
I.—	Up North	11
II.—	The Frozen Sea	16
III.—	The Dvina	20
IV.—	Archangel	24
V.—	Religious Life	29
VI.—	Pilgrims	34
VII.—	Father John	40
VIII.—	The Vladika	46
IX.—	A Pilgrim-boat	51
X.—	The Holy Isles	57
XI.—	The Local Saints	62
XII.—	A Monastic Household	68
XIII.—	A Pilgrim's Day	73
XIV.—	Prayer and Labor	78
XV.—	Black Clergy	84
XVI.—	Sacrifice	91
XVII.—	Miracles	96
XVIII.—	The Great Miracle	103
XIX.—	A Convent Spectre	110
XX.—	Story of a Grand Duke	114
XXI.—	Dungeons	118
XXII.—	Nicolas Ilyin	124
XXIII.—	Adrian Pushkin	130
XXIV.—	Dissent	135
XXV.—	New Sects	142
XXVI.—	More New Sects	146
XXVII.—	The Popular Church	151
XXVIII.—	Old Believers	158
XXIX.—	A Family of Old Believers	161
XXX.—	Cemetery of the Transfiguration	167
XXXI.—	Ragoski	173
XXXII.—	Dissenting Politics	179

CHAP.		PAGE
XXXIII.	—CONCILIATION	183
XXXIV.	—ROADS	187
XXXV.	—A PEASANT POET	192
XXXVI.	—FOREST SCENES	197
XXXVII.	—PATRIARCHAL LIFE	202
XXXVIII.	—VILLAGE REPUBLICS	208
XXXIX.	—COMMUNISM	213
XL.	—TOWNS	218
XLI.	—KIEF	222
XLII.	—PANSLAVONIA	225
XLIII.	—EXILE	229
XLIV.	—THE SIBERIANS	235
XLV.	—ST. GEORGE	241
XLVI.	—NOVGOROD THE GREAT	246
XLVII.	—SERFAGE	250
XLVIII.	—A TARTAR COURT	254
XLIX.	—ST. PHILIP	257
L.	—SERFS	262
LI.	—EMANCIPATION	267
LII.	—FREEDOM	272
LIII.	—TSEK AND ARTEL	278
LIV.	—MASTERS AND MEN	284
LV.	—THE BIBLE	289
LVI.	—PARISH PRIESTS	294
LVII.	—A CONSERVATIVE REVOLUTION	299
LVIII.	—SECRET POLICE	306
LIX.	—PROVINCIAL RULERS	312
LX.	—OPEN COURTS	318
LXI.	—ISLAM	324
LXII.	—THE VOLGA	330
LXIII.	—EASTERN STEPPE	336
LXIV.	—DON KOZAKS	341
LXV.	—UNDER ARMS	346
LXVI.	—ALEXANDER	351

FREE RUSSIA.

CHAPTER I.

UP NORTH.

"WHITE SEA!" laughs the Danish skipper, curling his thin red lip; "it is the color of English stout. The bed may be white, being bleached with the bones of wrecked and sunken men; but the waves are never white, except when they are ribbed into ice and furred with snow. A better name is that which the sailors and seal-fishers give it—the Frozen Sea!"

Rounding the North Cape, a weird and hoary mass of rock, projecting far into the Arctic foam, we drive in a south-east course, lashed by the wind and beaten by hail and rain, for two long days, during which the sun never sets and never rises, and in which, if there is dawn at the hour of midnight, there is also dusk at the time of noon.

Leaving the picturesque lines of fiord and alp behind, we run along a dim, unbroken coast, not often to be seen through the pall of mist, until, at the end of some fifty hours, we feel, as it were, the land in our front; a stretch of low-lying shore in the vague and far-off distance, trending away towards the south, like the trail of an evening cloud. We bend in a southern course, between Holy Point (Sviatoi Noss, called on our charts, in rough salt slang, Sweet Nose) and Kanin Cape, towards the Corridor; a strait some thirty miles wide, leading down from the Polar Ocean into that vast irregular dent in the northern shore of Great Russia known as the Frozen Sea.

The land now lying on our right, as we run through the Corridor, is that of the Lapps; a country of barren downs and deep black lakes; over which a few trappers and fishermen roam; subjects of the Tsar and followers of the Orthodox rite; but speaking a language of their own, not understood in the Winter Palace, and following a custom of their fathers, not yet recognized in St. Isaac's Church. Lapland is a tangle of rocks and pools; the rocks very big and broken, the pools very deep and black; with here and there a valley winding through them, on the slopes of which grows a little reindeer moss. Now and then you come upon a patch of birch and pine. No grain will grow in these Arctic zones, and the food of the natives is game and fish. Rye-bread, their only luxury, must be fetched in boats from the towns of Onega and Archangel, standing on the shores of the Frozen Sea, and fed from the warmer provinces in the south. These Lapps are still nomadic; cowering through the winter months in shanties; sprawling through the summer months in tents. Their shanty is a log pyramid thatched with moss to keep out wind and sleet; their tent is of the Comanche type; a roll of reindeer skins drawn slackly round a pole, and opened at the top to let out smoke.

A Lapp removes his dwelling from place to place, as the seasons come and go; now herding game on the hill-sides, now whipping the rivers and creeks for fish; in the warm months, roving inland in search of moss and grass; in the frozen months, drawing nearer to the shore in search of seal and cod. The men are equally expert with the bow, their ancient weapon of defense, and with the birding-piece, the arm of settlers in their midst. The women, looking any thing but lovely in their seal-skin tights and reindeer smocks, are infamous for magic and second sight. In every district of the North, a female Lapp is feared as a witch—an enchantress—who keeps a devil at her side, bound by the powers of darkness to obey her will. She can see into the coming day. She can bring a man ill-luck. She can throw herself out into space, and work upon ships that are sailing past her on the sea. Far out in the Polar brine, in waters where her countrymen fish for cod, stands a lump of rock, which the crews regard as a Woman and her Child. Such fantasies are common in these Arctic seas, where the waves wash in and out through the cliffs, and rend and carve them into wondrous shapes. A rock on the North Cape is called the Friar; a group of islets near that cape is known as the Mother and her Daughters. Seen through the veil of Polar mist, a block of stone may take a mysterious form; and that lump of rock in the Polar waste, which the cod-fishers say is like a woman with her child, has long been known to them as the Golden Hag. She is rarely seen; for the clouds in summer, and the snows in winter, hide her charms from the fishermen's eyes; but when she deigns to show her face in the clear bright sun, her children hail her with a song of joy, for on seeing her face they know that their voyage will be blessed by a plentiful harvest of skins and fish.

Woe to the mariner tossed upon their coast!

The land on our left is the Kanin peninsula; part of that region of heath and sand over which the Samoyed roams; a desert of ice and snow, still wilder than the countries hunted by the Lapp. A land without a village, without a road, without a field, without a name; for the Russians who own it have no name for it save that of the Samoyeds' Land; this province of the great empire trends away north and east from the walls of Archangel and the waters of Kanin Cape to the summits of the Ural chain and the Iron Gates of the Kara Sea. In her clefts and ridges snow never melts; and her shore-lines, stretching towards the sunrise upwards of two thousand miles, are bound in icy chains for eight months in the twelve. In June, when the winter goes away, suddenly the slopes of a few favored valleys grow green with reindeer moss; slight specks of verdure in a landscape which is even then dark with rock and gray with rime. On this green moss the reindeer feed, and on these camels of the Polar zone the wild men of the country live.

Samoyed means cannibal—man-eater; but whether the men who roam over these sands and bogs deserve their evil fame is one of the questions open to new lights. They use no fire in cooking food; and perhaps it is because they eat the reindeer raw that they have come to be accused of fondness for human flesh. In chasing the game on which they feed, the Samoyeds crept over the Ural Mountains from their far-off home in the north of Asia, running it down in a tract too cold and bare for any other race of men to dwell on. Here the Zarayny found them, thrashed them, set them to work.

These Zarayny, a clever and hardy people, seem connected in type and speech with the Finns; and they are thought to be the remnant of an ancient colony of trappers. Fairer than the Samoyeds, they live in log huts like other Russians, and are rich in herds of reindeer, which they compel the Samoyeds to tend like slaves. This service to the higher race is slowly changing the savage Samoyed into a civilized man; since it gives him a sense of property and a respect for life. A red man kills the beast he hunts; kills it beyond his need, in the animal wantonness of strength. A Samoyed would do the same; but the Zarayny have taught him to rear and tend, as well as to hunt and snare, his food. A savage, only one degree above the Pawnee and the Ute, a Samoyed builds no shed; plants no field; and owns no property in the soil. He dwells, like the Lapp, in a tent—a roll of skins, sewn on to each other with gut, and twisted round a shaft, left open at the top, and furnished with skins to lie on like an Indian lodge. No art is lavished on this roll of skin; not so much as the totem which a Cheyenne daubs on his prairie tent. Yet the Samoyed has notions of village life, and even of government. A collection of tents he calls a Choom; his choom is ruled by a medicine-man; the official name of whom in Russian society is a pope.

The reigning Emperor has sent some priests to live among these tribes, just as in olden times Marfa of Novgorod sent her popes and monks into Lapland and Karelia; hoping to divert the natives from their Pagan habits and bring them over to the church of Christ. Some good, it may be hoped, is done by these Christian priests; but a Russ who knows the country and the people smiles when you ask him about their doings in the Gulf of Obi and around the Kara Sea. One of these missionaries whom I chanced to meet had pretty well ceased to be a civilized man. In name, he was a pope; but he lived and dressed like a medicine-man; and he was growing into the likeness of a Mongol in look and gait. Folk said he had taken to his bosom a native witch.

Through the gateway held by these tribes we enter into Russia—Great Russia; that country of the old Russians, whose plains and forests the Tartar horsemen never swept.

Why enter Russia by these northern gates? If the Great

Mogul had conquered England in the seventeenth century; if Asiatic manners had been paramount in London for two hundred years; if Britain had recovered her ancient freedom and civil life, where would a foreign observer, anxious to see the English as they are, begin his studies? Would he not begin them in Massachusetts rather than in Middlesex, even though he should have to complete his observations on the Mersey and the Thames?

A student of the Free Russia born of the Crimean War, must open his work of observation in the northern zones; since it is only within this region of lake and forest that he can find a Slavonic race which has never been tainted by foreign influence, never been broken by foreign yoke. The zone from Onega to Perm—a country seven times larger than France — was colonized from Novgorod the Great, while Novgorod was yet a free city, rich in trade, in piety, in art; a rival of Frankfort and Florence; and, like London and Bruges, a station of the Hanseatic League. Her colonies kept the charter of their freedom safe. They never bent to the Tartar yoke, nor learned to walk in the German ways. They knew no masters, and they held no serfs. "We never had amongst us," said to me an Archangel farmer, "either a noble or a slave." They clung, for good and evil, to their ancient life; and when the Patriarch Nikon reformed the Church in a Byzantine sense (1667), as the Tsar Godunof had transformed the village in a Tartar sense (1601), they disowned their patriarch just as they had denied their Tsar. In spite of every force that could be brought against them by a line of autocrats, these free colonists have not been driven into accepting the reformed official liturgies in preference to their ancient rites. They kept their native speech, when it was ceasing to be spoken in the capital; and when the time was ripe, they sent out into the world a boy of genius, peasant-born and reared (the poet, Michael Lomonosof), to impose that popular language on the college, on the senate, on the court.

CHAPTER II.

THE FROZEN SEA.

At Cape Intsi we pass from the narrow straits dividing the Lapp country from the Samoyed country into this northern gulf.

About twice the size of Lake Superior in the United States, this Frozen Sea has something of the shape of Como; one narrow northern bay, extending to the town of Kandalax, in Russian Lapland; and two southern bays, divided from each other by a broad sandy peninsula, the home of a few villagers employed in snaring cod and hunting seal. These southern bays are known, from the rivers which fall into them, as Onega Bay and Dvina Bay. At the mouths of these rivers stand the two trading ports of Onega and Archangel.

The open part of this inland gulf is deep—from sixty to eighty fathoms; and in one place, off the entrance into Kandalax Bay, the line goes down no less than a hundred and sixty fathoms. Yet the shore is neither steep nor high. The gulf of Onega is rich in rocks and islets; many of them only banks of sand and mud, washed out into the sea from the uplands of Kargopol; but in the wide entrance of Onega Bay, between Orlof Point and the town of Kem, stands out a notable group of islets—Solovetsk, Anzersk, Moksalma, Zaet and others; islets which play a singular part in the history of Russia, and connect themselves with curious legends of the Imperial court.

In Solovetsk, the largest of this group of islets, stands the famous convent of that name; the house of Saints Savatie and Zosima; the refuge of St. Philip; the shrine to which emperors and peasants go on pilgrimage; the haunt of that Convent Spectre which one hears described in the cod-fisher's boat and in the Kozak's tent; the scene of many great events, and of one event which Russians have agreed to sing and paint as the most splendid miracle of these latter days.

Off the Dvina bar stands the new tower and lighthouse, where the pilots live; a shaft some eighty feet high, not often to be seen above the hanging drapery of fog. A pilot comes on board; a man of soft and patient face, with gray-blue eyes, and flow of brownish hair, who tells us in a bated tone—as though he feared we might be vexed with him and beat him—that the tide is ebbing on the bar, and we shall have to wait for the flow. "Wait for the tide!" snaps our Danish jarl; "stand by, we'll make our course." The sun has just peeped out from behind his veil; but the clouds droop low and dark, and every one feels that a gale is coming on. Two barks near the bar—the "Thera" and the "Olga"—bob and reel like tipsy men; yet our pale Russ pilot, urged by the stronger will, gives way with a smile; and our speed being lowered by half, we push on slowly towards the line of red and black signals floating in our front.

The "Thera" and the "Olga" are soon behind us, shivering in all their sheets, like men in the clutch of ague—left in our wake to a swift and terrible doom. In half an hour we pass the line of buoys, and gain the outer port.

Like all great rivers, the Dvina has thrown up a delta of isles and islets near her mouth, through which she pours her flood into the sea by a dozen arms. None of these dozen arms can now be laid down as her main entrance; for the river is more capricious than the sea; so that a skipper who leaves her by one outlet in August, may have to enter by another when he comes back to her in June. The main passage in the old charts flowed past the Convent of St. Nicolas; then came the turn of Rose Island; afterwards the course ran past the guns of Fort Dvina: but the storms which swept the Polar seas two summers since, destroyed that passage as an outlet for the larger kinds of craft. The port police looked on in silence. What were they to do? Archangel was cut off from the sea, until a Danish blacksmith, who had set up forge and hammer in the new port, proposed that the foreign traders should hire a steamer and find a deliverance for their ships. "If the water goes down," he said, "it must have made a way for itself. Let us try to find it out." A hundred pounds were lodged in the bank, a steamer was hired, and a channel, called the Maimax arm, was found to be deep enough for ships to pass. The work was done, the city opened to the sea; but then came the question of port authorities and their rules. No bark had ever left the city by this Maimax arm; no rules had been made for such a course of trade; and the port police could not permit a ship to sail unless her papers were drawn up in the usual forms. In vain the merchants told them the case was new, and must be governed by a rule to match. They might as well have reasoned with a Turkish bey. Here rode a fleet of vessels, laden with oats and deals for the Elbe, the Maas, and the Thames; there ran the abundant Maimax waters to the sea; but the printed rules of the port, unconscious of the freaks of nature and of the needs of man, forbade this fleet to sail.

Appeal was made to Prince Gagarine, governor of Archangel: but Gagarine, though he laughed at these port rules and their forms, had no deals and grain of his own on board the ships. Gospodin Sredine, a keen-witted master of the customs, tried to open the ports and free the ships by offering to put officers on the new channel; but the police were—the police. In vain they heard that the goods might spoil, that the money they cost was idle, and that every ruble wasted would be so much loss to their town.

To my question, "How was it arranged at last?" a skipper, who was one of the prisoners in the port, replies, "I will tell you in a word. We sent to Petersburg; the minister spoke to the Emperor; and here is what we have heard they said. 'What's all this row in Archangel about?' asks the Emperor. 'It is all about a new mouth being found in the Dvina, sir, and ships that want to sail down it, sir, because the old channel is now shoaled up, sir.' 'In God's name,' replied the Emperor, 'let the ships go out by any channel they can find.' "

Whether the thing was done in this sailor-like way, or by the more likely method of official report and order, the Maimax mouth was opened to the world in spite of the port police and their printed rules.

A Hebrew of the olden time would have called this sea a whited sepulchre. Even men of science, to whom wintry storms may be summed up in a line of figures—so many ships in the pack, so many corpses on the beach—can find in the records of this frozen deep some show of an excuse for that old

Lapland superstition of the Golden Hag. The year before last was a tragic time, and the memory of one dark day of wrack and death has not yet had time to fade away.

At the end of June, a message, flashed from the English consul at Archangel—a man to represent his country on these shores—alarmed our board of trade by such a cry for help as rarely reaches a public board. A hundred ships were perishing in the ice. These ships were Swedes, Danes, Dutch, and English; luggers, sloops, corvettes, and smacks; all built of wood, and many of them English manned. Could any thing be done to help them? "Help is coming," flashed the wires from Charing Cross; and on the first day of July, two steamers left the Thames to assist in rescuing those ships and men from the Polar ice. On the fifteenth night from home these English boats were off Cape Gorodetsk on the Lapland coast, and when morning dawned they were striving to cross the shallow Archangel bar. They could not pass; yet the work of humanity was swiftly and safely done by the English crews.

That fleet of all nations, English, Swedish, Dutch, and Danish, left the Dvina ports on news coming up the delta that the pack was breaking up in the gulf; but on reaching that Corridor through which we have just now come, they met the ice swaying to and fro, and crashing from point to point, as the changing wind veered round from north to south. By careful steering they went on, until they reached the straits between Kanin Cape and Holy Point. The ice in their front was now thick and high; no passage through it could be forced; and their vessels reeled and groaned under the blows which they suffered from the floating drifts. A brisk north wind arose, and blowing three days on without a pause, drove blocks and bergs of ice from the Polar Ocean down into the gut, forcing the squadrons to fall back, and closing up every means of escape into the open sea. The ships rolled to and fro, the helmsmen trying to steer them in mid-channel, but the currents were now too strong to stem, and the helpless craft were driven upon the Lapland reefs, where the crews soon saw themselves folded and imprisoned in the pack of ice.

Like shots from a fort, the crews on board the stronger ships could hear in the grim waste around them hull after hull crashing up, in that fierce embrace, like fine glass trinkets in a strong man's hand. When a ship broke up and sank, the crew leaped out upon the ice and made for the nearest craft, from which in a few hours more they might have to fly in turn. One man was wrecked five times in a single day; each of the boats to which he clung for safety parting beneath his feet and gurgling down into the frozen deep.

When the tale of loss was made up by the relieving steamers, this account was sent home to the Board of Trade:

The number of ships abandoned by their crews was sixty-four; of this great fleet of ships, fourteen were saved and fifty lost. Of the fifty ships lost in those midsummer days, eighteen were English built and manned; and the master mentions with a noble pride, that only one ship flying the English flag was in a state to be recovered from the ice after being abandoned by her crew.

It would be well for our fame if the natives had no other tales to tell of an English squadron in the Frozen Sea.

CHAPTER III.

THE DVINA.

By the Maimax arm we steam through the delta for some twenty miles; past low, green banks and isles like those in the Missouri bed; though the loam in the Dvina is not so rich and black as that on the American stream. Yet these small isles are bright with grass and scrub. Beyond them, on the main-land, lies a fringe of pines, going back into space as far as the eye can pierce.

The low island lying on your right as you scrape the bar is called St. Nicolas, after that sturdy priest, who is said to have smitten the heretic Arius on his cheek. No one knows where this Nicolas lived and died; for it is clear from the Acta that he had no part in the Council of Nice. The Book of Saints describes him as born in Liki and living in Mira; whence they call him the Saint of Mirliki; but not a line of his writing is extant, and the virtues assigned to him are of opposing kinds. He is a patron of nobles and of children, of sailors, of cadgers, and of pilgrims. Yet, in spite of his doubtful birth and genius, Nicolas is a popular saint. Poor people like him as one who is good to the poor; a friend of beggars, fishermen and tramps. A Russian turns to him as the hope of starving and drowning men; so that his name is often heard, his image often seen, in these northern wilds; more than all else, on the banks of rivers and on the margins of the Frozen Sea. A peasant learns with delight from his Book of Saints (his Bible, Epos, Drama, Code, and History all in one) that Nicolas is the most potent saint in heaven; sitting on the right hand of God; and having a cohort of three hundred angels, armed and ready to obey his nod. A mujik asked a foreign friend to tell him who will be God when God dies? "My good fellow," said he, smiling, "God will never die." At first the peasant seemed perplexed. "Never die!" and then a light fell on him. "Yes," he retorted, slowly; "I see it now. You are an unbeliever; you have no religion. Look you; I have been better taught. God will one day die; for He is very old; and then St. Nicolas will get his place."

Though he is common to all Russians—adored on the Dnieper, on the Volkhof, on the Moskva, no less than on the Dvina —he is worshipped with peculiar zeal in these northern zones. Here he is the sailor's saint, the adventurer's help; and all the paintings of him show that his watchful eyes are bent in eager tenderness upon the swirl and passion of the Frozen Sea. This delta might be called his province; for not only was the island on your right called after him, but also the ancient channel, and the bay itself. The oldest cloister in the district bears his name.

On passing into the Maimax arm, your eyes—long dimmed by the sight of sombre rock, dark cloud, and sullen surf—are charmed by soft, green grass and scrub; but the sight goes vainly out, through reeds and copse, in search of some cheery note of house and farm. One log hut you pass, and only one. Two men are standing near a bank, in a little clearing of the wood; a lad is idling in a frail canoe, which the wash of your steamer lifts and laves; but no one lodges in the shed; the men and boy have come from a village some miles away. Dropping down the river in their boat to cut down grass for their cows, and gather up fuel for their winter fires, they will jump into their canoe at vespers, and hie them home.

On the banks of older channels the villages are thick; slight groups of sheds and churches, with a cloister here and there, and a scatter of windmills whirling against the sky; each village and mill in its appointed place, without the freak and medley of original thought. Here nothing is done by individual force; a pope, an elder, an imperial officer, must have his say in every case; and not a mouse can stir in a Russian town, except by leave of some article in a printed code. Fort Dvina was erected on a certain neck of land in the ancient river-bed, and nature was expected to conform herself forever to the order fixed by imperial rule.

On all these banks you note a forest of memorial crosses. When a sailor meets with bad weather, he goes on shore and sets up a cross. At the foot of this symbol he kneels in prayer, and when a fair wind rises, he leaves his offering on the lonely coast. When the peril is sharp, the whole ship's crew will land, cut down and carve tall trees, and set up a memorial with names and dates. All round the margins of the Frozen Sea these pious witnesses abound; and they are most of all numerous on the rocks and banks of the Holy Isles. Each cross erected is the record of a storm.

Some of these memorial crosses are historic marks. One tree, set up by Peter the Great when he escaped from the wreck of his ship in the frozen deep, has been taken from the spot where he planted it, and placed in the cathedral at Archangel. "This cross was made by Captain Peter," says a tablet cut in the log by the Emperor's own knife; and Peter being a carver in wood and stone, the work is not without touches of art and grace. Might not a word be urged in favor of this custom of the sea, which leaves a picture and a blessing on every shore? An English mariner is apt to quit a coast on which he has been kept a prisoner by adverse winds with a curse in his heart and a bad name on his tongue. Jack is a very grand fellow in his way; but surely there is a beauty, not less winning than the piety, in this habit of the Russian tar.

Climbing up the river, you come upon fleets of rafts and praams, on which you may observe some part of the native life. The rafts are floats of timber—pine logs, lashed together with twigs of willow, capped with a tent of planks, in which the owner sleeps, while his woodmen lie about in the open air when they are not paddling the raft and guiding it down the stream. These rafts come down the Dvina and its feeders for a thousand miles. Cut in the great forests of Vologda and Nijni Konets, the pines are dragged to the water-side, and knitted by rude hands into these broad, floating masses. At the towns some sturdy helpers may be hired for nothing; many of the poor peasants being anxious to get down the river on their way to the shrines of Solovetsk. For a passage on the raft these pilgrims take a turn at the oar, and help the owners to guide her through the shoals.

In the praams the life is a little less bleak and rough than it is on board the rafts. In form the praam is like the toy called a Noah's ark; a huge hull of coarse pine logs, riveted and clamped with iron, covered by a peaked plank roof. A big one will cost from six to seven hundred rubles (the ruble may be reckoned for the moment as half a crown), and will carry from six to eight hundred tons of oats and rye. A small section of the praam is boarded off to be used as a room. Some bits of pine are shaped into a stool, a table, and a shelf. From the roof-beam swings an iron pot, in which the boatmen cook their food while they are out in the open stream; at other times—that is to say, when they are lying in port—no fire is allowed on board, not even a pipe is lighted, and the watermen's victuals must be cooked on shore. Four or five logs lashed together serve them for a launch, by means of which they can easily paddle to the bank.

Like the rafts, these praams take on board a great many pilgrims from the upper country; giving them a free passage down, with a supply of tea and black bread as rations, in return for their labor at the paddle and the oar. Not much labor is required, for the praam floats down with the stream. Arrived at Archangel, she empties her cargo of oats into the foreign ships (most of them bound for the Forth, the Tyne, and the Thames), and then she is moored to the bank, cut up, and sold. Some of her logs may be used again for building sheds, the rest is of little use, except for the kitchen and the stove.

The new port of Archangel, called Solambola, is a scattered handful of log houses, that would remind you of a Swiss hamlet were it not for the cluster of green cupolas and spires, reminding you still more strongly of a Bulgarian town. Each belfry bears a crescent, crowned by a cross. Along the brink of the river runs a strand, some six or eight feet above the level plain; beyond this strand the fields fall off, so that the country might be laid under water, while the actual strand stood high and dry. The new port is a water-village; for in the spring-time, when the ice is melting up stream, the flood goes over all, and people have to pass from house to magazine in boats.

Not a grain of this strand in front of the sheds is Russ; the whole line of road being built of ballast brought into the Dvina by foreign ships, and chiefly from English ports. This ridge of pebble, marl, and shells comes nearly all from London, Liverpool, and Leith; the Russian trade with England having this peculiarity, that it is wholly an export trade. A Russian sends us every thing he has for sale; his oats, his flax, his deals, his mats, his furs, his tar; he buys either nothing, or next to nothing, in return. A little salt and wine, a few saw-mills—chiefly for foreign account—are what come back from England by way of barter with the North. The payment is gold, the cargo ballast; and the balance of account between the two countries is—a strand of English marl and shells.

CHAPTER IV.

ARCHANGEL.

On passing up the Dvina from the Polar Sea, your first experience shows that you are sailing from the West into the East.

When scraping the bar, you notice that the pilot refuses to drop his lead. "Never mind," he says, "it is deep enough; we shall take no harm; unless it be the will of God." A pilot rarely throws out his line. The regulation height of water on the bar is so and so; and dropping a rope into the sea will not, he urges, increase the depth.

When climbing through the delta, you observe that every peasant on the shore, both man and woman, wears a sheepskin wrap—the garment of nomadic tribes; not worn as a rule by any of the settled races on the earth.

In catching a first glimpse of the city, you are struck by the forest of domes and spires; the domes all color and the spires all gold; a cluster of sacred buildings, you are apt to fancy, out of all proportion to the number of people dwelling in the town.

On feeling for the river-side, a captain finds no quay, no dock, no landing-pier, no stair. He brings-to as he can; and drags his boat into position with a pole, as he would have to do in the Turkish ports of Vidin and Rustchuk. No help is given him from the shore. Except in some ports of Palestine, you will nowhere find a wealthy trade conducted by such simple means.

When driving up that strand of English marl, towards the city of which you see the golden lights, you hear that in Archangel, as in Aleppo, there is no hotel; not even, as in Aleppo, a public khan.

Full of these signs, you turn to your maps, and notice that Archangel lies a little to the east of Mecca and Trebizond.

Yet these highways of the Dvina are not those of the genuine East. Baksheesh is hardly known. Your pilot may sidle up, and give your hand a squeeze (all Russians of the lower ranks are fond of squeezing!) on your safe arrival in the port; and if you fail to take his hint, as probably you will, he whispers meekly in your ear, as though he were telling you an important secret, that very few strangers come into the Dvina, but those few never fail to reward with na-chai (tea-money) the man who has brought them in from the sea of storms. But from the port officials nothing can be got by giving vails in the bad old way. Among the many wise things which have been done in the present reign, is that of reducing the number of men employed in the customs, and of largely increasing the salaries paid to them by the crown. No man is now underpaid for the service he has to do, and no one in the Customs is allowed to accept a bribe.

Prince Obolenski, chief of this great department, is a man of high courage as well as high principles, and under his eye the service has been purged of those old abuses which caused it to be branded with black and red in so many books. One case came under my notice, in which a foreign skipper had given to an officer in the port a dozen oranges; not as a bribe, but as a treat; oranges being rarely seen in this northern clime. Yet, when the fact was found out by his local superior, the man was reduced from a high post in the service to a low one. "If he will take an orange, he will take a ruble," said his chief; and a year elapsed before the offender was restored to his former grade.

The new method is not so Asiatic as the old; but in time it will lead the humblest officer in Russia to feel that he is a man.

Archangel is not a port and city in the sense in which Hamburg and Hull are ports and cities; clusters of docks and sheds, with shops, and wagons, and a busy private trade. Archangel is a camp of shanties, heaped around groups of belfries, cupolas and domes. Imagine a vast green marsh along the bank of a broad brown river, with mounds of clay cropping here and there out of the peat and bog; put buildings on these mounds of clay; adorn the buildings with frescoes, crown them with cupolas and crosses; fill in the space between church and convent, convent and church, with piles and planks, so as to make ground for gardens, streets, and yards; cut two wide lanes, from the church called Smith's Wife to the monastery of St. Michael, three or four miles in length; connect these lanes and the stream by a dozen clearings; paint the walls of church and convent white, the domes green and blue; surround the log houses with open gardens; stick a geranium, a fuschia, an oleander into every window; leave the grass growing everywhere in street and clearing—and you have Archangel.

Half-way from Smith's Wife's quarter to the Monastery, stand, in picturesque groups, the sites determined by the mounds of clay, the public buildings; fire-tower, cathedral, town-hall, court of justice, governor's house, museum; new and rough, with a glow of bright new paint upon them all. The collection in the museum is poor; the gilt on the cathedral rich. When seen from a distance, the domes and turrets of Archangel give it the appearance of some sacred Eastern city rather than a place of trade.

This sea-port on the Dvina is the only port in Russia proper. Astrachan is a Tartar port; Odessa an Italian port; Riga a Livonian port; Helsingfors a Finnish port. None of these outlets to the sea are in Russia proper, nor is the language spoken in any of them Russ. Won by the sword, they may be lost by the sword. As foreign conquests, they must follow the fate of war; and in Russia proper their loss might not be deeply felt; Great Russia being vast enough for independence and rich enough for happiness, even if she had to live without that belt of lesser Russias in which for her pride and punishment she has lately been clasped and strained. Archangel, on the other side, is her one highway to the sea; the outlet of her northern waters; her old and free communication with the world; an outlet given to her by God, and not to be taken away from her by man.

Such as they are, the port and city of Archangel owe their birth to English adventure, their prosperity to English trade.

In the last year of King Edward the Sixth, an English ship, in pressing her prow against the sand-banks of the Frozen Sea, hoping to light on a passage to Cathay, met with a broad sheet of water, flowing steadily and swiftly from the south. That ship was the "Bonaventure;" her master was Richard Challoner; who had parted from his chief, Sir Hugh Willoughby, in a storm. The water coming down from the south was fresh. A low green isle lay on his port, which he laid down in his chart as Rose Island; afterwards to be famous as the cradle of our northern trade. Pushing up the stream in search of a town, he came upon a small cloister, from the monks of which he learned that he was not in Cathay, but in Great Russia.

Great was a name given by old Russians, not only to the capital of their country, but to the country itself. Their capital was Great Novgorod; their country was Great Russia.

Sir Hugh Willoughby was driven by storms into "the harbor of death," in which he and his crews all perished in the ice; while his luckier lieutenant pushed up the Dvina to Vologda, whence he forced his way to Moscow, and saw the Grand Duke, Ivan the Fourth. In that age Russia was known to Europe as Moscovia, from the city of Moscow; a city which had ravaged her old pre-eminence from Novgorod, and made herself mistress of Great Russia.

Challoner was wrecked and drowned on his second voyage; but those who followed him built an English factory for trade on Rose Island, near the cloister; while the Russians, on their side, built a fort and town on the Dvina, some thirty miles from its mouth; in which position they could watch the strangers in their country, and exchange with them their wax and skins for cotton shirts and pewter pans. The builder of this fort and town was Ivan Vassilivitch, known to us as Ivan the Terrible—Ivan the Fourth.

Ivan called his town the New Castle of St. Michael the Archangel; an unwieldy name, which his raftmen and sailors soon cut down—as raftmen and sailors will—into the final word. On English lips the name would have been St. Michael; but a Russian shrinks from using the name of that prince of heaven. To him Michael is not a saint, as Nicolas and George are saints; but a power, a virtue, and a sanctity, before whose lance the mightiest of rebel angels fell. No Russian speaks of this celestial warrior as a saint. He is the archangel; greatest of the host; selected champion of the living God. Convents and churches are inscribed to him by his celestial rank; but never by his personal name. The great cathedral of Moscow is only known as the Archangel's church. Michael is understood; for who but Michael could be meant? Ivan Vassilivitch had such a liking for this fighting power, that on his death-bed he gave orders for his body to be laid, not in that splendid pile of St. Vassili, which he had spent so much time and money in building near the Holy Gate, but in a chapel of the Archangel's church; and there the grim old tyrant lies, in a plain stone coffin, covered with a velvet pall.

Peter the Great rebuilt Archangel on a larger scale with more enduring brick. Peter was fond of the Frozen Sea, and twice, at least, he sailed over it to pray in the Convent of Solovetsk; a place which he valued, not only as a holy shrine, but as a frontier fortress, held by his brave old Russ against the Lapps and Swedes. Archangel was made by Peter his peculiar care; and masons were fetched from Holland to erect his lines of bastions, magazines, and quays. A castle rose from the ground on the river bank; an island was reclaimed from the river and trimmed with trees; a summer palace was designed and built for the Tsar. A fleet of ships was sent to command the Dvina mouth. In fact, Archangel was one of the three sites—St. Petersburg and Taganrog being the other two—on which the Emperor designed to build cities that, unlike Novgorod and Moscow, should be at once fortresses and ports.

The city of Ivan and the city of Peter have each in turn gone by. Not a stone of Ivan's town remains; for his new castle and monastery, being built of logs, were duly rotted by rain and consumed by fire. A fort and a monastery still protect and adorn the place; but these have both been raised in more recent years. Of Peter's city, though it seemed to be solid as the earth itself, hardly a house is standing to show the style. A heap of arches, riven by frost and blackened by smoke, is seen on the Dvina bank; a pretty kiosk peeps out from between the birches on Moses Isle; and these are all!

In our western eyes Archangel may seem to be over-rich in domes, as the delta may appear to be over-rich in crosses; but then, in our western eyes, the city is a magazine of oats and tar, of planks and skins; while in native eyes it is the archangel's house, the port of Solovetsk, and the gate of God.

CHAPTER V.

RELIGIOUS LIFE.

A FRIEND is one day driving me from house to house in Archangel, making calls, when we observe from time to time a smart officer going into courtyards.

"This man appears to be dogging our steps."

"Ha!" laughs my friend; "that fellow is an officer of police."

"Why is he following us?"

"He is not following us; he is going his rounds; he is warning the owners of all good houses that four candles must be lighted in each front window to-night at eight o'clock."

"Four candles! For what?"

"The Emperor. You know it is his angel's day; you will see the streets all lighted—by police suggestion—at the proper time."

"Surely the police have no need to interfere. The Emperor is popular; and who can forget that this is St. Alexander's Day?"

"There you are wrong; our people hardly know the court at all. You see these shops are open, yon stalls are crowded, that mill is working, as they would be on the commonest day in all the year. A mujik cares but little for kings and queens; he only knows his own angel—his peculiar saint. If you would test his reverence, ask him to make a coat, repair a tarantass, or fetch in wood, on his angel's day. He would rather die at your feet than sully such a day with work. In fact, a mujik is not a courtier—he is only a religious man."

My friend is right in the main, though his illustration takes me as a stranger by surprise.

The first impulse in a Russian heart is duty to God. It is an impulse of observance and respect; at once moral and ceremonial; an impulse with an inner force and an outer form; present in all ranks of society, and in all situations of life; in an army on the march, in a crowd at a country fair, in a lecture-room full of students; showing itself in a princess dancing at a ball, in a huckster writing at his desk, in a peasant tugging at his cart, in a burglar rioting on his spoil.

This duty adorns the land with fane and altar, even as it touches the individual man with penitential grace. Every village must have its shrine, as every child must have his guardian angel and baptismal cross. The towns are rich in churches and convents, just as the citizens are rich in spiritual gifts. I counted twenty spires in Kargopol, a city of two thousand souls. Moscow is said to have four hundred and thirty churches and chapels; Kief, in proportion to her people, is no less rich. All public events are celebrated by the building of a church. In Kief, St. Andrew's Church commemorates the visit of an apostle; St. Mary's, the introduction of Christianity. In Moscow, St. Vassili's commemorates the conquest of Kazan; the Donskoi Convent, Fedor's victory over the Crim Tartars; St. Saviour's, the expulsion of Napoleon. In Petersburg, St. Alexander's commemorates the first victory won by Russians over Swedes; St. Isaac's, the birth of Peter the Great; Our Lady of Kazan's, the triumphs of Russian arms against the Persian, Turk, and Frank. Where we should build a bridge, the Russians raise a house of God: so that their political and social history is brightly written in their sacred piles.

By night and day, from his cradle to his grave, a Russian lives, as it were, with God; giving up to His service an amount of time and money which no one ever dreams of giving in the West. Like his Arabian brother, the Slavonian is a religious being; and the gulf which separates such men from the Saxon and the Gaul is broader than a reader who has never seen an Eastern town will readily picture to his mind.

An Oriental is a man of prayer. He seems to live for heaven and not for earth; and even in his commonest acts, he pays respect to what he holds to be a celestial law. One hand is clean, the other unclean. One cup is lawful, another cup is unlawful. If he rises from his couch a prayer is on his lips; if he sits down to rest a blessing is in his heart. When he buys and when he sells, when he eats and when he drinks, he remembers that the Holy One is nigh. If poor in purse, he may be rich in grace; his cabin a sanctuary, his craft a service, his daily life an act of prayer.

Enter into a Russian shed—you find a chapel. Every room in that shed is sanctified; for in every room there is a sacred image, a domestic altar, and a household god. The inmate steps into that room with reverence; standing for a moment at the threshold, baring his head, crossing himself, and uttering a saintly verse. Once in the house, he feels himself in the Presence, and every act of his life is dedicated to Him in whom we live and move. "Slava Bogu"—Glory to God—is a phrase forever on his lips; not as a phrase only, to be uttered in a light vein, as a formal act, but with an inward bending and confession of the soul. He fasts very much, and pays a respect beyond our measure to sacred places and to sacred things. He thinks day and night of his angel; and payments are made by him at church for prayers to be addressed in his name to that guardian spirit. He finds a divine enjoyment in the sound of cloister-bells, a foretaste of heaven in kneeling near the bones of saints. The charm of his life is a profound conviction of his own unworthiness in the sight of God, and no mere pride of rank ever robs him of the hope that some one higher in virtue than himself will prove his advocate at the throne of grace. He feels a rapture, strange to a Frank, in the cadence of a psalm, and the taste of consecrated bread is to him a fearful joy. Such things are to him not only things of life and death, but of the everlasting life and the ever-present death.

The church is with a Russian early and late. A child is hardly considered as born into the world, until he has been blessed by the pope and made by him a "servant of God."

As the child begins, so he goes on. The cross which he receives in baptism—which he receives in his cradle, and carries to his grave—is but a sign. Religion goes with him to his school, his play-ground, and his workshop. Every act of his life must begin with supplication and end with thanks. A school has a set of prayers for daily use; with forms to be used on commencing a term, on parting for holidays, on engaging a new teacher, on opening a fresh course. It is the same with boys who work in the mill and on the farm. Every one has his office to recite and his fast to keep. The fasting is severe; and more than half the days in a Russian year are days of fasting and humiliation. During the seven weeks before Easter, no flesh, no fish, no milk, no eggs, no butter, can be touched. For five or six weeks before St. Peter's Day, and for six weeks before Christmas Day, no flesh, no milk, no eggs, no butter, can be used. For fifteen days in August, a fast of great severity is held in honor of the Virgin's death. A man must fast on every Wednesday and Friday throughout the year, eating nothing save fish. Besides keeping these public fasts, a man should fast the whole week before making his confession and receiving his sacrament; abstaining from every dainty, from sugar, cigarettes, and every thing cooked with fire.

On the eve of Epiphany—the day for blessing the water—

no one is suffered to eat or drink until the blessing has been given, about four o'clock, when the consecrated water may be sipped and dinner must be eaten with a joyful heart. To fetch away the water, people carry into church their pots and pans, their jacks and urns; each peasant with a taper in his hand, which he lights at the holy fire, and afterwards burns before his angel until it dies.

Every new house in which a man lives, every new shop which he opens for trade, must be blessed. A man who moves from one lodging to another must have his second lodging purified by religious rites. Ten or twelve times a year, the parish priest, attended by his reader and his deacon, enters into every house in his district, sprinkles the rooms with holy water, cleanses them with prayer, and signs them with the cross.

In his marriage, on his dying bed, the Church is with a Russ even more than at his birth and baptism. Marriage, held to be a sacrament, and poetically called a man's coronation, is a long and intricate affair, consisting of many offices, most of them perfect in symbolism as they are lovely in art. Prayers are recited, rings exchanged, and blessings invoked; after which the ceremony is performed; an actual circling of the brows with a golden rim. "Ivan, servant of God," cries the pope, as he puts the circlet on his brows, "is crowned with Nadia, handmaid of God." The bride is crowned with Ivan, servant of God.

Some people wear their bridal crowns for a week, then put them back into the sacristy, and obtain a blessing in exchange. Religion touches the lowliest life with a passing ornament. The bride is always a queen, the groom is always a king, on their wedding-day.

A man's angel is with him early and late; a spirit with whom he dares not trifle; one whom he can never deceive. He puts a picture of this angel in his bedroom, over the pillow on which he sleeps. A light should burn before that picture day and night. The angel has to be propitiated by prayers, recited by a consecrated priest. His day must be strictly kept, and no work done, except works of charity, from dawn to dusk. A feast must be spread, the family and kindred called under one roof, presents made to domestics, and alms dispensed to the poor. On his angel's day a man must not only go to church, but buy from the priests some consecrated loaves, which he must give to servants, visitors, and guests. On that day he should send for his parish priest, who will bring his gospel and cross, and say a prayer to the angel, for which he must be paid a fee according to your means. A child receives his angel's name in baptism, and this angelic name he can never change. A peasant who was tried in the district court of Moscow on a charge of having forged a passport and changed his name, in order to pass for another man, replied that such a thing could not be done. "How," he asked in wonder, "could I change my name? I should lose my angel. I only forged my place of birth."

So closely have religious passions passed into social life, that civil rights are made to depend in no slight degree on the performance of religious duties. Every man is supposed to attend a weekly mass, and to confess his sins, and take a sacrament once a year. A man who neglects these offices forfeits his civil rights; unless, as sometimes happens in the best of cities, he can persuade his pope to give him a certificate of his exemplary attendance in the parish church!

CHAPTER VI.

PILGRIMS.

NEXT to his religious energy, the mastering passion of a Russ is the untamable craving of his heart for a wandering life.

All Slavonic tribes are more or less fond of roving to and fro; of peddling, and tramping, and seeing the world; of living, as it were, in tents, as the patriarchs lived; but the propensity to ramble from place to place is keener in the Russ than it is in the Bohemian and the Serb.

A while ago the whole of these Slavonic tribes were still nomadic; a people of herdsmen, driving their flocks from plain to plain, in search of grass and water; camping either in tents of skin, or in frames of wood not much more solid than tents of skin; carrying with them their wives and children, their weapons of war, and their household gods. They chased the wild game of their country, and when the wild game failed them, they ate their flocks. Some few among them tilled the soil, but only in a crude and fitful way—as an Adouan tends his patch of desert, as a Pawnee trifles with his stretch of plain; for the Slavonic husbandman was nearly as wild a wanderer as the driver of kine and goats. His fields were so vast, his kin so scattered, that the soil which he cropped was of no more value to him than the water he crossed, the air he breathed. He never dreamt of occupying his piece of ground after it had ceased to yield him, in the unbought bounty of nature, his easy harvest of oats and rye.

Some trace of these wandering habits may still be found, especially in the pilgrim bands.

These pilgrim bands are not a rabble of children and women, gay and empty folk, like those you meet when the vintage is gathered in Sicily and the south of France; mummers who take to the pilgrim's staff in wantonness of heart, and end a week of devotion by a feast in the auberge and a dance under the plaintain leaves. At best that French or Sicilian rabble is but a spent tradition and a decaying force. But these Northern pilgrims are grave and sad in their doings, even as the North is grave and sad. You never hear them laugh; you rarely see them smile; their movements are sedate; the only radiance on their life is the light of prayer and praise. Seeing these worshippers in many places and at many times —before the tomb of Sergie near Moscow, and before the manger at Bethlehem, I have everywhere found them the same, in reverence, in humility, in steadfastness of soul. One of these lowly Russ surprised me on the Jordan at Bethabara; and only yesterday I helped his brother to cross the Dvina on his march from Solovetsk. The first pilgrim had visited the tombs of Palestine, from Nazareth to Marsaba; the second, after toiling through a thousand miles of road and river to Solovetsk, is now on his way to the shrines at Kief. As my horses rattled down the Dvina bluffs I saw this humble pilgrim on his knees, his little pack laid by, and his forehead bent upon the ground in prayer. He was waiting at the ford for some one to come by—some one who could pay the boatman, and would give him a passage on the raft. The day had not yet dawned; the wind came up the river in gusts and chills; yet the face of that lowly man was good to see; a soft and tender countenance, shining with an inward light, and glad with unearthly peace. The world was not much with him, if one might judge from his sackcloth garb, his broken jar, his crust of black bread; but one could not help thinking, as he bowed in thanks, that it might be well for some of us who wear fine linen and dine off dainty food to be even as that poor pilgrim was.

This pilgrimage to the tombs and shrines of Russian saints, so far from being a holiday adventure, made when the year is spent and the season of labor past, is to the pilgrim a thing of life and death. He has degrees. A pilgrim perfect in his calling will go from shrine to shrine for several years. If God is good to him, he will strive, after making the round of his native shrines, to reach the valley of Nazareth, and the heights of Bethlehem and Zion. Some hundreds of these Russian pilgrims annually achieve this highest effort of the Christian life on earth; making their peace with heaven by kissing the stones in front of the Redeemer's tomb. Of course the poorer and weaker man can never expect to reach this point of grace; but his native soil is holy. Russia is a land of saints; and his map is dotted with sacred tombs, to which it is better for him to toil than rest at home in his sloth and sin.

These pilgrims go on foot, in bands of fifty or sixty persons, men, women, children, each with a staff in his hand, a water-bottle hanging from his belt; edifying the country as they march along, kneeling at the wayside chapel, and singing their canticles by day and night. The children whine a plaintive little song, of which the burden runs:

> "Fatherkins and motherkins,
> Give us bread to eat;"

and this appeal of the children is always heard, since all poor people fancy that the knock of a pilgrim at their window may be that of an angel, and will bring them luck.

A part—a very large part—of these rovers are simple tramps, who make a trade of piety; carrying about with them relics and rags which they vend at high rates to servant-girls and superstitious crones.

A man who in other days would have followed his sheep and kine, now seeks a wild sort of freedom as a pilgrim, hugging himself on his immunity from tax and rent, from wife and brat; migrating from province to province; a beggar, an impostor, and a tramp; tickled by the greeting of young and old as he passes their door, "Whither, oh friend, is the Lord leading thee?" Sooner or later such a man falls in with a band of pilgrims, which he finds it his good to join. The Russian Autolycus slings a water-bottle at his belt, and his female companion limps along the forest road on her wooden staff. You meet them on every track; you find them in the yard of every house. They creep in at back-doors, and have an assortment of articles for sale, which are often as precious in the eyes of a mistress as in those of her maid; a bit of rock from Nazareth, a drop of water from Jordan, a thread from the seamless coat, a chip of the genuine cross. These are the bolder spirits: but thousands of such vagrants roam about the country, telling crowds of gapers what they have seen in some holy place, where miracles are daily performed by the bones of saints. They show you a cross from Troitsa; they give you a morsel of consecrated bread from St. George. They can describe to you the defense of Solovetsk, and tell you of the incorruptible corpses of Pechersk.

These are the impostors—rank and racy impostors—yet some of these men and women who pass you on the roads are pious and devoted souls, wandering about the earth in search of what they fancy is a higher good. A few may be rich; but riches are dust in the eyes of God; and in seeking after His glory they dare not trust to an arm of flesh. Equally with his meekest brother, the rich pilgrim must take his staff, and march on foot, joining his brethren in their devotions and confessions, in their matins and their evening song.

Most of these pilgrim bands have to beg their crust of black bread, their sup of sour quass, from people as poor as themselves in money and almost as rich in the gifts of faith. Like the hadji going to Mecca, a pilgrim coming to Archangel, on his way to the shrines, is a holy man, with something of the character of a pope. The peasant, who thinks the crossing of his door-step by the stranger brings him blessings, not only lodges him by night, but helps him on the road by day. A pilgrim is a sacred being in rustic eyes. If his elder would let him go, he would join the band; but if he may not wend in person, he will go in spirit, to the shrine. A prayer shall be said in his name by the monks, and he will send his last kopeck in payment for that prayer by the hand of this ragged pilgrim, confident that the fellow would rather die than abuse his trust.

The men who escape from Siberian mines put on the pilgrim frock and seize the pilgrim staff. Thus robed and armed, a man may get from Perm to Archangel with little risk, even though his flesh may be burnt and his papers forged. Pietrowski has told the story of his flight, and many such tales may be heard on the Dvina praams.

A peasant living in a village near Archangel killed his father in a quarrel, but in such a way that he was not suspected of the crime; and he would never have been brought to justice had not Vanka, a friend and neighbor, been a witness of the deed. Now Vanka was weak and superstitious, and every day as he passed the image of his angel in the street, he felt an inner yearning to tell what he had seen. The murderer, watching him day and night, observed that he prayed very much, and crossed himself very often, as though he were deeply troubled in his mind. On asking what ailed him, he heard to his alarm that Vanka could neither eat nor sleep while that terrible secret lay upon his soul. But what could he do? Nothing; absolutely nothing? Yes; he could threaten to do for him what he had done by accident for a better man. "Listen to me, Vanka," he said, in a resolute tone; "you are a fool; but you would not like to have a knife in your throat, would you?" "God take care of me!" cried Vanka. "Mind me, then," said the murderer: "if you prate, I will have your blood." Vanka was so much frightened that he went to the police that very night and told them all he knew; on which his friend was arrested, brought to trial in Archangel, and condemned to labor on the public works for life. Vanka was the main witness, and on his evidence the judge pronounced his sentence. Then a scene arose in court which those who saw it say they shall not forget. The man in the dock was bold and calm, while Vanka, his accuser, trembled from crown to sole; and when the sentence of perpetual exile to the mines was read, the murderer turned to his friend and said, in a clear, firm voice, "Vanka! remember my words. To-day is yours: I am going to Siberia; but I shall come to your house again, and then I shall take your life. You know!" Years went by, and the threat, forgotten by every one else, was only remembered by Vanka, who, knowing his old friend too well, expected each passing night would be his last on earth. At length the tragedy came in a ghastly form. Vanka was found dead in his bed; his throat was cut from ear to ear; and in a drinking-den close by lay his murderer, snoring in his cups. He had made his escape from the mines; he had traversed the whole length of Asiatic Russia; he had climbed the Ural chain, and walked through the snow and ice of Perm, travelling in a pilgrim's garb, and singing the pilgrim's song, until he came to the suburbs of Archangel, where he slipped away from his raft, hid himself in the wood until nightfall, crept to the familiar shed and drew his knife across Vanka's throat.

No one suspects a pilgrim. With a staff in his hand, a sheepskin on his back, a water-bottle at his belt, and a clot of bass tied loosely round his feet, a peasant of the Ural Mountains quits his home, and makes no merit of trudging his two or three thousand miles. On the river he takes an oar, on the wayside he endures with incredible fortitude the burning sun by day, the biting frost at night. In Moscow I heard the history of three sisters, born in that city, who have taken up the pilgrim's staff for life. They are clever women, milliners by trade, and much employed by ladies of high rank. If they could only rest in their shop, they might live in comfort, and end their days in peace. But the religious and nomadic passions of their race are strong upon them. Every year they go to Kief, Solovetsk, and Jerusalem; and the journey occupies them forty-nine weeks. Every year they spend three weeks at home, and then set out again—alone, on foot—to seek, in winter snow and summer heat, salvation for their souls. No force on earth, save that which drives an Arab across the desert, and a Mormon across the prairie, is like this force.

In the hope of seeing these pilgrim bands, of going with

them to Solovetsk, and studying them on the spot, as also of inquiring about the convent spectre, and solving the mystery which for many years past connected that spectre with the Romanof family, I rounded the North Cape, and my regret is deep, when landing at Archangel, to hear that the last pilgrim band has sailed, and that no more boats will cross the Frozen Sea until the ice breaks up in May next year.

CHAPTER VII.

FATHER JOHN.

STUNG by this news of the pilgrim-boat having sailed, and haunting, unquietly, the Pilgrim's Court in the upper town, I notice a good many sheepskin garbs, with wearers of the burnt and hungry sort you meet in all seasons on the Syrian roads. They are exceedingly devout, and even in their rags and filth they have a certain grace of aspect and of mien. A pious purpose seems to inform their gestures and their speech. Yon poor old man going home with his morsel of dried fish has the air of an Arab sheikh. These pilgrims, like myself, have been detained by storms; and a hope shoots up into my heart that as the monks must either send away all these thirsty souls unslaked, or lodge and feed them for several months, they may yet contrive to send a boat.

A very small monk, not five feet high, with girl-like hair and rippling beard, which parts and flows out wildly in the wind, is standing in the gateway of the Pilgrim's Court; and hardly knowing how it might be best to put the matter in my feeble Russ, I ask him in that tongue where a man should look for the Solovetsk boat.

"English?" inquires the girl-like monk.

"Yes, English," I reply, in some surprise; having never before seen a monk in Russia who could speak in any other tongue than Russ. "The boat," he adds, "has ceased to run, and is now at Solovetsk laid up in dock."

In dock! This dwarf must be a wag; for such a conjunction as monks and docks in a country where you find a quay like that of Solambola is, of course, a joke. "In dock!"

"Oh yes, in dock."

"Then have you a dock in the Holy Isle?"

"A dock—why not? The merchants of Archangel have no docks, you say? Well, that is true; but merchants are not monks. You see, the monks of Solovetsk labor while the merchants of Archangel trade. Slava Bogu! A good monk does his work; no shuffling, and no waste. In London you have docks?"

"Yes, many: but they were not built by monks."

"In England you have no monks; once you had them; and then they built things—eh?"

This dwarf is certainly a wag. What, monks who work, and docks in the Frozen Sea! After telling me where he learned his English (which is of nautical and naughty pattern), the manikin comforts me with news that although the pilgrim-boat has gone back to Solovetsk (where her engines are to be taken out, and put by in warm boxes near a stove for the winter months), a provision-boat may sail for the monastery in about a week.

"Can you tell me where to find the captain of that boat?"

"Hum!" says the dwarf, slowly, crossing himself the while, and lipping his silent prayer, "*I* am the skipper!"

My surprise is great. This dwarf, in a monk's gown and cap, with a woman's auburn curls, the captain of a sea-going ship! On a second glance at his slight figure, I notice that his eyes are bright, that his cheek is bronze, that his teeth, though small, are bony and well set. In spite of his serge gown and his girl-like face, there *is* about the tiny monk that look of mastery which becomes the captain of a ship.

"And can you give me a passage in your boat?"

"You! English, and you wish to see the holy tombs? Well, that is something new. No men of your nation ever sail to Solovetsk. They come over here to buy, and not to pray. Sometimes they come to fight."

The last five words, spoken in a low key, come out from between his teeth with a snap which is highly comic in a man so lowly and so small. A lady living at Onega told me some days ago that once, when she was staying for a week at Solovetsk with a Russian party, she was compelled to hide her English birth, from fear lest the monks should kill her. A woman's fancy, doubtless; but her words came back upon my mind with a very odd sort of start as the manikin knits his brow and hisses at the English fleet.

"Where is your boat, and what is she called?"

"She lies in the lower port, by the Pilgrim's Wharf; her name is the 'Vera;' as you would say, the 'Faith.'"

"How do you call your captain?" I inquire of a second monk, who is evidently a sailor also; in fact, he is the first mate, serving on board the "Faith."

"Ivan," says the monk; a huge fellow, with hasty eyes and audacious front; "but we mostly call him Vanoushka, because he is little, and because we like him." Vanoushka is one of the affectionate forms of Ivan: Little Ivan, Little John. The skipper, then, is properly Father John.

As for the next ten days and nights we are to keep company, it may be best for me to say at once what I came to know of the queer little skipper in the long gown and with the woman's curls.

Father John is an infant of the soil. Born in a Lapland village, he had before him from his cradle the hard and hopeless life of a woodman and cod-fisher—the two trades carried on by all poor people in these countries, where the modes of life are fixed by the climate and the soil. In the summer he would cut logs and grass; in the winter he would hunt the sea in search of seal and cod. But the lad was smart and lively. He wished to see the world, and hoped in some future time to sail a boat of his own. In order to rise, he must learn; in order to become a skipper, he must study the art of guiding ships at sea. Some thirty miles from the hamlet where he lived stood Kem, an ancient town established on the Lapland coast by colonists from Novgorod the Great, in which town there was a school of navigation; rude and simple as became so poor a place, but better than none at all; and to this provincial school Father John contrived to go. That movement was his first great step in life.

From Kem you can see a group of high and wooded islands towards the rising sun, the shores of which shine with a peculiar light in the early dawn. They seem to call you, as it were, by a spell, into some paradise of the north. Every view is green, and every height is crowned by a church with a golden cross. These islands are the Solovetsk group; and once, at least, the lad went over from Kem in a boat to pray in that holy place. The lights, the music, and the ample cheer appealed to his fancy and his stomach; leaving on his mind an impression of peace and fullness never to be effaced.

He got his pass as a seaman, came over to Archangel, fell into loose ways, and meeting with some German sailors from the Baltic, listened to their lusty songs and merry tales, until he felt a desire to leave his own country and go with them on a voyage. Now sailors are scarce in the Russian ports; the Emperor Nicolas was in those days drafting his seamen into the Black Sea fleets; and for a man to quit Russia without a pass from the police was a great offense. Such a pass the lad felt sure he could never get; and when the German vessel was about to sail he crept on board her in the night, and got away to sea without being found out by the port police.

The vessel in which he escaped from his country was the "Hero," of Passenburg, in Hanover, plying as a rule between German and Danish ports, but sometimes running over to the Tyne and the Thames. Entered on the ship's books in a foreign name, Father John adopted the tastes of his new comrades; learned to eat English beef, to drink German beer, and to carry himself like a man of the world. But the teaching of his father and his pope was not lost upon him, even in the slums of Wapping and on the quays of Rotterdam. He began to pine for religion, as a Switzer pines for his Alp and an Egyptian for his Nile. What could he do? The thought of going home to Kem was a fearful dream. The lash, the jail, the mine awaited him—he thought—in his native land.

Cut off from access to a priest of his own religion, he talked to his fellows before the mast about their faith. Some laughed at him; some cursed him; but one old sailor took him to the house of a Catholic priest. For four or five weeks Father John received a lesson every day in the creed of Rome; but his mind misgave him as to what he heard; and when his vessel left the port he was still without a church. In the Levant, he met with creeds of all nations—Greek, Italian, Lutheran, Armenian—but he could not choose between them, and his mind was troubled with continual longings for a better life.

Then he was wrecked in the Gulf of Venice, and having nearly lost his life, he grew more and more uneasy about his soul. A few months later he was wrecked on the coast of Norway; and for the second time in one year he found himself at the gates of death. He could not live without religion; and the only religion to whisper peace to his soul was that of his early and better days. But then the service of his country is one of strict observance, and a man who can not go to church can not exercise his faith. How was he to seek for God in a foreign port?

A chance of coming back to Russia threw itself in his path. The ship in which be served—a German ship—was chartered by an English firm for Archangel; and as Father John was the only Russ on board, the skipper saw that his man would be useful in such a voyage. But the news was to John a fearful joy. He longed to see his country once more, to kneel at his native shrines, to give his mother some money he had saved; but he had now been twelve years absent without leave, and he knew that for such an offense he could be sent to Siberia, as he phrased it, "like a slave." His fear overcame his love, and he answered the skipper that he would not go, and must quit the ship.

But the skipper understood his trade. Owing John some sixteen pounds for pay, he told him that he had no money where he lay, and could not settle accounts until they arrived in Archangel, where he would receive his freight. "Money," says the Russ proverb, "likes to be counted," and when Father John thrust his hands into empty pockets, he began to think, after all, it might be better to go home, to get his wages, and see what would be done.

With a shaven chin and foreign name, he might have kept his secret and got away from Archangel undiscovered by the port police, had he not yielded the night before he should have sailed, and gone with some Germans of the crew to a drinking-den. Twelve years of abstinence from vodka had caused him to forget the power of that evil spirit; he drank too much, he lost his senses; and when he woke next day he found that his mates had left him, that his ship had sailed. What could he do? If he spoke to the German consul, he would be treated as a deserter from his post. If he went to the Russian police, he fancied they would knout him to death. Not knowing what to say or how to act, he was mooning in the port, when he met an old schoolfellow from Kem, one Jacob Kollownoff (whom I afterwards came to know). Like most of the hardy men of Kem, Jacob was prospering in the world; he was a skipper, with a boat of his own, in which he made distant and daring voyages. At the moment when he met Father John he was preparing for a run to Spitzbergen in search of cod, to be salted at sea, and carried to the markets of Cronstadt. Jacob saw no harm in a sailor drinking a glass too much, and knowing that John was a good hand, he gave him a place in his boat and took him out on his voyage. The cod was caught, and Cronstadt reached; but the return was luckless; and John was cast away for a third time in his life. A wrecked and broken man, he now made up his mind to quit the sea, and even to take his chance of what his people might do with him at home.

Returning to Kem with the skipper, he was seized by the police on the ground of his papers being out of order, and cast into the common jail of the town, where he lay for twelve months untried. The life in jail was not harder than his life on deck; for the Government paid him, as a prisoner, six kopecks a day; enough to supply his wants. He was never brought before a court. Once, if not more than once, the elder hinted that a little money would make things straight, and he might go his way. The sum suggested as enough for the purpose was seventy-five rubles—nearly ten pounds in English coin. "Tell him," said John to his brother, who brought this message to the jail, "he shall not get from me so much as one kopeck."

A week later he was sent in a boat from Kem to Archangel, under sentence, he was told, of two years' hard labor in the fort; but either the elder talked too big, or his message was misread; for on going up to the police-office in that city, the prisoner was examined and discharged.

A dream of the summer isles and golden pinnacles came back to him; he had lived his worldly life, and longed for rest. Who can wonder that he wished to become a monk of Solovetsk!

To the convent his skill in seamanship was of instant use.

A steamer had just been bought in Glasgow for the carriage of pilgrims to and fro; and on her arrival in Archangel, Feofan, Archimandrite of Solovetsk, discharged her Scottish crew and manned her with his monks. At first these holy men felt strange on deck; they crossed themselves; they sang a hymn; and as the pistons would not move, they begged the Scottish engineer to return; since the machine—being made by heretics—had not grace enough to obey the voice of a holy man. They made two or three midsummer trips across the gulf, getting hints from the native skippers, and gradually warming to their work. A priest was appointed captain, and monks were sent into the kitchen and the engine-room. All went well for a time; Savatie and Zosima—the local saints of Solovetsk—taking care of their followers in the fashion of St. Nicolas and St. George.

Yet Father John was a real God's gift to the convent, for the voyage is not often to be described as a summer trip; and even so good a person as an Archimandrite likes to know, when he goes down into the Frozen Sea, that his saints are acting through a man who has sailed in the roughest waters of the world.

CHAPTER VIII.

THE VLADIKA.

"You have a letter of introduction to the Archimandrite of Solovetsk?" asks Father John, as we are shaking hands under the pilgrim's lamp. "No! Then you must get one."

"Why? Are you so formal when a pilgrim comes to the holy shrine?"

"You are not quite a pilgrim. You will need a room in the guest-house for yourself. You may wish to have horses, boats, and people to go about. You will want to see the sacristy, the jewels, and the books. You may like to eat at the Archimandrite's board."

"But how are these things to be done?"

"You know the Most Sacred Vladika of Archangel, perhaps?"

"Well, yes, a little. One of the Vladika's closest friends has been talking to me of that sacred personage, and has promised to present me this very day."

"Get from him a line to the Archimandrite. That will make all things smooth," says Father John.

"Are they great friends?"

"Ha! who can tell? You see, the Most Sacred Vladika used to be master of every one in the Holy Isles; and now . . . . ; but then the Vladika of Archangel and the Archimandrite of Solovetsk are holy men, not likely to fall out. You'll get a line?"

"Yes, if he will give me one; good-bye."

"Count on a week for the voyage, and bring white bread," adds the dwarf. "Prosteté—Pardon me."

Of course, the Vladika (bishop or archbishop) is a monk; for every high-priest in the Orthodox Church, whether his rank be that of vicar, archimandrite, bishop, or metropolite, must wear the hood, and must have taken vows. The rule that a bishop must be "the husband of one wife," is set aside so far as regards the clergy of higher grades. A parish priest is a married man; must, in fact, be a married man; and no young deacon can obtain a church until he has first obtained a bride. The social offices of the Church are done by these family men; baptism, purifying, marriage, confession, burial; yet the higher seats in the hierarchy are all reserved (as yet) for celibates who are under vows.

The Holy Governing Synod—highest court of the Orthodox Church—consists of monks, with one lay member to assist them by his knowledge of the world. No married priest has ever had a seat on that governing board. The metropolites are monks; and not only monks, but actual rulers of monastic houses. Isidore, metropolite of Novgorod, is archimandrite of the great Convent of St. George. Arseny, metropolite of Kief, is archimandrite of the great Convent of Pechersk. Innocent, metropolite of Moscow, is archimandrite of the great Convent of Troitsa. All the vicars of these high-priests are monks. The case of Archangel and Solovetsk is, therefore, the exception to a general rule. St. George, Pechersk, and Troïtsa, are governed by the nearest prince of the Church; and in former times this was also the case with Solovetsk; but Peter the Great, in one of his fits of reverence, broke this old connection of the convent and the see of Archangel; endowing the Archimandrite of Solovetsk with a separate standing and an independent power. Some people think the Archbishop of Archangel nurses a grudge against the civil power for this infringement of his ancient rights; and this idea was probably present in the mind of Father John.

Acting on Father John's advice, I put on my clothes of state—a plain dress suit; the only attire in which you can wait on a man of rank—and drive to my friend's abode, and finding him ready to go with me, gallop through a gust of freezing rain to the palace-door.

The archbishop is at home, though it is not yet twelve o'clock. It is said of him that he seldom goes abroad; affecting the airs of an exile and a martyr; but doing—in a sad, submissive way, as if the weapon were unworthy of its work—a great deal of good; watching over his church, admonishing his clergy, both white and black, and thinking, like a father, for the poor.

Leaving our wraps in an outer hall (the proper etiquette of guests), we send in our cards by an usher, and are received at once.

The Most Sacred Vladika, pale as a ghost, dressed in a black gown, on which hangs a sapphire cross, and wearing his hood of serge, rises to greet us; and coming forward with a sweet and vanishing smile, first blesses his penitent, and then shakes hands with his English guest.

This Most Sacred Father Nathaniel is now an aged, shadowy man, with long white beard, and a failing light in his meek blue eyes. But in his prime he is said to have been handsome in person, eager in gait, caressing in style. In his youth he was a village pastor—one of the White Clergy—married, and a family man; but his wife died early; and as a pastor in his church can not marry a second time, he followed a fashion long ago set by his aspiring brethren—he took the vows of chastity, became a monk, and began to rise. His fine face, his courtly wit, his graceful bearing, brought him hosts of fair penitents, and these fair penitents made for him high friends at court. He was appointed Vicar of St.

Petersburg—a post not higher in actual rank than that of a Dean of St. Paul's, but one which a popular and ambitious man prefers to most of the Russian sees. Father Nathaniel was an idol of the city. Fine ladies sought his advice, and women of all classes came to confess to him their sins. Princes fell beneath his sway; princesses adored him; and no rank in the Church, however high, appeared to stand beyond his reach. But these court triumphs were his ruin. He was such a favorite with ladies that his brethren began to smile with malicious leer when his back was turned, and drop their poisonous hints about the ways in which he walked. They said he was too fond of power; they said he spent more time with his female penitents than became a monk. It is the misery of these vicars and bishops that they can not be married men, with wives of their own to turn the edges of such shafts. Men's tongues kept wagging against Nathaniel's fame; and even those who knew him to be earnest in his faith began to think it might be well for the Church if this fascinating father could be honorably sent to some distant see.

Whither was he to go?

While a place was being sought for him, he happened to give deep offense in high quarters; and as Father Alexander, Vladika of Archangel (hero of Solovetsk), was eager to go south and be near the court, Father Nathaniel was promoted to that hero's place.

He left St. Petersburg amidst the tears of fair women, who could not protect their idol against the malice of envious monks. Taking his promotion meekly as became his robe, he sighed to think that his day was come, and in the future he would count in his church as a fallen man. Arriving in Archangel, he shut himself up in his palace near the monastery of St. Michael; a house which he found too big for his simple wants. Soon after his coming he abandoned this palace for a smaller house; giving up his more princely pile to the monks of St. Michael for a public school.

A spirit of sacrifice is the pre-eminent virtue of the Russian Church.

The shadowy old man compels me to sit on the sofa by his side; talks of my voyage round the North Cape; shows me a copy in Russian of my book on the Holy Land; inquires whether I know the Pastor Xatli in London. Fancying that he means the Russian pope in Welbeck Street, I answer yes; on which we get into much confusion of tongues; until it flashes upon me that he is talking of Mr. Hatherley of Wolverhampton, the gentleman who has gone over from the English to the Russian rite, and is said to have carried some twenty souls of the Black Country with him. What little there is to tell of this Oriental Church in our Black Country is told; and in return for my scanty supply of facts, the Vladika is good enough to show me the pictures hanging on his wall. These pictures are of two classes, holy and loyal; first the sacred images—those heads of our Saviour and of the Virgin Mother which hang in the corners of every Russian room, the tutelary presence, to be adored with reverence at the dawn of day and the hour of rest; then the loyal and local pictures—portraits of the reigning house, and of former archbishops—which you would expect to find in such a house; a first Alexander, with flat and dreamy face; a Nicolas, with stiff and haughty figure; a second Alexander, hung in the place of honor, and wearing a pensive and benignant smile. More to my mind, as less familiar than these great ones of the hour, is the fading image of a lady, thoroughly Russ in garb and aspect—Marfa, boyarine of Novgorod and colonizer of the North.

Nathaniel marks with kindling eyes my interest in this grand old creature—builder alike of convents and of towns—who sent out from Novgorod two of her sons, and hundreds of her people, to the bleak north country, then inhabited by pagan Lapps and Karels, worshippers of the thunder-cloud, and children of the Golden Hag. Her story is the epic of these northern shores.

While Red and White Rose were wasting our English counties with sword and fire, this energetic princess sent her sons and her people down the Volkhoff, into Lake Ladoga, whence they crept up the Swir into Lake Onega; from the banks of which lake they marched upward, through the forests of birch and pine, into the frozen north. She sent them to explore the woods, to lay down rivers and lakes, to tell the natives of a living God. They came to Holmogory, on the Dvina, then a poor fishing-village occupied by Karels, a tribe not higher in type than the Samoyeds of the present day. They founded Suma, Soroka, and Kem. They took possession of the Frozen Sea and its clustering isles. In dropping down a main arm of the river, Marfa's two sons were pitched from their boat and drowned. Their bodies being washed on shore and buried in the sand, she caused a cloister to be raised on the spot, which she called the Monastery of St. Nicolas, after the patron of drowning men.

That cloister of St. Nicolas was the point first made by Challoner when he entered the Dvina from the Frozen Sea.

"You are going over to Solovetsk?" says the Vladika, coming back to his sofa. "We have no authority in the isles, although they lie within our See. It pleased the Emperor Peter, on his return from a stormy voyage, to raise the Convent of Savatie to independent rank, to give it the title of Lavra—making it the equal, in our ecclesiastical system, with Troitsa, Pechersk, and St. George. From that day Solovetsk became a separate province of the Church, dependent on the Holy Governing Synod and the Tsar. Still I can give you a line to Feofan, the Archimandrite."

Slipping into an inner room for five minutes, he composes a mandate in my favor, in the highest Oriental style.

CHAPTER IX.

A PILGRIM-BOAT.

A LADY, who knows the country, puts up in a crate such things as a pilgrim may chance to need in a monastic cell—good tea, calf's tongue, fresh butter, cheese, roast beef, and indispensable white bread. These dainties being piled on a drojki, propped on pillows and covered with quilts—my bedding in the convent and the boat—we rattle away to the Pilgrim's Wharf.

Yes, there it is, an actual wharf—the only wharf in Archangel along which boats can lie, and land their passengers by a common sea-side plank!

Moored to the capstan by a rope, lies the pretty craft; a

gilt cross on her foremast, a saintly pennant on her main. Four large gold letters tell her name:

ВѢРА

(pronounced Verra), and meaning Faith. Father John is standing on his bridge, giving orders in a low voice to his officers and crew, many of whom are monks—mate, steward, cook, and engineer—each and all arrayed in the cowl and frock.

On the Pilgrim's Wharf, which lies in a yard cut off by gates from the street, and paved with chips and shavings to form a dry approach, stands a new pile of monastic buildings; chapels, cells, store-rooms, offices, stalls, dormitories; in fact, a new Pilgrim's Court. A steamer can not reach the port in the upper town, where the original Pilgrim's Court was built; and the fathers, keeping pace with the times, have let their ancient lodgings in the town, and built a new house lower down the stream.

Crowds of men and women—pilgrims, tramps, and soldiers —strew the wharf with a litter of baskets, tea-pots, beds, dried-fish, felt boots, old rugs and furs, salt-girkins, black bread; through which the monks step softly and sadly; helping a child to trot on board, getting a free pass for a beggar, buying rye-loaves for a lame wretch, and otherwise aiding the poorest of these poor creatures in their need. For, even though the season is now far spent, nearly two hundred pilgrims are in waiting on the Pilgrim's Wharf; all hoping to get over to the Holy Isles. Most of these men have money to pay their fare; and some among the groups are said to be rich. A dozen of the better sort, natives of Archangel, too busy to pass over the sea in June, when their river was full of ships, are taking advantage of the lull in trade, and of the extra boat. Each man brings with him a basket of bread and fish, a box of tea, a thick quilt, and a pair of felt leggings, to be worn over his boots at night. These local pilgrims carry a staff; but in place of the leathern belt and water-bottle, they carry a teapot and a cup. One man wears a cowl and gown, who is not of the crew; a jolly, riotous monk, going back to his convent as a prisoner. "What has he been doing?" "Women and drink," says Father John. The fares are low: first-class, six rubles (fifteen shillings); second-class, four rubles. Third-class, three rubles. This tariff covers the cost of going out and coming back—a voyage of four hundred miles—with lodgings in the guest-house, and rations at the common tables, during a stay of five or six days. A dozen of these poor pilgrims have no rubles in their purse, and the question rises on the wharf, whether these paupers shall be left behind. Father John and his fellow-skipper have a general rule; they must refuse no man, however poor, who asks them for a passage to Solovetsk in the name of God.

A bell tolls, a plank is drawn, and we are off. As we back from the wharf, getting clear, a hundred heads bow down, a hundred hands sign the cross, and every soul commends itself to God. Every time that, in dropping down the river, we pass a church, the work of bowing and crossing begins afresh. Each head uncovers; each back is bent; each lip is moved by prayer. Some kneel on deck; some kiss the planks. The men look contrite, and the women are sedate. The crews on fishing-craft salute us, oftentimes kneeling and bowing as we glide past, and always crossing themselves with uncovered heads. Some beg that we will pray for them; and the most worldly sailors pause in their work and hope that the Lord will give us a prosperous wind.

A gale is blowing from west and north. In the river it is not much felt, excepting for the chill, which bites into your bone. Father John, with a monk's contempt for caution, gives the Maimax Channel a free berth, and having a boat in hand of very light draught, drops down the ancient arm as a shorter passage into the gulf.

Before we quit the river, our provident worshippers have begun to brew their tea and eat their supper of girkin and black bread.

The distribution on board is simple. Only one passenger has paid the first-class fare. He has the whole state cabin to himself; a room some nine feet square, with bench and mat to sleep on; a cabin in which he might live very well, had it not pleased the monks to stow their winter supply of tallow in the boxes beneath his couch. Two persons have paid the second-class fare—a skipper and his wife, who have been sailing about the world for years, have made their fortunes, and are now going home to Kem. "Ah!" says the fair, fat woman, "you English have a nice country to live in, and you get very good tea; but . . . ." The man is like his wife. "Prefer to live in Kem? Why not? In London you have beef and stout; but you have no summer and no winter; all your seasons are the same; never hot, never cold. If you want to enjoy life, you should drive in a reindeer sledge over a Lapland plain, in thirty degrees of frost."

The rest of our fellow-pilgrims are on deck and in the hold; rich and poor, lame and blind, merchant and beggar, charlatan and saint; a motley group, in which a painter might find models for a Cantwell, a Torquemada, a St. John. You see by their garb, and hear in their speech, that they have come from every province of the Empire; from the Ukraine and from Georgia, from the Crimea and from the Ural heights, from the Gulf of Finland and from the shores of the Yellow Sea. Some of these men have been on foot, trudging through summer sands and winter snows, for more than a year.

The lives of many of my fellow-passengers are like an old wife's tales.

One poor fellow, having no feet, has to be lifted on board the boat. He is clothed in rags; yet this poor pilgrim's face has such a patient look that one can hardly help feeling he has made his peace. He tells me that he lives beyond Viatka, in the province of Perm; that he lost his feet by frost-bite years ago; that he lay sick a long time; that while he was lying in his pain he called on Savatie to help him, promising that saint, on his recovery, to make a pilgrimage to his shrine in the Frozen Sea. By losing his legs he saved his life; and then, in his poverty and rags, he set forth on his journey, crawling on his stumps, around which he has twisted a coarse leather splinth, over fifteen hundred miles of broken road.

Another pilgrim, wearing a felt boot on one leg, a bass shoe on the other, has a most abject look. He is a drunkard, sailing to Solovetsk to redeem a vow. Lying tipsy on the canal bank at Vietegra, he rolled into the water, and narrowly escaped being drowned. As he lay on his face, the foam oozing slowly from his mouth, he called on his saints to save him, promising them to do a good work in return for such help. To keep that vow he is going to the holy shrines.

A woman is carrying her child, a fine little lad of six or

seven years, to be offered to the monks and educated for the cowl. She has passed through trouble, having lost her husband, and her fortune, and she is bent on sacrificing the only gift now left to her on earth. To put her son in the monastery of Solovetsk is to secure him, she believes, against all temporal and all spiritual harm. Poor creature! It is sad to think of her lot when the sacrifice is made; and the lonely woman, turning back from the incense and glory of Solovetsk, has to go once more into the world, and without her child.

An aged man, with flowing beard and priestly mien, though he is wrapped in rags, is noticeable in the groups among which he moves. He is a vowed pilgrim; that is to say, a pilgrim for life, as another man would be a monk for life; his whole time being spent in walking from shrine to shrine. He has the highest rank of a pilgrim; for he has been to Nazareth and Bethlehem, as well as to Novgorod and Kief. This is the third time he has come to Solovetsk; and it is his hope, if God should spare him for the work, to make yet another round of the four most potent shrines, and then lay up his dust in these holy isles.

Some of these pilgrims, even those in rags, are bringing gifts of no small value to the convent fund. Each pilgrim drops his offering into the box: some more, some less, according to his means. Many bear gifts from neighbors and friends who can not afford the time for so long and perilous a voyage, but who wish to walk with God, and lay up their portion with His saints.

On reaching the river mouth we find a fleet of fishing-boats in dire distress; and the two ships that we passed a week since, bobbing and reeling on the bar like tipsy men, are completely gone. The "Thera" is a Norwegian clipper, carrying deals; the "Olga" a Prussian bark, carrying oats; they are now aground, and raked by the wash from stem to stern. We pass these hulls in prayer; for the gale blows dead in our teeth; and we are only too well aware that before daylight comes again we shall need to be helped by all the spirits that wait on mortal men.

With hood and gown wrapped up in a storm-cape, made for such nights, Father John is standing on his bridge, directing the course of his boat like an English tar. His monks meet the wind with a psalm, in the singing of which the pilgrims and soldiers join. The passenger comes for a moment from his cabin into the sleet and rain; for the voices of these enthusiasts, pealing to the heavens through rack and roar, are like no sounds he has ever yet heard at sea. Many of the singers lie below in the hold; penned up between sacks of rye and casks of grease; some of them deadly sick, some groaning as though their hearts would break; yet more than half these sufferers follow with lifted eyes and strenuous lungs the swelling of that beautiful monkish chant. It is their even-song, and they could not let the sun go down into the surge until that duty to their Maker was said and sung.

Next day there comes no dawn. A man on the bridge declares that the sun is up; but no one else can see it; for a veil of mist droops everywhere about us, out of which comes nothing but a roar of wind and a flood of rain.

The "Faith" is bound to arrive in the Bay of Solovetsk by twelve o'clock; but early in the day Father John comes to tell me (apart) that he shall not be able to reach his port until five o'clock; and when five is long since past, he returns to tell me, with a patient shrug, that we want more room, and must change our course. The entrance to Solovetsk is through a reef of rocks.

"Must we lie out all night?"

"We must." Two hours are spent in feeling for the shore; Father John having no objection to use his lead. When anchorage is found, we let the chain go, and swinging round, under a lee shore, in eight fathoms of water, find ourselves lying out no more than a mile from land.

Then we drink tea; the pilgrims sing their even-song; and, with a thousand crossings and bendings, we commit our souls to heaven. Lying close in shore, under cover of a ridge of pines, we swing and lurch at our ease; but the storm howls angrily in our wake; and we know that many a poor crew, on their frail northern barks, are struggling all night with the powers of life and death. A Dutch clipper, called the "Ena," runs aground; her crew is saved, and her cargo lost. Two Russian sloops are shattered and riven in our track; one of them parting amidships and going down in a trough of sea with every soul on board.

In the early watch the wind goes down; sunlight streaks the north-eastern sky; and, in the pink dawn, we catch, in our front, a little to the west, a glimpse of the green cupolas and golden crosses of Solovetsk—a joy and wonder to all eyes; not more to pilgrims, who have walked a thousand miles to greet them, than they are to their English guest.

Saluting the holy place with prayer, and steaming by a coast-line broken by rocks and beautified by verdure, we pass, in a flood of soft warm sunshine, up a short inland reach, in which seals are plashing, over which doves are darting, each in their happy sport, and, by eight o'clock of a lovely August morning, swing ourselves round in a secluded bay under the convent walls.

CHAPTER X.

THE HOLY ISLES.

Chief in a group of rocks and banks lying off the Karel coast—a group not yet surveyed, and badly laid down in charts—Solovetsk is a small, green island, ten or twelve miles long, by eight or nine miles wide. The waters raging round her in this stormy sea have torn a way into the mass of stones and peat; forming many little coves and creeks; and near the middle, where the convent stands, these waters have almost met. Hardly a mile of land divides the eastern bay from the western bay.

Solovetsk stands a little farther north than Vatna Jökull; the sixty-fifth degree of latitude passing close to the monastic pile. The rocks and islets lying round her are numerous and lovely, for the sea runs in and out among them, crisp with motion and light with foam; and their shores are everywhere green with mosses and fringed with forests of birch and pine. The lines are not tame, as on the Karel and Lapland coasts, for the ground swells upward into bluffs and downs, and one at least of these ridges may be called a hill. Each height is crowned by a white church, a green cupola, and a golden cross. On the down which may be called a hill stands a larger church, the belfry of which contains a light. Land, sea, and sky are all in keeping; each a wonder and a beauty in the eyes of pilgrims of the stormy night.

Running alongside the wharf, on to which we step as easily as on to Dover Pier, we notice that beyond this beauty of nature, which man has done so much to point and gild, there is a bright and even a busy look about the commonest things. Groups of strange men dot the quays; Lopars, Karels, what not; but we soon perceive that Solovetsk is a civilized no less than an enchanted isle. The quay is spacious, the port is sweet and fresh. On our right lies that dock of which Father John was speaking with such pride. The "Hope," a more commodious pilgrim-boat than the "Faith," is lying on her stays. On our left stands a guest-house, looking so airy, light, and clean, that no hostelry on Italian lake could wear a more cheerful and inviting face. We notice a lift and crane, as things not seen in the trading ports; and one has hardly time to mark these signs of science ere noticing an iron tramway, running from the wharf to a great magazine of stôres and goods.

A line of wall, with gates and towers, extends along the upper quay; and high above this line of wall, spring convent, palace, dome, and cross. A stair leads up from the water to the Sacred Gates; and near the pathway from this stair we see two votive chapels; marking the spots on which the imperial pilgrims, Peter the Great and Alexander the Beneficent, landed from their boats.

Every thing looks solid, many things look old. Not to speak of the fortress walls and turrets, built of vast boulders torn up from the sea-bed in the days of our own Queen Bess, the groups of palace, church, and belfry rising within those walls are of older date than any other work of man in this far-away corner of the globe. One cathedral—that of the Transfiguration—is older than the fortress walls. A second cathedral—that of the Ascension—dates from the time when St. Philip was prior of Solovetsk. Besides having this air of antiquity, the place is alive with color, and instinct with a sense of art. The votive chapels which peep out here and there from among the trees are so many pictures; and these red crosses by the water-margin have been so arranged as to add a motive and a moral to the scene. Some broad but not unsightly frescoes brighten the main front of the old cathedral, and similar pictures light the spandrel of the Sacred Gates; while turrets and cupolas of church and chapel are everywhere gay with green and gold.

One dome, much noticed, and of rarest value in a pilgrim's eye, is painted azure, fretted with golden stars. That dome is the crown of a new cathedral built in commemoration of 1854—that year of wonders—when an English fleet was vanquished by the Mother of God. Within, the convent looks more durable and splendid than without. Wall, rampart, guest-house, prison, tower, and church, are all of brick and stone. Every lobby is painted; often in a rude and early style; but these rough passages from Holy Writ have a sense and keeping higher than the morals conveyed by a coat of lime. The screens and columns in the churches glow with a nobler art; though here, again, an eye accustomed to admire no other than the highest of Italian work will be only too ready to slight and scorn. The drawing is often weak, the pigment raw, the metal tawdry; yet these great breadths of gold and color impress both eye and brain, especially when the lamps are lit, the psalm is raised, the incense burning, and the monks, attired in their long black hoods and robes, are ranged in front of the royal gates.

This pretty white house under the convent wall, near the Sacred Gates, was built in witness of a miracle, and is known as the Miracle Church. A pilgrim, eating a bit of white bread, which a pope had given him, let a crumb of it fall to the ground, when a strange dog tried to snatch it up. The crumb seemed to rise into the dog's mouth and then slip away from him, as though it were alive. That dog was the devil. Many persons saw this victory of the holy bread, and the monks of Solovetsk built a shrine on the spot to keep the memory of that miracle alive; and here it stands on the bay, between the chapels erected on the spots where Peter the Great and Alexander the Second landed from their ships.

When we come to drive, and sail, and walk into the recesses of this group of isles, we find them not less lovely than the first sweet promise of the bay in which we land. Forests surround, and lakelets pursue us, at every step. The wood is birch and pine; birch of the sort called silver, pine of the alpine stock. The trees are big enough for beauty, and the undergrowths are red with berries and bright with Arctic flowers. Here and there we come upon a clearing, with a dip into some green valley, in the bed of which slumbers a lovely lake. A scent of hay is in the air, and a perfume new to my nostrils, which my companions tell me breathes from the cotton-grass growing on the margin of every pool. At every turn of the road we find a cross, well shaped and carved, and stained dark red; while the end of every forest lane is closed by a painted chapel, a lonely father's cell. A deep, soft silence reigns through earth and sky.

But the beauty of beauties lies in the lakes. More than a hundred of these lovely sheets of water nestle in the depths of pine-wood and birch-wood. Most famous of all these sheets is the Holy Lake, lying close behind the convent wall; most beautiful of all, to my poor taste, is the White Lake, on the road to St. Savatie's Cell and Striking Hill.

Holy Lake, a sheet of black water, deep and fresh, though it is not a hundred yards from the sea, has a function in the pilgrim's course. Arriving at Solovetsk, the bands of pilgrims march to this lake and strip to bathe. The waters are holy, and refresh the spirit while they purify the flesh. Without a word, the pilgrims enter a shed, throw off their rags, and leap into the flood; except some six or seven city-folk, who shiver in their shoes at the thought of that wholesome plunge. Their bath being finished, the pilgrims go to dinner and to prayers.

White Lake lies seven or eight miles from the convent, sunk in a green hollow, with wooded banks, and a number of islets, stopping the lovely view with a yet more lovely pause. If St. Savatie had been an artist, one need not have wondered at his wandering into such a spot.

Yet the chief islet in this paradise of the Frozen Sea has one defect. When looking down from the belfry of Striking Hill on the intricate maze of sea and land, of lake and ridge, of copse and brake, of lawn and dell; each tender breadth of bright green grass, each sombre belt of dark-green pine, being marked by a white memorial church; you gaze and wonder, conscious of some hunger of the sense; it may be of the eye, it may be of the ear; your heart declaring all the while that, wealthy as the landscape seems, it lacks some last poetic charm. It is the want of animal life. No flock is in the meadow, and no herd is on the slope. No bark of dog comes on the air; no low of kine is on the lake. Neither cow nor calf, neither sheep nor lamb, neither goat nor kid, is seen in all the length of country from Striking Hill to the convent gate. Man is here alone, and feels that he is alone.

This defect in the landscape is radical; not to be denied, and never to be cured. Not that cattle would not graze on these slopes and thrive in these woods. Three miles in front of Solovetsk stands the isle called Zaet, on which sheep and cattle browse; and five or six miles in the rear lies Moksalma, a large grassy isle, on which the poultry cackle, the horses feed, and the cows give milk. These animals would thrive on the holy isle, if they were not driven away by monastic rule; but Solovetsk has been sworn of the celibate order; and love is banished from the saintly soil. No mother is here permitted to fondle and protect her young; a great defect in landscapes otherwise lovely to eye and heart — a denial of nature in her tenderest forms.

The law is uniform, and kept with a rigor to which the imperial power itself must bend. No creature of the female sex may dwell on the isle. The peasants from the Karel coast are said to be so strongly impressed with the sin of breaking this rule, that they would rather leap into the sea than bring over a female cat. A woman may come in the pilgrim season to say her prayers, but that duty done she must go her way. Summer is a time of license—a sort of carnival season, during which the letter of a golden rule is suspended for the good of souls. A woman may lodge in the guest-house, feed in the refectory; but she must quit the wards before nine at night. Some of the more holy chapels she may not enter: and her day of privilege is always short. A male pilgrim can reside at Solovetsk for a year; a female must be gone with the boats that bring her to the shrine. By an act of imperial grace, the commander of his majesty's forces in the island—an army some sixty strong—is allowed to have his wife and children with him during the pilgrim's year; that is to say, from June to August; but when the last boat returns to Archangel with the men of prayer, the lady and her little folk must leave their home in this holy place. A reign of piety and order is supposed to come with the early snows, and it is a question whether the empress herself would be allowed to set her foot on the island in that better time.

The rule is easily enforced in the bay of Solovetsk, under the convent walls; not so easily enforced at Zaet, Moksalma, and the still more distant isles, where tiny little convents have been built on spots inhabited by famous saints. In these more distant settlements it is hard to protect the holy men from female intrusion; for the Karel girls are fond of mischief, and they paddle about these isles in their light summer craft by day and night. The aged fathers only are allowed to live in such perilous spots.

CHAPTER XI.

THE LOCAL SAINTS.

THIS exclusion of women from the Holy Isle was the doing of Savatie, first of the Local Saints.

Savatie, the original anchoret of Solovetsk, was one day praying near a lake, when he heard a cry, as of a woman in pain. His comrade said it must have been a dream: for no woman was living nearer to their "desert" than the Karel coast. The saint went forth again to pray; but once again his devotions were disturbed by cries and sobs. Going round by the banks of the lake to see, he found a young woman lying on the ground, with her flesh all bruised, her back all bleeding from recent blows. She was a fisherman's wife. On being asked who had done her this harm, she said that two young men, with bright faces and dressed in white raiment, came to her hut while her hushand was away, and telling her she must go after him, as the land belonged to God, and no woman must sleep on it a single night, they threw her on the ground, struck her with rods, and made her cry with pain.

When she could walk, the poor creature got into her boat, and St. Savatie saw her no more. The fisherman came to fish, but his wife remained at home; and in this way woman was driven by angels from the Holy Isle. No monk, no layman, ever doubts this story. How can he? Here, to this day, stands the log house in which Savatie dwelt, and twenty paces from it lies the mossy bank on which he knelt. Across the water there, beside yon clump of pines, rose the fisherman's shed. The sharp ascent on which the church and lighthouse glisten, is still called Striking Hill.

This St. Savatie was a monk from Novgorod living at the old convent of Belozersk, in which he served the office of tonsurer—shaver of heads; but longing for a life of greater solitude than his convent gave him, he persuaded one of his brethren, named Valaam, to go up with him into the deserts near the Polar Sea. Boyars from his country-side were then going up into the north; and why should holy men not bear as much for Christ as boyars and traders bore for pelf? On praying all night in their chapels, these boyars and traders ran to their archbishop with the cry: "Oh, give us leave, Vladika, to go forth, man and horse, and win new lands for St. Sophia." Settling in Kem, in Suma, in Soroka, and at other points, these men were adding a region larger than the mother-country to the territories ruled by Novgorod the Great. The story of these boyars stirred up Savatie to follow in their wake, and labor in the desolate land which they were opening up.

Toiling through the virgin woods and sandy plains, Savatie and his companion Valaam arrived on the Vieg (in 1429), and found a pious monk, named German, who had also come from the south country. Looking towards the east, these monks perceived, in the watery waste, a group of isles; and trimming a light skiff, Savatie and German crossed the sea. Landing on the largest isle, they made a "desert" on the shore of a lakelet, lying at the foot of a hill on which birch and pine trees grew to the top. Their lake was sheltered, the knoll was high; and from the summit they could see the sprinkle of isles and their embracing waves, as far as Orloff Cape to the south, the downs of Kem on the west.

Savatie brought with him a picture of the Virgin, not then known to possess miraculous virtues, which he hung up in a chapel built of logs. Near to this chapel he made for himself and his companion a hut of reeds and sticks, in which they lived in peace and prayer until the rigor of the climate wore them out. After six years spent in solitude, German sailed back to the Vieg; and Savatie, finding himself alone on the rock, in that desert from which he had banished woman and love, became afraid of dying without a priest being at hand to shrive and put him beneath the grass. Getting into his skiff, he also crossed to Soroka, where he obtained from Father Nathaniel, a prior who chanced to visit that town, the bread and cup; and then, his work on earth being done, he passed away to his eternal rest.

Laying him in the sands at Soroka, Nathaniel raised a chapel of pine logs, dedicated to the Holy Trinity, above his grave; and there Savatie would have lain forever, his name unknown, his saintly rank unrecognized on earth, had he not fallen in the path of a man of stronger and more enduring spirit.

One of the bold adventurers from Novgorod, named Gabriel, settling with his wife Barbara in the new village of Tolvui, on the banks of Lake Onega, had a son, whom he called Zosima, and devoted to God. Zosima, a monk while he was yet a child, took his vows in the monastery of Palaostrofsk, near his father's home; and on reaching the age when he could act for himself, he divided his inheritance among his kin, and taking up his pilgrim's staff departed for the north. At Suma he fell in with German, who told him of the life he had lived six years in his desert on the lonely rock. Zosima, taken by this tale, persuaded German to show him the spot where he and Savatie had dwelt so long. They crossed the sea. A lucky breeze bore them past Zaet, into a small and quiet bay; and when they leaped on shore—then strewn with boulders, and green with forest trees—they found themselves not only on the salt sea, but close to a deep and lustrous lake, the waters of which were sweet to the taste, and swarming with fish, the necessary food of monks.

Kneeling on the sand in prayer, Zosima was nerved by a miraculous vision to found a religious colony in that lonely island, even as Marfa's people were founding secular colonies at Suma, Soroka, and Kem. He saw, as in a dream, a bright and comely monastic pile, with swelling domes and lofty turrets, standing on the brink of that lovely sheet of water—

henceforth to be known as the Holy Lake. Starting from his knees, he told his companion, German, of the vision he had seen; described the walls, the Sacred Gates, the clusters of spires and domes; in a word, the convent in the splendor of its present form. They cut down a pine, and framed it into a cross, which they planted in the ground; in token that this island in the frozen deep belonged to God and to His saints. This act of consecrating the isle took place (in 1436) a year after St. Savatie died.

The monks erected cabins near this cross; in which cabins they dwelt, about a mile apart, so as not to crowd upon each other in their desert home. The sites are marked by chapels erected to perpetuate their fame.

The tale of these young hermits living in their desert on the Frozen Sea being noised abroad in cloisters, monks from all sides of the north country came to join them; bringing strong thews and eager souls to aid in their task of raising up in that wild region, and among those savage tribes, a temple of the living God. In time a church grew round and above the original cross; and as none of the hermits were in holy orders, they sent a messenger to Yon, then archbishop of Novgorod, asking him for a blessing on their work, and praying him to send them a prior who could celebrate mass. Yon gave them his benediction and his servant Pavel. Pavel travelled into the north, and consecrated their humble church; but the climate was too hard for him to bear. A second prior came out in Feodosie; a third prior in Yon; both of whom staid some time in the Frozen Sea, and only went back to Novgorod when they were broken in health and advanced in years.

When Yon, the third prior, left them, the fathers held a meeting to consider their future course. Sixteen years had now passed by since Zosima and German crossed the sea from Suma; ten or twelve years since Pavel consecrated their humble church. In less than a dozen years three priors had come and gone; and every one saw that monks who had grown old in the Volkhoff district could not live in the Frozen Sea. The brethren asked their archbishop to give them a prior from their own more hardy ranks; and all these brethren joined in the prayer that Zosima, leader of the colony from first to last, would take this office of prior upon himself. His poor opinion of himself gave place to a sense of the public good.

Marching on foot to Novgorod, a journey of more than a thousand miles, through a country without a road, Zosima went up to the great city, where he was received by the Vladika, and was ordained a priest. From the mayor and chief boyars he obtained a more definite cession of the isles than Prior Yon had been able to secure; and thus he came back to his convent as pope and prior, with the fame of a holy man, to whom nothing might be denied. Getting leave to remove the bones of Savatie from Soroka to Solovetsk, he took up his body from the earth, and finding it pure and fresh, he laid the incorruptible relics in the crypt of his infant church.

More and more monks arrived in the lonely isles; and pilgrims from far and near began to cross the sea; for the tomb of Savatie was said to work miraculous cures. But as the monastery grew in fame and wealth, the troubles of the world came down upon the prior and his monks. The men of Kem began to see that this bank in the Frozen Sea was a valuable prize; and the lords of Anzersk and Moksalma quarrelled with the monks; disputing their right over the foreshores, and pressing them with claims about the waifs and strays. At length, in his green old age, Zosima girded up his loins, and taking his pastoral staff in hand, set out for Novgorod, in the hope of seeing Marfa in person, and of settling, once and forever, the question of his claim to these rocks by asking for the lordship of Kem itself to be vested in the prior of Solovetsk!

On a column of the great cathedral of St. Sophia, in the Kremlin of Novgorod, a series of frescoes tells the story of this visit of St. Zosima to the parent state. One picture takes the eye with a singular and abiding force—a banquet in a noble hall, in which the table is surrounded by headless guests.

Passing through the city from house to house, Zosima was received in nearly all with honor, as became his years and fame; but not in all. The boyars of Kem had friends in the city; and the Marfa's ear had been filled with tales against his monkish guile and monkish greed. From her door he was driven with scorn; and her house was that in which he was most desirous of being received in peace. Knowing that he could do nothing without her aid, Zosima set himself, by patient waiting on events, to overcome her fury against the cause which he was there to plead. At length, her feeling being subdued, she granted him a new charter (dated 1470, and still preserved at Solovetsk), confirming his right over all the lands, lakes, forests and fore-shores of the Holy Isles, together with the lordship of Kem, made over, then and for all coming time, to the service of God.

Before Zosima left the great city, Marfa invited him to her table, where he was to take his leave, not only of herself, but of the chief boyars. As the prior sat at meat, the company noticed that his face was sad, that his eyes were fixed on space, that his soul seemed moved by some unseen cause. "What is the matter?" cried the guests. He would not speak; and when they pressed around him closely, they perceived that burning drops were rolling down his cheeks. More eagerly than ever, they demanded to know what he saw in his fixed and terrible stare. "I see," said the monk, "six boyars at a feast, all seated at a table without their heads!"

That dinner-party is the subject painted on the column in St. Sophia; and the legend says that every man who sat with him that day at Marfa's table had his head sliced off by Ivan the Third, when the proud and ancient republic fell before the destroyer of the Golden Horde.

Strengthened by his new titles, Zosima came back to Solovetsk a prince; and the pile which he governed took the style, which it has ever since borne, of

The Convent that Endureth Forever.

Zosima ruled his convent as prior for twenty-six years; and after a hermitage of forty-two years on his lowly rock he passed away into his rest.

On his dying couch he told his disciples that he was about to quit them in the flesh, but only in the flesh. He promised to be with them in the spirit; watching in the same cells, and kneeling at the same graves. He bade them thank God daily for the promise that their convent should endure forever; safe as a rock, and sacred as a shrine—even though it stood in the centre of a raging sea—in the reach of pitiless foes. And then he passed away—the second of these local saints—leaving, as his legacy to mankind, the temporal and spiritual germs of this great sanctuary in the Frozen Sea.

About that time the third monk also died—German, the companion of Savatie, in his cabin near Striking Hill; afterwards of Zosima, in his hut by the Holy Lake. He died at Novgorod, to which city he had again returned from the north. His bones were begged from the monks in whose grounds they lay, and being carried to Solovetsk, were laid in a shrine near the graves of his ancient and more famous friends.

Such was the origin of the convent over which the Archimandrite Feofan now rules and reigns.

CHAPTER XII.

A MONASTIC HOUSEHOLD.

My letter from his Sanctity of Archangel having been sent in to Feofan, Archimandrite of Solovetsk, an invitation to the palace arrives in due form by the mouth of Father Hilarion; who may be described to the lay world as the Archimandrite's minister for secular affairs. Father Hilarion is attended by Father John, who seems to have taken upon himself the office of my companion-in-chief. Attiring myself in befitting robes, we pass through the Sacred Gates, and after pausing for a moment to glance at the models of Peter's yacht and frigate, there laid up, and to notice some ancient frescoes which line the passage, we mount a flight of steps, and find ourselves standing at the Archimandrite's door.

The chief of this monastery is a great man; one of the greatest men in the Russian Church; higher, as some folks say, than many a man who calls himself bishop, and even metropolite. Since the days of Peter the Great, the monastery of Solovetsk has been an independent spiritual power; owning no master in the Church, and answering to no authority save that of the Holy Governing Synod.

Like an archbishop, the Archimandrite of Solovetsk has the right to bless his congregation by waving three tapers in his right hand over two tapers in his left. He lives in a palace; he receives four thousand rubles a year in money; and the cost of his house, his table, his vestments, and his boats, comes out of the monastic fund. He has a garden, a vineyard, and a country-house; and his choice of a cell in the sunniest nooks of these sacred isles. His personal rank is that of a prince, with a dignity which no secular rank can give; since he reigns alike over the bodies and the souls of men.

Dressed in his cowl and frock, on which hangs a splendid sapphire cross, Feofan, a small, slight man—with the ascetic face, the womanlike curls, and vanishing figure, which you note in nearly all these celibate priests—advances to meet us near the door, and after blessing Father John, and shaking me by the hand, he leads us to an inner room, hung with choice prints, and warmed by carpets and rugs, where he places me on the sofa by his side, while the two fathers stand apart, in respectful attitude, as though they were in church.

"You are not English?" he inquires, in a tender tone, just marked by a touch—a very light touch—of humor.

"Yes, English, certainly."

A turn of his eye, made slowly, and by design, directs my attention to his finger, which reclines on an object hardly to have been expected on an Archimandrite's table; an iron shell! The Tower-mark proves that it must have been fired from an English gun. A faint smile flits across the Archimandrite's face. There it stands; an English shell, unburst; the stopper drawn; and two plugs near it on a tray. That missile, it is clear, must have fallen into some soft bed of sand or peat.

"You are the first pilgrim who ever came from your country to Solovetsk," says Feofan, smiling. "One man came before you in a steamship; he was an engineer—one Anderson; you know him, maybe? No! He was a good man—he minded his engines well; but he could not live on fish and quass—he asked for beef and beer; and when we told him we had none to give him, he went away. No other English ever came."

He passes on to talk of the Holy Sepulchre and the Russian convent near the Jaffa Gate.

"You are welcome to Solovetsk," he says at parting; "see what you wish to see, go where you wish to go, and come to me when you like." Nothing could be sweeter than his voice, nothing softer than his smile, as he spake these words; and seeing the twinkle in his eye, as we stand near the English shell, I also smile and add: "On the mantel-piece of my writing-room in London there lies just such another shell, a trifle thinner in the girth."

"Yes?" he asks, a little curious—for a monk.

"My shell has the Russian mark; it was fired from Sebastopol, and picked up by a friend of my own in his trench before the Russian lines."

Feofan laughs, so far as an Archimandrite ever laughs—in the eyes and about the mouth. From this hour his house and household are at my disposal—his boat, his carriage, and his driver; every thing is done to make my residence in the convent pleasant; and every night my host is good enough to receive from his officers a full report of what I have seen and what I have said during the day!

Three hundred monks of all classes reside on the Holy Isle. The chief is, of course, the Archimandrite; next to him come forty monks, who are also popes; then come seventy or eighty monks who wear the hood and have taken the final vows; after these orders come the postulants, acolytes, singers, servants. Lodgers, scholars, and hired laymen fall into a second class.

These brethren are of all ages and conditions, from the pretty child who serves at table to the decrepit father who can not leave his cell; from the monk of noble birth and ample fortune to the brother who landed on these islands as a tramp. They wear the same habit, eat at the same board, listen to the same chants, and live the same life. Each brother has his separate cell, in which he sleeps and works; but every one, unless infirm with years and sickness, must appear in chapel at the hour of prayer, in refectory at the hour of meals. Hood and gown, made of the same serge, and cut in the same style, must be worn by all, excepting only by the priest who reads the service for the day. They suffer their beards and locks to grow, and spend much time in combing and smoothing these abundant growths. A flowing beard is the pride of monks and men; but while the beard is coming, a young fellow combs and parts his hair with all the coquetry of a girl. When looking at a bevy of boys in a church, their heads uncovered, their locks, shed down the centre, hanging about their shoulders, you might easily mistake them for singers of the sweeter sex.

Not many of these fathers could be truly described as ordinary men. A few are pure fanatics, who fear to lose their souls; still more are men with a natural calling for religious life. A goodly list are prisoners of the church, sent up from convents in the south and west. These last are the salt and wine of Solovetsk; the men who keep it sweet and make it strong. The offense for which they suffer is too much zeal: a learned and critical spirit, a disposition to find fault, a craving for reform, a wish to fall back on the purity of ancient times. For such disorders of the mind an ordinary monk has no compassion; and a journey to the desert of Solovetsk is thought to be for such diseases the only cure.

An Archimandrite, appointed to his office by the Holy Governing Synod, must be a man of learning and ability, able to instruct his brethren and to rule his house. He is expected to burn like a shining light, to fast very often, to pray very much, to rise very early, and to live like a saint. The brethren keep an eye upon their chief. If he is hard with himself he may be hard with them; but woe to him if he is weak in the flesh—if he wears fine linen about his throat, if savory dishes steam upon his board, if the riumka—that tiny glass out of which whisky is drunk—goes often to his lips. In every monk about his chamber he finds a critic; in nearly every one he fears a spy. It is not easy to satisfy them all. One father wishes for a sterner life, another thinks the discipline too strict. By every post some letters of complaint go out, and every member of the Holy Governing Synod may be told in secret of the Archimandrite's sins. If he fails to win his critics, the appeals against his rule increase in number and in boldness, till at length inquiry is begun, bad feeling is provoked on every side, and the offending chieftain is promoted—for the sake of peace—to some other place.

The Archimandrite of Solovetsk has the assistance of three

great officers, who may be called his manager, his treasurer, and his custodian; officers who must be not only monks but popes.

Father Hilarion is the manager, with the duty of conducting the more worldly business of his convent. It is he who lodges the guests when they arrive, who looks after the ships and docks, who employs the laborers and conducts the farms, who sends out smacks to fish, who deals with skippers, who buys and sells stores, who keeps the workshops in order, and who regulates the coming and going of the pilgrim's boat. It is he who keeps church and tomb in repair, who sees that the fathers are warmly clad, who takes charge of the buildings and furniture, who superintends the kitchen, who keeps an eye on corridor and yard, who orders books and prints, who manages the painting-room and the photographer's office, who inspects the cells, and provides that every one has a bench, a press, a looking-glass, and a comb.

Father Michael is the treasurer, with the duty of receiving all gifts and paying all accounts. The income of the monastery is derived from two sources: from the sale of what is made in the monkish workshops, and from the gifts of pilgrims and of those who send offerings by pilgrims. No one can learn how much they receive from either source; for the receiving-boxes are placed in corners, and the contributor is encouraged to conceal from his left hand what his right hand drops in. Forty thousand rubles a year has been mentioned to me as the sum received in gifts; but five thousand pounds must be far below the amount of money passing in a year under Father Michael's eye. It is probably eight or ten. The charities of these monks are bounded only by the power of the people to come near them; and in the harder class of winters the peasants and fishermen push through the floes of ice from beyond Orloff Cape and Kandalax Bay in search of a basket of convent bread. These folks are always fed when they arrive, are always supplied with loaves when they depart. The schools, too, cost no little; for the monks receive all boys who come to them—sent as they hold, by the Father whom they serve.

Father Alexander is the custodian, with the duty of keeping the monastic wardrobe, together with the ritual books, the charters and papers, the jewels and the altar plate. His office is in the sacristy, with the treasures of which he is perfectly familiar, from the letter, in Cyrilian character and Slavonic phrase, by which Marfa of Novgorod gave this islet to the monks, down to that pious reliquary in which are kept some fragments of English shells; kept with as much veneration as bones of saints and chips from the genuine cross!

CHAPTER XIII.

A PILGRIM'S DAY.

A PILGRIM'S day begins in the early morning, and lengthens late into the night.

At two o'clock, when it has hardly yet grown dark in our cells, a monk comes down the passage, tinkling his bell and droning out, "Rise and come to prayer." Starting at his cry, we huddle on our clothes, and rush from our hot rooms, heated by stoves, into the open air; men and women, boys and girls, boatmen and woodmen, hurrying through the night towards the Sacred Gates.

At half-past two the first matins commence in the new church — the Miracle Church — dedicated to the Victress, Mother of God; in which lie the bones of St. Savatie and St. Zosima, in the corner, as the highest place. A hundred lamps are lit, and the wall-screen of pictured saints glows richly in our sleepy eyes. Men and women, soldiers and peasants, turn into that sacred corner where the saints repose, cross themselves seven times, bow their foreheads to the ground, and kiss the pavement before the shrine.

Falling into our places near the altar-screen; arranging ourselves in files, rank behind rank, in open order, so that each can kneel and kiss the ground without pushing against his neighbor; we stand erect, uncovered, while the pope recites his office, and the monks respond their chant. These matins are not over until four o'clock.

A second service opens in the old cathedral at half-past three, and lasts until half-past five; and when the first pope has given his blessing, some of the more ardent pilgrims rush from the Virgin's church to the cathedral, where they stand in prayer, and kneel to kiss the stones for ninety minutes more; at the end of which time they receive a second benediction from a second pope.

An hour is now spent by the pilgrims in either praying at the tombs of saints, or pacing a long gallery, so contrived as to connect the several churches and other monastic buildings by a covered way. Along the walls of this gallery rude and early Russian artists have painted the joys of heaven, the pains of purgatory, and the pangs of hell. These pictures seize the eyes of my fellow-pilgrims, though in quaint and dramatic terror they sink below the level of such old work in the Gothic cloisters of the Rhine. A Russian painter has no variety of invention; a devil is to him a monkey with a spiked tail and a tongue of flame; and hell itself is only a hot place in which sinners are either fried by a fiend, or chawed up, flesh and bone, by a monstrous bear. Yet, children sometimes swoon, and women go mad from fright, on seeing these threats of a future state. My own poor time is given to scanning a miraculous picture of Jerusalem, said to have been painted on the staircase by a monk of Solovetsk, as a vision of the Holy City, seen by him in a dream. After studying the details for a while, I recognize in this vision of the holy man a plan of Olivet and Zion copied from an old Greek print!

All this time the pilgrims are bound to fast.

At seven o'clock the bells announce early mass, and we repair to the Miracle Church, where, after due crossings and prostration before the tomb, we fall into rank as before, and listen for an hour and a half to the sacred ritual, chanted with increasing fire.

When this first mass is over, the time being nearly nine o'clock, the weaker brethren may indulge themselves with a cup of tea; but the better pilgrim denies himself this solace, as a temptation of the Evil Spirit; and even his weaker brother has not much time to dally with the fumes of his darling herb. The great bell in the convent yard, a gift of the reigning Emperor, and one more witness to the year of wonders, warns us that the highest service of the day is close at hand.

Precisely at nine o'clock the monks assemble in the cathedral to celebrate high mass; and the congregation being already met, the tapers are lit, the deacon begins to read, the clergy take up the responses, and the officiating priest, arrayed in his shining cope and cap, recites the old and mystical forms of Slavonic prayer and praise. Two hours by the clock we stand in front of that golden shrine; stand on the granite pavement—all uncovered, many unshod—listening with ravished ears to what is certainly the noblest ceremonial music of the Russian Church.

High mass being sung and said, we ebb back slowly from the cathedral into the long gallery, where we have a few minutes more of purgatorial fire, and then a monk announces dinner, and the devoutest pilgrim in the band accepts his signal with a thankful look.

The dining-hall to which we adjourn with some irregular haste is a vaulted chamber below the cathedral, and in any other country than Russia would be called a crypt. But men must build according to their clime. The same church would not serve for winter and summer, on account of the cold and heat; and hence a sacred edifice is nearly always divided into an upper and a lower church; the upper tier being used in summer, the lower tier in winter. Our dining-hall at Solovetsk is the winter church.

Long tables run down the room, and curl round the circular shaft which sustains the cathedral floor. On these tables the first course is already laid; a tin plate for each guest, in which lies a wooden spoon, a knife and fork; and by the side of this tin platter a pound of rye bread. The pilgrims are expected to dine in messes of four, like monks. A small tin dish is laid between each mess, containing one salted sprat, divided into four bits by a knife, and four small slices of raw onion. To each mess is given a copper tureen of sour quass, and a dish of salt codfish, broken into small lumps, boiled down, and left to cool.

A bell rings briskly; up we start, cross ourselves seven times, bow towards the floor, sit down again. The captain of each mess throws pepper and salt into the dish, and stirs up our pottage with the ladle out of which he drinks his quass. A second bell rings; we dip our wooden ladles into the dish of cod. A reader climbs into the desk, and drawls the story of some saint, while a youth carries round a basket of white bread, already blessed by the priest and broken into bits. Each pilgrim takes his piece and eats it, crossing himself, time after time, until the morsel gets completely down his throat.

A third bell rings. Hush of silence; sound of prayer. Serving-men appear; our platters are swept away; a second course is served. The boys who wait on us, with rosy cheeks, smooth chins, and hanging locks, look very much like girls. This second course, consisting of a tureen of cabbage-soup, takes no long time to eat. A new reader mounts the desk, and gives us a little more life of saint. A fourth bell jangles; much more crossing takes place; the serving-men rush in; our tables are again swept clean.

Another course is served; a soup of fresh herrings, caught in the convent bay; the fish very good and sweet. Another reader; still more life of saint; and then a fifth bell rings.

A fourth and last course now comes in; a dainty of barley paste, boiled rather soft, and eaten with sour milk. Another reader; still more life of saint; and then sixth bell. The pilgrims rise; the reader stops, not caring to finish his story; and our meal is done.

Our meal, but not the ritual of that meal. Rising from our bench, we fall once more into rank and file; the women, who have dined in a room apart, crowd back into the crypt; and we join our voices in a sacred song. Then we stand for a little while in silence, each with his head bent down, as humbling ourselves before the screen, during which a pope distributes to each pilgrim a second morsel of consecrated bread. Brisk bell rings again; the monks raise a psalm of thanksgiving; a pope pronounces the benediction; and then the diners go their way refreshed with the bread and fish.

It is now near twelve o'clock. The next church service will not be held until a quarter to four in the afternoon. In the interval we have the long cloister to walk in; the holy lake to see; the shrine of St. Philip to inspect; the tombs of good monks to visit; the priestly robes and monastic jewels to admire; with other distractions to devour the time. We go off, each his own way; some into the country, which is full of tombs and shrines of the lesser saints; others to lave their limbs in the holy lake; not a few to the cells of monks who vend crosses, amulets, and charms. A Russian is a believer in stones, in rings, in rosaries, in rods; for he bears about him a hundred relics of his ancient pagan creeds. His favorite amulet is a cross, which he can buy in brass for a kopeck; one form for a man, a second form for a woman; the masculine form being Nikon's cross, with a true Greek cross in relief; the feminine form being a mixture of the two. Once tied round the neck, this amulet is never to be taken off, on peril of sickness and sudden death. To drop it is a fault, to lose it is a sin. A second talisman is a bone ball, big as a pea, hollow, drilled and fitted with a screw. A drop of mercury is coaxed into the hole, and the screw being turned, the charm is perfect, and the ball is fastened to the cross. This talisman protects the wearer from contagion in the public baths.

Some pilgrims go in boats to the farther isles; to Zaet, where two aged monks reside, and a flock of sheep browses on the herbage; to Moksalma, a yet more secular spot, where the cattle feed, and the poultry cluck and crow, in spite of St. Savatie's rule. These islets supply the convent with milk and eggs—in which holy men rejoice, as a relief from fish—in nature's own old-fashioned ways.

Not a few of the pilgrims, finding that a special pope has been appointed to show things to their English guest, perceive that the way to see sights is to follow that pope. They have to be told—in a kindly voice—that they are not to follow him into the Archimandrite's room. To-day they march in his train into the wardrobe of the convent, where the copes, crowns, staffs and crosses employed in these church services are kept; a rich and costly collection of robes, embroidered with flowers and gold, and sparkling with rubies, diamonds and pearls. Many of these robes are gifts of emperors and tsars. One of the costliest is the gift of Ivan the Terrible; but even this splendid garment pales before a gift of Alexander, the reigning prince, who sent the Archimandrite—in remembrance of the Virgin's victory—a full set of canonicals, from crown and staff to robe and shoe.

Exactly at a quarter before four o'clock, a bell commands us to return; for vespers are commencing in the Miracle Church. Again we kneel at the tombs and kiss the stones, the hangings, and the iron rails; after which we fall in as before, and listen while the vespers are intoned by monks and boys. This service concludes at half-past four. Adjourning to the long gallery, we have another look at the fires of purgatory and the abodes of bliss. Five minutes before six we file into the cathedral for second vespers, and remain there standing and uncovered—some of us unshod—until half-past seven.

At eight the supper-bell rings. Our company gathers at the welcome sound; the monks form a procession; the pilgrims trail on; all moving with a hungry solemnity to the crypt, where we find the long tables groaning, as at dinner, with the pound of black bread, the salt sprat, the onion parted into four small pieces with a knife, and the copper tureen of quass. Our supper is the dinner served up afresh, with the same prayers, the same bowing and crossing, the same bell-ringing, and the same life of saint. The only difference is, that in the evening we have no barley-paste and no stale milk.

When every one is filled and the fragments are picked up, we rise to our feet, recite a thanksgiving, and join the fathers in their evening song. A pope pronounces a blessing, and then we are free to go into our cells.

A pilgrim who can read, and may happen to have good books about him, is expected, on retiring to his cell, to read through a Psalm of David, and to ponder a little on the Lives of Saints. The convent gates are closed at nine o'clock; when it is thought well for the pilgrim to be in bed.

At two in the morning a monk will come into his lobby, tinkle the bell, and call him to the duties of another day.

CHAPTER XIV.

PRAYER AND LABOR.

BUT if the hours given up to prayer at Solovetsk are many, the hours given up to toil are more. This convent is a hive of industry, not less remarkable for what it does in the way of work than for what it is in the way of art and prayer.

"Pray and work" was the maxim of monastic houses, when monastic houses had a mission in the West. "Pray and work," said Peter the Great to his council. But such a maxim is not in harmony with the existing system; not in harmony with the Byzantine Church; and what you find at Solovetsk is traceable to an older and a better source. No monk in this sanctuary leads an idle life. Not only the fathers who are not yet popes, but many of those who hold the staff and give the benediction, devote their talents to the production of things which may be useful in the church, in the refectory, and in the cell. A few make articles for sale in the outer world; such articles as bread, clothes, rosaries and spoons. All round these ramparts, within the walls, you find a row of workshops, in which there is a hum of labor from early dawn until long after dark; forges, dairies, salting-rooms, studies, ship-yards, bake-houses, weaving-sheds, rope-walks, sewing-rooms, fruit-stores, breweries, boot-stalls, and the like, through all the forms which industry takes in a civilized age. These monks appear to be masters of every craft. They make nearly every thing you can name, from beads to frigates; and they turn out every thing they touch in admirable style. No whiter bread is baked, no sweeter quass is brewed, than you can buy in Solovetsk. To go with Father Hilarion on his round of inspection is to meet a dozen surprises face to face. At first the whole exhibition is like a dream; and you can hardly fancy that such things are being done by a body of monks, in a lonely islet, locked up from the world for eight months in the twelve by storms of sleet and deserts of ice.

These monks make seal-skin caps and belts; they paint in oil and carve in wood; they cure and tan leather; they knit woollen hose; they cast shafts of iron; they wind and spin thread; they polish stones; they cut out shoes and felts; they mould pewter plates; they dry fruit; they fell and trim forest trees; they clip paper flowers; they build carts and sledges; they embroider capes and bands; they bake bricks; they weave baskets and panniers of silver bark; they quarry and hew blocks of stone; they paint soup-ladles; they design altar-pieces, chapels, and convents; they refine bees'-wax; they twist cord and rope; they forge anchors and marling-spikes; they knit and sew, and ply their needles in every branch of useful and decorative art. In all these departments of industry, the thing which they turn out is an example of honest work.

Many of the fathers find a field for their talents on the farm: in breeding cattle, in growing potatoes, in cutting grass, in shearing sheep, in rearing poultry, in churning butter, and making cheese. A few prefer the more poetic labor of the garden: pruning grapes, bedding strawberries, hiving bees, and preserving fruit. The honey made at Mount Alexander is pure and good, the wax is also white and fine.

The convent bakehouse is a thing to see. Boats run over from every village on the coast to buy convent bread; often to beg it; and every pilgrim who comes to pray takes with him one loaf as a parting gift. This convent bread is of two sorts—black and white—leavened and unleavened—domestic and consecrated. The first is cheap, and eaten at every meal; the second is dear, and eaten as an act of grace. Both kinds are good. A consecrated loaf is small, weighing six or eight ounces, and is stamped with a sacred sign and blessed by a pope. The stamp is a cross, with a legend running round the border in old Slavonic type. These small white loaves of unleavened bread are highly prized by pious people; and a man who visits such a monastery as either Solovetsk, St. George, or Troitsa, can not bring back to his servants a gift more precious in their eyes than a small white loaf.

The brewery is no less perfect in its line than the bakehouse. Quass is the Russian ale and beer in one; the national drink; consumed by all classes, mixed with nearly every dish. Solovetsk has a name and fame for this Russian brew.

Connected with these good things of the table are the workshops for carving platters and painting spoons. The arts of life are simple in these northern wilds; forks are seldom seen; and knives are not much used. The instrument by which a man mostly helps himself to his dinner is a spoon. Nearly all his food is boiled; his cabbage-soup, his barley mess, his hash of salt-cod, his dish of sour milk. A deep platter lies in the centre of his table, and his homely guests sit round it, armed with their capacious spoons. Platter and spoon are carved of wood, and sometimes they are painted with skill and taste; though the better sorts are kept by pilgrims rather as keepsakes than for actual use.

A branch of industry allied to carving spoons and platters is that of twisting baskets and panniers into shape. Crockery in the forest is rude and dear, and in a long land-journey the weight of three or four pots and cups would be a serious strain. From bark of trees they weave a set of baskets for personal and domestic use, which are lighter than cork and handier than tin. You close them by a lid, and carry them by a loop. They are perfectly dry and sweet; with just a flavor, but no more, of the delicious resin of the tree. They hold milk. You buy them of all sizes, from that of a pepper-box to that of a water-jar; obtaining a dozen for a few kopecks.

The panniers are bigger and less delicate, made for rough passage over stony roads and through bogs of mire. These panniers are fitted with compartments, like a vintner's crate, in which you can stow away bottles of wine and insinuate knives and forks. In the open part of your pannier it is well (if you are packing for a long drive) to have an assortment of bark baskets, in which to carry such trifles as mustard, cream, and salt.

Among the odds and ends of workshops into which you drop, is that of the weaving-shed, in one of the turrets on the convent wall; a turret which is noticeable not only for the good work done in the looms, but for the part which it had to play in the defense of Solovetsk against the English fleet. The shot which is said to have driven off the "Brisk" was fired from this Weaver's Tower.

Peering above a sunny corner of the rampart stands the photographic chamber, and near to this chamber, in a new range of buildings, are the cells in which the painters and enamellers toil. The sun makes pictures of any thing in his range; boats, islets, pilgrims, monks; but the artists toiling in these cells are all employed in devotional art. Some are only copiers; and the most expert are artists only in a conventional sense. This country is not yet rich in art, except in that hard Byzantine style which Nikon the Patriarch allowed in private houses, and enforced in convent, shrine, and church.

But these fathers pride themselves, not without cause, on

being greater in their works by sea than even in their works by land. Many of them live on board, and take to the water as to their mother's milk. They are rich in boats, in rigging, and in nets. They wind excellent rope and cord. They know how to light and buoy dangerous points and armlets. They keep their own lighthouses. They build lorchas and sloops; and they have found by trial that a steamship can be turned off the stocks at Solovetsk, of which every part, from the smallest brass nail to the mainmast (with the sole exception of her engines), is the produce of their toil.

That vessel is called the "Hope." Her crew is mainly a crew of monks; and her captain is not only a monk—like Father John—but an actual pope. My first sight of this priestly skipper is in front of the royal gates where he is celebrating mass.

This reverend father takes me after service to see his vessel and the dock in which she lies. Home-built and rigged, the "Hope" has charms in my eyes possessed by very few ships. A steamer made by monks in the Frozen Sea, is, in her way, as high a feat of mind as the spire of Notre Dame in Antwerp, as the cathedral front at Wells. The thought of building that steamer was conceived in a monkish brain; the lines were fashioned by a monkish pen; monks felled the trees, and forged the bolts, and wove the canvas, and curled the ropes. Monks put her together; monks painted her cabin; monks stuffed her seats and pillows. Monks launched her on the sea, and, since they have launched her, they have sailed in her from port to port.

"How did you learn your trade of skipper?"

The father smiles. He is a young fellow—younger than Father John; a fellow of thirty or thirty-two, with swarthy cheek, black eye, and tawny mane; a man to play the pirate in some drama of virtuous love. "I was a seaman in my youth," he says, "and when we wanted a skipper in the convent, I went over to Kem, where we have a school of navigation, and got the certificate of a master; that entitled me to command my ship."

"The council of that school are not very strict?"

"No; not with monks. We have our own ways; we labor in the Lord; and He protects us in what we do for Him."

"Through human means?"

"No; by His own right hand, put forth under all men's eyes. You see, the first time that we left the convent for Archangel, we were weak in hands and strange to our work. A storm came on; the 'Hope' was driven on shore. Another crew would have taken to their boats and lost their ship, if not their lives. We prayed to the Most Pure Mother of God: at first she would not hear us on account of our sins; but we would not be denied, and sang our psalms until the wind went down."

"You were still ashore?"

"Yes; grooved in a bed of sand; but when the wind veered round, the ship began to heave and stir. We tackled her with ropes and got her afloat once more. Slava Bogu! It was her act!"

The dock of which Father John spoke with pride turns out to be not a dock only, but a dry dock! Now, a dock, even where it is a common dock, is one of those signs by which one may gauge—as by the strength of a city wall, the splendor of a court of justice and the beauty of a public garden—the height to which a people have attained. In Russia docks are extremely rare. Not a dozen ports in the empire can boast a dock. Archangel has no dock; Astrachan has no dock; Rostoff has no dock. It is only in such cities as Riga and Odessa, built and occupied by foreigners, that you find such things. The dry dock at Solovetsk is the only sample of its kind in the whole of Russia Proper! Cronstadt has a dry dock; but Cronstadt is in the Finnish waters—a German port, with a German name. The only work of this kind existing on Russian ground is the product of monkish enterprise and skill.

Priests take their share in all these labors. When a monk enters into orders he is free to devote himself, if he chooses, to the Church service only, since the Holy Governing Synod recognizes the right of a pope to a maintenance in his office; but in the Convent of Solovetsk, a priest rarely confines his activity to his sacred duties. Work is the sign of a religious life. If any man shows a talent for either art or business, he is excited by the praise of his fellows and superiors to pursue the call of his genius, devoting the produce of his labor to the glory of God. One pope is a farmer, a second a painter, a third a fisherman; this man is a collector of simples, that a copier of manuscripts, and this, again, a binder of books.

Of these vocations that of the schoolmaster is not the least coveted. All children who come to Solovetsk are kept for a year, if not for a longer time. The lodging is homely and the teaching rough; for the schools are adapted to the state of the country; and the food and sleeping-rooms are raised only a little above the comforts of a peasant's home. No one is sent away untaught; but only a few are kept beyond a year. If a man likes to remain and work in the convent he can hire himself out as a laborer, either in the fishing-boats or on the farms. He dines in summer, like the monks, on bread, fish and quass; in winter he is provided with salt mutton, cured on the farm—a luxury his masters may not touch. Many of these boys remain for life, living in a celibate state, like the monks; but sure of a dinner and a bed, safe from the conscription, and free from family cares. Some of them take vows. If they go back into the world they are likely to find places on account of their past; in any case they can shift for themselves, since a lad who has lived a few years in this convent is pretty sure to be able to fish and farm, to cook his own dinner, and to mend his own boots.

CHAPTER XV.

BLACK CLERGY.

ALL men of the higher classes in Russia talk of their Black Clergy as a body of worthless fellows; idle, ignorant, profligate; set apart by their vows as unsocial; to whom no terms should be offered, with whom no capitulations need be kept. "Away with them, root and branch!" is a general cry, delivered by young and liberal Russians in the undertone of a fixed resolve.

The men who raise this cry are not simply scoffers and scorners, making war on religious ideas and ecclesiastical institutions. Only too often they are men who love their church, who support their parish priests, and who wish to plant their country in the foremost line of Christian states. Russia, they say, possesses ten thousand monks; and these ten thousand monks they would hand over to a drill sergeant and convert into regiments of the line.

This rancor of the educated classes towards the monks—a rancor roused and fed by their undying hatred of reforms in Church and State—compels one to mark the extent and study the sources of monastic power. This study will take us far and wide: though it will also bring us in the end to Solovetsk once more.

"A desert dotted with cloisters," would be no untrue description of the country spreading southward from the Polar Sea to the Tartar Steppe. In New Russia, in the khanates of Kazan and Crimea, in the steppes of the Lower Volga, and in the wastes of Siberia, it would not be true. But Great Russia is a paradise of monks. In the vast regions stretching from Kem to Belgorod—an eagle's flight from north to south of a thousand miles—from Pskoff on Lake Peipus, to Vasil on the Middle Volga—a similar flight from west to east of seven hundred miles—the land is everywhere bright with cloisters, musical with monastic bells.

Nothing on this earth's surface can be drearier than a Russian forest, unless it be a Russian plain. The forest is a growth of stunted birch and pine; the trees of one height and girth; the fringe of black shoots unvaried save by some break of bog, some length of colorless lake. The plain is a stretch of moor, without a swell, without a tree, without a town, for perhaps a hundred leagues; on which the grass, if grass such herbage can be called, is brown; while the village, if such a scatter of cabins can be called by a name so tender and picturesque, is nothing but log and mud. A traveller's eye would weary, and his heart would sicken, at the long succession of such lines, were it not that here and there, in the opening of some forest glade, on the ridge of some formless plain, the radiant cross and sparkling towers of a convent spring towards heaven; a convent with its fringe of verdure, its white front, its clustering domes and chains. The woods round Kargopol, the marshes near Lake Ilmen, and the plains of Moscow, are alive with light and color; while the smaller convents on river bank and in misty wood, being railed and painted, look like works of art. One of my sweetest recollections in a long, dull journey, is that of our descent into the valley of Siya, when we sighted the great monastery, lying in a watery dell amidst groves of trees, with the rays of a setting sun on her golden cross and her shining domes—a happy valley and a consecrated home; not to speak of such trifles as the clean cell and the wholesome bread which a pilgrim finds within her walls!

The old cities of Great Russia—Novgorod, Moscow, Pskoff, Vladimir—are much richer in monastic institutions than their rivals of a later time. For leagues above and leagues below the ancient capital of Russia, the river Volkhoff, on the banks of which it stands, is bright with these old mansions of the Church. Novgorod enriched her suburbs with the splendid Convents of St. George, St. Cyril, and of St. Anton of Rome. Moscow lies swathed in a belt and mantle of monastic houses—Simonoff, Donskoi, Danieloff, Alexiefski, Ivanofski, and many more; the belfries and domes of which lighten the wonderful panorama seen from the Sparrow Hills. Pskoff has her glorious Convent of the Catacombs, all but rivalling that of Kief.

Within the walls, these cloisters are no less splendid than the promise from without. Their altars and chapels are always fine, the refectories neat and roomy, the sacristies rich in crosses and priestly robes. Many fine pictures—fine of their school—adorn the screens and the royal gates. Nearly all possess portraits of the Mother and Child encased in gold, and some have lamps and croziers worth their weight in sterling coin. The greater part of what is visible of Russian wealth appears to hang around these shrines.

These old monastic houses sprang out of the social life around them. They were centres of learning, industry, and art. A convent was a school, and in these schools a special excellence was sought and won. This stamp has never been effaced; and many of the convents still aspire to excellence in some special craft. The Convent of St. Sergie, near Strelna, is famed for music; the New Monastery, near Kherson, for melons; the Troitsa, near Moscow, for carving; the Catacombs, near Kief, for service-books.

In the belfry of the old Cathedral of St. Sophia at Novgorod you are shown a chamber which was formerly used as a treasure-room by the citizens—in fact, as their place of safety and their tower of strength. You enter it through a series of dark and difficult passages, barred by no less than twelve iron doors; each door to be unfastened by bolt and bar, secured in the catches under separate lock and key. In this strong place the burghers kept, in times of peril, their silver plate, their costly icons, and their ropes of pearl. A robber would not—and a boyar dared not—force the sanctuary of God. Each convent was, in this respect, a smaller St. Sophia; and every man who laid up gold and jewels in such a bank could sleep in peace.

"You must understand," said the antiquary of Novgorod, as we paddled in our boat down the Volkhoff, "that in ancient times a convent was a home—a family house. A man who made money by trade was minded in his old age to retire from the city and end his days in peace. In England such a man would buy him a country-house in the neighborhood of his native town, in which he would live with his wife and children until he died. In a country like Old Russia, with brigands always at his gates, the man who saved money had to put his wealth under the protection of his church. Selecting a pleasant site, he would build his house in the name of his patron saint, adorn it with an altar, furnish it with a kitchen, dormitory, and cellar, and taking with him his wife, his children, and his pope, would set up his tent in that secure and comfortable place for the remainder of his days on earth."

"Could such a man have his wife and children near him?"

"Near him! With him; not only in his chapel but in his cell. The convent was his home—his country-house; and at his death descended to his son, who had probably become a monk. In some such fashion, many of the prettiest of these smaller convents on the Volkhoff came to be."

Half the convents in Great Russia were established as country-houses; the other half as deserts—like Solovetsk; and many a poor fellow toiled like Zosima who has not been blessed with Zosima's fame.

But such a thing is possible, even now; for Russia has not yet passed beyond the legendary and heroic periods of her growth. The latest case is that of the new desert founded at Gethsemane, on the plateau of the Troitsa, near Moscow; one of the most singular notes of the present time.

In the year 1803 was born in a log cabin, in a small village called Prechistoe (Very Clean), near the city of Vladimir, a male serf, so obscure that his family name has perished. For many years he lived on his lord's estate, like any other serf, marrying in his own class (twice), and rearing three strapping sons. At thirty-seven he was freed by his owner; when he moved from his village to Troitsa, took the name of Philip, put on cowl and gown, and dug for himself a vault in the earth. In this catacomb he spent five years of his life, until he found a more congenial home among the convent graves, where he lived for twenty years. Too fond of freedom to take monastic vows, he never placed himself under convent rule. Yet seeing, in spite of the proverb, that the hood makes the monk in Russia, if not elsewhere, he robed his limbs in coarse serge, girdled his waist with a heavy chain, and walked to the palace of Philaret, Metropolite of Moscow, begged that dignitary's blessing, and craved permission to adopt his name. Philaret took a fancy to the mendicant; and from that time forth the whilom serf from Very Clean was known in every street as Philaret-oushka—Philaret the Less.

Those grave-yards of the Troitsa lay in a pretty and silent spot on the edge of a lake, inclosed in dark green woods. Among those mounds the mendicant made his desert. Buying a few images and crosses in Troitsa and Gethsemane at two kopecks apiece, he carried them into the streets and houses of Moscow, where he gave them to people, with his blessing; taking, in exchange, such gifts as his penitents pleased; a ruble, ten rubles, a hundred rubles each. He very soon had money in the bank. His images brought more rubles than his crosses; for his followers found that his images gave them luck, while his crosses sent them trouble. Hence a woman to whom he gave a cross went home with a heavy heart. Unlike the practice in western countries, no peasant woman adorns herself with this memorial of her faith; nor is the cross a familiar ornament even in mansions of the rich. A priest wears a cross; a spire is crowned by a cross; but this symbol of our salvation is rarely seen among the painted and plated icons in a private house. To "bear the cross" is to suffer pain, and no one wishes to suffer pain. One cross a man is bound to bear—that hung about his neck at the baptismal font; but few men care to carry a second weight.

An oddity in dress and speech, Philaret-oushka wore no shoes and socks, and his greeting in the market was, "I wish you a merry angel's day," instead of "I wish you well." In his desert, and in his rambles, he was attended by as strange an oddity as himself; one Ivanoushka, John the Less. This man was never known to speak; he only sang. He sang in his cell; he sang on the road; he sang by the Holy Gate. The tone in which he sang reflected his master's mood; and the voice of John the Less told many a poor creature whether Philaret the Less would give her that day an image or a cross.

This mendicant had much success in merchants' shops. The more delicate ladies shrank from him with loathing, not because he begged their money, but because he defiled their rooms. Though born in Very Clean, this serf was dirtier than a monk; but his followers saw in his rusty chains, his grimy skin, his unkempt hair, so many signs of grace. The women of the trading classes courted him. A lady told me, that on calling to see a female friend, the wife of a merchant of the first guild, she found her kneeling on the floor, and washing this beggar's feet. Her act was not a form; for the mendicant wore no shoes, and the streets of Moscow are foul with mire and hard with flints. One old maid, Miss Seribrikof, used to boast, as the glory of her life, that she had once been allowed to wash the good man's sores. Young brides would beg him to attend their nuptial feasts; at which he would "prophesy" as they call it; hinting darkly at their future of weal or woe. Sometimes he made a lucky hit. One day, at the wedding-feast of Gospodin Sorokine, one of the richest men in Moscow, he turned to the bride and said, "When your feastings are over, you will have to smear your husband with honey." No one knew what he meant, until three days later, when Sorokine died; on which event every one remembered that honey is tasted at all Russian funerals; and the words of Philaret the Less were likened to that Vision of Zosima, which has since been painted on the pillar in Novgorod the Great.

Madame Loguinof, one of his rich disciples, gave this mendicant money enough to build a church and convent, and when these edifices were raised in the grave-yard of Troitsa his "desert" was complete.

At the age of sixty-five, this idol of the people passed away. When his high patron died, Philaret the Less was not so happy in his desert as of yore; for Innocent, the new Metropolite, was a real missionary of his faith, and not a man to look with favor on monks in masquerade. Deserting his desert, the holy man went his way from Troitsa into the province of Tula, where, in the village of Tcheglovo, he built a second convent, in which he died about a year ago. The two convents built by his rusty chains and dirty feet are now occupied by bodies of regular monks.

In these morbid growths of the religious sentiment, the Black Clergy seek support against the scorn and malice of a reforming world.

These monks have great advantages on their side. If liberal thought and science are against them, usage and repute are in their favor. All the high places are in their gift; all the chief forces are in their hands. The women are with them; and the ignorant rustics are mostly with them. Monks have always attracted the sex from which they fly; and every city in the empire has some story of a favorite father followed, like Philaret the Less, by a female crowd. Vicar Nathaniel was not worshipped in the Nevski Prospect with a softer flattery than is Bishop Leonidas in the Kremlin gardens. Comedy but rarely touches these holy men; yet one may see in Moscow albums an amusing sketch of this gifted and fascinating man being lifted into higher place upon ladies' skirts.

The monks have not only got possession of the spiritual power; but they hold in their hands nearly all the sources of that spiritual power. They have the convents, catacombs, and shrines. They guard the bones of saints, and are themselves the stuff of which saints are made. In the golden book of the Russian Church there is not one instance of a canonized parish priest.

These celibate fathers affect to keep the two great keys of influence in a land like Russia—the gift of sacrifice, and the gift of miracles.

CHAPTER XVI.

SACRIFICE.

SACRIFICE is a cardinal virtue of the Church. To the Russian mind it is the highest form of good; the surest sign of a perfect faith. Sacrifice is the evidence of a soul given up to God.

A child can only be received into the church through sacrifice; and one of the forms in which a man gives himself up to heaven is that of becoming insane "for the sake of Christ."

Last year (1868), a poor creature called Ivan Jacovlevitch died in the Lunatic Asylum in Moscow, after winning for himself a curious kind of fame. One-half the world pronounced him mad; a second half respected him as a holy man. The first half, being the stronger, locked him up, and kept him under medical watch and ward until he died.

This Ivan, a burgher in the small town of Cherkesovo, made a "sacrifice" of his health and comfort to the Lord. By sacred vows, he bound himself never to wash his face and comb his hair, never to change his rags, never to sit on chair and stool, never to eat at table, never to handle knife and fork. In virtue of this sacrifice, he lived like a dog; crouching on the floor, and licking up his food with lips and tongue. When brought into the madhouse, he was washed with soap and dressed in calico; but he began to mess himself on purpose; and his keepers soon gave up the task of trying to keep him clean.

No saint in the calendar draws such crowds to his shrine as Ivan Jacovlevitch drew to his chamber in this lunatic's house. Not only servant girls and farmers' wives, but women of the trading classes, came to him daily; bringing him dainties to eat, making him presents in money, and telling him all the secrets of their hearts. Sitting on the ground, and gobbling up his food, he stared at these visitors, mumbling some words between his teeth, which his listeners racked their brains to twist and frame into sense. He rolled the crumbs of his patties into pills, and when sick persons came to him to be cured, he put these dirty little balls into their mouths. This man was said to have become "insane for the Lord."

The authorities of the asylum lent him a spacious room in which to receive his guests. They knew that he was mad; they knew that a crowded room was bad for him; but the public rush was so strong, that they could neither stand upon their science, nor enforce their rules. The lunatic died amidst the tears and groans of half the city. When the news of his death was noised abroad, a stranger would have thought the city was also mad. Men stopped in the street to kneel and pray; women threw themselves on the ground in grief; and a crowd of the lower classes ran about the bazars and markets, crying, "Ivan is dead! Ivan is dead! Ah! who will tell us what to do for ourselves, now Ivan is dead?"

On my table, as I write these words, lies a copy of the *Moscow Gazette*—the journal which Katkoff edits, in which Samarin writes—containing a proposal, made by the clergy, for a public monument to Ivan Jacovlevitch, in the village where this poor lunatic was born!

All monks prefer to live a life of sacrifice; the highest forms of sacrifice being that of the recluse and the anchorite.

Every branch of the Oriental Church—Armenian, Coptic, Greek—encourages this form; but no Church on earth has given the world so many hermits as the Russ. Her calendar is full of anchorites, and the stories told of these self-denying men and women are often past belief. One Sister Maria was nailed up in a niche at Hotkoff, fed through a hole in the rock, and lingered in her living tomb twelve years.

On the great plateau of the Troitsa, forty miles from Moscow, stands a monastic village, called Gethsemane. This monastic village is divided into two parts; the convent and the catacombs; separated by a black and silent lake.

A type of poverty and misery, the convent is built of rough logs, colored with coarse paint. Not a trace of gold or silver is allowed, and the only ornaments are of cypress. Gowns of the poorest serge, and food of the simplest kind, are given to the monks. No female is allowed to enter this holy place, excepting once a year, on the feast of the Virgin's ascent into heaven. Three women were standing humbly at the gate as we drove in; perhaps wondering why their sex should be shut out of Gethsemane, since their Lord was not betrayed in the garden by a female kiss!

Across the black lake lie the catacombs, cut off from the convent by a gate and fence; for into these living graves it is lawful for a female to descend. Deep down from the light of day, below the level of that sombre lake, these catacombs extend. We light each man his taper, as we stand above the narrow opening into the vaults. A monk, first crossing his breast and muttering his pass-words in an unknown tongue, goes down the winding stairs. We follow slowly, one by one in silence; shading the light and holding to the wall. A faint smell fills our nostrils; a dull sound greets our ears; heavily comes our breath in the damp and fetid air. The tapers faint and flicker in the gloom. Gaining a passage, we observe some grated windows, narrow holes, and iron-bound doors. These openings lead into cells. The roof above is wet with slime, the floor is foul with crawling, nameless things.

"Hush!" drones the monk, as he creeps past some grated window and some iron-clad door, as though he were afraid that we should wake the dead.

"What is this hole in the stone?" The monk stops short and waves his lurid light: "A cell; a good man lies here; hush! his soul is now with God!"

"Dead?"

"Yea—dead to the world."

"How long has he been here?"

"How long? Eleven years and more."

Passing this living tomb with a shiver, we catch the boom of a bell, and soon emerge from the narrow passage into a tiny church. A lamp is burning before the shrine; two monks are kneeling with their temples on the floor; a priest is singing in a low, dull tone. The fittings of this church are all of brass; for pine and birch would rot into paste in a single year. Beyond the chapel we come to the holy well, the water of which is said to be good for body and soul. It is certainly earthy to the taste.

On coming into the light of day, we question the father sharply as to that recluse who is said to have lived eleven years behind the iron-clad door; and learn without surprise that he comes out from time to time, to ring the convent-bell, to fetch in wood, and hear the news! We learn that a man retired with his son into one of these catacombs; that he remained in his grave—so to speak—two years and a half, and then came out completely broken in his health. My eminent Russian friend, Professor Kapoustin, turns to me and says, "When our country was covered with forests, when our best road was a rut, and our villages were all shut in, a man who wished for peace of mind might wall himself up in a cell; but the country is now open, monks read newspapers, travellers come and go, and the recluse likes to hear the news and see the light of day."

Instead of living in their catacombs, the monks now turn a penny by showing them to pilgrims, at the price of a taper, and by selling to visitors the portraits of monks and nuns who lived in the sturdier days of their church.

The spirit of sacrifice takes other and milder forms. In the court-yards of Solovetsk one sees a strange creature, dressed in rags, fed on garbage, and lodged in gutters, who belongs to the monastic order, without being vowed as a regular monk. He lives by sufferance, not by right. He offers himself up as a daily sacrifice. He follows, so to speak, the calling of abjectness; and makes himself an example of the worthlessness of earthly things. This strange being is much run after by the poorer pilgrims, who regard him as a holy man; and he is noticeable as a type of what the Black Clergy think meritorious in the Christian life.

Father Nikita, the name by which this man is known, is a dwarf, four feet ten inches high, with thin, gray beard, black face, and rat-like eyes. He never pollutes his skin with water and soap; for what is man that he should foster pride of the flesh? His garb is a string of rags and shreds; for he spurns the warmer and more decent habit of a monk. Instead of going to the store when he needs a frock, he crawls into the waste-closet, where he begs as a favor that the father having charge of the castaway clothes will give him the tatters which some poor brother has thrown aside. A room is left for his use in the cloister; but a bench of wood and a pillow of straw are things too good for dust and clay; and in token of his unworthiness, he lives on the open quay and sleeps in the convent yard. Nobody can persuade him to sit down to the common meal; the sup of sour quass, the pound of black bread, the morsel of salt cod being far too sumptuous food for him; but when the meal is over, and the crumbs are swept up, he will slink into the pantry, scrape into one dish the slops and bones, and make a repast of what peasants and beggars have thrown away.

He will not take his place in church; he will not pass through the Sacred Gates. When service is going on, he crouches in the darkest corner of the church, and listens to the prayers and chants with his head upon the ground. He likes to be spurned and buffeted by the crowd. A servant of every one, he is only too happy if folk will order him about; and when he can find a wretch so poor and dirty that every one else shuns him, he will take that dirty wretch to be his lord. In winter, when the snow lies deep on the ground, he will sleep in the open yard; in summer, when the heat is fierce, he will expose his shaven crown to the sun. He loves to be scorned, and spit upon, and robbed. Like all his class, he is fond of money; and this love of dross he turns into his sharpest discipline of soul. Twisting plaits of birch-bark into creels and crates, he vends these articles to boatmen and pilgrims at two kopecks apiece; ties the copper coins in a filthy rag; and then creeps away to hide his money under a stone, in the hope that some one will watch him and steal it when he is gone.

The first monk who held the chair of abjectness in Solovetsk, before Nikita came in, was a miracle of self-denial, and his death was commemorated by an act of the rarest grace. Father Nahum is that elder and worthier sacrifice to heaven.

Nahum is said to have been more abject in manner, more self-denying in habit, than Nikita; being a person of higher order, and having more method in his scheme of sacrifice. He abstained from the refuse of fish, as too great a delicacy for sinful men. He liked to sleep in the snow. He was only too happy to lie down at a beggar's door. Once, when he slept outside the convent gates all night, some humorous brother suggested that perhaps he had been looking out for girls;

and on hearing of this ribald jest he stripped himself nearly naked, poked a hole in the ice, and sat down in the frozen lake until his feet were chilled to the bone. A wing of the convent once took fire, and the monks began to run about with pails; but Nahum rolled a ball of snow in his palms and threw it among the flames; and as the tongues lapped higher and higher, he ran to the church, threw himself on the floor, and begged the Lord to put them out. Instantly, say the monks, the fire died down. An archimandrite saw him groping in a garden for potatoes, tearing up the roots with his fingers. "That is cold work, is it not, Nahum?" asked his kindly chief. "Humph!" said the monk; "try it." When the present emperor came to Solovetsk, and every one was anxious to do him service, Nahum walked up to him with a wooden cup, half full of dirty water, saying, "Drink; it is good enough."

When this professor of abjectness died, he was honored by his brethren with a special funeral, inside the convent gates. He was buried in the yard, beneath the cathedral dome; where all day long, in the pilgrim season, a crowd of people may be seen about the block of granite which marks his grave; some praying beside the stone, as though he were already a "friend of God," while others are listening to the stories told of this uncanonized saint. Only one other monk of Solovetsk has ever been distinguished by such a mark of grace. Time—and time only—now seems wanting to Father Nahum's glory. In another generation—if the Black Clergy hold their own—Nahum of Solovetsk, canonized already by the popular voice of monks and pilgrims, will be taken up in St. Isaac's Square, and raised by imperial edict to his heavenly seat.

CHAPTER XVII.

MIRACLES.

YET the gift of miracles is greater than the gift of sacrifice. The Black Clergy stand out for miracles; not in a mystical sense, but in a natural sense; not only in times long past, but in the present hour; not only in the dark and in obscure hamlets, but in populous places and in the light of day.

At Kief a friend drives me out to the caves of Anton and Feodosie, where we find some men and women standing by the gates, expecting the father who keeps the keys to bring them and unlock the doors. As these living pilgrims occupy us more than the dead anchorets, we join this party, pay our five kopecks, light our tapers, and descend with them the rocky stairs into the vault. Candle in hand, an aged monk goes forward, muttering in the gloom; stopping for an instant, here and there, to show us, lying on a ledge of rock, some coffin muffled in a pall. We thread a mile of lanes, saluting saint on saint, and twice or thrice we come into dwarf chapels, in each of which a lamp burns dimly before a shrine. The women kneel; the men cross themselves and pray. Moving forward in the dark, we come upon a niche in the wall, covered by a curtain and a glass door, on the ledge of which stands a silver dish, a little water, and a human skull. Our pilgrims cross themselves and mutter a voiceless prayer, while the aged monk lays down his taper and unlocks the door. A woman sinks on her knees before the niche, turns up her face, and shuts her eyes, while the father, dipping a quill into the water, drops a little of the fluid on her eyelids. One by one, each pilgrim undergoes this rite; and then, on rising from his knees, lays down an offering of a few kopecks on the ledge of rock.

"What does this ceremony mean?" I ask the father. "Mean?" says he: "a mystery—a miracle! This skull is the relic of a holy man whose eye had suffered from a blow. He called upon the Most Pure Mother of God; she heard his cry of pain; and in her pity she cured him of his wound."

"What is the name of that holy man?"—"We do not know."

"When did he live and die?"—"We do not know."

"Was he a monk of Kief?"—"He was; and after he died his skull was kept, because his fame was great, and every one with pain in his eyes came hither to obtain relief."

Not one of our fellow-pilgrims has sore eyes; but who, as the father urges, knows what the morrow may have in store? Bad eyes may come; and who would not like to insure himself forever against pain and blindness at the cost of five kopecks?

Such miracles are performed by the bones of saints in cities less holy and old than Kief.

Seraphim, a merchant of Kursk, abandoned his wife, his children, and his shop, to become a monk. Wandering to the cloister called the Desert of Sarof, in the province of Tambof, he dug for himself a hole in the ground, in which he lay down and slept. Some robbers came to his cave, where they beat and searched him; but, on finding his pockets empty, they knew that he must be a holy man. From that lucky day his fame spread rapidly abroad; and people came to see him from far and near; bringing presents of bread, of raiment, and of money; all of which he took into his cave, and doled out afterwards to the poor. A second window had to be cut into his cell; at one he received gifts, at the other he dispensed them. His desert became a populous place, and the Convent of Sarof grew into vast repute.

Seraphim founded a second desert for women, ten miles distant from his own. A gentleman gave him a piece of ground; merchants sent him money; for his favor was by that time reckoned as of higher value than house and land. Lovely and wealthy women drove to see him, and to stay with him; entering into the desert which he formed for them, and living apart from the world, without taking on their heads the burden of conventual vows. At length a miracle was announced. A lamp which hung in front of a picture of the Virgin died out while Seraphim was kneeling on the ground; the chapel grew dark and the face of the Virgin faint; the pilgrims were much alarmed; when, to the surprise of every one who saw it, a light came out from the picture and re-lit the lamp! A second miracle soon followed. One day, a crowd of poor people came to the desert for bread, when Seraphim had little in his cell to give. Counting his loaves, he saw that he had only two; and how was he to divide two loaves among all those hungry folk? He lifted up his voice —and lo! not two, but twenty loaves were standing on his board. From that time wonders were reported every year from Sarof; cures of all kinds; and the court in front of Seraphim's cell was thronged by the lame and blind, the deaf and dumb, by day and night.

Seraphim died in 1833; yet miracles are said to be effected

at his tomb to this very hour. Already called a saint, the people ask his canonization from the Church. Every new Emperor makes a saint; as in Turkey every new Sultan builds a mosque; and Seraphim is fixed upon by the public voice as the man whom Alexander the Third will have to make a saint.

One Motovilof, a landowner in the province of Penza, lame, unable to walk, applied for help to Seraphim, who promised the invalid, on conditions, a certain cure. Motovilof was to become a friend of Sarof; a supporter of the female desert. Yielding to these terms, he was told to go down to Voronej, and to make his reverence at the shrine of Metrofanes, a local saint, on which he would find himself free from pain. Motovilof went to Voronej, and came back cured. With grateful heart he gave Seraphim a patch of land for his female desert; and then, being busy with his affairs, he gradually forgot his pilgrimage and his miraculous cure. The pain came back into his leg; he could hardly walk; and not until he sent a supply of bread and clothes to Seraphim was he restored in health. Not once, but many times, the worldly man was warned to keep his pledge; a journey to the desert became a habit of his life; until he fell into love for one of Seraphim's fair penitents, and taking her home from her refuge, made that recluse his wife.

More noticeable still is the story of Tikhon, sometime Bishop of Voronej, now a recognized saint of the Orthodox Church. Tikhon is the official saint of the present reign; the living Emperor's contribution to the heavenly ranks.

Timothy Sokolof, son of a poor reader in a village church, was born (in 1724) in that province of Novgorod which has given to Russia most of her popular saints. The reader's family was large, his income small, and Timothy was sent to work on a neighbor's farm. Toiling in the fields by day, in the sheds by night; sleeping little, eating less; he yet contrived to learn how to read and write. Sent from this farm to a school, just opened in Novgorod, he toiled so patiently at his tasks, and made such progress in his studies, that on finishing his course he was appointed master of the school.

His heart was not in this work of teaching. From his cradle he had been fond of singing hymns and hearing mass, of being left alone with his books and thoughts, of flying from the face of man and the allurements of the world. A vision shaped for him his future course. "When I was yet a teacher in the school," he said to a friend in after life, "I sat up whole nights, reading and thinking. Once, when I was sitting up in May, the air being very soft, the sky very bright, I left my cell, and stood under the starry dome, admiring the lights, and thinking of our eternal life. Heaven opened to my sight—a vision such as human words can never paint! My heart was filled with joy, and from that hour I felt a passionate longing to quit the world."

A few years after he took the cowl and changed the name of Timothy for Tikhon, he was raised from his humble cell to the episcopal bench; first in Novgorod, afterwards at Voronej; the second a missionary see; the province of Voronej lying close to the Don Kozak country and the Tartar steppe.

The people of this district were lawless tribes; Kozaks, Kalmuks, Malo-Russ; a tipsy, idle, vagabond crew; the clergy worse, it may be, than their flocks. Voronej had no schools; the popes could hardly read; the services were badly sung and said. All classes of the people lived in sin. Tikhon began a patient wrestle with these disorders. Opening with the priests, and with the schools, he put an end to flogging in the seminaries; in order, as he said, to raise the standing of a priest, and cause the student to respect himself. This change was but a sign of things to come. By easy steps he won his clergy to live like priests; to drink less, to pray more; and generally to act as ministers of God. In two years he purged the schools and purified the Church.

No less care was given to lay disorders. Often he had to be plain in speech; but such was the reverence felt for him by burgher and peasant that no one dared to disregard his voice. "You must do so, if Tikhon tells you," they would say to each other; "if not, he will complain of you to God." He dressed in a coarse robe; he ate plain food; he sent the wine untouched from his table to the sick. He was the poor man's friend; and only waited on the rich when he found no wretched ones at his gates. The power of Tikhon lay in his faultless life, in his tender tones, and in his loving heart. "Want of love," he used to urge, "is the cause of all our misery; had we more love for our brothers, pain and grief would be more easy to bear; love soothes away all grief and pain."

Two years in Novgorod, five years in Voronej, he spent in these gracious labors, till the longing of his heart for solitude grew too strong. Laying down his mitre, he retired from his palace in Voronej to the convent of Zadonsk, a little town on the river Don, where he gave up his time to writing tracts and visiting the poor. These labors were of highest use; for Tikhon was among the first (if not the first of all) to write in favor of the serf. Fifteen volumes of his works are printed; fifteen more are said to lie in manuscript; and some of these works have gone through fifty editions from the Russian press.

Tikhon's great merit as a writer lies in the fact that he foresaw, prepared, and urged emancipation of the serfs.

For fifteen years he lived the life of a holy man. As a friend of serfs, he one day went to the house of a prince, in the district of Voronej, to point out some wrong which they were suffering on his estate, and to beg him, for the sake of Jesus and Mary, to be tender with the poor. The prince got angry with his guest for putting the thing so plainly into words; and in the midst of some sharp speech between them, struck him in the face. Tikhon rose up and left the house; but when he had walked some time, he began to see that he—no less than his host—was in the wrong. This man, he said to himself, has done a deed of which, on cooling down, he will feel ashamed. Who has caused him to do that wrong? "It was my doing," sighed the reprover, turning on his heel, and going straight back into the house. Falling at the prince's feet, Tikhon craved his pardon for having stirred him into wrath, and caused him to commit a sin. The man was so astonished, that he knelt down by the monk, and, kissing his hands, implored his forgiveness and his benediction. From that hour, it is said, the prince was another man; noticeable through all the province of Voronej for his kindness to the serfs.

Tikhon lived into his eightieth year. Before he passed away, he told the brethren of his convent he would live until such a day and then depart. He died, as he had told them he should die—on the day foreseen, and in the midst of his weeping friends. From the day of his funeral, his shrine in Zadonsk was visited by an ever-increasing crush; for cures of many kinds were wrought; the sick recovered, the lame walked home, the blind saw, the crooked became straight. A thousand voices claimed the canonization of this friend of serfs; until the reigning emperor, struck by this appeal, invited the Holy Governing Synod to conduct the inquiries which precede the canonization of a Russian saint.

The commission sat; the miracles were proved; and then the tomb was opened. Out from the coffin came a scent of flowers; the flesh was pure and sweet; and the act of canonization was decreed and signed in 1861, the emancipation year. Tikhon of Zadonsk is the emancipation saint.

Yet, according to the Black Clergy, the newest and the greatest miracle of modern times is the Virgin's defense of Solovetsk against the Anglo-French squadron in 1854.

The wardrobe of Solovetsk contains the chief treasures of the cloister; old charters and letters; original grants of lands; the rescript of Peter; manuscript lives of Savatie and Zosima; service-books, richly bound in golden plates; Pojarski's sword; cups, lamps, crosses, candlesticks in gold and silver; but the treasure of treasures is the evidence of that stupendous miracle wrought by the Most Pure Mother of God.

On the centre stand, under a glass case, strongly locked, lie an English shell and two round-shot. They are carefully inscribed. A reliquary in a closet holds a dozen bits of brass, the rent fusees of exploded shells. A number of prints are sold to the devout, in which the English gun-boats are moored under the convent wall, so near that men might easily have leaped on shore. Among this mass of evidence is a new and splendid ornamental cup; the gift of Russia to Solovetsk—in memory of the day when human help had failed, and "the convent that endureth forever" was saved by the Virgin Mother of God.

A scoffer here and there may smile. "Savatie! Zosima!" laughed a Russian cynic in my face; "you English made the fortune of these saints. How so? You see a peasant has but two notions in his pate—the Empire and the Church; a power of the flesh and a power of the spirit. Now, see what you have done. You wage war upon us; you send your fleets into the Black Sea and into the White Sea; in the first to fight against the Empire, in the second to fight against the Church. In one sea, you win; in the other sea, you lose. Sevastopol falls to your arms; while Solovetsk drives away your ships. The arm of the spirit is seen to be stronger than the arm of flesh. What then? 'Heaven,' says the rustic to his neighbor, as they dawdle home from church, 'is mightier than the Tsar.' For fifty years to come our superstitions will lie on English heads!"

The tale of that miracle, told me on the spot, will sound in some ears like a piece of high comedy, in others like a chapter from some ancient and forgotten book. A dry dispatch from Admiral Ommaney contains the little that we know of our "Operations in the White Sea;" the next chapter gives the story, as they tell it on the other side.

CHAPTER XVIII.

THE GREAT MIRACLE.

So soon as news arrived in the winter palace that an English fleet was under steam for the Polar seas, the War Office set to work in the usual way; sending out arms and men; such arms and men as could be found and spared in these northern towns. Six old siege-guns, fit for a museum, were shipped from Archangel to the convent, with five artillerymen, and fifty troopers of the line, selected from the Invalid Corps. An officer came with these forces to conduct the defense.

Just as the English ships were entering on their task this officer died (June, 1854); no doubt by the hand of God, in order to rebuke the pride of man, while adding fresh lustre to the auriol of His saints. The arm of flesh having failed, the fathers threw themselves on the only power that can never fail.

Father Alexander, then the Archimandrite, ordered a series of services to be held in the several chapels within the walls. A special office was appointed for Sunday, with a separate appeal to Heaven for guidance; first in the name of the Most

Sweet Infant Jesus; afterwards in that of the Most Pure Mother of God. Midnight services were also given; the effect of which is said to have been great and strange; firing the monks with a new and wonderful spirit of confidence in their cause. The Archimandrite sang mass in person before the tombs of Savatie and Zosima, in the crypt of the cathedral church, and also before the miracle-working picture of the Virgin brought by Savatie to his desert. This picture—so important in the story—came from Greece. The service sung before it filled the monks with gladness; warmth and comfort flowed from the Madonna's face; and her adorers felt themselves conquerors, in her name, before the English war-ships hove in sight.

In their first trouble, the copes and missals, charters and jewels, had been sent away into the inland towns. This act of doubt occurred before the officer died, and the monks had taken upon themselves the burden of defense. To those who carried away the cups and crosses, robes and books, the Archimandrite gave his blessing and his counsel. "Know," he said to them at parting, "that, whether you be on sea or land, every Friday we shall be fasting and praying for you; do you the same; and God will preserve the things which belong to His service, and which you are carrying away; follow my commands, and come back to me in a better time, sound in health, with the things of which you go in charge." When news came in that English ships were cruising off the bar of Archangel, some of the brethren fainted; "left by the Emperor," they sighed, "to be made a sacrifice for his sins." Ten days before the squadron came in sight, the Archimandrite held a service in his church, to encourage these feeble souls; and when his prayers were ended, he addressed them thus: "Grieve not that the defense seems weak while the foe is strong. Rely upon our Lord, upon His Most Pure Mother, upon the two excellent saints who have promised that this convent shall endure forever. Jesus will perform a miracle, for their sake, such as the world has never seen." A ray of comfort stole into their hearts; and rolling out barrels of pitch and tar, they smeared the wooden shingles of wall and tower, filled pails of water in readiness to drench out fires, and took down from the convent armory the rusty pikes and bills which had been lying up since the attack of Swedish ships in the days of Peter the Great.

A hundred texts were found to show that these old weapons could be used again, even as the arms of David were used once more by the Lion of Judah in defense of Solomon's shrine. Young children came into the monastery from Kem and Suma, vowed by their fathers to the cause of God; and many old pikes and bills were put into these infant hands. "The fire of your ships," said one of the monks, "did not frighten these innocents, who played with the shells as though they had been harmless toys." Not a child was hurt.

When the fleet was signalled from the outlooks, Alexander spoke to his brethren after meat: "Have a good heart," he cried; "we are not weak, as we appear; for God is on our side. If we were saved by an army, where would be our credit? With the soldiery, with the world! What would be our gain? But if by prayer alone we drive the squadron from our shores, the glory will belong to our convent and our faith. Have a good heart! Slava Bogu—Glory to God!"

On Tuesday morning (July 18th, 1854) the watchers signalled two frigates, which were rounding Beluga Point: the Archimandrite proclaimed a three days' fast. The two frigates anchored seven miles from the shore: the Achimandrite ordered the convent bell to toll for a special service to the Most Pure Mother of God. Like a Hebrew king, he took off his gorgeous robes, and, humbling himself before the fathers, read a prayer in front of the tombs of Savatie and Zosima, and, taking down the miraculous picture of the Virgin, marched with it in procession round the walls. Then—but not till then—the frigates sailed away.

As the ships steamed off towards Kem, it was feared they might still come back; and Ensign Niconovitch, commanding the Company of Invalids, went out to survey the shores, dragging two three-pounder guns through the sand; while many of the pilgrims and workmen offered their services as scouts. Niconovitch built a battery of sods and sand, behind which he trained his guns; and eight small pieces were laid upon the towers and walls, after which the fathers fell once more to prayer.

Next day a trail of smoke was seen in the summer sky.

The two ships, soon known to them as the "Brisk" and the "Miranda," steamed into the bay. The "Brisk," say the monks, was the first to speak, and she opened her parley with a rattling shot. Standing on the quay, the Archimandrite was nearly struck by a ball, and his people, frightened at the crashing roar, ran up into the convent yard, and tried to close behind them the Sacred Gates.

A petty officer, one Drushlevski, having charge of ten men and a gun in the Weaver's Tower, returned the fire; on which the English frigate is said to have opened her broadside on the tower and wall. Drushlevski took up her challenge; but with aim and prudence, having very little powder in his casks. The "Brisk," they say, fired thirty rounds, while the officer in the Weaver's Tower discharged his gun three times. The English then sheered off; a shot from the convent gun having struck her side, and killed a man.

That night was spent in joy and prayer. The Archimandrite kissed Drushlevski, and gave his blessing to every gunner in the Weaver's Tower. When night came on—the summer night of the Frozen Sea—the frigates were out of sight; but no one felt secure, and least of all Drushlevski, that this triumph of the cross was yet complete. Not a soul in the convent slept.

Dawn brought them one of the holiest festivals of the Russian year; Thursday, July 20th, the feast of our Lady of Kasan; a day on which no plough is driven, no mill is opened, no school is kept, in any part of Russia, from the White Sea to the Black. Matins were sung, as usual, in the Cathedral Church at half-past two; the Archimandrite steadily going through his chant, as though the peril were not nigh. Te Deum was just being finished, when a boat came ashore from the "Brisk," carrying a white flag, and bringing a summons for the convent to yield her keys. The letter was in English, accompanied by a bad translation, in which the word for "squadron of ships," was rendered by the Russian term for squadrons of horse. Consulting with his monks—who laughed in good hearty mood at the idea of being set upon by cavalry from the sea—the Archimandrite told the messenger to say his answer should be sent to the "Brisk" by an officer of his own.

Two "insolent conditions" were imposed by the admiral:

(1.) The commander was to yield his sword in person; (2.) The garrison were to become prisoners of war. Ommanney's letter informed the fathers that if a gun were fired from the wall, his bombardment would begin at once; alleging in explanation that on the previous day a gun in the convent had opened on his ship.

One Soltikoff, a pilgrim, carried the Archimandrite's answer to the "Brisk:"—a proud refusal to give up his keys. Denying that the convent had opened fire on the English boat, he said the first shot came from the frigate, and the convent simply replied to it in self-defense. The paper was unsigned; the monk declaring that as a man of peace he could not write his name on a document treating of blood and death.

Admiral Ommanney told the pilgrim there was nothing more to say; the bombardment would begin at once; and the convent would be swept from the earth. Soltikoff asked for time, and Ommanney offered him three hours' grace. It was now five in the morning, and the admiral gave the fathers until eight o'clock; but on the pilgrim saying the time was short, Ommanney is said to have sworn a great oath, and lessened his term of grace three-quarters of an hour. He kept his oath; the bombardment opened at a quarter to eight o'clock of that holy day—inscribed to Our Lady of Kazan—our Lady of Victory; the first shell flying over the convent shingles almost as soon as Soltikoff reached the Sacred Gates.

On the English frigates opening fire, the bell in the courtyard tolled the monks to prayer. Shot, shell, grenade and cartridge rained on the walls and domes; yet the services went on all day; a hurricane of fire without; an agony of prayer within! While the people were on their knees, a shell struck the cathedral dome—the rent of which is piously preserved — and, tearing through the wooden framework, dashed down the ceiling on the supplicants' heads. The rafters were on fire; the church was suddenly filled with smoke. A sacred image was grazed and singed. The windows cracked; the doors flew open; the buildings reeled and shivered; and the terrified people fell with their faces on the stones. One man only kept his feet. Standing before the royal gates, the Archimandrite cried: "Stay! stay! Be not afraid, the Lord will guard His own!" The monks and pilgrims, lifting up their eyes, beheld the old man standing before his altar, quiet and erect, with big tears rolling down his cheeks. They sprang to their feet; they ran to fetch water; they put out the flames; they swept off the wreck of dust and rafters; and when the floor was cleansed, they sank on their knees and bowed their heads once more in prayer.

When mass was over, three poor women remained in the cathedral on their knees; a shell came through the roof, and burst; on which the poor things crawled towards the shrines where men were praying, and women are not allowed to come. A good pope let them in, and suffered them to pray with the men; an act which the monks regard as one of the highest wonders of that miraculous day.

A petty officer named Ponomareff occupied with his gun a spit of rock, from which he could tease the frigates, and draw upon himself no little of their wrath. Every shot from the "Miranda" splashed the mire about his men, who were often buried, though they were not killed that day. Leaping to his feet, and shaking the dirt from his clothes, Ponomareff stood to his gun, until he was called away. He and three other men crept through the stones and trees, to places far apart; whence they discharged their carbines, and ran away into the scrub, after drawing upon these points a rattle of shot and shell. At length he was recalled. "It is a sad day for the monastery," sighed the gunner, "but we are willing to die with the saints."

Services were sung all day in front of the shrines of Savatie and Zosima. Once a shot struck the altar; the pope shrank back from his desk, and the people fell on their faces. Every one supposed that his hour was come, and many cried out in their fear for the bread and wine. Father Varnau, the confessor, took his seat, confessed the people, and gave them the sacrament. Alexander was the first to confess his sins, and make up his account with God. The elders followed; then the lay monks, pilgrims, soldiers, women; and when all were shriven, the body of penitents pressed around the shrines of Philip, Savatie, Zosima, and the Mother of God.

A little after noon, the convent bells in the yard were tolled, the monks and pilgrims gathered on the wall, and lines of procession were ordered to be formed. The monks stood first, the pilgrims next, the women and children last; and when they were all got ready to march, the Archimandrite took down from the screen beside his altar the Miraculous Virgin and the principal cross; and placing himself in front of his people, with the cross in his right hand, the Virgin in his left, conducted them round the ramparts under fire. He waved his cross, and blessed the pilgrims with the Miraculous Virgin as he strode along. The great bell tolled, the monks and pilgrims sang a psalm. Shot and shell rained overhead; the boulders trembled in the wall; the shingles cracked and split on the roof. Near the corner tower by the Holy Lake the procession came to a halt. A shell had struck the windmill, setting the fans on fire. Pealing their psalm, and calling on their saints, they waited till the flames died down, and then resumed their march. A shot came dashing through the rampart; splintering the logs and planks in their very midst, and cutting the line of procession into head and heel. "Advance!" cried the Archimandrite, waving his cross and picture, and the people instantly advanced. On reaching the Weaver's Tower, from which the shot of destiny had been fired the previous day, the Archimandrite, calling the monk Gennadie to his side, gave him the cross, with orders to carry it up into the tower, and let the gunners kiss the image of our Lord. While Gennadie was absent on this errand, the Archimandrite showed the monks and pilgrims that the convent doves were not fluttered in their nests by the English guns.

A miracle! When the procession moved from the Weaver's Tower, they came near some open ground, which they were obliged to cross, under showers of shot. No man of flesh and blood—unless protected from on high—could pass through that fire unscathed. But now was the time to try men's faith. A moment only the procession paused; the Archimandrite, holding up his miraculous picture of the Mother of God, advanced into the cloud of dust and smoke; the people pealed their psalm; and the shells and balls from the English ships were seen to curve in their flight, to whirl over dome and tower, and come down splashing into the Holy Lake! Every eye saw that miracle; and every heart confessed the Most Pure Mother of God.

The frigates then drew off, and went their way; to be seen

from the watch-towers of the sacred isles no more; vanquished and put to shame; though visibly not by the hand of man. Not a soul in the convent had been hurt; though hurricanes of brass and iron had been fired from the English decks.

A Norwegian named Harder, a visitor by chance to Solovetsk, was so much struck by this miraculous defense, that he cried in the convent yard, "How great is the Russian God!" and begged to be admitted a member of their Church.

The news of this attack by an English Admiral on Solovetsk was carried into every part of Russia, and the effect which it produced on the Russian mind may be conceived by any one who will take the pains to imagine how he would feel on hearing reports from Palestine that a Turkish Pasha had opened fire on the dome and cross of the Holy Sepulchre. Shame, astonishment, and fury filled the land, until the further news arrived that this abominable raid among the holy graves and shrines had come to naught. Since that year of miracles, young and old, rich and poor, have come to regard a journey to Solovetsk as only second in merit to a voyage to Bethlehem and the tomb of Christ. Peasants set the fashion, which Emperors and grand dukes are taking up. Alexander the Second has made a pilgrimage to these holy isles; his brother Constantine has done the same; and two of his sons will make the trip next year. The Empress, too, is said to have made a vow, that if Heaven restores her strength, she will pay a visit to Savatie's shrine.

Some people think these visits of the imperial race are due, not only to the wish to lead where they might otherwise have to follow, but to matters connected with that mystery of a buried grand duke which lends so dark a fame to the convent in the Frozen Sea.

CHAPTER XIX.

A CONVENT SPECTRE.

A LAND alive with goblins and sorceries, in which every monk sees visions, in which every woman is thought to be a witch, presents the proper scenery for such a legend as that of the convent spectre, called the Spirit of the Frozen Sea.

Faith in the existence of this phantom is widely spread. I have met with evidences of this faith not only in the northern seas, but on the Volga, in hamlets of the Ukraine, and among old believers in Moscow, Novgorod, and Kief. All the Ruthenians, most of the Don Kozaks, and many of the Poles, give credit to this tale, in either a spiritualized or physical form.

Rufin Pietrowski, the Pole who escaped from his Siberian mine, and, crossing the Ural Mountains, dropped down the river Dvina on a raft, and got as near to Solovetsk as Onega Point, reports the spectre as a fact, and offers the explanation which was given of it by his fellow-pilgrims. He says it is not a ghost, but a living man. Other and later writers than Pietrowski hint at such a mystery; but the tale is one of which men would rather whisper in corners than prate in books.

"You have been to Solovetsk?" exclaimed to me a native of Kalatch, on the Don, a man of wit and spirit. "May I ask whether you saw any thing there that struck you much?"

"Yes, many things; the convent itself, the farms and gardens, the dry-dock, the fishing-boats, the salt-pits, the tombs of saints."

"Ah! yes, they would let you see all those things; but they would not let you go into their secret prison."

"Why not?" I said, to lead him on.

"They have a prisoner in that building whom they dare not show."

The same thing happened to me several times, with variations of time and place.

Some boatman from the Lapland ports, while striving, in the first hard days of winter, with the floes of ice, is driven beneath the fortress curtain, where he sees, on looking up, in the faint light of dusk, a venerable figure passing behind a loop-hole in the wall; his white hair cut, which proves that he is not a monk; his eyes upraised to heaven; his hands clasped fervently, as though he were in prayer; his whole appearance that of a man appealing to the justice of God against the tyranny of man. A sentry passes the loop-hole, and the boatman sees no more.

This figure is not seen at other times and by other folk.

Three months in the year these islands swarm with pilgrims, many of whom come and go in their craft from Onega and Kem. These visitors paddle below the ramparts day and night; yet nothing is seen by them of the aged prisoner and his sentry on the convent wall. Clearly, then, if the figure is that of a living man, there must be reasons for concealing him from notice during the pilgrim months.

"Hush!" said a boatman once to a friend of mine, as he lay in a tiny cove under the convent wall; you must not speak so loud; these rocks can hear. One dares not whisper in one's sleep, much less on the open sea, that the phantom walks yon wall. The pope tells you it is an imp; the elder laughs in your face and calls you a fool. If you believe your eyes, they say you are crazed, not fit to pull a boat."

"You have not seen the figure?"

"Seen him—no; he is a wretched one, and brings a man bad luck. God help him . . . if he is yet alive!"

"You think he is a man of flesh and blood?"

"Holy Virgin keep us! who can tell?"

"When was he last seen?"

"Who knows? A boatman seldom pulls this way at dusk; and when he finds himself here by chance, he turns his eyes from the castle wall. Last year, a man got into trouble by his chatter. He came to sell his fish, and fetching a course to the south, brought up his yawl under the castle guns. A voice called out to him, and when he looked up suddenly, he saw behind the loop-hole a bare and venerable head. While he stood staring in his yawl, a crack ran through the air, and looking along the line of roof, he saw, behind a puff of smoke, a sentinel with his gun. A moment more and he was off. When the drink was in his head, he prated about the ghost, until the elder took away his boat and told him he was mad."

"What is the figure like?"

"A tall old man, white locks, bare head, and eyes upraised, as if he were trying to cool his brain."

"Does he walk the same place always?"

"Yes, they say so; always. Yonder, between the turrets, is the phantom's walk. Let us go back. Hist! That is the convent bell."

The explanation hinted by Pietrowski, and widely taken for the truth, is that the figure which walks these ramparts in the winter months is not only that of a living man, but of a popular and noble prince; no less a personage than the Grand Duke Constantine, elder brother of the late Emperor Nicolas, and natural heir to the imperial crown!

This prince, in whose cause so many patriots lost their lives, is commonly supposed to have given up the world for love; to have willingly renounced his rights of succession to the throne; to have acquiesced in his younger brother's reign; to have died of cholera in Minsk; to have been buried in the fortress of St. Peter and St. Paul. But many persons look on this story as a mere official tale. Their version is, that the prince was a liberal prince; that he married for love; that he never consented to waive his rights of birth; that the documents published by the Senate were forged; that the Polish rising of 1831 was not directed against him; that the attack on his summer palace was a feint; that his retirement to Minsk was involuntary; that he did not die of cholera, as announced; that he was seized in the night, and whisked away in a tarantass, while Russia was deceived by funeral rites; that he was driven in the tarantass to Archangel, whence he was borne to Solovetsk; that he escaped from the convent; that in the year of Emancipation he suddenly appeared in Penza; that he announced a reign of liberty and peace; that he was followed by thousands of peasants; that, on being defeated by General Dreniakine, he was suffered to escape; that he was afterwards seized in secret, and sent back to Solovetsk; where he is still occasionally seen by fishermen walking on the convent wall.

The facts which underlie these versions of the same historical events are wrapped in not a little doubt; and what is actually known is of the kind that may be read in a different sense by different eyes.

CHAPTER XX.

STORY OF A GRAND DUKE.

WHEN Alexander the First—elder brother of Constantine and Nicolas—died, unexpectedly, at Taganrog, on the distant Sea of Azof, leaving no son to reign in his stead, the crown descended, by law and usage, to the brother next in birth. Constantine was then at Warsaw, with his Polish wife; Nicolas was at St. Petersburg, with his guards. Constantine was called the heir; and up to that hour no one seems to have doubted that he would wear the crown, in case the Emperor's life should fail. There was, however, a party in the Senate and the barrack against him; the old Russian party, who could not pardon him his Polish wife.

When couriers brought the news from Taganrog to St. Petersburg, Nicolas, having formed no plans as yet, called up the guards, announced his brother's advent to the throne, and set them an example of loyalty by taking the oath of allegiance to his Imperial Majesty Constantine the First. The guards being sworn, the generals and staff-officers signed the act of accession and took the oaths. Cantering off to their several barracks, these officers put the various regiments of St. Petersburg under fealty to Constantine the First; and Nicolas sent news that night to Warsaw that the new Emperor had begun to reign.

But while the messengers were tearing through the winter snows, some members of the Senate came to Nicolas with yet more startling news. Alexander, they said, had left with them a sealed paper, contents unknown, which they were not to open until they heard that he was dead. On opening this packet, they found in it two papers; one a letter from the Grand Duke Constantine, written in 1822, renouncing his rights in the crown; the second, a manifesto by the dead Emperor, written in 1823, accepting that renunciation and adopting his brother Nicolas as his lawful heir. A similar packet, they alleged, had been secretly left with Philaret of Moscow, and would be found in the sacristy of his cathedral church. Nicolas scanned these documents closely; saw good reason to put them by; and urged the whole body of the Senate to swear fidelity to Constantine the First. In every office of the State the imperial functionaries took this oath. All Russia, in fact all Europe, saw that Constantine had opened his reign in peace.

Then followed a surprise. Some letters passed between the two grand dukes, in which (it was said) the brothers were each endeavoring to force the other to ascend the throne; Nicolas urging that Constantine was the elder born and rightful heir; Constantine urging that Nicolas had better health and a more active spirit. Ten days rolled by. The Empire was without a chief. A plot, of which Pestel, Rostovtsef, and Mouravief were leading spirits, was on the point of explosion. But on Christmas Eve, the Grand Duke Nicolas made up his mind to take the crown. He spent the night in drawing up a manifesto, setting forth the facts which led him to occupy his brother's seat; and on Christmas Day he read this paper in the Senate, by which body he was at once proclaimed Autocrat and Tsar. A hundred generals rode to the various barracks, to read the new proclamation, and to get those troops who had sworn but a week ago to uphold his majesty Constantine the First, to cast that oath to the winds, and swear a second time to uphold his majesty Nicolas the First. But, if most of the regiments were quick to unswear themselves by word of command, a part of the guards, and chiefly the marines and grenadiers, refused; and, marching from their quarters into St. Isaac's Square, took up a menacing position towards the new Emperor, while a cry rose wildly from the crowd, of "Long live Constantine the First!"

A shot was heard.

Count Miloradovitch, governor-general of St. Petersburg, fell dead; a brave general who had passed through fifty battles, killed as he was trying to harangue his troops. A line of fire now opened on the square. Colonel Stürler fell, at the head of his regiment of guards. When night came down, the ground was covered with dead and dying men; but Nicolas was master of the square. A charge of grape-shot swept the streets clear of rioters just as night was coming down.

When the trials to which the events of that day gave rise came on, it suited both the Government and the conspirators to keep the grand duke out of sight. Count Nesselrode told the courts that this revolt was revolutionary, not dynastic; and Nicolas denounced the leaders to his people as men who wished to bring "a foreign contagion upon their sacred soil."

The grand duke and his Polish wife remained in Warsaw, living at the summer garden of Belvedere, in the midst of woods and lakes, of pictures, and works of art. Once, indeed, he left his charming villa for a season; to appear, quite unexpectedly (the court declared), in the Kremlin, and assist in placing the Imperial crown on his brother's head. That act of grace accomplished, he returned to Warsaw; where he reigned as viceroy; keeping a modest court, and leading an almost private life. But the country was excited, the army was not content. One war was forced by Nicolas on Persia, a second on Turkey; both of them glorious for the Russian arms; yet men were said to be troubled at the sight of a younger brother on the throne; a sentiment of reverence for the elder son being one of the strongest feelings in a Slavonic breast; and all these troubles were kept alive by the social and political writhings of the Poles.

Two prosperous wars had made the Emperor so proud and haughty that when news came in from Paris, telling him of the fall of Charles the Tenth, he summoned his minister of war, and ordered his troops to march. He said he would move on Paris, and his Kozaks began to talk of picqueting their horses on the Seine. But the French have agencies of mischief in every town of Poland; and in less than five months after Charles the Tenth left Paris, Warsaw was in arms.

Every act of this Polish rising seems, so far as concerns the Grand Duke Constantine, to admit of being told in different ways.

A band of young men stole into the Belvedere in the gloom of a November night, and ravaged through the rooms. They killed General Gendre; they killed the vice-president of police, Lubowicki; and they suffered the grand duke to escape by the garden gate. These are the facts; but whether he escaped by chance is what remains in doubt. The Russian version was that these young fellows came to kill the prince, as well as Gendre and Lubowicki; that a servant, hearing the tumult near the palace, ran to his master's room, and led him through the domestic passages into the open air. The Polish version was, that these young men desired to find the prince; not to murder him, but to use him as either hostage or emperor in their revolt against his brother's rule.

Arriving in Warsaw from his country-house, the grand duke, finding that city in the power of a revolted soldiery, moved some posts on the road towards the Russian frontier. Agents came to assure him that no harm was meant to him; that he was free to march with his guards and stores; that no one would follow him or molest him on the road. Some Polish companies were with him; and four days after his departure from Belvedere, he received in his camp near Warsaw a deputation, sent to him by his own request, from the insurgent chiefs. Then came the act which roused the anger of his brother's court; and led, as some folk think, to the mystery and sympathy which cling around his name.

He asked the deputation to state their terms. "A living Poland!" they replied; "the charter of Alexander the First; a Polish army and police; the restoration of our ancient frontier." In return, he told these deputies that he had not sent to Lithuania for troops; and he consented that the Polish companies in his camp should return to Warsaw and join the insurgent bands! For such a surrender to the rebels any other general in the service would certainly have been tried and shot. The Emperor, when he heard the news, went almost mad with rage; and every one wishing to stand well at court began to whisper that the Grand Duke Constantine had forfeited his honor and his life.

Constantine died suddenly at Minsk. The disease was cholera; the corpse was carried to St. Petersburg; and the prince, who had lost a crown for love, was laid with honor among the ashes of his race, in the gloomy fortress of St. Peter and St. Paul.

But no gazetteer could make the common people believe that their prince was gone from them forever. Like his father Paul, and like his grandfather Peter, he was only hiding in some secret place; and putting their heads together by the winter fires they told each other he would come again.

In the year of emancipation (1861) a man appeared in the province of Penza, who announced himself not only as the grand duke, but as a prophet, a leader, and a messenger from the Tsar. He told the people they were being deceived by their priests and lords, that the Emperor was on their side, that the emancipation act gave them the land without purchase and rent-charge, and that they must support the Emperor in his design to do them good. A crowd of peasants, gathering to his voice, and carrying a red banner, marched through the villages, crying death to the priests and nobles. General Dreniakine, an aide-de-camp of the Emperor, a prompt and confidential officer, was sent from St. Petersburg against the grand duke, whom in his proclamation he called Egortsof, and after a smart affair, in which eight men were killed and twenty-six badly hurt, the peasants fled before the troops. The grand duke was suffered to escape; and nothing more has been heard of him, except an official hint that he is dead.

What wonder that a credulous people fancies the hero of such adventures may be still alive?

In every country which has virtue enough to keep the memory of a better day, the popular mind is apt to clothe its hopes in this legendary form. In England, the commons expected Arthur to awake; in Portugal, they expected Sebastian to return; in Germany they believed that Barbarossa sat on his lonely peak. Masses of men believe that Peter the Third is living, and will yet resume his throne.

Before landing in the Holy Isles, I gave much thought to this mystery of the grand duke, and nursed a very faint hope of being able to resolve the spectre into some mortal shape.

CHAPTER XXI.

DUNGEONS.

My mind being full of this story, I keep an eye on every gate and trap that might lead me either up or down into a prisoner's cell. My leave to roam about the convent-yards is free; and though I am seldom left alone, except when lodged in my private room, some chance of loitering round the ramparts falls in my way from time to time. The monks retire about seven o'clock, and as the sun sets late in the summer months, I stroll through the woods and round by the Holy Lake, while Father John is laying our supper of cucumbers and sprats. Sometimes I get a peep at strange places while the fathers are at mass.

One day, when strolling at my ease, I come into a small court-yard, which my clerical guides have often passed by. A flutter of wings attracts me to the spot, and, throwing a few crumbs of biscuit on the ground, I am instantly surrounded by a thousand beautiful doves. They are perfectly tame. Here, then, is that colony of doves which the Archimandrite told his people were not disturbed by the English guns; and looking at the tall buildings and the narrow yard, I am less surprised by the miracle than when the story was told me by the monks. Lifting my eyes to the sills from which these birds come fluttering down, I see that the windows are barred, that the door is strongly bound. In short, this well-masked edifice is the convent jail; and it flashes on me quickly that behind these grated frames, against which the doves are pecking and cooing, lies the mystery of Solovetsk.

In going next day round the convent-yards and walls, with my two attending fathers, dropping into the quass-house, the school, the dyeing-room, the tan-yard, and the Weaver's Tower, I lead the way, as if by merest chance, into this pigeons' court. Referring to the Archimandrite's tale of the doves, I ask to have that story told again. Hundreds of birds are cooing and crying on the window-sills, just as they may have done on the eventful feast of Our Lady of Kazan.

"How pretty these doves! What a song they sing!"

"Pigeons have a good place in the convent," says the father at my side. "You see we never touch them; doves being sacred in our eyes on account of that scene on the Jordan, when the Holy Ghost came down to our Lord in the form of a dove."

"They seem to build by preference in this court."

"Yes, it is a quiet corner; no one comes into this yard; yon windows are never opened from within."

"Ah! this is the convent prison?"

"Yes; this is the old monastic prison."

"Are any of the fathers now confined in the place?"

"Not one. We have no criminals at Solovetsk."

"But some of the fathers are in durance, eh? For instance, where is that monk whom we brought over from Archangel in disgrace? Is he not here?"

"No; he has been sent to the desert near Striking Hill."

"Is that considered much of a penalty?"

"By men like him, it is. In the desert he will be alone; will see no women, and get no drink. In twelve months he will come back to the convent another man."

"Let us go up into this prison and see the empty cells."

"Not now."

"Why not? I am curious about old prisons; especially about church prisons; and can tell you how the dungeons of Solovetsk would look beside those of Seville, Antwerp, and Rome."

"We can not enter; it is not allowed."

"Not allowed to see empty cells! Were you not told to show me every part of the convent? Is there a place into which visitors must not come?"

The two fathers step aside for a private talk, during which I feed the pigeons and hum a tune.

"We can not go in there—at least, to-day."

"Good!" I answer, in a careless tone; "get leave, and we will come this way to-morrow. . . . . Stay! To-morrow we sail to Zaet. Why not go in at once and finish what we have yet to see down here?"

They feel that time would be gained by going in now; but then, they have no keys. All keys are kept in the guard-room, under the lieutenant's eyes. More talk takes place between the monks; and doubt on doubt arises, as to the limit of their powers. Their visitor hums a tune, and throws more crumbs of bread among the doves, who frisk and flutter to his feet, until the windows are left quite bare. A father passes into a house; is absent some time; returns with an officer in uniform, carrying keys. While they are mounting steps and opening doors, the pilgrim goes on feeding doves, as though he did not care one whit to follow and see the cells.

But when the doors roll back on their rusty hinges, he carelessly follows his guides up the prison steps.

The first floor consists of a long dark corridor, underground; ten or twelve vaults arranged in a double row. These cells are dark and empty. The visitor enters them one by one, pokes the wall with his stick, and strikes a light in each, to be sure that no one lies there unobserved; telling the officer and the monks long yarns about underground vaults and wells in Antwerp, Rome, and Seville. Climbing the stairs to an upper floor, he finds a sentinel on duty, pacing a strong anteroom; and feels that here, at least, some prisoner must be kept under watch and ward. An iron-bound door is now unlocked, and the visitor passes with his guides into an empty corridor with cells on either side, corresponding in size and number with the vaults below. Every door in that corridor save one is open. That one door is closed and barred.

"Some one in there?"

"No one?" says the father; but in a puzzled tone of voice, and looking at the officer with inquiring eyes.

"Well, yes; a prisoner," says that personage.

"Let us go in. Open the door."

Looking at the monks, and seeing no sign of opposition on their part, the soldier turns the key; and as we push the door back on its rusty hinge, a young man, tall and soldier-like, with long black beard and curious eyes, springs up from a pallet; and snatching a coverlet, wraps the loose garment round his all but naked limbs.

"What is your name?" the visitor asks; going in at once, and taking him by the hand.

"Pushkin," he answers softly; "Adrian Pushkin."

"How long have you been confined at Solovetsk?"

"Three years; about three years."

"For what offense?"

He stares in wonder, with a wandering light in his eye that tells his secret in a flash.

"Have you been tried by any court?"

The officer interferes; the sentinel on guard is called; and we are huddled by the soldiers—doing what they are told—from the prisoner's cell.

"What has he done?" I ask the fathers, when the door is slammed upon the captive's face.

"We do not know, except in part. He is condemned by the Holy Governing Synod. He denies our Lord." More than this could not be learned.

"A mad young man," sighs the monk; "he might have gone home long ago; but he would not send for a pope, and kiss the cross. He is now of better mind; if one can say he has any mind. A mad young man!"

There is yet another flight of steps. "Let us go up and see the whole."

We climb the stair, and find a second sentinel in the second anteroom. More prisoners, then, in this upper ward! The door which leads into the corridor being opened, the visitor sees that here again the cells are empty, and the doors ajar —in every case but one. A door is locked; and in the cell behind that door they say an old man lodges; a prisoner in the convent for many years.

"How long?"

"One hardly knows," replies the monk: "he was here when most of us came to Solovetsk. He is an obstinate fellow; quiet in his ways; but full of talk; he worries you to death; and you can teach him nothing. More than one of our Archimandrites, having pity on his case, has striven to lead him into a better path. An evil spirit is in his soul."

"Who is he?"

"A man of rank; in his youth an officer in the army."

"Then you know his name?"

"We never talk of him; it is against the rules. We pray for him, and such as he is; and he needs our prayers. A bad Russian, a bad Christian, he denies our holy Church."

"Does he ever go out?"

"In winter, yes; in summer, no. He might go to mass; but he refuses to accept the boon. He says we do not worship God aright; he thinks himself wiser than the Holy Governing Synod—he! But in winter days, when the pilgrims have gone away, he is allowed to walk on the rampart wall, attended by a sentinel to prevent his flight."

"Has he ever attempted flight?"

"Attempted! Yes; he got away from the convent; crossed the sea; went inland, and we lost him. If he could have held his peace, he might have been free to this very hour; but he could not hold his tongue; and then he was captured and brought back."

"Where was he taken?"

"No one knows. He came back pale and worn. Since then he has been guarded with greater care."

Here, then, is the prisoner whom I wish to see; the spectre of the wall; the figure taken for the prince; the man in whom centre so many hopes. "Open the door!" My tone compels them either to obey at once or go for orders to the Archimandrite's house. A parley of the officer and monks takes place; ending, after much ado, in the door being unlocked (to save them trouble), and the whole party passing into the prisoner's cell.

An aged, handsome man, like Kossuth in appearance, starts astonished from his seat; unused, as it would seem, to such disturbance of his cell. A small table, a few books, a pallet bed, are the only furnishings of his room, the window of which is ribbed and crossed with iron, and the sill bespattered with dirt of doves. A table holds some scraps of books and journals; the prisoner being allowed, it seems, to receive such things from the outer world, though he is not permitted to send out a single line of writing. Pencils and pens are banished from his cell. Tall, upright, spare; with the bearing of a soldier and a gentleman; he wraps his cloak round his shoulder, and comes forward to meet his unexpected guests. The monks present me in form as a stranger visiting Solovetsk, without mentioning *his* name to me. He holds out his hand and smiles; receiving me with the grace of a gentleman offering the courtesies of his house. A man of noble presence and courtly bearing: *not*, however, the Grand Duke Constantine, as fishermen and pilgrims say!

"Your name is—?"

"Ilyin; Nicolas Ilyin."

"You have been here long?"

Shaking his head in a feeble way, he mutters to himself, as it were, like one who is trying to recall a dream. I put the question again; this time in German. Then he faintly smiles; a big tear starting in his eye. "Excuse me, sir," he sighs,

"I have forgotten most things; even the use of speech. Once I spoke French easily. Now I have all but forgotten my mother tongue."

"You have been here for years?"

"Yes; many. I wait upon the Lord. In His own time my prayer will be heard, and my deliverance come."

"You must not speak with this prisoner," says the officer on duty; "no one is allowed to speak with him." The lieutenant is not uncivil; but he stands in a place of trust; and he has to think of duty to his colonel before he can dream of courtesy to his guest.

In a moment we are in the pigeons' court. The iron gates are locked; the birds are fluttering on the sills; and the prisoners are alone once more.

CHAPTER XXII.

NICOLAS ILYIN.

LEAVING Solovetsk for the south, I keep the figure of this aged prisoner in my mind, and by asking questions here and there, acquire in time a general notion of his course of life. But much of it remains dark to me, until, on my return from Kertch and Kief to St. Petersburg, the means are found for me of opening up a secret source.

The details now to be given from this secret source—controlled by other and independent facts—will throw a flood of light into some of the darkest corners of Russian life, and bring to the front some part of the obstacles through which a reforming Emperor has to march.

It will be also seen that in the story of Ilyin's career, there are points—apart from what relates to the convent spectre, and the likeness to Constantine the First—which might account for some of the sympathy shown for him by Poles.

Ilyin seems to have been born in Poland; his mother was certainly a Pole. His father, though of Swedish origin, held the rank of general in the imperial service. At an early age the boy was sent by General Ilyin to the Jesuits' College in

Polotsk; that famous school in which, according to report, so many young men of family were led astray in the opening years of Alexander the First. The names he bore inclined him to devote his mind to sacred studies. Nicolas is the poor man's saint, and Ilyin is the Russian form of Elias, the Hebrew prophet. It is not by chance, he thought, that men inherit and receive such names.

He was highly trained. In the school-room he was noted for his gentle ways, his studious habits, his religious turn of mind. He neither drank nor swore; he neither danced nor gamed. When the time arrived for him to leave his college and join the army, he passed a good examination, took a high degree, and entered an artillery corps with the rank of ensign. By his new comrades he was noted for his power of work, for his scorn of pleasure, for his purity of life. A hard reader, he gave up his nights and days to studies which were then unusual in the mess-room and the camp. While other young men were drinking deep and dancing late in their garrison-towns, he was giving up the hours that could be snatched from drill and gunnery to Newton on the Apocalypse, to Swedenborg on Heaven and Hell, to Bengel on the Number of the Beast. What his religious doctrines were in these early days, we can only guess. His father seems to have been a Greek Catholic, his mother a Roman Catholic; and we know too much of the genius which inspired the Jesuits' College in Polotsk to doubt that every effort would be made by the fathers to win such a student as Nicolas Ilyin to their side.

In Polotsk, as in nearly all Polish towns, reside a good many learned Jews. Led by his Apocalyptic studies to seek the acquaintance of Rabbins, Ilyin talked with these new friends about his studies, and even went with them to their synagogue; in the ritual of which he found a world of mystical meaning not suspected by the Jews themselves. In conning the Mishna and Gemara, he began to dream that a confession of faith, a form of prayer, a mode of communion, might be framed, by help of God's Holy Spirit, which would place the great family of Abraham under a common flag. A dream, it may be, yet a noble dream!

Ilyin toyed with this idea, until he fancied that the time for a reconciliation of all the religious societies owning the God of Abraham for their father was close at hand; and that he, Nicolas Ilyin—born of a Greek father and a Catholic mother; bearing the names of a Hebrew prophet and a Russian saint; instructed, first by Jesuits and then by Rabbins; serving in the armies of an Orthodox emperor—was the chosen prophet of this reign of grace and peace. A vision helped him to accept his mission, and to form his plan.

Taking the Hebrew creed, not only as more ancient and venerable, but as simpler in form than any rival, he made it the foundation for a wide and comprehensive church. Beginning with God, he closed with man. Setting aside, as things indifferent, all the points on which men disagree, he got rid of the immaculate conception, the symbol of the cross, the form of baptism, the practice of confession, the official Church, and the sacerdotal caste. In his broad review, nothing was of first importance save the unity of God, the fraternity of men.

Gifted with a noble presence and an eloquent tongue, he began to teach this doctrine of the coming time; announcing his belief in a general reconciliation of all the friends of God. The monks who have lodged him in the Frozen Sea, accuse him of deceit; alleging that he affected zeal for the Orthodox faith; and that on converting General Vronbel, his superior officer, from the Roman Church to the Russian Church, he sought, as a reward for this service, a license to go about and preach. The facts may be truly stated; yet the moral may be falsely drawn. A general in the Russian service, not of the national creed, has very few means of satisfying his spiritual wants. Unless he is serving in some great city, a Roman Catholic can no more go to mass than a Lutheran can go to sermon; and an officer of either confession is apt to smoke a pipe and play at cards, while his Orthodox troops are attending mass. Ilyin may have deemed it better for Vronbel to become a good Greek than remain a bad Catholic. In these early days of his religious strife, he seems to have dreamt that the Orthodox Church afforded him the readiest means of reconciling creeds and men. In bringing strangers into that fold, he was putting them into the better way. Anyhow, he converted his general, and obtained from his bishop the right to preach.

It was the hope of his bishop that he would bring in stragglers to the fold; not that he should set up for himself a broader camp in another name and under a bolder flag. Ilyin went out among the sectaries who abound in every province of the empire; and to these men of wayward mind he preached a doctrine which his ecclesiastical patrons fancied to be that of the Orthodox faith. In every place he drew to himself the hearts of men; winning them alike by the splendor of his eloquence and by the purity of his life.

Early married, early blessed with children, happy in his home, Ilyin could give up hand and heart to the work he had found. He took from the Book of Revelation the name of Right-hand Brethren, as an appropriate title for all true members of the church; his purpose being to proclaim the present unity and future salvation of all the friends of God.

A good soldier, a good man of business, Ilyin was sent to the government works, in the province of Perm, in the Ural Mountains, where he found time, in the midst of his purely military duties, for preaching among the poor, and drawing some of those who had strayed into separation back into the orthodox fold. His enemies admit that in those days of his work in the Ural Mountains he lived a holy life. Going on state affairs to the mines of Barancha, where the Government owns a great many iron works and steel works, he saw among the sectaries of that district, most of whom were exiles suffering for their conscience' sake, a field for the exercise of his talents as a preacher of the word, a reconciler of men. But the martyrs of free thought whom he met in the mines of Barancha, were to him what the Kaffir chieftains were to the Bishop of Natal. They put him to the test. They showed him the darker side of his cause. They led him to doubt whether reconciliation was to be expected from metropolites and monks. Forced into a sharper scrutiny of his own belief, Ilyin at length gave up his advocacy of the Orthodox faith, and even ceased to attend the Orthodox mass.

A secret Church was slowly formed in the province of Perm, of which Ilyin was the chief. Not much was known in high quarters about his doings, until Protopopoff, one of his pupils, was accused of some trifling offense, connected with the public service, and brought to trial. Protopopoff was a leading man among the Ural dissenters. His true offense was some expression against the Church. Ilyin appeared in public as his friend and advocate. Protopopoff was condemned: and Ilyin closely watched. Ere long, the director-general of the Ural Mines reported to his chief, the minister of finance in St. Petersburg, that in one of his districts he had found existing among the miners a new religious body, calling themselves, in secret, Right-hand Brethren, of which body Nicolas Ilyin, captain of artillery in the Emperor's service, was the chief and priest.

Not a little frightened by his discoveries, the director-general lost his head. In his report to the minister of finance, he said a good deal of these reconcilers that was not true. He charged them with circumcising children, with advocating a community of goods and lands, with propagating doctrines fatally at war with imperial order in Church and State.

It is true that under the name of Gospel love, the followers of Ilyin taught very strongly the necessity and sanctity of mutual help. They spoke to the poor, and bade them take heart of grace; bidding them look, not only for bliss in a better world, but for a reign of peace and plenty on the earth. In the great questions of serf and soil, two points around which all popular politics then moved, they took a part with the peasant against his lord, though Ilyin was himself of noble birth. These things appeared to the director-general of mines anarchical and dangerous, and Ilyin was denounced by him to the minister of finance as a man who was compromising the public peace.

But the fact which more than all else struck the council in St. Petersburg, was the zeal of Ilyin's pupils in spreading his doctrine of the unity and brotherhood of mankind. The new society was said to be perfect in unity. The first article of their association was the need for missionary work; and every member of the sect was an apostle, eager to spend his strength and give his life in building up the friends of God. A man who either could not or would not convert the Gentile was considered unworthy of a place on His right hand. At the end of seven years a man who brought no sheep into the fold was expelled as wanting in holy fire. Ilyin is alleged to have declared that there was no salvation beyond the pale of this new church, and that all those who professed any other creed would find their position at the last day on the left hand of God, while the true brethren found their seats on His right. This story is not likely to be true; and an intolerant Church is always ready with such a cry. It is not asserted that the new Church had any printed books, or even circulars, in which these things were taught. The doctrine was alleged to be contained in certain manuscript gospels, copied by proselytes and passed from one member to another; such manuscript gospels having been written, in the first instance at least, by Ilyin himself.

A special commission was named by the ministers to investigate the facts; and this commission, proceeding at once into the Ural Mines, arrested many of the members, and seized some specimens of these fugitive gospel sheets. Ilyin, questioned by the commissioners, avowed himself the author of these Gospel tracts, which he showed them were chiefly copies of sayings extracted from the Sermon on the Mount. In scathing terms, he challenged the right of these commissioners to judge and condemn the words of Christ. Struck by his eloquence and courage, the commission hardly knew what to say; but as practical men, they hinted that a captain of the imperial artillery holding such doctrines must be unsound in mind.

A report from these commissioners being sent, as usual, to the Holy Governing Synod, that board of monks made very short work of this pretender to sacred gifts. The reconciler of creeds and men was lodged in the Convent of the Frozen Sea until he should put away his tolerance, give up his dream of reconciliation, and submit his conscience to the guidance of a monk.

And so the reconciler rests in his convent ward. The Holy Governing Synod treats such men as children who have gone astray; looking forward to the wanderer coming round to his former state. The sentence, therefore, runs in some such form as this: "You will be sent to . . . ., where you will stay, under sound discipline, until you have been brought to a better mind." Unless the man is a rogue, and yields in policy, one sees how long such sentences are likely to endure!

Nicolas Ilyin is a learned man, with whom no monk in the

Convent of Solovetsk is able to contend in speech. A former Archimandrite tried his skill; but the prisoner's verbal fence and knowledge of Scripture were too much for his feeble powers; and the man who had repulsed the English fleet retired discomfited from Ilyin's cell.

Once the prisoner got away, by help of soldiers who had known him in his happier days. Escaping in a boat to Onega Point, he might have gone his way overland, protected by the people; but instead of hiding himself from his pursuers, he began to teach and preach. Denounced by the police, he was quickly sent back to his dungeon; while the soldiers who had borne some share in his escape were sent to the Siberian mines for life.

The noble name and courtly family of Ilyin are supposed to have saved the arrested fugitive from convict labor in the mines.

My efforts to procure a pardon for the old man failed; at least, for a time; the answer to my plea being sent to me in these vague words: "Après l'examin du dossier de l'affaire d'Ilyin, il resulte qu'il n'y a pas eu d'arrêt de mise en liberté." Yet men like Nicolas Ilyin are the salt of this earth; men who will go through fire and water for their thought; men who would live a true life in a dungeon rather than a false life in the richest mansions of the world!

CHAPTER XXIII.

ADRIAN PUSHKIN.

EXCEPT the fact of their having been lodged in the Convent of Solovetsk in neighboring cells, under the same hard rule, Adrian Pushkin and Nicolas Ilyin have nothing in common; neither age nor rank; neither learning nor talent; not an opinion; not a sympathy; not a purpose. Pushkin is young, Ilyin is old. Pushkin is of burgher, Ilyin of noble birth. Pushkin is uneducated in the higher sense; Ilyin is a scholar to whom all systems of philosophy lie open. Pushkin is not clever; Ilyin is considered, even by his persecutors, as a man of the highest powers.

Yet Pushkin's story, from the man's obscurity, affords a still more curious instance of the dark and difficult way through which a beneficent and reforming government has to pass.

Early in the spring of 1866, a youth of good repute in his class and district, that of a small burgher, in the town of Perm, began to make a stir on the Ural slopes, by announcing to the peasant dissenters of that region the second coming of our Lord, and offering himself as the reigning Christ!

Such an event is too common to excite remark in the upper ranks, until it has been seen by trial whether the announcement takes much hold on the peasant mind. In Pushkin's case, the neighbors knew their prophet well. From his cradle he had been frail in body and flushed in mind. When he was twenty years old, the doctors were consulted on his state of mind; and though they would not then pronounce him crazy, they reported him as a youth of weak and febrile pulse, afflicted with disease of the heart; a boy who might, at any moment of his life, go mad. Easy work, in country air, was recommended. A place was got for him in the country, on the Countess Strogonof's estate, not far from Perm. He was made a kind of clerk and overseer; a place of trust, in which the work was light; but even this light labor proved too great for him to bear. In doing his duty to his mistress, his mind gave way; and when the light went out on earth, the poor idiot offered his help in leading other men up to heaven.

Many of the people near him knew that he was crazed; but his unsettled wits were rather a help than hindrance to his success in stirring up the village wine-shop and the workman's shed. In every part of the East some touch of idiotcy is looked for in a holy man; the wandering eye, the broken phrase, the distracted mien, being read as signs of the Holy Spirit. The province of Perm is rich in sectaries; many of whom watch and pray continually for the second coming of our Lord. Among these sectaries, Adrian found some listeners to his tale. He spoke to the poor, and of the poor. Calling the peasants to his side, he pictured to them a kingdom of heaven in which they would owe no taxes and pay no rent. The earth, he told them, was the Lord's; a paradise given by

Him as a possession to His saints. What peasant would not hear such news with joy? A gospel preached in the village wine-shop and the workman's shed was soon made known by its fruits; and the Governor of Perm was told that tenants were refusing to pay their rent and to render service, on the ground that the kingdom of heaven was come and that Christ had begun to reign.

Adrian was now arrested, and being placed before the Secret Consultative Committee of Perm, he was found guilty of having preached false doctrine and advocated unsocial measures; of having taught that the taxes were heavy, that the peasants should possess the land, that dues and service ought to be refused. Knowing that the young man was mad, the Secret Consultative Committee saw that they could never treat his case like that of a man in perfect health of body and mind. They thought the Governor of Perm might request the Holy Governing Synod to consent that Pushkin should be simply lodged in some country convent, where he might live in peace, and, under gentle treatment, hope to regain his wandering sense.

But the Holy Governing Synod pays scant heed to lay opinion. Judging the young man's fault with sharper anger than the Secret Consultative Committee of Perm had done, they sent him to Solovetsk; not until he should recover his sense and could resume his duties as a clerk, but until such time as he should recant his doctrines and publicly return to the Orthodox fold.

Valouef, Minister of the Interior, received from Perm a copy of this synodal resolution, which he saw, as a layman, that he could not carry out, except by flying in the face of Russian law. The man was mad. The Holy Governing Synod treated him as sane. But how could he, a jurist, cast a man into prison for being of unsound mind? No code in the world would sanction such a course; no court in Russia would sustain him in such an act. Of course, the Holy Governing Synod was a light unto itself; but here the civil power was asked to take a part which in the minister's conscience was against the spirit and letter of the imperial code.

It was a case of peril on either side. Such things had been done so often in former years, that the Church expected them to go on forever; and the monks were certain to resist, to slander, and destroy the man who should come between them and their prey. Valouef, acting with prudence, brought the report before a council of ministers, and after much debate, not only of the special facts but of the guiding rules, the council of ministers agreed upon these two points: first, that such a man as Pushkin could not be safely left at large in Perm; second, that it would be against the whole spirit of Russian law to punish a man for being out of his mind.

On these two principles being adopted, Valouef was recommended by the Council of Ministers to procure the Emperor's leave for Adrian Pushkin to be brought from Perm to St. Petersburg, for the purpose of undergoing other and more searching medical tests. Carrying his minute-book to the Emperor, Valouef explained the facts, together with the rules laid down, and his majesty, adopting the suggestion, wrote with his own hand these words across the page: "Let this be done according to the Minister of the Interior's advice. Oct. 21, 1866."

On this humane order, Pushkin was brought from Perm to St. Petersburg, where he was placed before a board of medical men. After much care and thought had been given to the subject, this medical board declared that Pushkin was unsound of brain, and could not be held responsible for his words and acts.

So far then as Emperor and ministers could go, the course of justice was smooth and straight; but then came up the question of what the Church would say. A board of monks had ordered Pushkin to be lodged in the dungeons of Solovetsk until he repented of his sins. A board of medical men had found him out of his mind; and a council of ministers, acting on their report, had come to the conclusion that, according to law, he could not be lodged in jail. His majesty was become a party to the course of secular justice by having signed, with his own hand, the order for Adrian to be fetched from Perm and subjected to a higher class of medical tests. Emperor, ministers, physicians, stood on one side; on the other side stood a board of monks. Which was to have their way?

The Holy Governing Synod held their ground; and in a

question of false teaching it was impossible to oppose their vote. They knew, as well as the doctors, that Adrian was insane; but then, they said, all heretics are more or less insane. The malady of unbelief is not a thing for men of science to understand. They, and not a medical board, could purge a sufferer like Pushkin of his evil spirit. They said he must be sent, as ordered, to the Frozen Sea.

No minister could sign the warrant for his removal after what had passed; and, powerful as they are, the Holy Governing Synod have to use the civil arm. The dead-lock was complete. But here came into play the silent and inscrutable agency of the secret police. These secret police have a life apart from that of every other body in the State. They think for every one; they act for every one. So long as law is clear and justice prompt, they may be silent—looking on; but when the hour of conflict comes, when great tribunals are at feud, when no one else can see their way, these officers step to the front, set aside codes and rules, precedents and decisions, as so much idle stuff, assume a right to judge the judges, to replace the ministers, and, in the name of public safety, do what they consider, in their wisdom, best for all.

The men who form this secret body are not called police, but "members of the third section of his imperial majesty's chancellery." They are highly conservative, not to say despotic, in their views; and said to feel a particular joy when thwarting men of science and overruling judgments given in the courts of law. One general rule defines the power which they can bring to bear in such a case as that of Adrian Pushkin. If justice seems to them to have failed, and they are firmly persuaded—they must be "firmly persuaded"—that the public service requires "exclusive measures" to be adopted, they are free to act.

On the whole, these secret agents side with power against law, with usage against reform, with all that is old against every thing that is new. In Pushkin's case they sided with the monks. Overriding Emperor, minister, council, medical board, they carried Pushkin to the White Sea, where he was placed by the Archimandrite, not in a monastic cell, but in the dismal corridor in which I found him. He is perfectly submissive, and clearly mad. He goes to mass without ado, says his prayers, confesses his sins, and seems to have returned into the arms of the official Church. The monks in charge of him have told their chiefs that he is now of right mind with regard to the true faith; and the Governor of Archangel has written to advise that he should be allowed to go back to his friends in Perm.

It is hard, however, for a man to get away from Solovetsk. A year ago, General Timashef, who has now replaced Valouef in the Ministry of the Interior, wrote to ask whether the Holy Governing Synod had not heard from the Archimandrite of Solovetsk in favor of the prisoner; and whether the time had not come for him to be given up to his friends. No answer to that letter has been received to the present day (Dec., 1869). The board of monks are slow to undo their work; the dissidents in Perm are gaining ground; and this poor madman remains a prisoner in the pigeons' yard!

CHAPTER XXIV.

DISSENT.

THESE dissidents, who ruffle so much the patient faces of the monks, are gaining ground in other provinces of the empire as well as Perm.

Such tales as those of Ilyin and Pushkin open a passage, as it were, beneath an observer's feet; going down into crypts and chambers below the visible edifice of the Orthodox Church and Government; showing that, in the secret depths of Russian life there may be other contentions than those which are arming the married clergy against the monks. On prying into these crypts and chambers, we find a hundred points on which some part of the people differ from their Official Church.

The Emperor Nicolas would not hear of any one falling from his Church; "autocracy and orthodoxy" was his motto; and what the master would not deign to hear, the Minister of Education tried his utmost not to see. That millions of Mussulmans, Jews, and Buddhists lived beneath his sceptre, Nicolas was fond of saying; but for a countryman of his own to differ in opinion from himself was like a mutiny in his camp. The Church had fixed the belief of one and all; the only terms on which they could be saved from hell. Had *he* not sworn to observe those terms? While Nicolas lived it was silently assumed in the Winter Palace that the dissenting bodies were all put down. One Christian church existed in his empire; and never, perhaps, until his dying hour did Nicolas learn the truth about those men whom the breath of his anger was supposed to have swept away!

Outside the Winter Palace and the Official Church dissent was growing and thriving throughout his reign. No doubt some few conformed—with halters round their throats. When autocrat and monk combined to crush all those who held aloof from the State religion, the sincere dissenter had to pass through bitter times; but spiritual passion is not calmed by firing volleys into the house of prayer; and the result of thirty years of savage persecution is, that these non-conformists are to-day more numerous, wealthy, concentrated, than they were on the day when Nicolas began his reign.

No man in Russia pretends to know the names, the numbers, and the tenets of these sects, still less the secrets of their growth. A mystery is made of them on every side. The Minister of Police divides them into four large groups, which he names and classifies as follows:

I.—DUKHOBORTSI, Champions of the Holy Spirit.
II.—MOLOKANI, Milk Drinkers.
III.—KHLYSTI, Flagellants.
IV.—SKOPTSI, Eunuchs.

In our day it is rare to find self-deception carried to so high a point as in this official list. Four groups! Why, the Russian dissenters boast, like their Hindoo brethren, of a hundred sects. The classification is no less strange. The Champions of the Holy Spirit are neither an ancient nor a strong society. The Milk Drinkers are of later times than the Flagellants and the Eunuchs. The Flagellants are not so numerous as the Eunuchs, though they probably surpass in strength the Champions of the Holy Spirit.

The Flagellants and Eunuchs are of ancient date—no one

knows how ancient; the Flagellants going back to the fourteenth century at least; the Eunuchs going back to the Scythian ages; while the Milk Drinkers and the Champions of the Holy Spirit sprang into life in the times of Peter the Great.

CHAMPIONS OF THE HOLY SPIRIT.

Though standing first in the official list, the Champions of the Holy Spirit are one of the less important sects. They write nothing, and never preach. The only book which contains their doctrine is "The Dukhobortsi," written by a satirist and a foe! Novitski, a professor in the University of Kief, having heard of these champions from time to time, threw what he learned about them into a squib of some eighty pages; meaning to laugh at them, and do his worst to injure them, according to his lights. His tract was offered for twenty kopecks, but no one seemed disposed to buy, until the Champions took it up, read it in simple faith, and sent a deputation to thank the professor for his service to their cause! Novitski was amused by their gravity; especially when they told him a fact of which he was not aware; that the articles of their creed had never until then been gathered into a connected group! Of this droll deputation the police got hints. Novitski, being an officer of state, was, of course, orthodox; and his book bore every sign of having been written to expose and deride the non-conforming sect. Yet the police, on hearing of that deputation, began to fear there was something wrong; and in the hope of setting things right, they put his tract on their prohibited list of books. What more could an author ask? On finding the work condemned by the police, the Champions sent to the writer, paying him many compliments and buying up every copy of his tract at fifty rubles each. Novitski made a fortune by his squib; and now, in spite of his jokes, the laughing Professor of Kief is held to be the great expounder of their creed!

The Champions build no churches and they read no Scriptures; holding, like some of our Puritan sects, that a church is but a house of logs and stones, while the temple of God is the living heart; that books are only words, deceitful words, while the conscience of man must be led and ruled by the inner light. They show a tendency towards the most ancient form of worship; holding that every father of a family is a priest. Many of them join the Jews, and undergo the rite of circumcision. Now and then they buy a copy of the Hebrew Bible, though they can not read one word of the sacred text. They keep it in their houses as a charm.

MILK DRINKERS.

The Milk Drinkers are of more importance than these Champions of the Holy Spirit.

Critics dispute the meaning of Molokani. The original seats of the Milk Drinkers are certain villages in the south country, lying on the banks of a river called the Molotchnaya (Milky Stream); a river flowing past the city of Melitopol into the Sea of Azof, through a district rich in saltpetre, and pushing its waters into the sea as white as milk. But some of the secretaries whom I meet at Volsk, on the Lower Volga, tell me this resemblance of name is an accident, no more. According to my local guides, the term Milk Drinker, like that of Shaker, Mormon, and, indeed, of Christian, is a term of contempt applied to them by their enemies, because they decline to keep the ordinary fasts in Lent. Milk—and what comes of milk; butter, whey, and cheese—are staples of food in every house; and a sinner who breaks his fast in Lent is pretty sure to break it on one of the articles derived from milk; chiefly by frying his potato in a pat of butter instead of in a drop of vegetable oil.

These milk people deny the sanctity and the use of fasts, holding that men who have to work require good food, to be eaten in moderation all the year round; no day stinted, no day in excess. They prefer to live by the laws of nature; asking and giving a reason for every thing they do. They set their faces against monks and popes. They look on Christ with reverence, as the purest being ever born of woman; but they deny his oneness with the Father, and treat the miraculous part of his career on earth as a tale of later times. In a word, the Milk Drinkers are Rationalists.

The name which they give themselves is Gospel Men; for they profess to stand by the Evangelists; live with exceeding purity, and base their daily lives on what they understand to be the laws laid down for all mankind in the Sermon on the

Mount. Under Nicolas they were sorely harried. Sixteen thousand men and women were seized by the police; arranged in gangs; and driven with rods and thongs across the dreary steppes and yet more dreary mountain crests into the Caucasus. In that fearful day a great many of the Milk Drinkers fled across the Pruth into Turkey, where the Sultan gave them a village, called Tulcha, for their residence. Wise and tolerant Turk! These emigrants carried their virtues and their wealth into the new country, prospered in their shops and farms, and made for their protectors beyond the Danube a thousand friends in their ancient homes.

FLAGELLANTS.

The Flagellants are older in date, stronger in number than the Champions and the Milk Drinkers. They go back to the first year of Alexie (1645); to a time of deep distress, when the heads of men were troubled with a sense of their guilty neglect of God.

One Daniel Philipitch, a peasant in the province of Kostroma, serving in the wars of his country, ran away from his flag, declared himself the Almighty, and wandered about the empire, teaching those who would listen to his voice his doctrine in the form of three great assertions: I. I am God, announced by the prophets; there is no other God but me. II. There is no other doctrine. III. There is nothing new.

To these three assertions were added nine precepts: (1.) drink no wine; (2.) remain where you are, and what you are; (3.) never marry; (4.) never swear, or name the devil; (5.) attend no wedding, christening, or other feast; (6.) never steal; (7.) keep my doctrine secret; (8.) love each other, and keep my laws; (9.) believe in the Holy Spirit. Daniel roamed about the country, preaching this gospel for several years, gathering to himself disciples in many places, though his head-quarters remained at Kostroma. He was God; and his converts called themselves God's people. Daniel chose a son, one Ivan Susloff, a peasant of Vladimir; and this Ivan Susloff chose a pretty young girl as his Virgin Mother, together with twelve apostles. Flung into prison with forty of his disciples, Susloff saw the heresy spread. It ran through the empire, and it has followers at this hour in every part of Central Russia. "God's House," Daniel's residence in the village of Staroï, still remains—held in the utmost veneration by country folk.

The chief article of their faith is the last precept given by Daniel, "Believe in the Holy Ghost." All their discipline and service is meant to weaken the flesh and strengthen the spirit; to which end they fast very often and flog each other very much.

Great numbers of these Flagellants have been sent into the Caucasus and Siberia, where many of them have been forced to serve in the armies and in the mines.

EUNUCHS.

A more singular body is that of the Beliegolubi (White Doves), called by their enemies Skoptsi (Eunuchs). These people "make themselves eunuchs for the kingdom of heaven's sake," and look on Peter the Third, whom they take to be still alive, as their priest and king. They profess to lead a life of absolute purity in the Lord; spotless, they say, as the sacrificial doves! The White Doves are believed to live like anchorites; all except a few of their prophets and leading men. They drink no whisky and no wine. They think it a sin to indulge in fish; their staple food is milk, with bread and walnut oil. White, weak, and wasting, they appear in the shops and streets like ghosts. The monks admit that they are free from most of the vices which afflict mankind. It is affirmed of them that they neither game nor quarrel; that they neither lie nor steal. The sect is secret; and any profession of the faith would make a martyr of the man upon whom was found the sign of his high calling. Seeming to be what other men are, they often escape detection, not for years only, but for life; many of them filling high places in the world; their tenets unknown to those who are counted in the ranks of their nearest friends.

The White Doves have no visible church, no visible chief. Christ is their king, and heaven their church. But the reign of Christ has not yet come; nor will the Prince of Light appear until the earth is worthy to receive Him. Two or three persons, gathered in His name, may hope to find Him in the spirit; but not until three hundred thousand saints confess

His reign will He come to abide with them in visible flesh. One day that sacred host will be complete; the old earth and the old heaven will pass away, consumed like a scroll in the fire.

So far as I can see (for the Eunuchs print no books, and frame no articles), their leading tenet, borrowed from the East, appears to be that of a recurring Incarnation of the Word. Just as a pundit of Benares teaches that Vishnu has been born into the world many times, probably many hundred times, a White Dove holds that the Messiah is for evermore being born again into the world which He has saved. Once He came as a peasant's child in Galilee, when the soldiers and high-priests rose on Him and slew Him. Once again He came as an emperor's grandson in Russia, when the soldiers and high-priests rose on Him again and slew Him. He did not die; for how could God be killed by man? But He withdrew into the unseen until His hour should come. Meantime he is with His Church, though not in His majestic and potential shape, as hero, king, and God.

The White Doves have amongst them, only known to few, a living Virgin and a living Christ. These incarnations are not Son and Mother in their mortal shapes; in fact, the Son is generally older than the Mother; and they are not of kin, except in the Holy Spirit. The present Christ exists in his lower form; holy, not royal; pure, not perfect; waiting for the ripeness of his time, when he will once again take flesh in all his majesty as God. A Virgin is chosen in the hope that when the ripeness of His time has come, He will be born again from that Virgin's side.

Alexander the First was deeply moved by what he heard of these sectaries. He went amongst them, and held much talk with their learned men. It has been imagined that he joined their church. Under Nicolas, the "Doves" were chased and seized by the police. On proof of the fact they were tied in gangs, and sent into the Caucasus, where they lived—and live—at the town of Maran, a post on the road from Poti to Kutais, waiting for Peter to arrive. A second colony exists in the town of Shemakha, on the road from Tiflis to the Caspian Sea. They are said to be docile men, doing little work on scanty food, giving no trouble, and leading an innocent and sober life. At present, they are not much worried by the police; except when some discovery, like the Plotitsen case in Tambof, excites the public mind. A Dove who keeps his counsel, and refrains from trying to convert his neighbors, need not live in fear. The law is against him; his faith is forbidden; he is not allowed to sing in the streets, to hold public meetings, and to bury his dead with any of his adopted rites; these ceremonies of his faith must be done in private and in secret; yet this singular body is said to be increasing fast. They are known to be rich; they are reported to be generous. A poor man is never suspected of being a Eunuch. When the love of woman dies out, from any cause, in a man's heart, it is always succeeded by the love of money; and all the bankers and goldsmiths who have made great fortunes are suspected of being Doves. In Kertch and Moscow, you will hear of vast sums in gold and silver being paid to a single convert for submitting to their rite.

The richest Doves are said to pay large sums of money to converts, on the strength of a prophecy made by one of their holy men, that so soon as three hundred thousand disciples have been gathered into his fold, the Lord will come to reign over them in person, and to give up to them all the riches of the earth.

CHAPTER XXV.

NEW SECTS.

THESE groups, so far from ending the volume of dissent, do little more than open it up to sight. Stories of the Flagellants and the Eunuchs are like old-world tales, the sceneries of which lie in other ages and other climes. These sects exist, no doubt; but they draw the nurture of their life from a distant world; and they have little more enmity to Church and State than what descends with them from sire to son. Committees have sat upon them; laws have been framed to suit them; ministerial papers have described them. They figure in many books, and are the subjects of much song and art. In short, they are historical sects, like the Anabaptists in Germany, the Quakers in England, the Alumbradros in Spain.

But the genius of dissent is change; and every passing day gives birth to some new form of faith. As education spreads, the sectaries multiply. "I am very much puzzled," said to me a parish priest, "by what is going on. I wish to think the best; but I have never known a peasant learn to read, and think for himself, who did not fall away into dissent." The minds of men are vexed with a thousand fears, excited by a thousand hopes; every one seems listening for a voice; and every man who has the daring to announce himself is instantly followed by an adoring crowd. These births are in the time, and of the time; apostles born of events, and creeds arising out of present needs. They have a political side as well as a religious side. Some samples of these recent growths may be described from notes collected by me in provinces of the empire far apart; dissenting bodies of a growth so recent, that society—even in Russia—has not yet heard their names.

LITTLE CHRISTIANS.

In the past year (1868) a new sect broke out in Atkarsk, in the province of Saratof, and diocese of the Bishop of Tsaritzin. Sixteen persons left the Orthodox Church, without giving notice to their parish priest. They set up a new religion, and began to preach a gospel of their own devising. Saints and altar-pieces, said these dissidents, were idols. Even the bread and wine were things of an olden time. They had a call of their own to teach, to suffer, and to build a Church. This call was from Christ. They obeyed the summons by going down into the Volga, dipping each other into the flood, changing their names, and holding together a solemn feast. This scene took place in winter—Ash Wednesday, February 26th, when the waters of the Volga are locked in ice, and had to be pierced with poles. From that day they have called themselves humbly, after the Lord's name, Little Christians.

They have no priests, and hardly any form of prayer. They keep no images, use no wafers, and make no sacred oil. Instead of the consecrated bread, they bake a cake, which they afterwards worship, as a special gift from God. This cake is like a penny bun in shape and size; but in the minds of these Little Christians it possesses a potent virtue and a mystic charm.

Hearing of these secessions from his flock, the Bishop of Tsaritzin wrote to Count Tolstoi, Minister of Education, who in turn dispatched his orders to the district police. These orders were, that the men were to be closely watched; that no more baptisms in the ice were to be allowed; that no more cakes were to be baked of the size and shape of a penny bun. All preaching of these new tenets was to be stopped. The bishop, living on the spot, was to be consulted on every point of procedure against the sectaries. All these orders, and some others, have been carried out; the police are happy in their labor of repression; and the heresy of the Little Christians is increasing fast.

HELPERS.

A few months ago the Governor of Kherson was amused by hearing that some villagers in his province had been arrested by the police on the ground of their being a great deal too good for honest men. It was said the men who had been cast into prison never drank, never swore, never lied, owed no money, and never confessed their sins to the parish priest. Nobody could make them out; and the police, annoyed at not being able to make them out, whipped them off their fields, threw them into prison, and laid a statement of their suspicions before the prince.

These over-good peasants were brothers, by name Ratushni, living in the hamlet of Osnova, in which they owned some land. Not far from Osnova stands a small town called Ananief, in which lived a burgher named Vonsarski, who was also marked by the police with a black line, as being a man too good for his class. Vonsarski paid his debts and kept his word; he lived with his wife in peace; and he never attended his parish church. He, too, was seized by the police and lodged in jail, until such time as he should explain himself, and the governor's pleasure could be learned.

It is surmised that the monks set the police at work; in the hope that if nothing could be proved at first against these offenders, tongues might be loosened, tattle might come out, and some sort of charge might be framed, so soon as the fact of their lying in jail was noised abroad through the southern steppe.

Ratushni and Vonsarski were known to be clever men; to have talked with Moravian settlers in the south. They were suspected of looking with a lenient eye on the foreign style of harnessing bullocks and driving carts. They were accused of underrating the advantages of rural communes, in favor of a more equitable and religious system of mutual help. They were called the Helpers. But their chief offense appears to have been their preference for domestic worship over that of the parish priest.

The Governor of Kherson thought his duty in the matter clear; he set the prisoners free. When the Black Clergy of his province stormed upon him, as a man abetting heresy and schism, he quoted Paragraph 11 in his imperial master's minute on the treatment of Dissent; a paragraph laying down the rule that every man is free to believe as he likes, so long as he abstains from troubling his neighbors by attempting to convert them to his creed. The prince added a recommendation of his own, that the clergy of his province should strive in their own vocation to bring these wanderers back into the fold of God.

NON-PAYERS OF RENT.

Near Kasan I hear of a new sect having sprung up in the province of Viatka, which is giving the ministry much trouble. It may have been the fruit of poor Adrian Pushkin's labor (though I have not heard his name in connection with it); the main doctrine of the Non-payers of Rent being the second article of Pushkin's creed.

The canton of Mostovinsk, in the district of Sarapul, is the scene of this rising of poor saints against the tyrants of this world. Viatka, lying on the frontiers of Asia, with a mixed population of Russ, Finns, Bashkirs, Tartars, is one of the most curious provinces of the empire. Every sort of religion flourishes in its difficult dales; Christian, Mussulman, Buddhist, Pagan; each under scores of differing forms and names. Twenty Christian sects might be found in this single province;

and as all aliens and idolaters living there have the right of being ruled by their own chiefs, it is not easy for the police to follow up all the clues of discovery on which they light. But such a body as the Non-payers of Rent could hardly conceal themselves from the public eye. If they were to live their life and obey their teachers, they must come into the open day, avow their doctrine, and defend their creed. Such was the necessary logic of their conversion, and when rents became due they refused to pay. The debt was not so much a rental, as a rent-charge on their land. Like all crown-peasants (and these reformers had been all crown-peasants), they had received their homesteads and holdings subject to a certain liquidating charge. This charge they declined to meet on religious grounds.

Alarmed by such a revolt, the Governor of Viatka wrote to St. Petersburg for orders. He was told, in answer, to make inquiries; to arrest the leaders; and to watch with care for signs of trouble. Nearly two hundred Non-payers of Rent were seized by the police, parted into groups, and put under question. Some were released on the governor's recommendation; but when I left the neighborhood, twenty-three of these Non-paying prisoners were still in jail.

They could not see the error of their creed; they would not promise to abstain from teaching it; and, worst of all, they obstinately declined to bear the stipulated burdens on their land.

What is a practical statesman to do with men who say their conscience will not suffer them to pay their rent?

CHAPTER XXVI.

MORE NEW SECTS.

ON my arrival in the province of Simbirsk, every one is talking of a singular people, whose proceedings have been recently brought to light. One Peter Mironoff, a private soldier in the Syzran regiment, has set up a new religion, which is to be professed in secret and to have no name. Peter is known as a good sort of man; pious, orderly, sedate; a soldier never absent from his drill; a penitent who never shirked his priest. Nothing fantastic was expected from him. It is said that he began by converting fourteen of his comrades, all of whom swore that they would hold the truth in private, that they would act so as to divert suspicion, that they would suffer exile, torture, death itself, but never reveal the gospel they had heard.

Not being a learned man, and having no respect for books, Peter rejects all rituals, derides all services, tears up all lives of saints. He holds that reading and writing are dangerous things, and takes tradition and a living teacher for his guides. Though waging war against icons and crosses, on which he stamps and frowns in his secret rites, he ostentatiously hangs a silver icon in his chamber, and wears a copper cross suspended from his neck. Teaching his pupils that true religion lies in a daily battle with the flesh, he urges them to fast and fast; abstaining, when they fast, from every kind of food, so as not to mock the Lord; and when they indulge the senses, to reject as luxuries unfit for children of grace such food as meat and wine, as milk and eggs, as oil and fish. He warns young people against the sin of marriage, and he bids the married people live as though they were not; urging them to lead a life of purity and peace, even such as the angels are supposed to lead in heaven. By day and night he declares that the heart of man is full of good and evil; that the good may be encouraged, the evil discouraged; that fasting and prayer are the only means of driving out the evil spirits which enter into human flesh.

The men whom Peter has drawn into order reject all mysteries and signs; they wash themselves in quass, and then drink the slops. They live in peace with the world, they help each other to get on, and they implicitly obey a holy virgin whom they have chosen for themselves.

This virgin, a peasant-woman named Anicia, living in the village of Perevoz, in the province of Tambof, is their actual ruler; one who is even higher in authority than Peter Mironoff himself. Anicia has been married about nineteen years. Fallen man, they say, can only have one teacher; and that one teacher must be a woman and a virgin. After Anicia, they recognize the Saviour and St. Nicolas as standing next in rank.

Their service, held in secret, with closed doors and shutters, begins and ends with songs; brisk music of the romping sort, accompanied by jumping, hopping, twirling; and a part of their worship has been borrowed from the Tartar mosques. They stand in prayer. They bow to the ground in adoration. They make no sign of the cross. Instead of crying "Save me, pardon me, Mother Mary!" they cry "Save me, pardon me, Mother Anicia Ivanovna!"

Like all the sectaries, these Nameless Ones reject the official empire and the official church.

A long time passed before Peter and his fellows were betrayed to the police, and now that the prophet and virgin have been seized, attempts are made to pass the matter by as a harmless joke. The Government is puzzled how to act; nearly all the men and women accused of belonging to this lawless and blasphemous sect being known through the province of Simbirsk for their sober and decent lives. The leaders are noted men, not only as church-goers, but supporters of the clergy in their struggles against the world. Every man whom the police has seized on suspicion holds a certificate from his priest, in which his regularity in coming to confess his sins and receive the sacrament is duly set forth and signed. Nay, more, the parish priests come forward to testify in their behalf; for in a society which does not commonly regard priests with favor, the men who are now accused of irreligion have set an example of respect for God's ministers by asking them, on suitable occasions, to their homes.

Mother Anicia, arrested in her village, has been put under the severest trials; yet nothing has been found against her credit and her fame. She is forty years old. She has been married nineteen years. A medical board, appointed by the governor, reports that she is still a virgin, and her neighbors, far and near, declare that she has lived amongst them a perfectly blameless life.

The police are not yet beaten in their game. An agent of their own has sworn to having been present in one of the sheds in which they conducted their indecent rites. Peter Mironoff, he declares, took down the ordinary icons from the wall, spat on them, cursed them, banged them on the floor, leaped on them, and ground them beneath his feet. After cursing the images, Mironoff kneaded a peculiar cake of ashes, foul water, and paste, in mockery of the sacred bread, and gave to every man in the shed a piece of this cake to eat. When they had eaten this cake, he called on them to strip, each one as naked as when he was born—garments being a sign of sin; and when they had all obeyed his words he bade them sing and pray together, in testimony against the world.

Each man, says this agent, is bound by the rules to choose for himself a bride of the Spirit, with whom he must live in the utmost purity of life.

What can a reforming minister do in such a case? A jurist would be glad to leave such folk alone; but the Holy Governing Synod will not suffer them to be left alone. Peter and Anicia remain in jail; their case is under consideration; and the model soldier and blameless villager will probably end their days in a Siberian mine.

COUNTERS.

In the province of Saratof, a wild steppe country, lying between the lands of the Kalmuks and the Don Kozaks, I hear of a new sect, called the Counters or Enumerators (Chislenniki). The high-priest of this congregation is one Taras Maxim, a peasant of Semenof, one of the bleak log villages in the black-soil country.

Taras speaks of having been out one night in a wood, when he met a venerable man, holding in his hands a book. This book had been given to the old man by an angel, and the old man offered to let Taras read it. Parting the leaves, he found the writing in the sacred Slavonic tongue, and the words a message of salvation to all living men. The book declared that the people of God must be counted and set apart from the world. It spoke of the Official Church as the Devil's Church. It showed that men have confused the order of time, so as to profane with secular work the day originally set apart for rest; that Thursday is the seventh day, the true Sabbath, to be kept forever holy in the name of God. It mentioned saints and angels with contempt; denounced the official fasts as works of Satan; and proclaimed in future only one fast a year. It spoke of the seven sacraments as delusions, to be wholly banished from the Church of God. It said the priesthood was unnecessary and unlawful; every man was a priest, empowered by Heaven to confess penitents, to read the service, and inter the dead.

Having read all these things, and some others, in the book, Taras Maxim left his venerable host in the wood, and going back into Semenof, told a friend what he had seen and learned. Men and women listened to his tale, and, being anxious for salvation, they counted themselves off from a corrupt society, and founded the Secret Semenof Church.

So far as I could learn—the sect being unlawful, and the rites performed in private—one great purpose seems to inspire these Counters; that of pouring contempt, in phrase and gesture, on the forms of legal and official life. Sometimes, I can hardly doubt, they carry this protest to the length of indecent riot. Holding that Sunday is not a holy day, they meet in their sheds and barns on Sunday morning, while the village pope is saying mass, and having closed the door and planted watchers in the street, they sing and dance, they gibe and sneer; using, it is said, the roughest Biblical language to denounce, the coarsest Oriental methods to defile, the neighbors whom they regard as enemies of God.

Semenof stands east of Jerusalem, and even east of Mecca.

Maxim's chief theological tenet refers to sin. Man has to be saved from sin. Unless he sins, he can not be saved. To commit sin, is therefore the first step towards redemption. Hence it is inferred by the police that Maxim and his pupils rather smile on sinners, especially on female sinners, as persons who are likely to become the objects of peculiar grace. Outside their body, these Counters are regarded, even by liberal men, as an immoral and unsocial sect.

NAPOLEONISTS.

In Moscow I hear of a body of worshippers who have the singular quality of drawing their hope from a foreign soil. These men are Napoleonists. Like all the dissenting sects, they hate the official empire and deride the Official Church. Seeing that the chief enemy of Russia in modern times was Napoleon, they take him to have been, literally, that Messiah which he assumed to be, in a certain mystical sense, to the oppressed and divided Poles; and they have raised the Corsican hero into the rank of a Slavonic god.

Their society is secret, and their worship private. That they live and thrive, as an organized society, is affirmed by those who know their country well. Their meetings are held with closed doors and windows, under the very eyes of the police; but this is the case with so many sects in Moscow, that their immunity from detection need excite no wonder in our eyes. Making a sort of altar in their room, they place on it a bust of the foreign prince, and fall on their knees before it. Busts of Napoleon are found in many houses; in none more frequently than in those of the imperial race. I have been in most of these imperial dwellings, and do not recollect one, from the Winter Palace to the Farm, in which there was not a bust of their splendid foe.

The Napoleonists say their Messiah is still alive, and in the flesh; that he escaped from the snares of his enemies; that he crossed the seas from St. Helena to Central Asia; that he dwells in Irkutsk, near Lake Baikal, on the borders of Chinese Tartary; that in his own good time he will come back to them, heal their sectional quarrels, raise a great army, and put the partisans of Satan, the reigning dynasty and acting ministers, to the sword.

CHAPTER XXVII.

THE POPULAR CHURCH.

THESE secret sects and parties would be curious studies—and little more—if they stood apart, and had to live or die by forces of their own. In such a case they would be hardly more important than the English Levellers and the Yankee Come-outers; but these Russian dissidents are symptoms of a disease in the imperial body, not the disease itself. They live on the popular aversion to an official church.

It is not yet understood in England and America that a Popular Church exists in Russia side by side with the Official Church. It is not yet suspected in England and America that this Popular Church exists in sleepless enmity and eternal conflict with this Official Church. Yet in this fact of facts lies the key to every estimate of Russian progress and Russian power.

This Popular Church consists of the Old Believers; men who reject the pretended "reforms" of Patriarch Nikon, and follow their fathers in observing the more ancient rite. "You will find in our country," said to me a priest of this ancient faith, "a Church of Byzantine, and a Church of Bethlehem; a new voice and an old voice; a system framed by man, and a gospel given by God."

No one has ever yet counted the men who stand aloof from the State Church as Old Believers. By the Government they have been sometimes treated in a vague and foolish way as dissenters; though the governments have never had the courage to count them as dissenters in the official papers. Known to be sources of weakness in the empire, they have been hated, feared, cajoled, maligned; observed by spies, arrested by police, entreated by ministers; every thing but counted; for the governments have not dared to face the truths which counting these Old Believers would reveal. A wiser spirit rules to-day in the Winter Palace; and this great question—greatest of all domestic questions—is being studied under all its lights. Already it is felt in governing circles—let the monks say what they will—that nothing can be safely done in Russia, unless these Old Believers like it. Every new suggestion laid before the Council of Ministers is met (I have been told) by the query—"What will the Old Believers say?"

The points to be ascertained about these Old Believers are these: How many do they count? What doctrines do they profess? What is their present relation to the empire? What concessions would reconcile them to the country and the laws?

How many do they count?

A bishop, who has travelled much in his country, tells me they are ten or eleven millions strong. A minister of state informs me they are sixteen or seventeen millions strong. "Half the people, even now, are Old Believers," says a priest from Kem; "more than three-fourths will be, the moment we are free." My own experience leads me to think this priest is right. "I tell you what I find in going through the country," writes to me a German who has lived in Russia for thirty years, knowing the people well, yet standing free (as a Lutheran) from their local brawls; "I find, on taking the population, man by man, that *four* persons *in five* are either Old Believers now, or would be Old Believers next week, if it were understood among them that the Government left them free." This statement goes beyond my point; yet I see good reason every day to recognize the fact—so long concealed in official papers—that the Old Believers are the Russian people, while the Orthodox Believers are but a courtly, official, and monastic sect.

Nearly all the northern peasants are Old Believers; nearly all the Don Kozaks are Old Believers; more than half the population of Nijni and Kazan are Old Believers; most of the Moscow merchants are Old Believers. Excepting princes and generals, who owe their riches to imperial favor, the wealthiest men in Russia are Old Believers. The men who are making money, the men who are rising, the captains of industry, the ministers of commerce, the giants of finance—in one word, the men of the instant future—are members of the Popular Church.

Driving through the streets of Moscow, day by day, admiring the noble houses in town and suburb, your eye and ear are taken by surprise at every turn. "Whose house is this?" you ask. "Morozof's." "What is he?" "Morozof! why, sir, Morozof is the richest man in Moscow; the greatest mill-owner in Russia. Fifty thousand men are toiling in his mills. He is an Old Believer."

"Who lives here?" "Soldatenkof." "What is he!" "A great merchant; a great manufacturer; one of the most powerful men in Russia. He is an Old Believer."

"Who lives in yonder palace?"

"Miss Rokhmanof. In London you have such a lady; Miss Burdett Coutts is richer, perhaps, than Miss Rokhmanof, but not more swift to do good deeds. Her house, as you see, is big; it has thirty reception-rooms. She is an Old Believer." So you drive on from dawn to dusk. You go into the bazar—to find Old Believers owning most of the shops; you go into the University—to find Old Believers giving most of the burses; you go into the hospitals—to find Old Believers feeding nearly all the sick. The old Russ virtues—even the old Russ vices—will be found among these Old Believers; not among the polite and enervated followers of the official form. "In Russia," said to me a judge of men, "society has a ritual of her own; a ritual for the palace, for the convent, for the camp; a gorgeous ritual, fit for emperors and princes, such as the purple-born might offer to barbaric kings, not such as fishermen in Galilee would invent for fishermen on the Frozen Sea."

An Old Believer clings to the baldest forms of village worship, and the simplest usages of village life. Conservative in the bad sense, as in the good, he objects to every new thing, whether it be a synod of monks, a capital on foreign soil, a cup of tea sweetened with sugar, a city lit by gas. Show him a thing unknown to his fathers in Nikon's time, and you show him a thing which he will spurn as a work of the nether fiend.

These Old Believers are as much the enemies of an official empire as they are of an official church. The test of loyalty in Russia is praying for the reigning prince as a good Emperor and a good Christian; but many of these Old Believers will not pray for the reigning prince at all. Some will pray for him as Tsar, though not as Emperor; but none will pray for him as a Christian man. They look on him as reigning by a dubious title and a doubtful right. The word emperor, they say, means Chert—Black One; the double eagle an evil spirit; the autocracy a kingdom of Antichrist.

All this confusion in her moral and political life is traceable to the times of Nikon the Patriarch; a person hardly less important to a modern observer of Russia, than the great prince who is said by Old Believers to have been his bastard son.

About the time when our own Burton and Prynne were being laid in the pillory, when Hampden and Cromwell were being stayed in the Thames, a man of middle age and sour expression landed from a boat at Solovetsk to pray at the shrine of St. Philip, and beg an asylum from the monks. He described himself as a peasant from the Volga, his father as a field laborer in a village near Nijni. He was a married man and his wife was still alive. In his youth he had spent some time in a monastery, and after trying domestic life for ten years, he had persuaded his partner to become a bride of Christ. Leaving her in the convent of St. Alexie in Moscow, he had pushed out boldly into the frozen north.

At that time certain hermits lived on the isle of Anzersk, where the farm now stands, in whose "desert" this stranger found a home. There he took the cowl, and the name of Nikon; but his nature was so rough, that he was soon engaged in bickering with his chief as he had bickered with his wife. Eleazar, founder of the desert, desired to build a church of stone in lieu of his church of pines, and the two men set out for Moscow to collect some funds. They quarrelled on their road; they quarrelled on their return. At length, the brethren rose on the new-comer, expelled him from the desert, placed him in a canoe, with bread and water, and told him to go whither he pleased, so that he never came back. Chance threw him on shore at Ki, a rock in Onega Bay; where he set up a cross, and promised to erect a chapel, if the virgin whom he served would help him to get rich.

On crossing to the main land, he became the organizer of a band of hermits on Leather Lake (Kojeozersk) in the province of Olonetz. From Leather Lake he made his spring into power and fame; for having an occasion to see the Tsar Alexie on some business, he so impressed that very poor judge of men that in a few years he was raised to the seats of Archimandrite, Bishop, Metropolite, and Patriarch.

Combining the pride of Wolsey with the subtlety of Cranmer, Nikon set his heart on governing the Church with a sharper rod than had been used by his faint and shadowy predecessors. A burly fellow, flushed of face, red of nose, and bleary of eye, Nikon resembled a Friesland boor much more than a Moscovite monk. He revelled in pomp and show; he swelled with vanity as he sat enthroned in his cathedral near the Tsar. Feeling a priest's delight in the splendor of the Byzantine clergy, even under Turkish rule, he sought to model his own ceremonial rites on those of the Byzantine clergy, not aware that in going back to the Lower Empire he was seeking guidance from the Greeks in their corruptest time. His earlier steps were not unwise. Sending out a body of scribes, he obtained from Mount Athos copies of the most ancient and authentic sacred books, which he caused to be translated into Slavonic and compared with the books in ordinary use; and finding that errors had crept into the text, he bade his scribes prepare for him a new edition of the Scriptures and Rituals, in which the better readings should be introduced. But here his merit ends. Nikon knew no Greek; yet when the work was done for him by others, he proceeded, with an arrogant frown on his brow, to force his version on the Church. The Church objected; Nikon called upon the Tsar. The priests demurred to this intrusion of the civil power; and Nikon handed the protesting clergy over to the police. Alexie lent him every aid in carrying out his scheme. Yet the opposition was strong, not only in town and village, but in the council, in the convent, and in the Church. Peasants and popes were equally against the changes he proposed to make. The service-books were old and venerable; they sounded musical in every ear; their very accents seemed divine. These books had been used in their sacred offices time out of mind, and twenty generations of their fathers had by them been christened, married, and laid at rest. Why should these books be thrown aside? The writings offered in their stead were foreign books. Nikon said they were better; how could Nikon know? The Patriarch was not a critic; many persons denied that he was a learned man. Instead of trying to gain support for his innovations, he forced them on the Church. Nor was he satisfied to deal with the texts alone. He changed the old cross. He trifled with the sacraments. He brought in a new mode of benediction. He altered the stamp on consecrated bread. By order of the Tsar, who could not see the end of what he was about, the Council adopted Nikon's reforms in the Church; and these new Scriptures, these new services, these new sacraments, this new cross, and this new benediction, were introduced, by order of the civil power, in every church and convent throughout the land. The Nikonian Church was recognized as an Official Church.

Most of the people and their parish clergy stood up boldly for their ancient texts, especially in the far north countries, where the court had scarcely any power over the thoughts of men. The view taken in the north appears to have been something like that of our English Puritans when judging the merits and demerits of King James's version: they thought the new Scriptures rather too worldly in tone; over-just to high dignitaries in Church and State; less likely to promote holy living and holy dying than the old. In a word, they thought them too political in their accent and their spirit.

No convent in the empire showed a sterner will to reject these innovations than the great establishment in the Frozen Sea. When Nikon's service-books arrived at Solovetsk, the brethren threw them aside in scorn. The Archimandrite, as an officer of state, took part with the Patriarch and the Tsar; but the fathers put their Archimandrite in a boat and carried him to Kem. Having called a council of their body, they chose two leaders; Azariah, whom they elected caterer; and Gerontie, whom they elected bursar. All the Kozaks in the fortress joined them; and, supported from the mainland by people who shared their minds, the monks of Solovetsk maintained their armed revolt against the Nikonian Church for upward of ten years, and only fell by treachery at last.

In Orthodox accounts of this siege the captors are represented as behaving as men should behave in war. They are said to have put to the sword only such as they took in arms; and borne the rest away from Solovetsk, to be placed in convents at a distance till they came to a better mind. But many old books, possessed by peasants round the Frozen Sea, put another face on such tales. A peasant, living in the Delta, pulled up a book from a well under his kitchen floor, and showed me a passage in red and black ink, to the effect that the whole brotherhood of resisting monks was put to the sword and perished to a man.

What the besiegers won, the nation lost. This victory clove the Church in twain, and the end of Nikon's triumph has not yet been reached.

CHAPTER XXVIII.

OLD BELIEVERS.

THE new service-books and crosses were ordered to be used in every Church. The Church which used them was declared official, orthodox, and holy. Every other form of public worship was put under curse and ban.

Princes, Vladikas, generals, all made haste to pray in the form most pleasing to their Tsar. Cajoled and terrified by turns, the monks became in a few years orthodox enough; and many of the parish priests, on being much pressed by the police, marched over to the stronger side. Not all; not nearly all; for thousands of the country clergymen resisted all commands to introduce into their services these suspected books; contending that the changes wrought in the sacred texts were neither warranted by fact nor justified by law. They treated them as the daring labor of a single man. Not all of those who held out against Nikon could pretend to be scholars and critics; but neither, they alleged, was Nikon himself a scholar and a critic. When he came to Solovetsk he was an ignorant peasant, too old to learn; when he was driven from Anzersk by his outraged brethren, he was as ignorant of letters as when he came. Since that time he had led a life of travel and intrigue. If they were feeble judges, he was also a feeble judge.

Clinging fast to their venerable forms, the clergy kept their altars open to a people whom neither soldiers nor police could drive to the new matins and the new mass. Many of the burghers, most of the peasants, doggedly refused to budge from their ancient chapels, to forego their favorite texts. They were Old Believers; they were the Russian Church; Nikon was the heretic, the sectarian, the dissident; and, strong in these convictions, they set their teeth against every man who fell away from the old national rite to the new official rite.

From those evil times, the people have been parted into two hostile camps; a camp of the Ancient Faith, and a camp of the Orthodox Faith; a parting which it is no abuse of words to describe as the heaviest blow that has ever fallen upon this nation; heavier than the Polish invasion, heavier than the Tartar conquest; since it sets brother against brother, and puts their common sovereign at the head of a persecuting board of monks.

One consequence of these Old Believers being driven into relations of enmity towards the Government is the weakening of Russia on every side. The Church is shorn of her native strength; the civil power usurps her functions; and the man who brought these evils on her was deposed from his high rank. Nikon was hardly in his grave before the office of Patriarch was abolished; and the Church was virtually absorbed into the State. The Orthodox Church became a Political Church; extending her limits, and ruling her congregations by the secular arm. Imperious and intolerant, she allows no reading of the Bible, no exercise of thought, no freedom of opinion, within her pale. The Old Believers suffer, in their turn, not only from the persecutions to which their "obstinacy" lays them open, but from the isolation into which they have fallen.

From the moment of their protest down to the present time, these Old Believers have been driven, by their higher virtues, into giving an unnatural prominence to ancient habits and ancient texts. Living in an old world, they see no merit in the new. According to their earnest faith, the reign of Antichrist began with Nikon; and since the time of Nikon every word spoken in their country has been false, every act committed has been wrong.

Like a Moslem and like a Jew, an Old Believer of the severer classes may be known by sight. "An Old Believer?" says a Russian friend, as we stand in a posting-yard, watching some pilgrims eat and drink; "an Old Believer? Yes."

"How do you read the signs?"

"Observe him; see how he puts the potatoes from him with a shrug. That is a sign. He eats no sugar with his glass of tea; that also is a sign. The chances are that he will not smoke."

"Are all these notes of an Old Believer?"

"Yes; in these northern parts. At Moscow, Nijni, and Kazan, you will find the rule less strict—especially as to drinking and smoking—least of all strict among the Don Kozaks."

"Are the Don Kozaks Old Believers?"

"Most of them are so; some say all. But the Government of Nicolas strove very hard to bring them round; and seeing that these Kozaks live under martial law, their officers could press them in a hundred ways to obey the wishes of their Tsar. Their Atamans conformed to the Emperor's creed; and many of his troopers so far yielded as to hear an official mass. Yet most of them stood out; and many a fine young fellow from the Don country went to the Caucasus, rather than abandon his ancient rite. You should not trust appearances too far, even among those Don Kozaks; for it is known that in spite of all that popes and police could do, more than half the Kozaks kept their faith; and fear of pressing them too far has led, in some degree, to the more tolerant system now in vogue."

"You find some difference, then, even as regards adherence to the ancient rite, between the north country and the south?"

"It must be so; for in the north we live the true Russian life. We come of a good stock; we live apart from the world; and we walk in our fathers' ways. We never saw a noble in our midst; we hold to our native saints and to our genuine Church."

The signs by which an Old Believer is to be distinguished from the Orthodox are of many kinds; some domestic—such as his way of eating and drinking; others devotional—such as his way of making the cross and marking the consecrated bread.

An Old Believer has a strong dislike to certain articles; not because they are bad in themselves, but simply because they have come into use since Nikon's time. Thus, he eats no sugar; he drinks no wine; he repudiates whisky; he smokes no pipe.

An Old Believer of the sterner sort has come to live alone; even as a Hebrew or a Parsee lives alone. He has taken hold of the Eastern doctrine that a thing is either clean or unclean, as it may happen to have been touched by men of another creed. Hence he must live apart. He can neither break bread with a stranger, nor eat of flesh which a heretic has killed. He can not drink from a pitcher that a stranger's lip has pressed. In his opinion false belief defiles a man in body and in soul; and when he is going on a journey, he is tortured like a Hebrew with the fear of rendering himself unclean. He carries his water-jug and cup, from which no stranger is allowed to drink. He calls upon his comrades only, since he dares not eat his brown bread, and drain his basin of milk in a stranger's house. Yet homely morals cling to these men no less than homely ways. An Old Believer is not more completely set apart from his neighbors of the Orthodox rite by his peculiar habits, than by his personal virtues. Even in the north country, where folk are sober, honest, industrious, far beyond the average Russian, these members of the Popular Church are noticeable for their probity and thrift. "If you want a good workman," said to me an English mill-owner, "take an Old Believer, especially in a flax-mill."

"Why in a flax-mill?"

"You see," replied my host, "the great enemy of flax is fire; and these men neither drink nor smoke. In their hands you are always safe."

CHAPTER XXIX.

A FAMILY OF OLD BELIEVERS.

In the forest village of Kondmazaro lives a family of Old Believers, named Afanasevitch; two brothers, who till the soil, fell pines, and manufacture tar. Their house is a pile of logs; a large place, with barn and cow-shed, and a patch of field and forest. These brothers are wealthy farmers, with manly ways, blue eyes, and gentle manners. Fedor and Michael are the brothers, and Fedor has a young and dainty wife.

The family of Afanasevitch is clerical, and the two men, Fedor and Michael, were brought up as priests. On going into their house you see the signs of their calling, and on going into their barn you see a chapel, with an altar and sacred books.

That barn was built by their grandfather, in evil days, as a chapel for his flock; and during many years, the father of these men—now gone to a better place—kept up, in the privacy of his farm, the forms of worship which had come down to him from his sire, and his sire's sire. This barn has no cupola, no cross, no bell. So far as takes the eye, it is a simple barn. Inside, it is a quaint little chapel, with screen and cross, with icon and crown. It has a regular altar, with step and desk, and the customary pair of royal gates.

The father of Fedor and Michael, following in his father's wake, appeared to the outside world a farmer and woodman, while to his faithful people he was a priest of God.

These lads assisted him in the service, while his neighbors took their turn of either dropping in to mass, or mounting guard in the lane. His altars were often stripped, his books put in a well, his pictures hidden in a loft; for the police, informed of what was going on by monkish spies, were often at his gates. At length a brighter day is dawning on the Popular Church. A new prince is on the throne; and under the White Tsar, the congregations which keep within the rules laid down are left in peace.

"You hold a service in this church?"

"My brother holds it; not myself," says Fedor, with a sigh. "My priesthood is gone from me."

"Your priesthood gone? How can a priesthood go away? Is not the law, once a priest always a priest?"

"Yes, in a regular church; but we are not now a regular church, with a sacred order and an apostolic grace. We are a village priesthood only; chosen by our neighbors to serve the Lord in our common name."

"How was your personal priesthood lost?"

"By falling into sin through love. My wife, though village born, had scruples about the form of marriage in use among our people, and begged me to indulge her weakness on that point by marrying her in the parish church. It was a proper thing for her to ask; a very hard thing for me to grant; for law and right are here at strife, and one must take his chance of rejecting either man or God. The time is not a reign of grace, and nothing that we do is lawful in the sight of Heaven. We take no sacraments; for the apostolic priesthood has passed away. No man alive has power to bind and loose, or even to marry and to shrive."

"Still you marry?"

"Yes; outwardly, according to a form; not inwardly, according to the Spirit. Besides, the law does not admit our form; the Orthodox say we are not married, and the courts declare our children basely born. Hence, some of our women crave to be wedded as the code directs, in the parish church, by an Orthodox priest. I could not blame poor Mary for her weakness, though she wished me to marry her in a way that would insult my kindred, harass my mother, and cause me to be removed from my office, and degraded from my rank as priest. I loved the girl and we went to church."

Fedor stands beside me, tall and lank, with mild blue eyes and yellow locks, a serge blouse hanging round his figure, caught at the waist by a broad red belt; his figure and face suggesting less of the meek Russ peasant than of the fiery northern skald. Quaint books, with old bronze clasps and leather ties, are in his arms. These books he spreads before me with mysterious silence, pointing out passage after passage, written in a dashing style—partly in red letters, partly in black—in the dead Slavonic tongue. He looks a very unlikely man to have lost the world for love.

"Your marriage got you into trouble?"

"Yes; a man who marries plunges into care."

"But though you have lost your priesthood, you are not expelled from the community?"

"Not expelled in words; yet I am not received into fellowship; not having yet performed the necessary acts."

"What acts?"

"The acts of penitence. Being married, I am not allowed to pass the church door; only to stand on the outer steps, salute the worshippers, and listen to the sacred sounds. I am expected to stand in the street, bareheaded, through the summer's sun and the winter frost; to bend my knee to every one going in; to beg his pardon of my offense; and to solicit his prayers at the throne of grace."

"How long will your time of penitence last?"

"Years, years!" he answers sadly; "if I were rich enough to do nothing else, I could be purified in six weeks. The penance is for forty days; but forty successive days; and I have never yet found time to give up forty days, in any one season, to the cleansing of my fame. But some year I shall find them."

"How does this failure affect your wife? Is she received into the church?"

"If you note this house of God, you will observe a part railed off behind the screen; this is the female side, and has an entrance by a separate door. No woman goes in at the principal gate. The space behind the screen is not considered as lying within the church; and there my wife can stand during service; bending to our neighbors as they enter, asking every woman to forgive her offense, and help her in prayer with her patron saint."

"Are you considered impure?"

"Yes; until our peace is made. You see, an Old Believer thinks that for most people a single life is better than a wedded life. It is the will of God that some should marry, in order that His children shall not die off the earth. Sometimes it is the will of Satan, that hell may be replenished with fallen souls. In either case, it is a sign of our lost estate; an act to be atoned by penitence and prayer. But getting married is not the whole of our offense. We went into the world: we held communion with the heathen; and we put ourselves beyond the pale of law."

"You hold the outer world to be unclean?"

"In one sense, yes. The world has been defiled by sin. A man who goes from our village into the world—who crosses the river in order to sell his deals and buy white flour—must purify himself on coming back. He may have to cut his bread with an unclean knife, to drink his water from an unclean glass. He carries his knife and cup beneath his girdle for common use; yet he may be forced, by accident, to eat with a strange knife, to drink out of a strange mug. On his return, he has to stand at the chapel door, and beg the forgiveness of every member of the community for his sins."

"Yet you are said to differ from the Orthodox clergy only in a few points?"

"On many points. We differ on the existence of a State Church; on the Holy Governing Synod; on the number of sacraments; on the benediction; on the cross; on the service-books; on the apostolical succession; and on many more. We object to the civil power in matters of faith; object to Byzantine pomp in our worship. What we want in our Church is the old Russian homeliness and heartiness; priests who are learned and sober men; bishops who are actual fathers of their flocks."

"Show me how you give the benediction."

"Christ and His apostles gave the blessing so; the first and second finger extended; the thumb on the third finger; not as the Byzantines give it, with the thumb on the first finger. We follow the usage introduced by Christ."

"You make much of that form?"

"Much for what it proves; not much for what it is. Pardon me, and I will show you. Here is a small bronze figure of our Lord; the work good and ancient; older than Nikon, older than St. Vladimir; it is said to have come from Kherson, on the Black Sea. This figure proves our case against Nikon the Monk, who altered things without reason, only to puff himself out with pride. Our Lord, you will observe, is giving the blessing, just as our saints, from Philip to Vladimir, gave it. The Greek fathers in Bethlehem bless a pilgrim in this way now. Our form is Syrian Greek, the Orthodox form is Byzantine Greek."

"And the cross?"

"We keep the old traditions of the cross. On every ancient spire and belfry in the land you find a true cross. Observe the spires in Moscow, Novgorod, and Kief. In places it has been removed, to make way for the Latin cross; but on many towers and steeples it remains; a lofty and silent witness for the truth."

"How do you prove that your cross is the true one? Think of it; the cross was a Roman gibbet: a thing unknown to either Jew or Greek. Are not the Latins likely to have known the shape of their own penal cross?"

"All that is true; but the Holy Cross on which our Lord expired in the flesh was not a common cross, made of two logs. We know that it was built of four different trees;

cypress, cedar, palm, and olive; therefore it must have had three arms."

"You take no sacraments?"

"At present, none. We have no priests ordained to bless the bread and wine. Saved without them? Yes; in the providence of God. Men were saved before sacraments; Judas Iscariot took them and was lost. A sacrament is a good form, not a saving means."

Fedor is a type of those Old Believers who are said to be slackening at the joints, in consequence of their present freedom from persecution. He has not learned to smoke; but he sees no harm in a pipe, except so far as it might cause a brother to fail and fall. He does not care for wine; but he will toss off his glass of whisky like a genuine child of the north. Some strict ones in his village drink no tea, having doubts on their mind whether tea came into use before Nikon's reign; and nearly all his neighbors refuse to mix sugar with their food, to put pipes into their mouths, to plant potatoes in their soil. Fedor objects to sugar, as being a devil's offering, purified with blood. Whisky he thinks lawful and beneficial, St. Paul having commanded Timothy to drink a little wine—which Fedor says is a shorter name for whisky—for his stomach's sake. Fedor is willing to obey St. Paul.

Fedor is a Bible-reader. Every phrase from his lips is streaked with text, and every point in his argument backed by chapter and verse. Except in some New England homesteads, I have never heard such floods of reference and quotation in my life.

"You say your Church has lost the priesthood?"

"Yes; our priests are all destroyed; the heavenly gift is lost, and we are wandering in the desert without a guide. This is our trial. Our bishops have all died off; we can not consecrate a priest; the consecrating power is in the devil's camp."

"How can you get back this gift?"

"By miracle; in no other way. The priesthood came by miracle; by miracle it will be restored."

"In our own day?"

"No; we do not hope it. Miracles come in an age of faith. *We* are not worthy of such a sign. We have to walk in our fathers' ways; to keep our children true; and hope that they may live into that better day."

"You think the Orthodox rite will be overthrown?"

"In time. In God's own time His kingdom will be restored; and Russia will be one people and one Church."

"What would you like the Government to do?"

"We want a free Church; we want to walk with our fathers; we want our old Church discipline; we want our old books, our old rituals, our old fashions; we want to read the Bible in our native tongue."

"Are the Old Believers all of one mind about these points?"

"Ha, no! There are Old Believers and Old Believers. In the north we are pretty nearly of one mind; in the south they are divided into two bodies, if not more. The Government is active in Moscow; Moscow being our ancient capital; and most of the traders in that city Old Believers. Ministers are trying to win them over to the Orthodox Church. Visit the Cemetery of the Transfiguration near Moscow; there you will see what Government has done."

Let us follow Fedor's hint.

CHAPTER XXX.

CEMETERY OF THE TRANSFIGURATION.

FOUR or five miles from the Holy Gate, beyond the walls of Moscow, in a populous suburb, near the edge of a pool of water, lies a field containing multitudes of graves—the graves of people who were long ago struck down by plague. This field is fenced with stakes, and part of the inclosure guarded by a wall. Within this wall stand a hospital and a convent; hospital on your left, convent on your right. A huge gateway, built of stones from older piles, and quaintly colored in Tartar panels, opens in your front. Driving up to this gate, we send in our cards — a councillor of state, an English friend, and myself—and are instantly admitted by the chief.

"This cemetery," says our friendly guide, "is called Preobrajenski (Transfiguration), from the village close by. In the plague time (1770) it was steppe, and people threw out their dead upon it, laying them in trenches, hardly covered with a pinch of dust. The plague growing worse and worse, the village elder got permission from Empress Catharine to build a house on the spot, to keep the peace and fumigate the dead. That house was built among the trenches. Ten years later (1781), Elia Kovielin, a brickmaker in Moscow, built among these graves a church, a cloister, and a hospital. This Kovielin was a clever man; rich in money and in friends; living in a fine house, and having the master of police, with governors, generals, princes, always at his board. Catharine was not aware of his being an Old Believer; but her ministers and courtiers knew him well enough. His house was a church; the pictures in his private chapel cost him fifty thousand rubles. Kovielin *was* a rich man. The monks were afraid of him, because he had friends at court; the priests, because he had the streets and suburbs at his back. Besides, what monk or priest could rail against a man for building a cemetery for the dead? A very clever man! You have heard the story of his magic loaf? You have not! Then you shall hear it. Paul the First, becoming aware that this edifice of the Transfiguration was an Old Believer's church, resolved to have it taken down. Kovielin drove to St. Petersburg, and found the Emperor deaf to his pleas. Voiékof, master of police in Moscow, having the Emperor's orders to pull down tower and wall, rode out to the cemetery, where he was received by Kovielin, and on going away was honored by the present of a convent loaf. A loaf! A magic loaf! Voiékof liked that lump of bread so well, that he went home and forgot to pull the cemetery about our ears. Folk say that loaf contained a purse — five thousand rubles coined in gold. Who knows? Elia Kovielin was a clever man.

Our guide through the courts and chapels is not an Old Believer, but an officer of state. In 1852, Nicolas seized the cemetery, sequestered the funds, and threw the management into official hands. The hospital he left to the Old Believers; for this great hospital is maintained in funds by the gifts of pious men; and the Emperor saw that if his officers seized the hospital, either his budget must be charged with a new burden, or the sick and aged people must be thrown into the streets. He seized their church, and left them their sick and aged poor.

"Kovielin's magic loaf was not the best," says the officer in charge; "these Old Believers are always rogues. When Bonaparte was lodging at the Kremlin, they went to him with gift and speech—the gift, a dish of golden rubles; saying, they came to greet him, and acknowledge him as Tsar."

"They thought he would deliver them from the tyranny of monks and priests?"

"Yes; that was what they dreamt. Napoleon humored them like fools, and even rode down hither to see them in their village. Kovielin was dead; *he* would not have done such things. Napoleon rode round their graves, and ate of their bread and porridge; but he could not make them out. They wanted a White Tsar; not a soldier in uniform and spurs. He went away puzzled; and when he was gone the rascals took to forging government notes."

"Odd trade to conduct in a cemetery!"

"You doubt me! Ask the police; ask any friend in Moscow; ask the councillor."

"They were suspected," says the councillor of state, "and their chapel was suppressed; but these events occurred in a former reign."

"What became of their chapel? Was it pulled down?"

"No; there it stands. The chapel is a rich one; Kovielin transferred to it all those pictures from his private house which had cost him fifty thousand rubles; and many rich merchants of Moscow graced it with works of art. It has been purified since, and turned into an Orthodox Church."

"An Orthodox Church?"

"Well, yes; in a sort of way. You see, the people here about are Old Believers; warm in their faith; attached to their ancient rites. In numbers only they are strong: ten millions—fifteen millions—twenty millions; no one knows how many. Long oppressed, they have lost alike their love of country and their loyalty to the Tsar; some looking wistfully for help to the Austrian Kaiser; others again dreaming of a king of France. It is of vast political moment to recover their lost allegiance; and the ministers of Nicolas conceived a plan which has been steadily carried out. The Old Believers are to be reconciled to the empire by—what shall we say?"

"A trick?"

"Well, this is the plan. The chapel is to be declared orthodox; it is to be opened by thirty monks and a dozen priests; but the monks are to be dressed in homely calico, and the ritual to be used is that employed before Nikon's time."

"You mean me to understand that the Official Church is willing to adopt the Ancient Rites, if she may do so with her present priests?"

"Yes; the object of the Government is to prove that custom, not belief, divides the Ancient from the Orthodox Church."

"It is an object that compels the Government to meet the Old Believers more than half-way; for to give up Nikon's ritual is to give up all the principle at stake. Has the experiment of an Orthodox priest performing the Ancient Rite succeeded in bringing people to the purified church?"

"Old Believers say it has completely failed. The chapel is now divided from the hospital by a moral barrier; and outside people scorn to pass the door and fall into what they call a trap. Last year the chiefs of the asylum prayed for leave to build a new wall across this courtyard, cutting off all communication with what they call their desecrated shrine. The home minister saw no harm in their request; but on sending their petition to the Holy Governing Synod, he met a firm refusal of the boon. The Popular Church has nothing to expect from these mitred monks."

On passing into this "desecrated shrine," we find a sombre church, in which vespers are being chanted by a dozen monks, without a single soul to listen. Most of these monks are aged men, with long hair and beards, attired in black calico robes, and wearing the ancient Russian cowl. Each monk has a small black pillow, on which he kneels and knocks his head. Church, costume, service, every point is so arranged as to take the eye and ear as homely, old and weird, in fact, the Ancient Rite.

"Do any of the Old Believers come to see you?"

"Yes, on Sundays, many," says the chief pope; "for on Sundays we allow them to dispute in church, and they are fond of disputing with us, phrase by phrase, and rite by rite. Five or six hundred come to us—after service—to hear us questioned by their popes. We try to show them that we all belong to one and the same Church; that the difference between us lies in ceremony and not in faith."

"Have you made converts to that view?"

"In Moscow, no; in Vilna, Penza, and elsewhere, our work of conciliation is said to have been more blessed."

"Those places are a long way off."

"Yes; bread that is scattered on the waters may be found in distant parts."

When I ask in official quarters, on what pretense the Emperor Nicolas seized the Popular Cemetery, the answer is—that under the guise of a cemetery, the Old Believers were establishing a college of their faith; from which they were sending forth missionaries, full of Bible learning, into other provinces; and that these priests and elders were attracting crowds of men from the Orthodox Church into dissent. It was alleged that they were spreading far and fast; that the parish priests were favoring them; and that every public trouble swelled their ranks. To wit, the cholera is said to have changed a thousand Orthodox persons into Old Believers every week. If it had raged two years, the Orthodox faith would have died a natural death. For in cases of public panic the Russian people have an irresistible longing to fall back upon their ancient ways. It is the cry of Hebrews in dismay: "Your tents! back to your tents!" All Eastern nations have this homely and conservative passion in their blood.

"These were the actual reasons," says the councillor of state; "but the cause assigned for interference was the scandal of the forged bank-notes."

"Surely no one believes that scandal?"

"Every one believes it. Only last year this scandal led to the perpetration of a curious crime."

"What sort of crime?"

"At dusk on a wintry day, when all the offices in the cemetery were closed, a cavalcade dashed suddenly to the door. A colonel of gendarmes leaped from a drojki, followed by a master of police. Four gendarmes and four citizens of Moscow came with them. Pushing into the chief office, they asked to see the strong-box, and to have it opened in their presence. As the clerk looked shy, the colonel of gendarmes was sharp and rude. They were accused, he said, of forging ruble notes, and he had come by order of the Governor-general, Prince Vladimir Dolgorouki, to open their strong-box under the eyes of four eminent merchants and the master of police. He laid the prince's mandate down; he showed his own commission; and then in an imperial tone, demanded to have the keys! The keys could not be found; the treasurer was gone to Moscow, and would not return that night. 'Then seal your box,' said the colonel of gendarmes; 'the police will keep it! Come to-morrow, with your keys, to Prince Dolgorouki's house in the Tverskoi Place, at ten o'clock.' The box was sealed; the police master hauled it into his drojki; in half an hour the cavalcade was gone. Next day the treasurer, with his clerk and manager, drove into Moscow with their keys, and on arriving in the Tverskoi Place were smitten pale with news that no search for ruble notes had been ordered by the prince."

"Who, then, was that colonel of gendarmes?"

"A thief; the master of police a thief; the four gendarmes were thieves; the four eminent citizens thieves!"

"And what was done?"

"Prince Dolgorouki sent for Rebrof, head of the police (a very fine head), and told him what these thieves had done. 'Superb!' laughed Rebrof, as he heard the tale; and when the prince had come to an end of his details, he again cried out, in genuine admiration, 'Ha! superb! One man, and only one in Moscow, has the brain for such a deed. The thief is Simonoff. Give me a little time, say nothing to the world, and Simonoff shall be yours.' Rebrof kept his word; in three months Simonoff was tried, found guilty on the clearest proof, and sentenced to the mines for life. Rebrof traced him through the cabmen, followed him to his haunts, learned what he had done with the scrip and bonds, and then arrested him in a public bath. The money—two hundred thousand rubles—he had shared and spent. 'Siberia,' cried the brazen rogue, when the judge pronounced his doom, 'Siberia is a jolly place; I have plenty of money, and shall have a merry time.' Had there been no false reports about the cemetery, a theft like Simonoff's could hardly have taken place."

CHAPTER XXXI.

RAGOSKI.

RAGOSKI, another cemetery of the Old Believers, in the suburbs of Moscow, has a different story, and belongs to a second branch of the Popular Church. There is a party of Old Believers "with priests" and a party "without priests." Ragoski belongs to the party with priests; Preobrajenski to the party without priests.

One party in the Popular Church believes that the priesthood has been lost; the other party believes that it has been saved. Both parties deny the Orthodox Church; but the more liberal branch of the Popular Church allows that a true priesthood may exist in other Greek communions, by the bishops of which a line of genuine pastors may be ordained.

"You wish to visit the Ragoski?" asks my host. "Then we must look to our means. The chiefs of Ragoski are suspicious; and no wonder; the times of persecution are near them still. In the reign of Nicolas, the Ragoski was shut up, the treasury was seized, and many of the worshippers were sent away—no one knows whither; to Siberia, to Archangel, to Imeritia—who shall say? Alexander has given them back their own; but they can not tell how long the reign of grace may last. An order from Prince Dolgorouki might come to-morrow; their property might be seized, their chapel closed, their hospital emptied, and their graves profaned. It is not likely; it is not probable; for the favor shown to this cemetery is a part of our general progress, not an isolated act of imperial grace. But these Old Believers, caring little about general progress, give the glory to God. If you told them they are tolerated, as Jews are tolerated, they would think you mad; 'The Lord giveth, and the Lord taketh away;

blessed be the name of the Lord.' Who among them knows when the evil day may come? Hence, they suspect a stranger. Not twenty men in Moscow, out of their own communion, have been within their gates. The cemetery will be hard to enter; hard as to enter your own Abode of Love."

By happy chance, a gentleman calls while we are talking of ways and means, who is not only an Old Believer, but an Old Believer of the branch with priests. A short man, white and wrinkled, with a keen gray eye, a serious face, and speech that takes you by its wonderful force and fire, this gentleman is a trader in the city, living in a fine house, and giving away in charities the income of a prince. I know one man to whom he sends every year a thousand rubles, as a help for poor students at the university. This good citizen is a banker, trader, mill-owner, what not; he is able, prompt, adroit; he gives good dinners; and is hand-and-glove with every one in power. I have heard folks say—by way of parable, no doubt—that all the police of Moscow are in his pay. You also hear whispers that this banker, trader, what not, is a priest; not of the ordained and apostolic order, but one of those popular priests whom the Synod hunts to death. Who knows?

"You are an Old Believer," he begins, addressing his speech to me. "I know that from your book on The Holy Land; every word of which expresses the doctrines held by the Russian Church in her better days."

My host explains my great desire to see the cemetery of Ragoski. "You shall be welcomed there like a friend. Let me see; shall I go with you? No; it will be better for you to go alone. The governor, Ivan Kruchinin, shall be there to receive you. I will write." He dashes off a dozen lines of introduction, written in the tone and haste of a recognized chief.

Armed with this letter we start next day, and driving through the court-yards of the Kremlin, have to pull up our drojki, to allow a train of big black horses to go prancing by. It is the train of Innocent, metropolite of Moscow, taking the air in a coach-and-six!

"This Ragoski cemetery," says the councillor of state, as we push through the China Town into the suburbs, "had an origin like that of the Transfiguration. It was opened on account of plague (1770), not by a single founder, like its rival, but by a company of pious persons, anxious to consecrate the ground in which they had already begun to lay their dead. A chapel was erected, and a daily service was performed in that chapel for eighty-six years. Of late, the police are said to have troubled them very much; no one knows why; and no one dares to ask any questions on such a point. We are all too much afraid of the gentlemen in cowl and gown."

In about an hour we are at the gates. The place is like a desert, brightened by one gaudy pile. An open yard and silent office; a wall of brick; a painted chapel, in the old Russ style; a huge tabernacle of plain red brick; a wilderness of mounds and tombs: this is Ragoski. Not a soul is seen except one aged man in homely garb, who is carrying logs of wood. This man uncaps as we drive past; but turns and watches us with furtive eyes. Our letter is soon sent in; but we are evidently scanned like pilgrims at Marsaba; and twenty minutes elapse before the governor comes to us, cap in hand, and begs us to walk in.

A small, round man, with ruddy face and laughing eyes, and tender, plaintive manner, Ivan Kruchinin is not much like the men we see about—men who have a lean, sad look and fearful eyes, as though they lived in the conscious eclipse of light and faith. Coming to our carriage-door, he begs us to step in, and puts his service smilingly at our will.

"What is this new edifice with the gay old Tartar lozenges and bars?"

"Ugh?" sighs the governor.

"One of the last efforts made to win these Old Believers over," says the councillor of state. "You see the monks have gone to work with craft. The pile is Russ outside, like many old chapels in Moscow; piles which catch the eye and impress the mind. They call it an Old Believers' Chapel; they have built it as the Roman centurion built the Jews a synagogue; and they hold a service in it, as they hold a service in the Transfiguration; said and sung by Orthodox popes, but in the language and the forms employed before Nikon's time."

Inside, the chapel is arranged to suit an Old Believer's taste; and every point of ritual, phrase and form is yielded to such as will accept the ministry of an Orthodox priest.

"Do they draw any part of your flock?"

"Not a soul," says the governor. "A few of those 'without priests,' have joined them in despair; not many—not a hundred; while thousands of their people are coming round to us."

"These converts, who accept an Orthodox priest and the ancient ritual, are called the United Old Believers—are they not?"

"United! They—the new schismatics! We know them not; we hate all sects; and these misguided men are adding to our country another sect."

Passing the cemetery yards, ascending some broad stone steps, we stand at a chapel door. This door is closed, and all around us reigns the silence which befits a tomb. Kruchinin makes a sign; his tap is answered from within; a door swings back; and out upon us floats a low, weird chant. Going through the door, we find ourselves in a spacious church, columned and pictured, with a noble dome. This is the Old Believers' church. A few dim lamps are burning on the shrines; some tapers flit and mingle near the royal gates; a crowd of women kneel on the iron floor, not only in the aisles, but across the nave. Advancing with our guide, up the central aisle, we come upon a line of men, some prostrate on the ground, some standing erect in prayer. A group of singers and readers stands apart, in front of the royal gates, with service-books and candles in their hands, reciting in a sweet, monotonous drone the ritual of the day.

As a surprise the scene is perfect.

"Who are these readers and singers?"

"Citizens of Moscow," says the governor; "bankers, farmers, men of every trade and class."

We stand aside until the service ends—a most impressive service, with louder prayers and livelier bendings than you hear and see in Orthodox cathedrals. Then we move about. "What is the service just concluded?" Kruchinin bends his eyes to the ground, and answers, "Only a layman's service; one that can be said without a priest. You noticed, perhaps, that neither the royal gates nor the deaccn's doors were opened?"

"Yes; how is that?'

"Our altars have been sealed."

"Your altars sealed?"

"Yes; you shall see. Come round this way," and the governor leads us to the deacon's door. Sealed; certainly sealed; the door being nailed by a piece of leather to the screen; and the leather itself attached by a fresh blotch of official wax. It looks as if the persecution were come again.

"How can such things be done?"

"Our Emperor does not know it," sighs the governor, who seems to be a thoroughly patriotic man; "it is the doing of our clerical police. We ask to have the use of our own altar, in our own church, according to the law. They say we shall have it, on one condition. They will give us our altar, if we accept their priest!"

"And you refuse?"

"What can we do? Their priests have not been properly ordained; they have lost their virtue; they can not give the blessing and absolve from sin. We have declined; our altars continue sealed; and our people have to sing and pray, as in the synagogues of Galilee, without a priest."

"That was not always so?"

"In other days we had our clergy, living with us openly in the light of day; but when our cemetery was restored to us by our good Emperor in 1856, some trouble came upon us from the Synod on the subject of consecration, and we have not yet lived that trouble down."

"The prelates in St. Isaac's Square object to your priests receiving ordination at the hands of foreign bishops?"

"Yes; they wish us to receive the Holy Spirit from them; from men who have it not to give! We can not live a lie; and we decline their offer to consecrate our priests."

"You have no popular priests?" "No."

"If you have no priests, how can you marry and baptize infants?"

"According to the law of God."

"Without a priest?"

"No; with a priest. We have a priest for such things; though we can not suffer him to risk Siberia by performing a public office in our church. Father Anton lives in secret. In the bazar of Moscow he is known as a merchant, dealing in grain and stuffs. The world knows nothing else about him; even the police have never suspected *him* of being a priest."

"He is ordained?"

"You know that some of our brethren live in Turkey and in Austria, where the Turks and Germans grant them asylums which they have not always found at home. A good many Old Believers dwell in a village, called Belia Krinitza, in the country lying at the feet of the Carpathians, just beyond the frontiers of Podolia and Bessarabia. One Ambrosius, a Greek prelate from Bulgaria, visited these refugees, and consecrated their Bishop Cyril, who is still alive. Cyril consecrated Father Anton, our Moscow priest."

"Father Anton marries and christens the members of your church?"

"He does, in secret. In his worldly name he buys and sells, like any other dealer in his shop."

"You live in hope that the persecution will not come again?"

"We live to suffer, and *not* to yield."

Passing into the hospital, we find a hundred men, in one large edifice; four hundred women in a second large edifice. The rooms are very clean; the beds arranged in rows, the kitchens and baking houses bright. A woman stands at a desk, before a Virgin, and reads out passages from the gospels and the psalms. Each poor old creature drops a courtesy as we pass her bed, and after we have eaten of their bread and salt, in the common dining-hall, they gather in a line and cross themselves, bending to the ground, thanking us, as though we had conferred on them some special grace.

These asylums of the Old Believers are the only free charities in Russia; for the hospitals in towns are Government works, supported by the state. The Black Clergy does little for the poor, except to supply them with crops of saints, and bring down persecution on the Popular Church.

On driving back to Moscow, in the afternoon—pondering on what we have seen and heard—the lay singers, the clean asylum, and the sealed-up altar—we arrive under the Kremlin wall in time to find the mitred monk in our front again, just dashing with his splendid coach and six black horses through the Holy Gate!

CHAPTER XXXII.

DISSENTING POLITICS.

THE revolution made by Nikon, ending in the rupture of his Church, gave vast importance to dissenting bodies, while opening up a field for missionaries and impostors of every kind. Before his reign as patriarch, the chief dissidents were the Eunuchs, the Self-burners, the Flagellants, the Sabbath-keepers, and the Silent Men; all of whom could trace their origin to foreign sources and distant times. They had no strong grip on the public mind. But, in setting up a state religion—an official religion—a persecuting religion—from which a majority of the people held aloof, in scorn and fear, the patriarch provided a common ground on which the wildest spirits could meet and mix. Aiming at one rule for all, the Government put these Old Believers on a level with Flagellants and Eunuchs; the most conservative men in Russia with the most revolutionary men in Europe. All shades of difference were confounded by an ignorant police, inspired in their malign activities by a band of ignorant monks. So long as the persecution lasted, a man who would not go to his parish church, pray in the new fashion, cross himself in the legal way, and bend his knee to Baal, was classed as a separatist, and treated by the civil power as a man false to his Emperor and his God.

Thus the Old Believers came to support such bodies as the Milk Drinkers and Champions of the Holy Spirit, much as the old English Catholics joined hands with Quakers and Millennialists in their common war against a persecuting Church. These dissidents have learned to keep their own secrets, and to fight the persecutor with his own carnal weapons. They, too, keep spies. They have secret funds. They place their friends on the press. They send agents to court whom the Emperor never suspects. They have relations with monks and ministers, with bishops and aides-de-camp; they not unfrequently occupy the position of monk and minister, bishop and aide-de-camp. They go to church; they confess their sins; they help the parish priest in his need; they give money to adorn convents; and in some important cases they don the cowl and take religious vows. These persons are not easily detected in their guile; unless, indeed, fanaticism takes with them a visible shape. In passing through the province of Harkof, I hear in whispers of a frightful secret having come to light; no less than a discovery by the police that in the great monastery of Holy Mount, in that province, a number of Eunuchs are living in the guise of Orthodox monks!

Every day the council is surprised by reports that some man noted for his piety and charity is a dissenter; nay, is a dissenting pope; though he owns a great mill and seems to devote his energies to trade.

The reigning Emperor, hating deceit, and most of all self-deceit, looks steadily at the facts. No doubt, if he could put these dissidents down he would; but, like a man of genius, he knows that he must work in this field of thought by wit and not by power. "No illusions, gentlemen." From the first year of his reign he has been asking for true reports, and searching into the statements made with a steadfast yearning to find the truth.

What comes of his study is now beginning to be seen of men. The Official Church has not ceased to be official, and even tyrannical; but the violence of her persecution is going down; the regular clergy have been softened; the monkish fury has been curbed; and lay opinion has been coaxed into making a first display of strength.

A minute was laid by the Emperor before his council of ministers so early as Oct. 15 and 27, 1858, for their future guidance in dealing with dissenters; under which title the Holy Governing Synod still classed the Old Believers with the Flagellants and Eunuchs! The minute written by his father was not removed from the books; it was simply explained and carried forward; yet the change was radical; since the police, in all their dealings with religious bodies, were instructed to talk in a gentler tone, and to give accused persons the benefit of every doubt which should occur on points of law. A change of spirit is often of higher moment than a change of phrase. Without implying that either his father was wrong, or the Holy Governing Synod unjust, the Emperor opened a door by which many of the nonconformists could at once escape. But what was done only shows too plainly how much remains to do. The Emperor has checked the persecutor's arm; he has not crushed the persecuting spirit.

A special committee was named by him to study the whole subject of dissent; with the practical view of seeing how far it could be conscientiously tolerated, and in what way it could be honestly repressed.

This committee made their report in August, 1864; a voluminous document (of which some folios only have been printed); and adopting their report, the Emperor added to the paper a second minute, which is still the rule of his ministers in dealing with such affairs. In this minute he recognizes the existence of dissent. He acknowledges that dissidents may have civil and religious rights. Of course, as head of the Church, he can not suffer that Church to be injured; but he desires his ministers, after taking counsel with the Holy Governing Synod, and obtaining their consent at every step, to see that justice is always done.

The spirit of this imperial minute is so good that the monks attack it; not in open day and with honest words; for such is not their method and their manner; but with sly suggestions in the confessor's closet and serpentine whispers near the sacred shrines. It is unpopular with the Holy Governing Synod. But the conservatives and sectaries, long cast down, look up into what they call a new heaven and a new earth. They say the day of peace has come, and finding a door of appeal thrown open to them in St. Petersburg, they are sending in hundreds of petitions; here requesting leave to open a cemetery, there to construct an altar, here again to build a church. In thirty-two months (Jan. 1866 to Sept. 1868), the home ministry received no less than three hundred and sixty-seven petitions of various kinds.

Valouef, the minister in power when this imperial minute was first drawn up, had a difficult part to play between his liberal master and the retrograde monks. No man is strong enough to quarrel with the tribunal sitting in St. Isaac's

Square; and Valouef was wrecked by his zeal in carrying out the imperial plan. The minister had to get these fathers to consent in every case to the petitioner's prayer; these fathers, who thought dissenters had no right to live, and kept on quoting to him the edicts of Nicolas, as though that sovereign were still alive! On counting his papers at the end of those thirty-two months of trial, Valouef found that out of three hundred and sixty-seven petitions in his office, the Holy Governing Synod consented to his granting twenty-one, postponing fifty, and rejecting all the rest.

A man, who said he was born in the Official Church, begged leave to profess dissenting doctrine, which he had come to see was right: refused. A merchant offered to build a chapel for dissenters in a dissenting village: refused. A builder proposed to throw a wall across a convent garden, so as to divide the male from the female part: refused. A dissenting minister asked to be relieved from the daily superintendence of his city police: refused. Michaeloff, a rich merchant of St. Petersburg, offered to found a hospital for the use of dissenters near the capital, at his personal charge: refused. Last year an asylum for poor dissenters was opened at Kluga; an asylum built by peasants for persons of their class: the Synod orders it to be closed.

Hundreds of petitions come in from Archangel, Siberia, and the Caucasus, from men who were in other days transported to those districts for conscience' sake, requesting leave to come back. These petitions are divided by the Holy Governing Synod, into two groups: (1.) those of men who have been judged by some kind of court; (2.) those of men who have been exiled by a simple order of the police. The first class are refused in mass without inquiry; a few of the second class, after counsel taken with the provincial quorum, are allowed.

From these examples, it will be seen that the liberal movement is not reckless; but the movement is along the line; the work goes on; and every day some progress is being made. A minister who has to work with a board of monks must feel his way.

CHAPTER XXXIII.

CONCILIATION.

ONE point has been gained in the mere fact of the imperial minute having drawn a distinction between things which may be thought and things which may be done. The right of holding a particular article of faith stands on a different ground to the right of preaching that article of faith in open day. The first is private, and concerns one's self; the second is public, and concerns the general weal. What is private only may be left to conscience; what is public must be always subject to the law.

The ministers have come to see that every man has a right to think for himself about his duty to God; and under their directions the police have orders to leave a man alone, so long as he refrains from exciting the public mind, and disturbing the public peace. In fact, the Russians have been brought into line with their neighbors the Turks.

In Moscow a man is now as free to believe what he likes as he would be in Stamboul; though he must exercise his liberty in both these cities with the deference due from the unit to the mass. He must not meddle with the dominant creed. He must not trifle with the followers of that creed; though his action on other points may be perfectly free. Having full possession of the field, the Church will not allow herself to be attacked; even though it should please her to fall on you with fire and sword.

In Moscow, a Mussulman may try to convert a Jew; in Stamboul, an Armenian may try to convert a Copt; but woe to the Mussulman in Russia who tempts a Christian to his mosque, to the Christian in Turkey who tempts a Mussulman to his church! As on the higher, so it stands on the lower plane. The right of propagand lies with the ruling power. In Russia, a monk may try to convert a dissenter; the dissenter will be sent to Siberia should he happen to convert the monk. A rule exactly parallel holds in Turkey and in Persia, where a mollah may try to convert a giaour; but the giaour will be beaten and imprisoned should he have the misfortune to convert the mollah.

Some men may fancy that little has been gained so long as toleration stops at free thought, and interdicts free speech. In England or America that would seem true and even trite; but the rules applied to Moscow are not the rules which would be suitable in London or New York. The gain is vast when a man is permitted to say his prayers in peace.

One day last week I came upon striking evidence of the value of this freedom. Riding into a large village, known to me by fame for its dissenting virtues, I exclaimed, on seeing the usual Orthodox domes and crosses—"Not many dissidents here!" My companion smiled. A moment later we entered the elder's house. "Have you any Old Believers here?"

"Yes, many."

"But here is a church, big enough to hold every man, woman, and child in your village."

"Yes, that is true. You find it empty now; in other times you might have found it full."

"How was that? Were your people drawn away from their ancient rites?"

"Never. We were driven to church by the police. When God gave us Alexander we left off going to mass."

"Was the persecution sharp?"

"So sharp, that only four stout men lived through it; never going to church for a dozen years. When Nicolas died, the police pretended that we had only those four Old Believers in this place; the next day it was suspected, the next year it was known, that every soul in it was an Old Believer."

All these dissenting bodies are political parties, more or less openly pronounced; and have to be dealt with on political, no less than on religious grounds. Rejecting the State Church, they reject the Emperor, so far as he assumes to be head of that Church. A State Church, they say, is Antichrist; a devil's kingdom, set up by Satan himself in the form of Nikon the Monk. So far as Alexander is a royal prince they take him, and even pray for him; but they will not place his image in their chapel; they refuse to pray for him as a true believer; and they fear he is dead to religion, and lost to God.

The Popular Church contends that since the reign of Peter the Great every thing has been lawless and provisional. Peter, they say, was a bastard son of Nikon the Monk; in other words, of the devil himself. The first object of this child of the Evil One being to destroy the Russian people, he abandoned the country, and built him a palace among the Swedes and Finns. His second object being to destroy the Russian Church, he abolished the office of Patriarch, and made himself her spiritual chief.

The consequences which they draw from these facts are instant and terrible; for these consequences touch with a deadly sorcery the business of their daily lives.

Since Satan began his reign in the person of Peter the Great, all authorities and rules have been suspended on the earth. According to them, nothing is lawful, for the reign of law is over. Contracts are waste; no trust can be executed; no sacrament can be truly held; not even that of marriage. Hence, it is a matter of conscience with thousands of Old Believers, that they shall not undergo the nuptial rite. They live without it, in the hope of heaven providing them with a remedy on earth for what would otherwise be a wrong in heaven. And thus their lives are passed in the shadow of a terrible doom.

The absence of marriage-ties among the best of these Old Believers is not the most frightful evil. So far as the men and women are concerned, the case is bad enough; but as regards their children, it is worse. These children are regarded by the law as basely born. "By the devil's law," say the Old Believers sadly; but the fact remains, that under the Russian code these "bastards" do not inherit their fathers' wealth. In other states, an issue might be found in the making of a will, by which a father could dispose of his property to his children as he pleased. But an Old Believer dares not make a will. A will is a public act, and he disclaims the present public powers. The common course is, for an Old Believer to *give* his money to some friend whom he can trust, and for that friend to *give it back* to his children when he is no more.

The Emperor, studying remedies for these grave disorders among his people, has conceived the bold idea of legalizing in Russia the system of civil marriage, already established in every free country of Europe, and in each of the United States. A bill has been drawn, so as to spare the Orthodox clergy, as much as could be done. The Council of State is favorable to this bill; but the Holy Governing Synod, frightened at all these changes, refuse to admit that a "sacrament" can be given by a magistrate; and a bill which would bring peace and order into a million of households is delayed, though it is not likely to be sacrificed, in deference to their monastic doubts.

"What else would you have the Emperor do?" I ask a man of confidence in this Popular Church.

"Do! Restore our ancient rights. In Nikon's time the crown procured our condemnation by a council of the Eastern Churches; we survive the curse; and now we ask to have that ban removed."

"You stand condemned by a council?"

"Yes; by a deceived and corrupted council. That curse must be taken off our heads."

"Is the Government aware of your demands?"

"It is aware."

"Have any steps been taken to that end?"

"A great one. Alexander has proposed to remove the ban; and even the Synod, calling itself holy, has consented to recall the curse; but we reject all offers from this band of monks; they have no power to bind and loose. The Eastern Churches put us in the wrong; the Eastern Churches must concur to set us right. They cursed us in their ignorance; they must bless us in their knowledge. We have passed through fire, and know our weakness and our strength. No other method will suffice. We ask a general council of the Oriental Church."

"Can the Emperor call that council?"

"Yes; if Russia needs it for her peace; and who can say she does not need it for her peace?"

CHAPTER XXXIV.

ROADS.

A MAN who loads himself with common luggage would find these Russian roads rather rough, whether his journey lay through the forest or across the steppe. An outfit for a journey is a work of art. A hundred things useful to the traveller are needed on these roads, from candle and cushion down to knife and fork; but there are two things which he can not live without—a tea-pot and a bed.

My line from the Arctic Sea to the southern slopes of the Ural range, from the Straits of Yeni Kale to the Gulf of Riga runs over land and lake, forest and fen, hill and steppe. My means of travel are those of the country; drojki, cart, barge, tarantass, steamer, sledge, and train. The first stage of my journey from north to south is from Solovetsk to Archangel; made in the provision-boat, under the eyes of Father John. This stage is easy, the grouping picturesque, the weather good, and the voyage accomplished in the allotted time. The second stage is from Archangel to Vietegra; done by posting in five or six days and nights; a drive of eight hundred versts, through one vast forest of birch and pine. My cares set in at this second stage. There is trouble about the podorojna—paper signed by the police, giving you a right to claim horses at the posting stations, at a regulated price. As very few persons drive to Holmogory, the police make a fuss about my papers, wondering why the gentleman could not sail in a boat up the Dvina like other folk, instead of tearing through a region in which there is hardly any road. Wish to see the birthplace of Lomonosof! What is there to see? A log cabin, a poor town, a scrubby country—that is all! Yet after some delays the police give in, the paper is signed. Then comes the question: carriage, cart, or sledge? No public vehicle runs to the capital; nothing but a light cart, just big enough to hold a bag of letters and a boy. That cart goes twice a week through the forest-tracks, but no one save the boy in charge can ride with the imperial mail. A stranger has to find his means of getting forward, and his choice is limited to a cart, a tarantass, and a sledge.

"A sledge is the thing," says a voice at my elbow; "but to use a sledge you must wait until the snow is deep and the frost sets in. In summer we have no roads; in some long reaches not a path; but from the day when we get five degrees of frost, we have the noblest roads in the world."

"That may be six or seven weeks hence?"

"Yes, true; then you must have a tarantass. Come over with me to the maker's yard."

A tarantass is a better sort of cart, with the addition of splash-board, hood, and step. It has no springs; for a carriage slung on steel could not be sent through these desert wastes. A spring might snap; and a broken coach some thirty or forty miles from the nearest hamlet, is a vehicle in which very few people would like to trust their feet. A good coach is a sight to see; but a good coach implies a smooth road, with a blacksmith's forge at every turn. A man with rubles in his purse can do many things; but a man with a million rubles in his purse could not venture to drive through forest and steppe in a carriage which no one in the country could repair.

A tarantass lies lightly on a raft of poles; mere lengths of green pine, cut down and trimmed with a peasant's axe, and lashed on the axles of two pairs of wheels, some nine or ten feet apart. The body is an empty shell, into which you drop your trunks and traps, and then fill up with hay and straw. A leather blind and apron to match, keep out a little of the rain; not much; for the drifts and squalls defy all efforts to shut them out. The thing is light and airy, needing no skill to make and mend. A pole may split as you jolt along; you stop in the forest skirt, cut down a pine, smooth off the leaves and twigs; and there, you have another pole! All damage is repaired in half an hour.

On scanning this vehicle closely in and out, my mind is clear that the drive to St. Petersburg should be done in a tarantass—not in a common cart. But I am dreaming all this while that the tarantass before me can be hired. A sad mistake! No maker can be found to part from his carriage on any terms short of purchase out and out. "St. Petersburg is a long way off," says he; "how shall I get my tarantass back?"

"By sending your man along with it. Charge me for his time, and let him bring it home."

The maker shakes his head.

"Too far! Will you send him to Vietegra, near the lake?"

"No," says the man, after some little pause, "not even to Vietegra. You see, when you pay off my man, he has still to get back; his journey will be worse than yours, on account of the autumn rains; he may sink in the marsh; he may stick in the sand; not to speak of his being robbed by bandits. and devoured by wolves."

"He is not afraid of robbers and wolves?"

"Why not? The forests are full of wild men, runaways, and thieves; and three weeks hence the wolves will be out in packs. How, then, can he be sure of getting home with my tarantass?"

Things look as though the vehicle must be bought. How much will it cost? A strong tarantass is said to be worth three hundred and fifty rubles. But the waste of money is not all. What can you do with it, when it is yours? A tarantass in these northern forests is like the white elephant in the Eastern story. "Can one sell such a thing in Vietegra?"

"Ha, ha!" laughs my friend. "In Vietegra, the people are not fools; in fact, they are rather sharp ones. They will say they have no use for a tarantass; they know you can't wait to chaffer about the price. Your best plan will be to drive into a station, pay the driver, and run away."

"Leaving my tarantass in the yard?"

"Exactly; that will be cheaper in the end. Some years ago I drove to Vietegra in a fine tarantass; no one would buy it from me. One fellow offered me ten kopecks. Enraged at his impudence, I put up my carriage in a yard to be kept for me; and every six months I received a bill for rent. In ten years' time that tarantass had cost me thrice its original price. In vain I begged the man to sell it; no buyer could be found. I offered to give it him, out and out; he declined my gift. At length I sent a man to fetch it home; but when my servant got to Vietegra he could find neither keeper nor tarantass. He only learned that in years gone by the yard was closed, and my tarantass sold with the other traps."

A God-speed dinner is the happy means of lifting this cloud of trouble from my mind. "The man," says our helpful consul, "thinks he will never see his tarantass again. Now, take my servant, Dimitri, with you; he is a clever fellow, not afraid of wolves and runaways; he may be trusted to bring it safely back."

"If Dimitri goes with you," adds a friendly merchant, "I will lend you my tarantass; it is strong and roomy; big enough for two."

"You will!" A grip of hands, a flutter of thanks, and the thing is done.

"Why, now," cries my host, "you will travel like a Tsar."

This private tarantass is brought round to the gates; an empty shell, into which they toss our luggage; first the hard pieces—hat-box, gun-case, trunk; then piles of hay to fill up chinks and holes, and wisps of straw to bind the mass; on all of which they lay your bedding, coats and skins. A woodman's axe, a coil of rope, a ball of string, a bag of nails, a pot of grease, a basket of bread and wine, a joint of roast beef, a tea-pot, and a case of cigars are afterwards coaxed into nooks and crannies of the shell.

Starting at dusk, so as to reach the ferry, at which you are to cross the river by day-break, we plash the mud and grind the planks of Archangel beneath our hoofs. "Good-bye! Look out for wolves! Take care of brigands! Good-bye, good-bye!" shout a dozen voices; and then that friendly and frozen city is left behind.

All night, under murky stars, we tear along a dreary path; pines on our right, pines on our left, and pines in our front. We bump through a village, waking up houseless dogs; we reach a ferry, and pass the river on a raft; we grind over stones and sand; we tug through slush and bog; all night, all day; all night again, and after that, all day; winding through the maze of forest leaves, now burnt and sear, and swirling on every blast that blows. Each day of our drive is like its fellow. A clearing, thirty yards wide, runs out before us for a thousand versts. The pines are all alike, the birches all alike. The villages are still more like each other than the trees. Our only change is in the track itself, which passes from sandy rifts to slimy beds, from grassy fields to rolling logs. In a thousand versts we count a hundred versts of log, two hundred versts of sand, three hundred versts of grass, four hundred versts of water-way and marsh.

We smile at the Russians for laying down lines of rail in districts where they have neither a turnpike road nor a country lane. But how are they to blame? An iron path is the natural way in forest lands, where stone is scarce, as in Russia and the United States.

If the sands are bad, the logs are worse. One night we spend in a kind of protest; dreaming that our luggage has been badly packed, and that on daylight coming it shall be laid in some easier way. The trunk calls loudly for a change. My seat by day, my bed by night, this box has a leading part in our little play; but no adjustment of the other traps, no stuffing in of hay and straw, no coaxing of the furs and skins suffice to appease the fretful spirit of that trunk. It slips and jerks beneath me; rising in pain at every plunge. Coaxing it with skins is useless; soothing it with wisps of straw is vain. We tie it with bands and belts; but nothing will induce it to lie down. How can we blame it? Trunks have rights as well as men; they claim a proper place to lie in; and my poor box has just been tossed into this tarantass, and told to lie quiet on logs and stones.

Still more fretful than this trunk are the lumbar vertebræ in my spine. They hate this jolting day and night; they have been jerked out of their sockets, pounded into dust, and churned into curds. But then these mutineers are under more control than the trunk; and when they begin to murmur seriously, I still them in a moment by hints of taking them for a drive through Bitter Creek.

Ha! here is Holmogory! Standing on a bluff above the river, pretty and bright, with her golden cross, her grassy roads, her pink and white houses, her boats on the water, and her stretches of yellow sands; a village with open spaces; here a church, there a cloister; gay with gilt and paint, and shanties of a better class than you see in such small country towns; and forests of pine and birch around her—Holmogory looks the very spot on which a poet of the people might be born!

CHAPTER XXXV.

A PEASANT POET.

In the grass-grown square of Archangel, between the fire-tower and the court of justice, stands a bronze figure on a round marble shaft; a figure showing a good deal of naked chest, and holding (with a Cupid's help) a lyre on the left arm. A Roman robe flows down the back. You wonder what such a figure is doing in such a place; a bit of false French art in a city of monks and trade! The man in whose name it has been raised was a poet; a poet racy of the soil; a village genius; who, among merits of many kinds, had the high quality of being a genuine Russian, and of writing in his native tongue.

For fifty years Lomonosoff was called a fool—a clever fool—for having wasted his genius on coachmen and cooks. Court ladies laughed at his whimsy of writing verses for the common herd to read; and learned dons considered him crazy for not doing all his more serious work in French. A change has come; the court speaks Russ; and society sees some merit in the phrases which it once contemned. The language of books and science is no longer foreign to the soil; and all classes of the people have the sense to read and speak in their musical and copious native speech. This happy change is due to Michael Lomonosoff, the peasant boy!

Born in this forest village on the Dvina bluffs (in 1711), he sprang from that race of free colonists who had come into the north country from Novgorod the Great. His father, Vassili Lomonosoff, a boatman, getting his bread by netting and spearing fish on the great river, brought him up among nets and boats, until the lad was big enough to slip his chain, throw down his pole, and push into the outer sea. Not many books were then to be got in a forest town like Holmogory, and some lives of saints and a Slavonic Bible were his only reading for many years. A good priest (as I learn on the spot) took notice of the child, and taught him to read the old Slavonic words. These books he got by heart; making heroes of the Hebrew prophets, and reading with ardor of his native saints. The priest soon taught him all he knew, and being a man of good heart, he sought around him for the means of sending the lad to school. But where, in those dark ages, could a school be found? He knew of schools for priests, and for the sons of priests; but schools for peasants, and for the sons of peasants, did not then exist. Could he be placed with a priest and sent to school? The village pastor wrote to a friend in Moscow, who, though poor himself, agreed to take the lad into his house. A train of carts came through the village on its way to Moscow, carrying fur and fish for sale; and the priest arranged with the drivers that Michael should go with them, trudging at their side, and helping them on the road. At ten years old he left his forest home, and walked to the great city, a distance of nearly a thousand miles.

The priest in Moscow sent him to the clerical school, where he learned some Latin, French, and German; in all of which tongues, as well as in Russian, he afterwards spoke and wrote. He also learned to work for his living as a polisher and setter of stones. A lad who can dine off a crust of rye bread and a cup of cabbage broth, is easily fed; and Michael, though he stuck to his craft, and lived by it, found plenty of time for the cultivation of his higher gifts. He was a good artist; for the time and place a very good artist; as the Jove-like head in the great hall of the University of Moscow proves. This head—the poet's own gift—was executed in mosaic by his hands.

After learning all that the monks could teach him in Moscow, he left that city for Germany, where he lived some years as artist, teacher, and professor; mastering thoroughly the modern languages and the liberal arts. When he came back to his native soil he was one of the deepest pundits of his time; a man of name and proof; respected in foreign universities for his wonderful sweep and grasp of mind. Studying many branches of science, he made himself a reputation in every branch. A Russian has a variety of gifts, and Michael was in every sense a Russ. While yet a lad it was said of him that he could mend a net, sing a ditty, drive a cart, build a cabin, and guide a boat with equal skill. When he grew up to be a man, it was said of him with no less truth, that he could at the same time crack a joke and heat a crucible; pose a logician and criticise a poet; draw the human figure and make a map of the stars. Coming back to Russia with such a name, he found the world at his feet; a professor's chair, with the rank of a nobleman, and the office of a councillor of state; dignities which a professor now enjoys by legal right. A strong Germanic influence met him, as a native intruder in a region of learning closed in that age to the Russ; but he joked and pushed, and fought his way into the highest seats. He not only won a place in the academy which Peter the Great had founded on the Neva, but in a few years he became its living soul.

Yet Michael remained a peasant and a Russian all his days. He drank a great many drams, and was never ashamed of being drunk. One day—as the members of that academy tell the tale—he was picked up from the gutter by one who knew him. "Hush! take care," said the good Samaritan softly; "get up quietly and come home, lest some one of the academy should see us." "Fool!" cried the tipsy professor, "Academy? I am the Academy!"

Not without cause is this proud boast attributed to the peasant's son; for Lomonosoff was the academy, at least on the Russian side. The breadth of his knowledge seems a marvel, even in days when a special student is expected to be an encyclopedic man, with the whole of nature for his province. He wrote in Latin and in German before he wrote in Russ. He was a miner, a physician, and a poet. He was a painter, a carver, and draughtsman. He wrote on grammar, on drugs, on music, and on the theory of ice. One of his best books is a criticism on the Varegs in Russia; one of his best papers is a treatise on microscopes and telescopes. He wrote on the aurora borealis, on the duties of a journalist, on the uses of a barometer, and on explorations in the Polar Sea. In the records of nearly every science and art his name is found. Astronomy owes him something, chemistry something, metallurgy something. But the glory of Lomonosoff was his verse, of which he wrote a great deal, and in many different styles; lays, odes, tragedies, an unfinished epic, and moral pieces without end.

The rank of a great poet is not claimed for Michael Lomonosoff by judicious critics. No creation like Oneghin, not even like Lavretski, came from his pen. His merit lies in the fact that he was the first writer who dared to be Russian in his art. But though it is the chief, it is far from being the only distinction which Lomonosoff enjoys, even as a poet. The mechanism of literature owes to his daring a reform, of which no man now living will see the end. The Russ are a religious people, to whom phrases of devotion are as their daily bread; but the language of their Church is not the language of their streets; and their books, though calling themselves Russ, were printed in a dialect which few except their popes and the Old Believers could understand. This dialect Lomonosoff laid aside, and took up in its stead the fluent and racy idiom of the market and the quay. But he had a poetic music to invent, as well as a poetic idiom to adapt. The poetry of a kindred race—the Poles—supplied him with a model, on which he built for the Russ that tonical lilt and flow, which ever since his time has been adopted by writers of verse as the most perfect vehicle for their poetic speech.

But greater than his poetic merit is the fact on which writers like Lamanski love to dwell, that Lomonosoff was a thorough Russian in his habits and ideas; and that after his election into the academy, he set his heart upon nationalizing that body, so as to render it Russian; just as the Berlin Academy was German, and the Paris Academy was French.

In his own time Lomonosoff met with little encouragement from the court. That court was German; the society nearest it was German; and German was the language of scientific thought. A Russian was a savage; and the speech of the common people was condemned to the bazars and streets. Lomonosoff introduced that speech into literature and into the discussions of learned men.

A statue to such a peasant marks a period in the nation's upward course. A line on the marble shaft records the fact that this figure was cast in 1829; and a second line states that it was removed in 1867 to its present site. Here, too, is progress. Forty years ago, a place behind the courts was good enough for a poet who was also a fisherman's son; even though he had done a fine thing in writing his verses in his native tongue; but thirty years later it had come to be understood by the people that no place is good enough for the man who has crowned them with his own glory; and as they see that this figure of Michael Lomonosoff is an honor to the province even more than to the poet, they have raised his pedestal in the public square.

Would that it had fallen into native hands! Modelled by a French sculptor, in the worst days of a bad school, it is a stupid travestie of truth and art. The rustics and fishermen, staring at the lyre and Cupid, at the naked shoulders and the Roman robe, wonder how their poet came to wear such a dress. This man is not the fellow whom their fathers knew—that laughing lad who laid down his tackle to become the peer of emperors and kings. Some day a native sculptor, working in the local spirit, will make a worthier monument of the peasant bard. A tall young fellow, with broad, white brow and flashing eyes, in shaggy sheep-skin wrap, broad belt, capacious boots, and high fur cap; his right hand grasping a pole and net, his left hand holding an open Bible; that would be Michael as he lived, and as men remember him now that he is dead.

Four years ago (the anniversary of his death in 1765), busts were set up, and burses founded in many colleges and schools, in honor of the peasant's son. Moscow took the lead; St. Petersburg followed; and the example spread to Harkof and Kazan. A school was built at Holmogory in the poet's name; to smooth the path of any new child of genius who may spring from this virgin soil. May it live forever!

CHAPTER XXXVI.

FOREST SCENES.

FROM Holgomory to Kargopol, from Kargopol to Vietegra, we pass through an empire of villages; not a single place on a road four hundred miles in length that could by any form of courtesy be called a town. The track runs on and on, now winding by the river bank, now eating its way through the forest growths; but always flowing, as it were, in one thin line from north to south; ferrying deep rivers; dragging through shingle, slime, and peat; crashing over broken rocks; and crawling up gentle heights. His horses four abreast, and lashed to the tarantass with ropes and chains, the driver tears along the road as though he were racing with his Chert—his Evil One; and all in the hope of getting from his thankless fare an extra cup of tea. It is the joke of a Russian jarvy, that he will "drive you out of your senses for ten kopecks." From dawn to sunset, day by day, it is one long race through bogs and pines. The landscape shows no dikes, no hedges, and no gates; no signs that tell of a personal owning of the land. We whisk by a log-fire, and a group of tramps, who flash upon us with a sullen greeting, some of them starting to their feet. "What are those fellows, Dimitri?"

"They seem to be some of the runaways."

"Runaways! Who are the runaways, and what are they running away from?"

"Queer fellows, who don't like work, who won't obey orders, who never rest in one place. You find them in the woods about here everywhere. They are savages. In Kargopol you can learn about them."

At the town of Kargopol, on the river Onega, in the province of Olonetz, I hear something of these runaways, as of a troublesome and dangerous set of men, bad in themselves, and still worse as a sign. I hear of them afterwards in Novgorod the Great, and in Kazan. The community is widely spread. Timashef is aware that these unsocial bodies exist in the provinces of Yaroslav, Archangel, Vologda, Novgorod, Kostroma, and Perm.

These runaways are vagabonds. Leaving house and land, throwing down their rights as peasants and burghers, they dress themselves in rags, assume the pilgrim's staff, retire from their families, push into forest depths, and dwell in quagmires and sandy rifts, protesting against the official empire and the official church. Some may lead a harmless life; the peasants helping them with food and drink; while they spend their days in dozing and their nights in prayer. Even when their resistance to the world is passive only; it is a protest hard to bear and harder still to meet. They will not labor for the things that perish. They will not bend their necks to magistrate and prince. They do not admit the law under which they live. They hold that the present imperial system is the devil's work; that the Prince of Darkness sits enthroned in the winter palace; that the lords and ladies who surround him are the lying witnesses and the fallen saints. Their part is not with the world, from which they fly, as Abraham fled from the cities of the plain.

Many of the peasants, either sympathizing with their views or fearing their vengeance, help them to support their life in the woods. No door is ever closed on them; no voice is ever raised against them. Even in the districts which they are said to ravage occasionally in search of food, hardly any thing can be learned about them, least of all by the masters of police.

Fifteen months ago the governor of Olonetz reported to General Timashef, minister of the interior, that a great number of these runaways were known to be living in his province and in the adjoining provinces, who were more or less openly supported by the peasantry in their revolt against social order and the reigning prince. On being asked by the minister what should be done, he hinted that nothing else would meet the evil but a seizure of vagabonds on all the roads, and in all the forest paths, in the vast countries lying north of the Volga, from Lake Ilmen to the Ural crests. His hints were taken in St. Petersburg, and hundreds of arrests were made; but whether the real runaways were caught by the police was a question open to no less doubt than that of how to deal with them when they were caught—according to the new and liberal code.

Roused by a sense of danger, the Government has been led into making inquiries far and near, the replies to which are of a kind to flutter the kindest hearts and puzzle the wisest heads. To wit: the Governor of Kazan reports to General Timashef that he has collected proof—(1.) that in his province the runaways have a regular organization; (2.) that they have secret places for meeting and worship; (3.) that they have chiefs whom they obey and trust. How can a legal minister deal with cases of an aspect so completely Oriental? Is it a crime to give up house and land? Is it an offense to live in deserts and lonely caves? What article in the civil code prevents a man from living like Seraphim in a desert; like Philaret the Less, in a grave-yard? Yet, on the other side, how can a reforming Emperor suffer his people to fall back into the nomadic state? A runaway is not a weakness only, but a peril; since the spirit of his revolt against social order is precisely that which the reformers have most cause to dread. In going back from his country, he is going back into chaos.

The mighty drama now proceeding in his country, turns on the question raised by the runaway. Can the Russian peasant live under law? If it shall prove on trial that any large portion of the Russian peasantry shares this passion for a vagabond life—as some folk hope, and still more fear—the great experiment will fail, and civil freedom will be lost for a hundred years.

The facts collected by the minister have been laid before a special committee, named by the crown. That committee is now sitting; but no conclusion has yet been reached, and no suggestion for meeting the evil can be pointed out.

Village after village passes to the rear!

Russ hamlets are so closely modelled on a common type, that when you have seen one, you have seen a host; when you have seen two, you have seen the whole. Your sample may be either large or small, either log-built or mud-built, either hidden in forest or exposed on steppe; yet in the thousands on thousands to come, you will observe no change in the prevailing forms. There is a Great Russ hamlet and a Little

Russ hamlet; one with its centre in Moscow, as the capital of Great Russia; the second with its centre in Kief, the capital of Little Russia.

A Great Russ village consists of two lines of cabins parted from each other by a wide and dirty lane. Each homestead stands alone. From ten to a hundred cabins make a village. Built of the same pine-logs, notched and bound together, each house is like its fellow, except in size. The elder's hut is bigger than the rest; and after the elder's house comes the whisky shop. Four squat walls, two tiers in height, and pierced by doors and windows; such is the shell. The floor is mud, the shingle deal. The walls are rough, the crannies stuffed with moss. No paint is used, and the log fronts soon become grimy with rain and smoke. The space between each hut lies open and unfenced; a slough of mud and mire, in which the pigs grunt and wallow, and the wolf-dogs snarl and fight. The lane is planked. One house here and there may have a balcony, a cow-shed, an upper story. Near the hamlet rises a chapel built of logs, and roofed with plank; but here you find a flush of color, if not a gleam of gold. The walls of the chapel are sure to be painted white, the roof is sure to be painted green. Some wealthy peasant may have gilt the cross.

Beyond these dreary cabins lie the still more dreary fields, which the people till. Flat, unfenced, and lowly, they have nothing of the poetry of our fields in the Suffolk and Essex plains; no hedgerow ferns, no clumps of fruit-trees, and no hints of home. The patches set apart for kitchen-stuff are not like gardens even of their homely kind; they look like workhouse plots of space laid out by yard and rule, in which no living soul had any part. These patches are always mean, and you search in vain for such a dainty as a flower.

Among the Little Russ—in the old Polish circles of the south and west, you see a village group of another kind. Instead of the grimy logs, you have a predominant mixture of green and white; instead of the formal blocks, you have a scatter of cottages in the midst of trees. The cabins are built of earth and reeds; the roof is thatched with straw; and the walls of the homestead are washed with lime. A fence of mats and thorns runs round the group. If every house appears to be small, it stands in a yard and garden of its own. The village has no streets. Two, and only two, openings pierce the outer fence—one north, one south; and in feeling your way from one opening in the fence to another, you push through a maze of lanes between reeds and spines, beset by savage dogs. Each new-comer would seem to have pitched his tent where he pleased; taking care to cover his hut and yard by the common fence.

A village built without a plan, in which every house is surrounded by a garden, covers an immense extent of ground. Some of the Kozak villages are as widely spread as towns. Of course there is a church, with its glow of color and poetic charm.

From Kief on the Dnieper to Kalatch on the Don, you find the villages of this second type. The points of difference lie in the house and in the garden; and must spring from difference of education, if not of race. The Great Russians are of a timid, soft, and fluent type. They like to huddle in a crowd, to club their means, to live under a common roof, and stand or fall by the family tree. The Little Russians are of a quick, adventurous, and hardy type; who like to stand apart, each for himself, with scope and range enough for the play of all his powers. A Great Russian carries his bride to his father's shed; a Little Russian carries her to a cabin of his own.

The forest melts and melts! We meet a woman driving in a cart alone; a girl darts past us in the mail; anon we come upon a wagon, guarded by troops on foot, containing prisoners, partly chained, in charge of an ancient dame.

This service of the road is due from village to village; and on a party of travellers coming into a hamlet, the elder must provide for them the things required—carts, horses, drivers—in accordance with their podorojna; but in many villages the party finds no men, or none except the very young or the very old. Husbands are leagues away; fishing in the Polar seas, cutting timber in the Kargopol forests, trapping fox and beaver in the Ural Mountains; leaving their wives alone for months. These female villages are curious things, in which a man of pleasant manners may find a chance of flirting to his heart's content.

Villages, more villages, yet more villages! We pass a gang

of soldiers marching by the side of a peasant's cart, in which lies a prisoner, chained; we spy a wolf in the copse; we meet a pilgrim on his way to Solovetsk; we come upon a gang of boys whose clothes appear to be out at wash; we pass a broken wagon; we start at the howl of some village dogs; and then go winding forward hour by hour, through the silent woods. Some touch of grace and poetry charms our eyes in the most desolate scenes. A virgin freshness crisps and shakes the leaves. The air is pure. If nearly all the lines are level, the sky is blue, the sunshine gold. Many of the trees are rich with amber, pink and brown; and every vagrant breeze makes music in the pines. A peasant and his dog troop past, reminding me of scenes in Kent. A convent here and there peeps out. A patch of forest is on fire, from the burning mass of which a tongue of pale pink flame laps out and up through a pall of purple smoke. A clearing, swept by some former fire, is all aglow with autumnal flowers. A bright beck dashes through the falling leaves. A comely child, with flaxen curls and innocent northern eyes, stands bowing in the road, with an almost Syrian grace. A woman comes up with a bowl of milk. A group of girls are washing at a stream, under the care of either the Virgin Mother or some local saint. On every point, the folk, if homely, are devotional and polite; brightening their forest breaks with chapel and cross, and making their dreary road, as it were, a path of light towards heaven.

We dash into a village near a small black lake.

CHAPTER XXXVII.

PATRIARCHAL LIFE.

"No horses to be got till night!"

"You see," smirks the village elder, "we are making holiday; it is a bridal afternoon, and the patriarch gives a feast on account of Vanka's nuptials with Nadia."

"Nadia! Well, a pretty name. We shall have horses in the evening, eh? Then let it be so. Who are yon people?

Ha! the church! Come, let us follow them, and see the crowning. Is this Vanka a fine young fellow?"

"Vanka! yes; in the bud. He is a lad of seventeen years; said to be eighteen years—the legal age—but, hem! he counts for nothing in the match."

"Why, then, is he going to take a wife?"

"Hem! that is the patriarch's business. Daniel wants some help in the house. Old Dan, you see, is Vanka's father, and the poor old motherkin has been worn by him to the skin and bone. She is ten years older than he, and the patriarch wants a younger woman at his beck and call; a woman to milk his cow, to warm his stove, and to make his tea."

"He wants a good servant?"

"Yes; he wants a good servant, and he will get one in Nadia."

"Then this affair is not a love-match?"

"Much as most. The lad, though young, is said to have been in love; for lads are silly and girls are sly; but he is not in love with the woman whom his father chooses for him."

"One of your village girls?"

"Yes, Lousha; a pretty minx, with round blue eyes and pouting lips; and not a ruble in the world. Now, Nadia has five brass samovars and fifteen silver spoons. The heart of Daniel melted towards those fifteen silver spoons."

"And what says Vanka to the match?"

"Nothing. What can he say? The patriarch has done it all: tested the spoons, accepted the bride, arranged the feast, and fixed the day."

"Russia is the land for you fathers, eh?"

"Each in his time; the father first, the offspring next. Each in his day; the boy will be a patriarch in his turn. A son is nobody till his parent dies."

"Not in such an affair as choosing his own wife?"

"No; least of all in choosing his own wife. You see our ways are old and homely, like the Bible ways. A patriarch rules under every roof—not only lives but rules; and where in the patriarchal times do you read that the young men went out into the world and chose them partners for themselves? Our patriarch settles such things; he and the proposeress."

"Proposeress! Pray what is a proposeress?"

"An ancient crone, who lives in yon cabin, near the bridge; a poor old waif, who feeds upon her craft, who tells your fortune by a card, who acts as agent for the girls, and is feared by every body as a witch."

"Have you such a proposeress in every village?"

"Not in every one. Some villages are too poor, for these old women must be paid in good kopecks. The craftier sisters live in towns, where they can tell you a good deal more. These city witches can rule the planets, while the village witches can only rule the cards."

"You really think they rule the planets?"

"Who can tell? We see they rule the men and women; yet every man has his planet and his angel. You must know, the girls who go to the proposeress leave with her a list of what they have—so many samovars, so much linen and household stuff. It is not often they have silver spoons. These lists the patriarchs come to her house and read. A sly fellow, like Old Dan, will steal to her door at dusk, when no one is about, and putting down his flask of whisky on the table, ask the old crone to drink. 'Come, motherkin,' he will giggle, 'bring out your list, and let us talk it over.' 'What are you seeking, Father Daniel?' leers the crone. 'A wife for Vanka, motherkin, a wife! Here, take a drink; the dram will do you good; and now bring out your book. A fine stout lass, with plenty of sticks and stones for me!' 'Ha!' pouts the witch, her finger on the glass, 'you want to see my book! Well, fatherkin, I have two nice lasses on my hands—good girls, and well to do; either one or other just the bride for Vanka. Here, now, is Lousha; pretty thing, but no household stuff; blue eyes, but not yet twenty; teeth like pearls, but shaky on her feet. Not do for you and your son? Why not? Well, as you please; I show my wares, you take them or you leave them. Lousha is a dainty thing—you need not blow the shingles off! Come, come, there's Dounia; well-built, buxom lassie; never raised a scandal in her life; had but one lover, a neighbor's boy. What sticks and stones? Dounia is a prize in herself—she eats very little, and she works like a horse. She has four samovars (Russian tea-urns). Not do for you! Well, now you *are* in luck to-night, little father. Here's Nadia!'—on which comes out the story of her samovars and her silver spoons."

"And so the match is made?"

"A fee is paid to the parish priest, a day for the rite is fixed, and all is over—except the feast, the drinking, and the headache."

"Tell me about Nadia?"

"You think Nadia such a pretty name. For my part, I prefer Marfousha. My wife was Marfa; called Marfousha when the woman is a pet."

"Is Nadia young and fair?"

"Young? Twenty-nine. Fair? Brown as a turf."

"Twenty-nine, and Vanka seventeen!"

"But she is big and bony; strong as a mule, and she can go all day on very little food."

"All that would be well enough, if what you wanted was a slave to thrust a spade and drive a cart."

"That is what the patriarch wants; a servant for himself, a partner for his boy."

"How came Vanka to accept her?"

"Daniel shows him her silver spoons, her shining urns, and her chest of household stuff. The lad stares wistfully at these fine things; Lousha is absent, and the old man nods. The woman kisses him, and all is done."

"Poor Lousha! where is she to-day?"

"Left in the fields to grow. She is not strong enough yet to marry. She could not work for her husband and her husband's father as a wife must do. Far better wait awhile. At twenty-nine she will be big and bony like Nadia; then she will be fit to marry, for then her wild young spirits will be gone."

We walk along the plank-road from the station to the church; which is crowded with men and women in their holiday attire; the girls in red skirts and bodices, trimmed with fur, and even with silver lace; the men in clean capotes and round fur caps, with golden tassels and scarlet tops. The rite is nearly over; the priest has joined the pair in holy matrimony; and the bride and groom come forth, arrayed in their tinsel crowns. The king leads out the queen, who certainly looks old enough to be his dam. One hears so much about marital rights in Russia, and the claim of women to be thrashed in evidence of their husband's love, that one can hardly help wondering how long it will be before Vanka can beat his wife. Not at present, clearly; so that one would feel some doubt of their "sober certainty of bliss," except for our knowledge that if Vanka fails, the patriarch will not scruple to use his whip.

Crowned with her rim of gilt brass, the bony bride, in stiff brocade and looking her fifteen silver spoons, slides down the sloppy lane to her future home.

The whisky-shops—we have two in our village for the comfort of eighty or ninety souls—are loud and busy, pouring out nips and nippets of their liquid death. Fat, bearded men are hugging and kissing each other in their pots, while the younger fry of lads and lasses wend in demure and pensive silence to an open ground, where they mean to wind up the day's festivities with a dance. This frolic is a thing to see. A ring of villagers, old and young, get ready to applaud the sport. The dancers stand apart; a knot of young men here, a knot of maidens there, each sex by itself, and silent as a crowd of mutes. A piper breaks into a tune; a youth pulls off his cap, and challenges his girl with a wave and bow. If the girl is willing, she waves her handkerchief in token of assent; the youth advances, takes a corner of the kerchief in his hand, and leads his lassie round and round. No word is spoken, and no laugh is heard. Stiff with cords and rich with braid, the girl moves heavily by herself, going round and round, and never allowing her partner to touch her hand. The pipe goes droning on for hours in the same sad key and measure; and the prize of merit in this "circling," as the dance is called, is given by spectators to the lassie who in all that summer revelry has never spoken and never smiled!

Men chat with men, and laugh with men; but if they approach the women, they are speechless; making signs with their caps only; and their dumb appeal is answered by a wave of the kerchief — answered without words. These romps go on till bed-time; when the men, being warm with drink, if not with love, begin to reel and shout like Comus and his tipsy crew.

The patriarch stops at home, delighted to spend his evening with Nadia and her silver spoons.

Even when her husband is a grown-up man, a woman has to come under the common roof, and live by the common rule. If she would like to get her share of the cabbage soup and the buckwheat pudding, not to speak of a new bodice now and then, she must contrive to please the old man, and she can only please him by doing at once whatever he bids her do. The Greek church knows of no divorce; and once married, you are tied for life: but neither party has imagination enough to be wretched in his lot, unless the beans should fail or the patriarch lay on the whip.

"Would not a husband protect his wife?"

"No," says the elder, "not where his father is concerned."

A patriarch is lord in his own house and family, and no man has a right to interfere with him; not even the village elder and the imperial judge. He stands above oral and written law. His cabin is not only a castle, but a church, and every act of his done within that cabin is supposed to be private and divine.

"If a woman flew to her husband from blows and stripes?"

"The husband must submit. What would you have? Two wills under one roof? The shingles would fly off."

"The young men always yield?"

"What should they do but yield? Is not old age to be revered? Is not experience good? Can a man have lived his life and not learned wisdom with his years? Now, it is said, the fashion is about to change; the young men are to rule the house; the patriarchs are to hide their beards. But not in my time; not in my time!"

"Do the women readily submit to what the patriarch says?"

"They must. Suppose Nadia beaten by Old Dan. She comes to me with her shoulders black and blue. I call a meeting of patriarchs to hear her tale. What comes of it? She tells them her father beats her. She shows her scars. The patriarchs ask her why he beats her? She owns that she refused to do this or that, as he bade her; something, it may be, which he ought not to have asked, and she ought not to have done; but the principle of authority is felt to be at stake; for, if a patriarch is not to rule his house, how is the elder to rule his village, the governor his province, the Tsar his empire? All authorities stand or fall together; and the patriarchs find that the woman is a fool, and that a second drubbing will do her good."

"They would not order her to be flogged?"

"Not now; the new law forbids it; that is to say, in public. In his own cabin Daniel may flog Nadia when he likes."

This "new law" against flogging women in public is an edict of the present reign; a part of that mighty scheme of social reform which the Emperor is carrying out on every side. It is not popular in the village, since it interferes with the rights of men, and cripples the patriarchs in dealing with the defenseless sex. Since this edict put an end to the open flogging of women, the men have been forced to invent new modes of punishing their wives, and their sons' wives, since they fancy that a private beating does but little good, because it carries no sting of shame. A news-sheet gives the following as a sample: Euphrosine M——, a peasant woman living in the province of Kherson, is accused by her husband of unfaithfulness to her vows. The rustic calls a meeting of patriarchs, who hear his story, and without hearing the wife in her defense, condemn her to be walked through the village stark naked, in broad daylight, in the presence of all her friends. That sentence is executed on a frosty day. Her guilt is never proved; yet she has no appeal from the decision of that village court!

A village is an original and separate power; in every sense a state within the state.

CHAPTER XXXVIII.

VILLAGE REPUBLICS.

A VILLAGE is a republic, governed by a law, a custom, and a ruler of its own.

In Western Europe and the United States a hamlet is no more than a little town in which certain gentlefolk, farmers, tradesmen, and their dependents dwell; people who are as free to go away as they were free to come. A Russian village is not a small town, with this mixture of ranks, but a collection of cabins, tenanted by men of one class and one calling; men who have no power to quit the fields they sow; who have to stand and fall by each other; who hold their lands under a common bond; who pay their taxes in a common sum; who give up their sons as soldiers in the common name.

These village republics are confined in practice to Great Russia, and the genuine Russ. In Finland, in the Baltic provinces, they are unknown; in Astrakhan, Siberia, and Kazan, they are unknown; in Kief, Podolia, and the Ukraine steppe, they are unknown; in the Georgian highlands, in the Circassian valleys, on the Ural slopes, they are equally unknown. In fact, the existence of these peasant republics in a province is the first and safest test of nationality. Wherever they are found, the soil is Russian, and the people Russ.

The provinces over which they spread are many in number, vast in extent, and rich in patriotic virtue. They extend from the walls of Smolensk to the neighborhood of Viatka; from the Gulf of Onega to the Kozak settlements on the Don. They cover an empire fifteen or sixteen times as large as France; the empire of Ivan the Terrible; that Russia which lay around the four ancient capitals—Novgorod, Vladimir, Moscow, Pskoff.

What is a village republic?

Is it Arcady, Utopia, New Jerusalem, Brook Farm, Oneida Creek, Abode of Love? Not one of these societies can boast of more than a passing resemblance to a Russian commune.

A village republic is an association of peasants, living like a body of monks and nuns, in a convent; living on lands of their own, protected by chiefs of their own, and ruled by customs of their own; but here the analogy between a commune and a convent ends; for a peasant marries, multiplies, and fills the earth. It is an agricultural family, holding an estate in hand like a Shaker union; but instead of flying from the world and having no friendship beyond the village bounds, they knit their interests up, by marrying with those of the adjacent communes. It is an association of laymen like a phalanx; but instead of dividing the harvest, they divide the land; and that division having taken place, their rule is for every man to do the best he can for himself, without regard to his brother's needs. It is a working company, in which the field and forest belong to all the partners in equal shares, as in a Gaelic clan and a Celtic sept; but the Russian rustic differs from a Highland chiel, and an Irish kerne, in owning no hereditary chief. It is a socialistic group, with property—the most solid and lasting property—in common, like the Bible votaries at Oneida Creek; but these partners in the soil never dream of sharing their goods and wives. It is a tribal unit, holding what it owns under a common obligation, like a Jewish house; but the associates differ from a Jewish house in bearing different names, and not affecting unity of blood.

By seeing what a village republic is not, we gain some insight into what it is.

We find some sixty or eighty men of the same class, with the same pursuits; who have consented, they and their fathers for them, to stay in one spot; to build a hamlet; to elect an elder with unusual powers; to hold their land in general, not in several; and to dwell in cabins near each other, face to face. The purpose of their association is mutual help.

A pack of wolves may have been the founders of the first village republic. Even now, when the forests are thinner, and the villages stronger than of yore, the cry of "wolf" is no welcome sound; and when the frost is keen, the village homesteads have to be watched in turns, by day and night. A wolf in the Russian forests is like a red-skin on the Kansas plains. The strength of a party led by an elder, fighting in defense of a common home, having once been proved by success against wolves, it would be easy to rouse that strength against the fox and the bear, the vagabond and the thief. In a region full of forests, lakes, and bogs, a lonely settler has no chance, and Russia is even yet a country of forests, lakes, and bogs. The settlers must club their means and powers, and bind themselves to stand by each other in weal and woe. Wild beasts are not their only foes. A fall of snow is worse than a raid of wolves; for the snow may bury their sheds, destroy their roads, imprison them in tombs, from which a single man would never be able to fight his way. The wolves are now driven into the woods, but the snow can never be beaten back into the sky; and while the northern storms go raging on, a peasant who tills the northern soil will need for his protection an enduring social bond.

These peasant republicans find this bond of union in the soil. They own the soil in common, not each in his own right, but every one in the name of all. They own it forever, and in equal shares. A man and his wife make the social unit, recognized by the commune as a house, and every house has a claim to a fair division of the family estate; to so much field, to so much wood, to so much kitchen-ground, as that estate will yield to each. Once in three years all claims fall in, all holdings cease, a fresh division of the land is made. A commune being a republic, and the men all peers, each voice must be heard in council, and every claim must be considered in parcelling the estate. The whole is parted into as many lots as there are married couples in the village; so much arable, so much forest, so much cabbage-bed for each. Goodness of soil and distance from the home are set against each other in every case.

But the principle of association passes, like the needs out of which it springs, beyond the village bounds. Eight or ten communes join themselves into a canton (a sort of parish); ten or twelves cantons form a volost, (a sort of hundred). Each circle is self-governed; in fact, a local republic.

From ancient times the members of these village democracies derive a body of local rights; of kin to those family rights which reforming ministers and judges think it wiser to leave alone. They choose their own elders, hold their own courts, inflict their own fines. They have a right to call meetings, draw up motions, and debate their communal affairs. They have authority over all their members, whether these are rich or poor. They can depose their elders, and set up others in their stead. A peasant republic is a patriarchal circle, exercising powers which the Emperor has not given, and dares not take away,

The elder—called in Russian starosta—is the village chief.

This elder is elected by the peasants from their own body;

elected for three years; though he is seldom changed at the end of his term; and men have been known to serve their neighbors in this office from the age of forty until they died. Every one is qualified for the post; though it seldom falls, in practice, to a man who is either unable or unwilling to pay for drink. The rule is, for the richest peasant of the village to be chosen, and a stranger driving into a hamlet in search of the elder will not often be wrong in pulling up his tarantass at the biggest door. These peasants meet in a chapel, in a barn, in a dram-shop, as the case may be; they whisper to each other their selected name; they raise a loud shout and a clatter of horny hands; and when the man of their choice has bowed his head, accepting their vote, they sally to a drinking-shop, where they shake hands and kiss each other over nippets of whisky and jorums of quass. An unpaid servant of his village, the Russian elder, like an Arab sheikh, is held accountable for every thing that happens to go wrong. Let the summer be hot, let the winter be dure, let the crop be scant, let the whisky be thin, let the roads be unsafe, let the wolves be out—the elder is always the man to blame. Sometimes, not often, a rich peasant tries to shirk this office, as a London banker shuns the dignity of lord mayor. But such a man, if he escape, will not escape scot free. A commune claims the service of her members, and no one can avoid her call without suffering a fine in either meal or malt. The man who wishes to escape election has to smirk and smile like the man who wishes to win the prize. He has to court his neighbor in the grog-shop, in the church, and in the field; flattering their weakness, treating them to drink, and whispering in their ear that he is either too young, too old, or too busy, for the office they would thrust upon him. When the time comes round for a choice to be made, the villagers pass him by with winks and shrugs, expecting, when the day is over, to have one more chance of drinking at his expense.

An elder chosen by this village parliament is clothed with strange, unclassified powers; for he is mayor and sheikh in one; a personage known to the law, as well as a patriarch clothed with domestic rights. Some of his functions lie beyond the law, and clash with articles in the imperial code.

To wit: an elder sitting in his village court, retains the

power to beat and flog. No one else in Russia, from the lord on his lawn and the general on parade, down to the merchant in his shop and the rider on a sledge, can lawfully strike his man. By one wise stroke of his pen, the Emperor made all men equal before the stick; and breaches of this rule are judged with such wholesome zeal, that the savage energy of the upper ranks is completely checked. Once only have I seen a man beat another—an officer who pushed and struck a soldier, to prevent him getting entangled in floes of ice. But a village elder, backed by his meeting, can defeat the imperial will, and set the beneficent public code aside.

A majority of peasants, meeting in a barn, or even in a whisky-shop, can fine and flog their fellows beyond appeal. Some rights have been taken from these village republicans in recent years; they are not allowed, as in former times, to lay the lash on women; and though they can sentence a man to twenty blows, they may not club him to death. Yet two-thirds of a village mob, in which every voter may be drunk, can send a man to Siberia for his term of life!

CHAPTER XXXIX.

COMMUNISM.

SUCH cases of village justice are not rare. Should a man have the misfortune, from any cause, to make himself odious to his neighbors, they can "cry a meeting," summon him to appear, and find him worthy to be expelled. They can pass a vote which may have the effect of sending for the police, give the expelled member into custody, and send him up to the nearest district town. He is now a waif and stray. Rejected from his commune, he has no place in society; he can not live in a town, he can not enter a village; he is simply a vagabond and an outcast, living beyond the pale of human law. The provincial governor can do little for him, even if he be minded to do any thing at all. He has no means of forcing the commune to receive him back; in fact, he has no choice, beyond that of sending such a waif to either the army or the public works. If all the forms have been observed, the village judgment is final, and the man expelled from it by such a vote is pretty sure of passing the remainder of his days on earth in either a Circassian regiment or a Siberian mine.

In the more serious cases dealt with by courts of law, a commune has the power of reviewing the sentence passed, and even of setting it aside.

Some lout (say) is suspected of setting a barn on fire. Seized by his elder and given in charge to the police, he is carried up to the assize town, where he is tried for his alleged offense, and after proof being given on either side, he is acquitted by the jury and discharged by the judge. It might be fancied that such a man would return to his cabin and his field, protected by the courts. But no; the commune, which has done him so much wrong already, may complete the injury by refusing to receive him back. A meeting may review the jurors and the judge, decline their verdict, try the man once more in secret, and condemn him, in his absence, to the loss—not simply of his house and land—but of his fame and caste.

The communes have other, and not less curious, rights. No member of a commune can quit his village without the general leave, without a passport signed by the elder, who can call him home without giving reasons for his acts. The absent brother must obey, on penalty of being expelled from his commune: that is to say—in a Russian village, as in an Indian caste—being flung out of organized society into infinite space.

Nor can the absent member escape from this tribunal by forfeiting his personal rights. An elder grants him leave to travel in very rare cases, and for very short terms; often for a month, now and then a quarter, never for more than a year. That term, whether long or short, is the limit of a man's freedom; when it expires, he must return to his commune, under penalty of seizure by the police as a vagabond living without a pass.

A village parliament is holden once a year, when every holder of house and field has the right to be heard. The suffrage is general, the voting by ballot. Any member can bring up a motion, which the elder is compelled to put. An unpopular elder may be deposed, and some one else elected in his stead. Subjects of contention are not lacking in these peasant parliaments; but the fiercest battles are those fought over roads, imperial taxes, conscripts, wood-rights, water-rights, wkisky licenses, and the choice of lots.

What may be termed the external affairs of the village—highways, fisheries, and forest-rights—are settled, not with imperial officers, but with their neighbors of the canton and the volost. The canton and the volost treat with the general, governor, and police. A minister looks for what he needs to the association, not to the separate members, and when rates are levied and men are wanted, the canton and the volost receive their orders and proceed to raise alike the money and the men. The crown has only to send out orders; and the money is paid, the men are raised. A system so effective and so cheap, is a convenience to the ministers of finance and war so great that the haughtiest despots and the wisest reformers have not dared to touch the interior life of these peasant commonwealths.

Thus the village system remains a thing apart, not only from the outer world, but from the neighboring town. The men who live in these sheds, who plough these fields, who angle in this lake, are living by an underived and original light. Their law is an oral law, their charter bears no seal, their franchise knows no date. They vote their own taxes, and they frame their own rules. Except in crimes of serious dye, they act as an independent court. They fine, they punish, they expel, they send unpopular men to Siberia; and even call up the civil arm in execution of their will.

Friends of these rustic republics urge as merits in the village system, that the men are peers, that public opinion governs, that no one is exempt from the general law, that rich men find no privilege in their wealth. All this sounds well in words; and probably in seven or eight cases out of ten the peasants treat their brethren fairly; though it will not be denied that in the other two or three cases gross and comical burlesques of justice may be seen. I hear of a man being flogged for writing a paragraph in a local paper, which half, at least, of his judges could not read. Still worse, and still more flagrant, is the abuse of extorting money from the rich. A charge is made, a meeting cried, and evidence heard. If the offender falls on his knees, admits his guilt, and offers to pay a fine, the charge is dropped. The whole party marches to the whisky shop, and spends the fine in drams. Now the villagers know pretty well the brother who is rich enough to give his rubles in place of baring his back; and when they thirst for a dram at some other man's cost, they have only to get up some flimsy charge on which that yielding brother can be tried. The man is sure to buy himself off. Then comes the farce of charge and proof, admission and fine; followed by the drinking bout, in which from policy the offender joins; until the virtuous villagers, warm with the fiery demon, kiss and slobber upon each other's beards, and darkness covers them up in their drunken sleep.

In Moscow I know a man, a clerk, a thrifty fellow, born in the province of Tamboff, who has saved some money, and the fact coming out, he has been thrice called home to his village, thrice accused of trumpery offenses, thrice corrected by a fine. In every case, the man was sentenced to be flogged; and he paid his money, as they knew he would, to escape from suffering and disgrace. His fines were instantly spent in drink. A member of a village republic who has prospered by his thrift and genius finds no way of guarding himself from such assaults, except by craftily lending sums of money to the heads of houses, so as to get the leading men completely into his power.

In spite of some patent virtues, a rural system which compels the more enterprising and successful men to take up such a position against their fellows in actual self-defense, can hardly be said to serve the higher purposes for which societies exist.

These village republics are an open question; one about which there is daily strife in every office of Government, in every organ of the press. Men who differ on every other point, agree in praising the rural communes. Men who agree on every other point, part company on the merits and vices of the rural communes.

Not a few of the ablest reformers wish to see them thrive; royalists, like Samarin and Cherkaski, and republicans, like

Herzen and Ogareff, see in these village societies the germs of a new civilization for East and West. Men of science, like Valouef, Bungay, and Besobrazof, on the contrary, find in these communes nothing but evil, nothing but a legacy from the dark ages, which must pass away as the light of personal freedom dawns.

That the village communes have some virtues may be safely said. A minister of war and a minister of finance are keenly alive to these virtues, since a man who wishes to levy troops and taxes in a quick, uncostly fashion, finds it easier to deal with fifty thousand elders, than with fifty million peasants. A minister of justice thinks with comfort of the host of watchful, unpaid eyes that are kept in self-defense on such as are suspected of falling into evil ways. These virtues are not all, not nearly all. A rural system, in which every married man has a stake in the soil, produces a conservative and pacific people. No race on earth either clings to old ways or prays for peace so fervently as the Russ. Where each man is a landholder, abject poverty is unknown; and Russia has scant need for poor-laws and work-houses, since she has no such misery in her midst as a permanent pauper class. Every body has a cabin, a field, a cow; perhaps a horse and cart. Even when a fellow is lazy enough and base enough to ruin himself, he can not ruin his sons. They hold their place in the commune, as peers of all, and when they grow up to man's estate, they will obtain their lots, and set up life on their own account. The bad man dies, and leaves to his province no legacy of poverty and crime. The communes cherish love for parents, and respect for age. They keep alive the feeling of brotherhood and equality, and inspire the country with a sentiment of mutual dependence and mutual help.

On the other side, they foster a parish spirit, tend to separate village from town, strengthen the ideas of class and caste, and favor that worst delusion in a country—of there being a state within a state! Living in his own republic, a peasant is apt to consider the burgher as a stranger living under a different and inferior rule. A peasant hears little of the civil code, except in his relations with the townsfolk; and he learns to despise the men who are bound by the letter of that civil code. Between his own institutions and those of his burgher neighbors there is a chasm, like that which separates America from France.

CHAPTER XL.

TOWNS.

A TOWN is a community lying beyond the canton and volost, in which people live by burgher right and not by communal law. Unlike the peasant, a burgher has power to buy and sell, to make and mend, to enter crafts and guilds; but he is chained to his trade very much as the rustic is chained to his field. His house is built of logs, his roads are laid with planks; but then his house is painted green or pink, and his road is wide and properly laid out. In place of a free local government, the town finds a master in the minister, in the governor, in the chief of police. While the village is a separate republic, the town is a parcel of the empire; and as parcel of the empire it must follow the imperial code.

Saving the great cities, not above five or six in number, all Russian towns have a common character, and when you have seen two or three in different parts of the empire, you have seen them all. Take any riverside town of the second class (and most of these towns are built on the banks of streams) from Onega to Rostoff, from Nijni to Kremenchug. A fire-tower, a jail, a fish-market, a bazar, and a cathedral, catch the eye at once. Above and below the town you see monastic piles. A bridge of boats connects the two banks, and a poorer suburb lies before the town. The port is crowded with smacks and rafts; the smacks bringing fish, the rafts bringing pines. What swarms of people on the wharf! How grave, how dirty, and how pinched, they look! Their sadness comes of the climate, and their dirt is of the East. "Yes, yes!" you may hear a mujik say to his fellow, speaking of some neighbor, "he is a respectable man—quite; he has a clean shirt once a week." The rustic eats but little flesh; his dinner, even on days that are not kept as fasts, being a slice of black bread, a girkin, and a piece of dried cod. Just watch them, how they higgle for a kopeck! A Russ craftsman is a fellow to deal with; ever hopeful and acquiescent; ready to please in word and act; but you are never sure that he will keep his word. He has hardly any sense of time and space. To him one hour of the day is like another, and if he has promised to make you a coat by ten in the morning, he can not be got to see the wrong of sending it home by eleven at night.

The market reeks with oil and salt, with vinegar and fruit, with the refuse of halibut, cod, and sprats. The chief articles of sale are rings of bread, salt girkins, pottery, tin plates, iron nails, and images of saints. The street is paved with pools, in which lie a few rough stones, to help you in stepping from stall to stall. To walk is an effort; to walk with clean feet a miracle. Such filth is too deep for shoes.

A fish-wife is of either sex; and even when she belongs of right to the better side of human nature, she is not easy to distinguish from her lord by any thing in her face and garb. Seeing her in the sharp wind, quilted in her sheep-skin coat, and legged in her deer-skin hose, her features pinched by frost, her hands blackened by toil, it would be hard to say which was the female and which the male, if Providence had not blessed the men with beards. By these two signs a Russ may be known from all other men—by his beard and by his boots; but since many of his female folk wear boots, he is only to be safely known from his partner in life by the bunch of hair upon his chin.

In the bazar stand the shops; dark holes in the wall, like the old Moorish shops in Seville and Granada; in which the dealer stands before his counter and shows you his poor assortment of prints and stuffs, his pots and pans, his saints, his candles, and his packs of cards. Next to rye-bread and salt fish, saints and cards are the articles mostly bought and sold; for in Russia every body prays and plays; the noble in his club, the dealer at his shop, the boatman on his barge, the pilgrim by his wayside cross. The propensities to pray and gamble may be traced to a common root; a kind of moral fetichism, a trust in the grace of things unseen, in the merit of dead men, and even in the power of chance. A Russian takes, like a child, to every strange thing, and prides himself on the completeness of his faith. When he is not kneeling to his angel, nothing renders him so happy as the sight of a pack of cards.

Nearly every one plays high for his means; and nothing is more common than for a burgher to stake and lose, first his money, then his boots, his cap, his caftan, every scrap of his garments, down to his very shirt. Whisky excepted, nothing drives a Russian to the devil so quickly as a pack of cards.

But see, these gamblers throw down their cards, unbonnet their heads, and fall upon their knees. The priest is coming down the street with his sacred picture and his cross. It is market-day in the town, and he is going to open and bless some shop in the bazar; and fellows who were gambling for their shirts are now upon their knees in prayer.

The rite by which a shop, a shed, a house, is dedicated to God is not without touches of poetic beauty. Notice must be given aforetime to the parish priest, who fixes the hour of consecration, so that a man's kinsfolk and neighbors may be present if they like. The time having come, the priest takes down his cross from the altar, a boy lights the embers in his censer, and, preceded by his reader and deacon, the pope moves down the streets through crowds of kneeling men and women, most of whom rise and follow in his wake, only too eager to catch so easily and cheaply some of the celestial fire.

Entering the shop or house, the pope first purges the room by prayer, then blesses the tenant or dweller, and lastly sanctifies the place by hanging in the "corner of honor" an image of the dealer's guardian angel, so that in the time to come no act can be done in that house or shop except under the eyes of its patron saint.

Though poor as art, such icons, placed in rooms, have power upon men's minds. Not far from Tamboff lived an old lady who was more than commonly hard upon her serfs, until the poor wretches, maddened by her use of the whip and the black hole, broke into her room at night, some dozen men, and told her, with a sudden brevity, that her hour had come and she must die. Springing from her bed, she snatched her image from the wall, and held it out against her assailants, daring them to strike the Mother of God. Dropping their clubs, they fled from before her face. Taking courage from her victory, she hung up the picture, drew on her wrapper, and followed her serfs into the yard, where, seeing that she was unprotected by her image, they set upon her with a shout, and clubbed her instantly to death.

In driving through the town we note how many are the dram-shops, and how many the tipsy men. Among the smaller reforms under which the burgher has now to live is that of a thinner drink. The Emperor has put water into the whisky, and reduced the price from fifteen kopecks a glass to five. The change is not much relished by the topers, who call their thin potation, dechofka—cheap stuff; but simpler souls give thanks to the reformer for his boon, saying, "Is he not good—our Tsar—in giving us three glasses of whisky for the price of a single glass!" Yet, thin as it is, a nippet of the fiery spirit throws a sinner off his legs, for his stomach is empty, his nerves are lax, and his blood is poor. If he were better fed he would crave less drink. Happily a Russian is not quarrelsome in his cups; he sings and smiles, and wishes to hug you in the public street. No richer comedy is seen on any stage than that presented by two tipsy mujiks riding on a sledge, putting their beards together and throwing their arms about each other's neck. A happy fellow lies in the gutter, fast asleep; another, just as tipsy, comes across the roadway, looks at his brother, draws his own wrapper round his limbs, and asking gods and men to pardon him, lies down tenderly in the puddle by his brother's side.

The social instincts are, in a Russian, of exceeding strength. He likes a crowd. The very hermits of his country are a social crew—not men who rush away into lonely nooks, where, hidden from all eyes, they grub out caves in the rock and burrow under roots of trees; but brothers of some popular cloister, famous for its saints and pilgrims, where they drive a shaft under the convent wall, secrete themselves in a hole, and receive their food through a chink, in sight of wondering visitors and advertising monks. Such were the founders of his church, the anchorets of Kief.

The first towns of Russia are Kief and Novgoròd the Great; her capitals and holy places long before she built herself a kremlin on the Moskva, and a winter palace on the Neva. Kief and Novgorod are still her pious and poetic cities; one the tower of her religious faith, the other of her imperial power. From Vich Gorod at Kief springs the dome which celebrates her conversion to the Church of Christ; in the Kremlin of Novgorod stands the bronze group which typifies her empire of a thousand years.

CHAPTER XLI.

KIEF.

KIEF, the oldest of Russian sees, is not in Russia Proper, and many historians treat it as a Polish town. The people are Ruthenians, and for hundreds of years the city belonged to the Polish crown. The plain in front of it is the Ukraine steppe; the land of hetman and zaporogue; of stirring legends and riotous song. The manners are Polish and the people Poles. Yet here lies the cradle of that church which has shaped into its own likeness every quality of Russian political and domestic life.

The city consists of three parts, of three several towns—Podol, Vich Gorod, Pechersk; a business town, an imperial town, and a sacred town. All these quarters are crowded with offices, shops, and convents; yet Podol is the merchant quarter, Vich Gorod the Government quarter, and Pechersk the pilgrim quarter. These towns overhang the Dnieper, on a range of broken cliffs; contain about seventy thousand souls; and hold, in two several places of interment, all that was mortal of the Pagan duke who became her foremost saint.

Kief is a city of legends and events; the preaching of St. Andrew, the piety of St. Olga, the conversion of St. Vladimir; the Mongolian assault, the Polish conquest, the recovery by Peter the Great. The provinces round Kief resemble it, and rival it, in historic fame. Country of Mazeppa and Gonta, the Ukraine teems with story; tales of the raid, the flight, the night attack, the violated town. Every village has its legend, every town its epic, of love and war. The land is aglow with personal life. Yon chapel marks the spot where a grand duke was killed; this mound is the tomb of a Tartar horde; that field is the site of a battle with the Poles. The men are brighter and livelier, the houses are better built, and the fields are better trimmed than in the North and East. The music is quicker, the brandy is stronger, the love is warmer, the hatred is keener, than you find elsewhere. These provinces are Gogol's country, and the scenery is that of his most popular tales.

Like all the southern cities, Kief fell into the power of Batu Khan, the Mongol chief, and groaned for ages under the yoke of Asiatic begs. These begs were idol-worshippers, and under their savage and idolatrous rule the children of Vladimir had to pass through heavy trials; but Kief can boast that in the worst of times she kept in her humble churches and her underground caves the sacred embers of her faith alive.

Below the tops of two high hills, three miles from that Vich Gorod in which Vladimir built his harem, and raised the statue of his Pagan god, some Christian hermits, Anton, Feodosie, and their fellows, dug for themselves in the loose red rock a series of corridors and caves, in which they lived and died, examples of lowly virtue and the Christian life. The Russian word for cave is pechera, and the site of these caves was called Pechersk. Above the cells in which these hermits dwelt, two convents gradually arose, and took the names of Anton and Feodosie, now become the patron saints of Kief, and the reputed fathers of all men living in Russia a monastic life.

A green dip between the old town, now trimmed and planted, parts the first convent—that of Anton—from the city; a second dip divides the convent of Feodosie, from that of his fellow-saint. These convents, nobly planned and strongly built, take rank among the finest piles in Eastern Europe. Domes and pinnacles of gold surmount each edifice; and every wall is pictured with legends from the lives of saints. The ground is holy. More than a hundred hermits lie in the catacombs, and crowds of holy men lie mouldering in every niche of the solid wall. Mouldering! I crave their pardons. Holy men never rust and rot. For purity of the flesh in death is evidence of purity of the flesh in life; and saints are just as incorruptible of body as of soul. In Anton's Convent you are shown the skull of St. Vladimir; that is to say, a velvet pall in which his skull is said to be wrapped and swathed. You are told that the flesh is pure, the skin uncracked, the odor sweet. A line of dead bodies fills the underground passages and lanes—each body in a niche of the rock; and all these martyrs of the faith are said to be, like Vladmir, also fresh and sweet.

A stranger can not say whether this tale of the incorruptibility of early saints and monks is true or not; since nothing can be seen of the outward eye except a coffin, a velvet pall, and an inscription newly painted in the Slavonic tongue. A great deal turns on the amount of faith in which you seek for proof. For monks are men, and a critic can hardly press them with his doubts. Suppose you try to persuade your guides to lift the pall from St. Anton's face. Your own opinion is that even though human frames might resist the dissolving action of an atmosphere like that of Sicily and Egypt, nothing less than a miracle could have preserved intact the bodies of saints who died a thousand years ago, in a cold, damp climate like that of Kief. You wish to put your science to the test of fact. You wish in vain. The monk will answer for the miracle, but no one answers for the monk.

Fifty thousand pilgrims, chiefly Ruthenians from the populous provinces of Podolia, Kief, and Volhynia, come in summer to these shrines.

When Kief recovered her freedom from the Tartar begs, she found herself by the chance of war a city of Polonia, not of Moscovy — a member of the Western, not of the Eastern section of her race. Kief had never been Russ, as Moscow was Russ; a rude, barbaric town, with crowds of traders and rustics, ruled by a Tartarized court; and now that her lot was cast with the more liberal and enlightened West, she grew into a yet more Oriental Prague. For many reigns she lay open to the arts of Germany and France; and when she returned to Russia, in the times of Peter the Great, she was not alone the noblest jewel in his crown, but a point of union, nowhere else to be found, for all the Slavonic nations in the world.

As an inland city Kief has the finest site in Russia. Standing on a range of bluffs, she overlooks a splendid length of steppe, a broad and navigable stream. She is the port and capital of the Ukraine; and the Malo-Russians, whether settled on the Don, the Ural, or the Dniester, look to her for orders of the day. She touches Poland with her right hand, Russia with her left; she flanks Galicia and Moldavia, and keeps her front towards the Bulgarians, the Montenegrins, and the Serbs. In her races and religions she is much in little; an epitome of all the Slavonic tribes. One-third of her population is Moscovite, one-third Russine, and one-third Polack; while in faith she is Orthodox, Roman Catholic, and United Greek. If any city in Europe offers itself to Panslavonic dreamers as their natural capital, it is Kief.

CHAPTER XLII.

PANSLAVONIA.

UNTIL a year ago, these Panslavonic dreamers were a party in the State; and even now they have powerful friends at Court. Their cry is Panslavonia for the Slavonians. Last year the members of this party called a congress in Moscow, to which they invited—first, their fellow-countrymen, from the White Sea to the Black, from the Vistula to the Amoor; and next, the representatives of their race who dwell under foreign sceptres—the Czeck from Prague, the Pole from Cracow, the Bulgar from Shumla, the Montenegrin from Cettigne, the Serb from Belgrade; but this gathering of the clans in Moscow opened the eyes of moderate men to the dangerous nature of this Panslavonic dream. A deep distrust of Russian life, as now existing, lies at the root of it; the dreamers hoping to fall back upon forms inspired by what they call a nobler national spirit. They read the chronicles of their race, they collect popular songs, they print peasant tales; and in these Ossianic legends of the steppe they find the germ of a policy which they call a natural product of their soil.

Like the Old Believers, these Panslavonians deny the Emperor and own the Tsar. To them Peter the Great is Antichrist, and the success of his reforms a temporary triumph of the Evil Spirit. He left his country, they allege, in order to study in foreign lands the arts by which it could be overthrown. On his return to Russia no one recognized him as their prince. He came with a shaven face, a pipe in his mouth, a jug of beer in his hand. A single stroke of his pen threw down an edifice which his people had been rearing for a thousand years. He carried his government beyond the Russian soil; and, in a strange swamp, by the shores of a Swedish gulf, he built a palace for his court, a market for his purveyors, a fortress for his troops. This city he stamped with a foreign genius and baptized with a foreign name.

For these good reasons, the Panslavonians set their teeth against all that Peter did, against nearly all that his followers on the throne have done. They wish to put these alien things away, to resume their capital, to grow their beards, to wear their fur caps, to draw on their long boots, without being mocked as savages, and coerced like serfs. They deny that civilization consists in a razor and a felt hat. Finding much to complain of in the judicial sharpness of German rule, they leaped to the conclusion that every thing brought from beyond the Vistula is bad for Russia and the Russ. In the list of things to be kept out of their country they include German philosophy, French morals, and English cotton-prints.

A thorough Panslavonian is a man to make one smile; with him it is enough that a thing is Russian in order to be sworn the best of its kind. Now, many things in Russia are good enough for proud people to be proud of. The church-bells are musical, the furs warm and handsome, the horses swift, the hounds above all praise. The dinners are well-served; the sterlet is good to eat; but the wines are not first-rate and the native knives and forks are bad. Yet patriots in Kief and Moscow tell you, with gravest face, that the vintage of the Don is finer than that of the Garonne, that the cutlery of Tula is superior to that of Sheffield. Yet these dreamers say and unsay in a breath, as seems for the moment best; for while they crack up their country right and wrong, in the face of strangers; they abuse it right and wrong when speaking of it among themselves. "We are sick, we are sick to death," was a saying in the streets, a cry in the public journals, long before Nicolas transferred the ailment of his country to that of his enemy the Turk. "We have never done a thing," wrote Khomakof, the Panslavonic poet; "not even made a rat-trap."

A Panslavonian fears free trade. He wants cheap cotton shirts, he wants good knives and forks; but then he shudders at the sight of a cheap shirt and a good fork on hearing from his priest that Manchester and Sheffield are two heretical towns, in which the spinners who weave cloth, the grinders who polish steel, have never been taught by their pastors how to sign themselves with the true Greek cross. What shall it profit a man to have a cheap shirt and lose his soul? The Orthodox clergy, seizing the Panslavonic banner, wrote on its front their own exclusive motto: "Russia and the Byzantine Church;" and this priestly motto made a Panslavistic unity impossible; since the Western branches of the race are not disciples of that Byzantine Church. At Moscow every thing was done to keep down these dissensions; and the question of a future capital was put off, as one too dangerous for debate. Nine men in ten of every party urge the abandonment of St. Petersburg; but Moscow, standing in the heart of Russia, can not yield her claims to Kief.

The partisans of Old Russia join hands with those of Young Russia in assailing these Panslavistic dreamers, who prate of saving their country from the vices and errors of Europe, and offer—these assailants say—no other plan than that of changing a German yoke for either a Byzantine or a Polish yoke.

The clever men who guide this party are well aware that the laws and ceremonies of the Lower Empire offer them no good models; but in returning to the Greeks, they expect to gain a firmer hold on the practices of their Church. For the rest, they are willing to rest in the hands of God, in the Oriental hope of finding that all is well at last. If nothing else is gained, they will have saved their souls.

"Their souls!" laugh the Young Russians, trained in what are called the infidel schools of France; "these fellows who have no souls to be saved!" "Their souls!" frown the Old

Believers, strong in their ancient customs and ancient faith; "these men whose souls are already damned!" With a pitiless logic, these opponents of the Panslavonic dreamers call on them to put their thoughts into simple words. What is the use of dreaming dreams? "How can you promote Slavonic nationality," ask the Young Russians, "by excluding the most liberal and enlightened of our brethren? How can you promote civilization by excluding cotton-prints?" The Old Believers ask, on the other side, "How can you extend the true faith by going back to the Lower Empire, in which religion was lost? How can you, who are not the children of Christ, promote his kingdom on the earth? You regenerate Russia! you, who are not the inheritors of her ancient and holy faith!"

Reformers of every school and type have come to see the force which lies in a Western idea—not yet, practically, known in Russia—that of individual right. They ask for every sort of freedom; the right to live, the right to think, the right to speak, the right to hold land, the right to travel, the right to buy and sell, *as personal rights.* "How," they demand from the Panslavonians, "can the Russian become a free man while his personality is absorbed in the commune, in the empire, and in the church?"

"An old Russian," replies the Panslavonian, "was a free man, and a modern Russian is a free man, but in a higher sense than is understood by a trading-people like the English, an infidel people like the French. Inspired by his Church, a Russian has obtained the gifts of resignation and of sacrifice. By an act of devotion he has conveyed his individual rights to his native prince, even as a son might give up his rights to a father in whose love and care he had perfect trust. A right is not lost which has been openly lodged in the hands of a compassionate and benevolent Tsar. The Western nations have retained a liberty which they find a curse, while the Russians have been saved by obeying the Holy Spirit."

Imagine the mockery by which an argument so patriarchal has been met!

"No illusion, gentlemen," said the Emperor to his first deputation of Poles. So far as they are linked in fortune with their Eastern brethren, the Poles are invited to an equal place in a great empire, having its centre of gravity in Moscow, its port of communication in St. Petersburg; not to a Japanese kingdom of the Slavonic tribes, with a mysterious and secluded throne in Kief.

Yet the Poles and Ruthenians who people the western provinces and the southern steppe will not readily give up their dream; and their genius for affairs, their oratorical gifts, their love of war, all tend to make them enemies equally dangerous in the court and in the field. Plastic, clever, adroit, with the advantage of speaking the language of the country, these dreamers get into places of high trust; into the professor's chair, into the secretary's office, into the aid-de-camp's saddle; in which they carry on their plot in favor of some form of government other than that under which they live.

CHAPTER XLIII.

EXILE.

A WEEK before the last rising of the Poles took place, an officer of high rank in the Russian service came in the dead of night, and wrapped in a great fur cloak, to a friend of mine living in St. Petersburg, with whom he had little more than a passing acquaintance—

"I am going out," he said, "and I have come to ask a favor and say good-bye."

"Going out!"

"Yes," said his visitor. "My commission is signed, my post is marked. Next week you will hear strange news."

"Good God!" cried my friend; "think better of it. You, an officer of state, attached to the ministry of war!"

"I am a Pole, and my country calls me. You, a stranger, can not feel with the passions burning in my heart. I know that by quitting the service I disgrace my general; that the Government will call me a deserter; that if we fail, I shall be deemed unworthy of a soldier's death. All this I know, yet go I must."

"But your wife—and married one year!"

"She will be safe. I have asked for three months' leave. Our passes have been signed; in a week she will be lodged in Paris with our friends. You are English; that is the reason why I seek you. In the drojki at your door is a box; it is full of coin. I want to leave this box with you; to be given up only in case we fail; and then to a man who will come to you and make this sign. I need not tell you that the money is all my own, and that the charge of it will not compromise you, since it is sacred to charity, and not to be used for war."

"It is a part, I suppose," said my friend, "of your Siberian fund?"

"It is," said the soldier; "you will accept my trust?"

The box was left; the soldier went his way. In less than a week the revolt broke out in many places; slight collisions took place, and the Poles, under various leaders, met with the success which always attends surprise. Three or four names, till then unknown, began to attract the public eye; but the name of my friend's midnight visitor was not amongst them. General ——— grew into sudden fame; his rapid march, his dashing onset, his daily victory, alarmed the Russian court, until a very strong corps was ordered to be massed against him. Then he was crushed; some said he was slain. One night, my friend was seated in his chamber, reading an account of this action in a journal, when his servant came into the room with a card, on which was printed:

THE COUNTESS R———.

The lady was below, and begged to see my friend that night. Her name was strange to him; but he went out into the passage, where he found a pale, slim lady of middle age, attired in the deepest black.

"I have come to you," she said at once, "on a work of charity. A young soldier crawled to my house from the field of battle, so slashed and shot that we expected him to die that night. He was a patriot; and his papers showed that he was the young General ———. He lived through the night, but wandered in his mind. He spoke much of Marie; perhaps she is his wife. By daylight he was tracked, and carried from my house; but ere he was dragged away, he gave me this card, and with the look of a dying man, implored me to place it in your hands."

"You have brought it yourself from Poland?"

"I am a sufferer too," she said; "no time could be lost; in three days I am here."

"You knew him in other days?"

"No; never. He was miserable, and I wished to help him. I have not learned his actual name."

Glancing at the card, my friend saw that it contained nothing but his own name and address written in English letters; as it might be:

George Herbert,
Sergie Street,
St. Petersburg.

He knew the handwriting. "Gracious heavens!" he exclaimed, "was this card given to you by General ——— ?"

"It was."

In half an hour my friend was closeted with a man who might intervene with some small hope. The minister of war was reached. Surprised and grieved at the news conveyed to him, the minister said he would see what could be done. "General Mouravieff," he explained, "is stern, his power unlimited; and my poor adjutant was taken on the field. Deserter, rebel—what can be urged in arrest of death?" In truth, he had no time to plead, for Mouravieff's next dispatch from Poland gave an account of the execution of General ——— *by the rope.* On my friend calling at the war-office to hear if any thing could be done, he was told the story by a sign.

"Can you tell me," inquired the minister, "under what name my second adjutant is in the field? He also is missing." The caller could not help a smile. "You are thinking," said the minister, "that this Polish revolt was organized in my office? You are not far wrong."

Archangel, Caucasus, Siberia—every frontier of the empire had her batch of hapless prisoners to receive. The present reign has seen the system of sending men to the frontiers much relaxed; and the public works of Archangel occupied, for a time, the place once held in the public mind by the Siberian mines. Not that the Asiatic waste has been abandoned as an imperial Cayenne. Many great criminals, and some unhappy politicians, are still sent over the Ural heights; but the system has been much relaxed of late, and the name of Siberia is no longer that word of fear which once appalled the imagination like a living death. It is no uncommon thing to meet bands of young fellows going up the Ural slopes from Mesen and Archangel, in search of fortune; going over into Siberia as into a promised land!

Many of the terrors which served to shroud Siberia in a pall have been swept away by science. The country has been opened up. The tribes have become better known. Tomsk, a name at which the blood ran cold, is seen to be a pleasant town, lying in a green valley at the foot of a noble range of heights. It is not far from Perm, which may be regarded as a distant suburb of Kazan. The tracks have been laid down, and in a few months a railroad will be made from Perm to Tomsk.

The world, too, has begun to see that a penal settlement has, at best, a limited lease of life. A man will make his home anywhere, and when a place has become his home, it must have already ceased to be his jail. It is in the nature of every penal settlement to become unsafe in time; and a province of Siberia, peopled by Poles, would be a vast embarrassment to the empire, a second Poland in her rear. Even now, long heads are counting the years when the sons of political exiles will occupy all the leading posts in Asia. Will they not plant in that region the seeds of a Polish power, and of a Catholic Church? It is the opinion of liberal Russians that Siberia will one day serve their country as England is served by the United States.

The exiles sent to the frontiers are of many kinds; noble, ignoble; clerical, lay; political offenders, cut-throats, heretics, coiners, schismatics; prisoners of the Court, prisoners of the Law, and prisoners of the Church. The exiles sent away by a minister of police, by the governor of a province, are not kept in jail, are not compelled to work. The police has charge of them in a certain sense; they are numbered, and registered in books; and they have to report themselves at head-quarters from time to time. Beyond these limits they are free. You meet them in society; and if you guess they are exiles, it is mainly on account of their keener intelligence and their greater reserve of words. They either live on their private means, or follow the professions to which they have been trained. Some teach music and languages, some practise medicine or law; still more become secretaries and clerks to the official Russ. A great many occupy offices in the village system. In one day's drive in a tarantass I saw a dozen hamlets, in which every man serving as a justice of the peace was a Pole.

Not less than three thousand of the insurgents taken with arms in their hands during the last rising at Warsaw, were sent on to Archangel. At first the number was so great that an insurrection of prisoners threatened the safety of the town. The governor had to call in troops from the surrounding country, and the war-office had to fetch back all the Prussian and Austrian Poles whom, in the first hours of repression, they had hurried to the confines of the Frozen Sea.

They lived in a great yellow building, once used as the arsenal of Archangel, before the Government works were carried to the South; and their lot, though hard enough, was not harder than that of the people amongst whom they lived. They were gently used by the officers, who felt a soldierly respect for their courage, and a committee of foreign residents was allowed to visit them in their rooms. The food allowed to them was plentiful and good, and many a poor sentinel standing with his musket in their doorways must have envied them the abundance of bread and soup.

In squads and companies these prisoners have been brought back to their homes; some to their families, others to the provinces in which they had lived. Many have been freed without terms; some have been suffered to return to Poland on the sole condition of their not going to Warsaw. A hundred, perhaps, remain in the arsenal building, waiting for their turn to march. Their lot is hard, no doubt; but where is the country in which the lot of a political prisoner is not hard? Is it Virginia? is it Ireland? is it France?

These prisoners are closely watched, and the chances of escape are faint; not one adventurer getting off in a dozen years. A Pole of desperate spirit, who had been sent to Mesen as a place of greater security than the open city of

Archangel, slipped his guard, crawled through the pine woods to the sea, hid himself in the forest, until he found an opportunity of stealing a fisherman's boat, and then pushed boldly from the shore in his tiny craft, in the hope of being picked up by some English or Swedish ship on her outward voyage. Four days and nights he lived on the open sea; suffering from chill and damp, and torn by the pangs of hunger and thirst, until the paddle dropped from his hands. His strength being spent, he drifted with the tide on shore, only too glad to exchange his liberty for bread. When the officer sent to make inquiries drove into Mesen, he found the poor fellow lying half dead in the convict ward.

Beyond this confinement in a bleak and distant land, the Polish insurgents do not seem to be physically ill-used. Their tasks are light, their pay is higher than that of the soldiers guarding them, and some of the better class are allowed to work in cities as messengers and clerks. At one time they were allowed to teach—one man dancing, a second drawing, a third languages; but this privilege has been taken from them on the ground that in the exercise of these arts they were received into families, and abused their trust.

It is no easy thing to mix these Polish malcontents with the general race, without producing these results which a jealous police regard as a "corruption" of youth.

Man for man, a Pole is better taught than a Russian. He has more ideas, more invention, more practical talent. Having more resources, he can not be thrown in the midst of his fellows without taking the lead. He can put their wishes into words, and show them how to act. A prisoner, he becomes a clerk: an exile, he becomes on overseer, a teacher—in fact, a leader of men. Sent out into a distant province, he gradually but surely asserts his rank. An order from the police can not rob him of his genius; and when the ban is taken from his name, he may remain as a citizen in the town which gives him a career and perhaps supplies him with a wife. He may get a professor's chair; he may be made a judge; if he has been a soldier, he may be put on the general's staff.

All this time, and through all these changes, he may hold on to his hope; continuing to be a Pole at heart, and cherishing the dream of independence which has proved his bane. The country that employs him in her service is not sure of him. In her hour of trial he may betray her to an enemy; he may use the power in which she clothes him to deal her a mortal blow. She can not trust him. She fears his tact, his suppleness, his capacity for work. In fact, she can neither get on with him nor without him.

In the mean time, Poles who have passed through years of exile into a second freedom are coming to be known as a class apart, with qualities and virtues of their own—the growth of suffering and experience acting on a sensitive and poetic frame. These men are known as the Siberians. A Pole with whom I travel some days is one of these Siberians, and from his lips I hear another side of this strange story of exile life.

CHAPTER XLIV.

THE SIBERIANS.

"He is one of the Siberians," says my comrade of the road, after quoting some verses from a Polish poet.

"One of the Siberians?"

"Yes," replies the Pole. "In these countries you find a people of whom the world has scarcely heard; a new people, I might say; for, while in physique they are like the fighting men who followed Sobieski to the walls of Vienna, they are in mind akin to the patient and laborious monks who have built up the shrines of Solovetsk. Time has done his work upon them. A sad and sober folk, they go among us by the name of our Siberians."

"They are Poles by birth?"

"Yes, Poles by genius and by birth. They are our children who have passed through fire; our children whom we never hoped to see in the living world. Once they were called our Lost Ones. In Poland we have a tragic phrase, much used by parting friends: 'We never meet again!' For many years that parting phrase was fate. An exile, sent beyond the Ural Mountains, never came back; he was said to have joined our Lost Ones; he became to us a memory like the dead. We could not hope to see his face again, except in dreams. To-day that line is but a song, a recollection of the past; a refrain sung by the waters of Babylon. In Vilna, in Kazan, in Kief, in a hundred cities widely parted from each other, you will find a colony of Poles, now happy in their homes, who have crossed and recrossed those heights; men of high birth, and of higher culture than their birth; men who have ploughed through the snows of Tomsk; who have brought back into the West a pure and bruised, though not a broken spirit."

"Are these pardoned men reconciled to the Emperor?"

"They are reconciled to God. Do not mistake me. No one doubts that the reigning Emperor is a good and brave man; high enough to see his duty; strong enough to face it, even though his feet should have to stumble long and often on the rocks. But God is over all, and his Son died for all. Alexander is but an instrument in His hands. You think me mystical! Because my countrymen believe in the higher powers, they are described by Franks, who believe in nothing, as dreamers and spiritualists. We dream our dreams, we see our signs, we practise our religion, we respect our clergy, we obey our God."

"I have heard the Poles described as women in prayer, as gods in battle!"

"Like the young men of my circle," he continues, after a pause, "I took a part in the rising of '48; a poor affair, without the merit of being either Polish or Slavonic. That rising was entirely French. While young in years I had travelled with a comrade in the west of Europe; living on the Rhine, and on the Seine, where we forgot the religion of our mothers and our country, and learned to think and to speak of Poland as of a northern France. We called ourselves republicans, and thought we were great philosophers; but the idol of our fancies was Napoleon the Great, under whose banner so many of our countrymen threw away their lives. We ceased to appear at church, and even denied ourselves to the Polish priest. We hated the Tsar, and we despised the Russians with all our souls. Two years before the republic was proclaimed in the streets of Paris, we returned to Warsaw, in the hope of finding some field of service against the Tsar; but the powers had been too swift for us; and Cracow, the last free city of our country, was incorporated with the kaisar's empire on the day when I was dropped from the tarantass at my father's door. France bade us trust in her, and in the secret meetings which we called among our youthful friends, we gave up the good old Polish psalms and signs for Parisian songs and passwords. In other days we sang 'The Babe in Bethlehem,' but now, inspired with a foreign hope, we rioted through the Marseillaise. We had become strangers in the land, and the hearts of our people were not with us. The women fell away, the clergy looked askance, but the unpopularity of our new devices only made us laugh. We said to ourselves, we could do without these priests and fools; men who were always slaves, and women who were always dupes. As to the crowd of grocers and bakers—we thought of them only with contempt. Who ever heard of a revolution made by chandlers? We were noble, and how could we accept their help? The year of illusion came at length. That France to which every Polish eye was strained, became a republic; and then a troop of revellers, strong enough to whirl through a polka, threw themselves on the Russian guns, and were instantly sabred and shot down. Ridden over in the street, I was carried into a house; and, when my wounds were dressed, was taken to the castle royal, with a hundred others like myself, to await our trial by commission, and our sentence of degradation from nobility, exile to Siberia, and perpetual service in the mines. My friend was with me in the street, and shared my doom."

"Had you to go on foot?"

"Well—no. For Nicolas, though stern in temper, was not a man to break the law. Himself a prince, he felt a proud respect for the rights of birth; and as a noble could not be reduced to march in the gangs like a peddler and a serf, our papers were made out in such a way that our privileges were not to end until we reached Tobolsk. There the permanent commission of Siberia sat; and there each man received his order for the mines. We rode in a light cart, to which three strong ponies were tied with ropes; and when the roads were hard, we made two hundred versts a day. Our feet were chained, so that we could not take off our boots by night or day; but the people of the steppe over which we tore at our topmost speed, were good and kind to us, as they are to exiles; giving us bread, dried fish, and whisky, on the sly. They knew that we were Poles, and, as a rule, their popes are only too much inclined to abuse the Poles as enemies of God; but the Russians, even when they are savages, have a tenderness of heart. They know the difference between a political exile and a thief; for the Government stamps the thief and murderer on the forehead and the two cheeks with a triple vor; a black and ghastly stamp which neither fire nor acid will remove; and if they think a Pole very wicked in being a Catholic they feel for his sufferings as a man. Twice I tried to escape from the mines; and on both occasions, though I failed to get away, the kindness of the poor surprised me. They dared not openly assist my flight, but they were sometimes blind and deaf; and often, when in hunger and despair I ventured to crawl near a cabin in the night, I found a ration of bread and fish, and even a cup of quass, laid ready on the window-ledge."

"Who put them there, and why?"

"Poor peasants, to whom bread and fish are scarce; in order to relieve the wants of some poor devil like myself."

"Then you began to like the people?"

"Like them! To understand them, and to see they were my brothers; but my heart was hard with them for years. I was a man of science, as they call it; and I told myself that in giving food to the hungry they were only obeying the first rude instincts of a savage horde. At length a poor priest came in a cart to the mines. Before his coming I had heard of him—his name—his mission—and his perils; for Father Paul was a free agent in his travels; having chosen this service in the desert snows, instead of a stall in some cathedral-town, from a belief that poor Catholic exiles had a higher claim on him than sleek and fashionable folk. I knew, from the report of others, that he made the round of Siberia, sledging from mine to mine, from mill to mill, in order to keep alive in these Catholic exiles some remembrance of their early faith; to say mass, to hear confessions, to marry and baptize, to sanctify the new-made grave. Yet I hardly gave to him a second thought. What could he do for me; a poor priest, dwelling by choice in a savage waste, with no high sympathies and no great friends? He was not likely to adore Napoleon, and he was certain to detest Mazzini's name. How could I talk with such a man? The night when he arrived was cold, his sledge was injured, and the wolves had been upon his track. Some natural pity for his age and danger drew me to his side in our wooden shed, and after he was thawed into life, he spoke to us, even before he tasted food, of that love of God which was his only strength. When he had supped on our coarse turnip soup and a little black bread, he lay down on a mattress and fell asleep. For hours that night I sat and gazed into his face, his white hair falling on his pillow, and his two arms folded like a cross upon his breast. If ever man looked like an angel in his sleep it was Father Paul. Of such men is the Church of Christ.

"Next day I sought him in his shed, for our inspector turned this visit into a holiday for his Catholic prisoners; and there he spoke to me of my country and of my mother, until my heart was softened, and the tears ran down my face. Pausing softly in his speech, he bent his eyes upon me, as my father might have looked, and pressing me tenderly by the hand, said: 'Come unto me all ye that labor and are heavy laden, and I will give you rest.' 'Blessed are they that mourn; for they shall be comforted. Blessed are the meek; for they shall inherit the earth.' I had read these words a hundred times, for I was fond of the New Testament as a book of democratic texts; but I had never felt their force until they fell from the lips of Father Paul. I saw they were addressed to me. My mother was about me in the air. I laid down my philosophy, and felt once more like a little child."

His voice is low and mellow, but the tones are firm, and touch my ear like strings in perfect tune. After a pause, I asked him how his change of feeling worked in his relations to the Russians.

"A Christian," he replies, "is not a slave of the flesh. His first consideration is for God; his second for the children of God, not as they chance to dwell on the Vistula, on the Alps, on the Frozen Sea, but in every land alike. He yields up the sword to those who will one day perish by the sword. His weapon is the spirit, and he hopes to subdue mankind by love."

"Then you would yield the sword to any one who is proud and prompt enough to seize it."

"No; the sword is God's to give, not mine to yield; and for His purposes He gives it unto whom He will. It is a fearful gift, and no man can be happy in whose grasp it lies."

"Yet many would like to hold it?"

"That is so. The man who first sees fire will burn himself. Observe how differently one thinks of war when one comes to see that men are really the sons of God. All war means killing some one. Which one? Would you like to think that in a future world some awful coil of fate should draw you into slaying an angel?"

"No; assuredly."

"Yet men are angels in a lower stage! We see things as we feel them. Men are blind, until their eyes are opened by the love of God; and God is nearest to the bruised and broken heart. Hosts of Siberians have come back to Poland; but among these exiles there is hardly one who has returned as he went forth."

"They are older."

"They are wiser. Father Paul, and priests like Father Paul—for he is not alone in his devotion—have not toiled in vain. Perhaps I should say they have not lived in vain; for the service which they render to the proud and broken spirit of the exile, is not the word they utter, but the doctrine they live. The poets and critics who have passed through fire are known by their chastened style. They have put away France and the French. They read more serious books; they speak in more sober phrase. In every thing except their love of God and love of country you might think them tame. They preach but little, and they practise much; above all, they look to what is high and noble, if remote, and set their faces sternly against the wanton waste of blood. They know the Russians better, and they did not need the amnesty, and what has followed it, in order to feel the brotherhood of all the Slavonic tribes."

"You are a Panslavonist?"

"No! We want a wider policy and a nobler word. The Panslavonic party has built a wall round Kief, and they would build a wall round Russia. They have a Chinese love of walls. Just look at Moscow; one wall round the Kremlin, a second wall round China-town, a third wall round the city proper. What we need is the old war-cry of St. George—the patron of our early dukes, our free cities, and our missionary church."

CHAPTER XLV.

ST. GEORGE.

St. George is a patron saint of all the Slavonic nations; whether Wend or Serb, Russine or Russ, Polack or Czeck; but he is worshipped with peculiar reverence by the elder Russ. His days are their chief festivals; the days on which it is good for them to buy and sell, to pledge and marry, to hire a house, to lease a field, to start an enterprise. Two days in the year are dedicated in his name, corresponding in their idiom and their climate to the first day of spring and the last day of autumn; days of gladness to all men and women who live by tending flocks and tilling fields. On the first of these days the sheds are opened, the cattle go forth to graze, the shepherd takes up his crook, the dairy-maid polishes her pots and pans. The second day is a kind of harvest-home, the labor of the year being over, the harvest garnered, and the flocks penned up. But George is a city saint as well as a rustic saint. His image is the cognizance of their free cities, and of their old republics; and the figure of the knight in conflict with the dragon has been borne in every period by their dukes, their grand dukes, and their Tsars. His badge occurs on a thousand crosses, amulets, and charms; dividing the affections of a pious and superstitious race with images of the Holy Trinity and the Mother of God. The knight in conflict with the dragon was proudly borne on the shield of Moscow hundreds of years before the Black Eagle was added to the Russian flag. That eagle was introduced by Ivan the Third; a prince who began the work (completed by his grandson, Ivan the Fourth) of crushing the great boyars and destroying the free cities. Ivan copied that emblem from the Byzantine flag; a symbol of his autocratic power, which many of his people read as a sign that devil-worship was the new religion of his army and his court. They saw in this black and ravening bird the Evil Spirit, just as they saw in the white and innocent dove the Holy Ghost. To soothe their fears, St. George was quartered on the Black Eagle; not in his talons, but on his breast; and in this form the Christian warrior figures on every Russian flag and Russian coin.

St. George was the patron of an agricultural and pacific race; a country that was pious, rich, and free; and what he was in ancient times he still remains in the national heart. As the patron of soldiers he is hardly less popular with princes than peasants. Peter the Great engraved the figure of St. George on his sword; the Empress Catharine founded an order in his name; and Nicolas built in his honor a magnificent marble hall. Yet the high place and typical shrine of St. George is Novgorod the Great.

For miles above and miles below the red kremlin walls at Novgorod, the Volkhof banks are beautiful with gardens, country houses, and monastic piles. These swards are bright with grass and dark with firs; the houses are of Swiss-like pattern; and the convents are a wonder of the land. St. Cyril and St. Anton lend their names to masses of picturesque building; but the glory of this river-side scenery is the splendid monastery of St. George.

Built by Jaroslav, a son of St. Vladimir, on a ridge of high ground, near the point where Lake Ilmen flows into the river Volkhoff, the Convent of St. George stood close to an ancient town called Gorod Itski—City of Strength—literally, Fenced Town. Of this fenced town, a church, with frescoes older than those of Giotto, still remains; a church on a bluff, with a quaint old name of Spas Nereditsa: literally, Our Saviour Beyond Bounds. In these old names old tales lie half-entombed. From this fenced town, the burghers, troubled by a fierce democracy, appear to have crossed the river and built for themselves a kremlin (that is to say, a stone inclosure) two miles lower down the stream, on a second ridge of ground, separated from the first by an impassable swamp. This new city, called Novgorod (New Town), was to become a wonder of the earth; a trading republic, a rival of Florence and Augsburg, a mother of colonies, a station of the Hanseatic League.

The old Church of our Saviour Beyond Bounds, and the still older Convent of St. George on the opposite bank, were left in the open country; left to the neglects of time and to the ravages of those Tartar begs who swept these plains from Moscow to the gates of Pskof.

Neglect, if slow, was steady in her task of ruining that ancient church, now become a landmark only; but a landmark equally useful to the critic of church history, and to the raftsman guiding his float across the lake. As we leave the porch, an old man, standing uncovered near the door, calls out, "You come to see the church—the poor old church—but no one gives a ruble to repair the poor old church! It is St. George's Day; yet no one here remembers the dear old church! Look up at the Mother of God; see how she is tumbling down; yet no man comes to save her! Give some rubles, Gospodin, to our Blessed Lady, Mother of God!" The old man sighs and sobs these words in a voice that seems to come from a breaking heart.

St. George was able to defend his cells and shrines; and in all the ravages committed by Tartar hordes, the rich convent near Lake Ilmen was never profaned by Moslem hoof. Cold critics assume that the belt of peat and bog lying south of Novgorod for a hundred miles was the true defense; but the poets of Novgorod assert, in many a song and tale, that they owed their safety from the infidel spoilers to no freak of nature and no arm of flesh. St. George defended his convent and his city by a standing miracle; and, in return for his protecting grace, the people of this province came to kneel and pray, as their fathers for a thousand years have knelt and prayed, before his holy shrine.

My visit to the Convent of St. George is paid (in company with Father Bogoslovski, Russian pope, and Mr. Michell, English diplomat) on the autumnal festival of the saint. Three or four thousand pilgrims, chiefly from the town and province of Novgorod, camp in a green meadow; their carts unyoked; their horses tethered to the ground; their camp-fires lighted here and there. Each pilgrim brings a present to St. George;

a load of hay, a sack of flour, a pot of wax, a roll of linen, an embroidered flag. That poor old creature, who can hardly walk, has brought him a ball of thread; a widow's mite, as welcome as an offering in gold and silver. Booths are built for the sale of bread and fruit; tea is fizzing on fifty stalls; grapes, nuts, and apples are sold on every side. The peasants are warmly and brightly clad: the men in sheep-skin vests, fur caps, and boots; the women in damask gowns and jackets, quilted and puckered, the edges fringed with silver lace. A fine day tempts the women and children to throw themselves on the green in groups. Monks move among the crowd; country folk stare at the finery; hawkers chaffer with the girls; and more than one transparent humbug makes a market of relics and pious ware. Every one is in holiday humor; and the general aspect of the field in front of the convent gates is that of a village fair, with just a dash of the revival camp.

The worshippers are a placid, kindly, and (for the moment) a sober folk, with quaint expressions and old-world manners. On the boat we hear a rustic say to his neighbor, "If you are not a noble, take your bundle off that bench and let me sit down; if you are a noble, go into the best cabin, your proper place." The neighbor sets his bundle down, and the new-comer drops into his seat, saying, "See, there is room for all Christians; we are equal here, being all baptized." An English churl might have said he had "paid his fare." On board the same boat a man replies to the steward, who wishes to turn him out of the dining-room, "Am I not a Christian, and why should I go out?" On hiring a boat to cross the river, Father Bogoslovski says to the oarsman, "Take your sheep-skin; you will get a cold." "No; thank you," answers the waterman, "we never take cold if God is with us." Another boatman tells us we are doing a "good work" in visiting the shrines. "Once," he says, "I was sick, and died; but I prayed to my angel Lazarus to let me live again. He listened to my prayers, not for my own sake, but for that of my brother, who had just come back from Solovetsk. My soul came back, and we were very glad. Your angel can always fetch back your soul, unless it has gone too far." Here stands a group of men; a young fellow with a basket of red apples, two or three lads, and an old peasant, evidently a stranger to these parts. "Eat an apple with me, uncle," says the young fellow to his elder; for a rustic, who addresses a stranger of his own age as "brother," always speaks to elderly ones as "uncle." "Very nice apples," says the stranger, "where were they blessed?" "In St. Sophia's, yonder; try them." Apples are blessed in church on August 6th, the feast of the transfiguration; the earliest day on which such garden fruit is certain to be ripe. It is an old popular custom, maintained by the Church, in the simple interest of the public health.

The scene is lovely. From the belfry of St. George — a shaft to compare with the Porcelain Tower—you command a world of encircling pines, through which flow, past your feet, the broad and idle waters of the Volkhof; draining the ample lake, here shining on your right. Below you spreads the deep and difficult marsh; and on the crests of a second ridge of land springs up a forest of spires and battlements, rich in all radiant hues; red walls, white towers, green domes, and golden pinnacles; here the kremlin and cathedral, there the city gate and bridge; and yonder, across the stream, the trading town, the bazar, and Yaroslav's Tower; the long and picturesque line of Novgorod the Great.

A bell of singular sweetness soothes the senses like a spell. At one stall you drink tea; no stronger liquor being sold at the convent gate. At a second stall you buy candles; to be lighted and left on the shrines within. At a third you get consecrated bread; a present for your friends and domestics far away. This fine white bread, being stamped with the cross and blessed, is not to be bought with money; for how could the flesh of our Lord be sold for coin? It is exchanged. You give a man twenty kopecks; he gives you a loaf of bread. Gift for gift is not barter—you are told—but brotherly love. On trying the same thing at an apple-stall, the result appears to you much the same. You pay down so many kopecks; you take up so much fruit; the quantity strictly measured by the amount of coin laid down. You see no difference between the two? Then you are not an Oriental, not a pilgrim of St. George.

Some twelve or fifteen thousand men and women bring their offerings, in kind and money, every spring and autumn, to the shrine of this famous saint.

CHAPTER XLVI.

NOVGOROD THE GREAT.

SITTING at my window, gazing into space—in front of me that famous tower of Yaroslav, from which once pealed the Vechie bell; and, lying beyond this tower, the public square, the bridge, the Kremlin walls, Sophia's golden domes, and that proud pedestal of the present reign, which tells of a Russia counting already her thousand years of political life—I fall a dreaming of the past, until the sceneries and the people come and go in a procession; not of dead things, but of quick and passionate men, alive with the energies of past and coming times.

What were the shapes and meanings of that dream? A wide expanse of wood and waste; forests of fir and silver-birch; with tarns and lakes on which the wild fowl of the country feed their young; and by the shores of which the shepherds and herdsmen watch their scanty flocks. In the midst of this wood and water stands a low red wall of stone, engirding a mass of cabins, with here and there a bigger cabin, from the peak of which springs a cross. A river rolls beneath the wall, the waters of which come from a dark and sombre lake. The space within the wall is a kremlin, an inclosure, and in this kremlin dwell a band of traders and craftsmen; holding their own, with watchful eye and ready hand, like the lodgers in a Syrian khan, against wild and predatory tribes. The life of these men is hard and mean; the air is bleak, the soil unfruitful; and the marauders prowl forever at their gates.

A mist of time rolls up and hides the red stone wall and shingles from my sight, and, when it clears away, a vast and shining city stands exposed to view, with miles of street and garden, and an outer wall, of sweep so vast that the eye can hardly take it in, with massive gates and towers to defend these gates, of enormous strength. The river is now alive with boats and rafts; the streets are thronged with people, and a hundred domes and steeples glitter in the sun. The red kremlin, not now used as a castle of defense, is covered with public buildings; one a cathedral of gigantic size and surpassing beauty; another, a palace with a garden, belted by a moat; the citadel in which the traders nestled together for their common safety having now become the seat of temporal and spiritual power. Long trains of horses file through the city gates, bringing in the produce of a thousand hamlets, which the merchants store in their magazines for export and expose in their bazars for sale. These merchants bring their wares from East and West, and send them in exchange to the farthest ports and cities of the earth. Their town is a free town, to which men from all nations come and go; a republic in the wilderness; a station of the Hanseatic league, devoting itself to freedom, commerce, and the liberal arts. The life of a great country flows into their streets and squares; from which run out again the prosperous purple tides into the unknown regions of ice and storm. Forth from her gates march out the colonists of the North; the men of Kem and Holmogory; men who are going forth to plant on the shores of the Arctic Sea the free institutions under which they live at home. A prince, elected by the people, serving while they list, sits in the chair of state, like a Podesta in Italian towns; but the actual power is in the hands of the Vetchie: a popular council, summoned by the ringing of a bell—the great city bell—which swings in Yaroslav's Tower.

Now comes a change, which seems to be less a change in the outward show than in the inner spirit of the place. The merchant has become a boyar, the nobleman a prince. Pride of the eye, and lust of the heart, are stamped upon every face. The rich are very rich; the poor are very poor; and men in cloth of gold affront and trample on men in rags. The streets—so spacious and so busy!—are disturbed by faction fights; and the Vetchie bell is swinging day and night, as though some Tartar horde were at the gates. The boyars have grown too rich for freedom, and the ancients of the city sell their consciences for gold and state. Deeming themselves the equals of kings, they give their city not only the name of Great, but the name of Lord. On public documents they ask—as if in mockery—Who can stand against God, and Novgorod the Great?

Again falls the mist of time; and as it rolls away, the city, still as vast, though not so busy as of yore, seems troubled in her splendor by a sudden fear. The bell which tolls her citizens to council, seems wild with pain, and men are hurrying to and fro along her streets; none daring, as in olden days, to snatch down lance and sword, and counsel his fellows to go forth and fight. For an enemy is nigh their gates, whom they have much offended, without having virtue enough to resist his arms. Ivan the Fourth, returning from a disastrous raid on the Baltic seaboard, hears that in his absence from Moscow, the citizens of Novgorod, hating his rule, have sent an embassy to the Prince of Sweden, praying him to take them under his protection; and in his fury the tyrant swears to destroy that city, and to sow the site with salt. An army of Tartars and Kozaks is at the gates; an army sullen from defeat and loss, and only to be rallied by an orgy of drink and blood. Pale with terror, the citizens run to and fro; the women shriek and swoon; and help for them is none, until Father Nicolas, an ancient man, with flowing beard and saintly face, stands forward in their midst. A wild creature; an Elisha the prophet, a John the Baptist; he stands up in their meeting, naked from head to feet. Such a man suits the times; and as he offers to go forth and save the city from ruin, they gladly let him try. Nicolas marches forth, in his nakedness, to denounce his prince in the midst of his ravenous hordes; and when he comes into the camp, he walks up boldly to the Tsar. Ivan, himself a fanatic, listens to this naked man with a patience which his guards and ministers observe with wonder. "Bloodsucker and unbeliever!" cries the hermit, "thou who art a devourer of Christian flesh—listen to my words. If thou, or any of these thy servants, touch a hair of a child's head in yon city—which God preserves for a great purpose—then, I swear by the angel whom God has given unto me to serve me, thou shalt surely die; die on the instant, by a flash from heaven!" As he speaks, the sky grows dark, a storm springs up, and rages through the tents. A pall comes down, and covers the earth. "Spare me, fearful saint," shrieks the Tsar, "the city is forgiven; and let me, in remembrance of this day, have thy constant prayers." On these conditions Nicolas withdraws his curse; and Ivan, marching into the city with his captives and his treasures, lodges in the Kremlin and the palace, and kneeling before the shrine of St. Sophia, makes himself gracious to the people for the hermit's sake.

Once more a mist comes down—a thin white veil, which passes like a pout from an infant's face. The city is the same in size, in splendor, in the fullness of her fearful life. The Tsar, who went away from her gates low and humble, has come back, like a wild beast thirsting for blood and prey. His army camps beyond the walls, and a whisper passes through the city that the place is to be razed, the women given up to the Tartars, while the men and boys are to be put without mercy to the sword. The city razed! No fancy can take in the fact; for Novgorod is one of the largest cities in Europe, a republic older than Florence, a capital larger than London, a shrine more sacred than Kief. Her walls measure fifty miles, her houses contain eight hundred thousand souls. Yet Ivan has doomed her to the dust. Telling off ten thousand gunners of his guard, and thirty thousand Tartars from the steppe, he gives up the republic to their lust, bidding them sack and burn, and spare neither man nor maid. They rush upon the gates; they scale the wall; they seize the bridge, the Kremlin, the cathedral; and they make themselves masters of the city, quarter by quarter and street by street. No pen will paint the horrors of that sack. The wines are drunk, the people butchered, the houses fired. Day by day, and week after week, the club, the musket, and the torch are in constant use. The streets run blood, the river is choked with bodies of the slain. When the work of slaughter stops, and the Tartars are recalled into their camp, the tale of murdered men, women, and children is found to be greater than the population of Petersburg in the present day. The desolation is Oriental and complete.

The city bell—the bell of council and of prayer—is taken down from Yaroslav's Tower and sent to Moscow, where it hangs beside the Holy Gate—an exile from the city it roused to arms, and haply speaking to some burgher's ear and student's heart of a time when Russian cities were equal to those of Italy and England, and her people were as free as those of Germany and France!

CHAPTER XLVII.

SERFAGE.

SERFAGE has but a vague resemblance to the system of villeinage once so common in the West; and serfage was not villeinage under another name. Villeinage was Occidental, serfage Oriental.

Villein, aldion, colonus, fiscal, homme de pooste, are words which, in various tongues of Western Europe, mark the man who belonged to a master, and was bound by law to serve him. Whether he lived in England, Italy, or France, the man was stamped with the same character, and laden with the same obligation. He was a hedger and ditcher—churl, clod, lout, and boor—heavy as the earth he tilled, and swinish as the herds he fed. He could not leave his lord; he could not quit his homestead and his field. In turn, his master could not drive him from the soil, though he might beat him, force him to work, throw him into prison, and sell his services when he sold the land. But here the likeness of serf to either villein, aldion, colonus, fiscal, or homme de pooste ends sharply. No one thought the villein was an actual owner of the soil he tilled, and in no country was the emancipation of his class accompanied by a cession of the land.

Serfage sprang from a different root, and in a different time. The great settlement, which is the glory of Alexander's reign, can only be understood by reference to the causes from which serfage sprang.

Some of the facts which prove this difference between Western villeinage and Eastern serfage lie beyond dispute. Villeinage was introduced by foreign princes, serfage by native tsars. Villeinage followed a disastrous war; serfage followed liberation from a foreign yoke. Villeinage came with the dark ages and passed away with them. Serfage came with the spreading light, with the rising of independence, with the sentiment of national life. Villeinage was forgotten by the Rhine, the Severn, and the Seine, before serfage was established on the Moskva and the Don.

In short, serfage is a historical phase.

In one of the book-rooms of the Academy of Sciences, in Vassile Ostrof, St. Petersburg, you turn over the leaves of an early copy—said to be the first—of "Nestor's Chronicle," in which are many fine drawings of scenes and figures, helping you to understand the text. This copy is known as the Radzivil codex. Nestor wrote his book in Kief, a hundred years before that city was sacked by Batu Khan; and the pictures in the Radzivil codex give you the early Russian in his dress, his garb, and his ways of life. Was he in that early time an Asiatic, dressed in a sheep-skin robe and a sheep-skin cap? In no degree. The Russian boyar dressed like a German knight; the Russian mujik dressed like an English churl.

In Nestor's time the Russians were a free people, ruled in one place by elective chiefs, in another place by family chiefs. They were a trading and pacific race; in the western countries settled in towns; in the eastern countries living in tents and huts. Novgorod, Pskof, and Hlynof, were free cities, ruled by elected magistrates, on the pattern of Florence and Pisa, Hamburg and Lubeck. In those days there was neither serf nor need of serf. But this old Russia fell under the Mongol yoke. Broken in the great battle on the Kalka, the country writhed in febrile agony for a hundred and eighty years; during which time her fields were scorched, her cities sacked, her peasants driven from their homes into the forest and the steppe. She had not yet raised her head from this blow, when Timur Beg swept over her prostrate form; an Asiatic of higher reach and nobler type than Batu Khan; a scholar, an artist, a statesman; though he was still an Asiatic in faith and spirit. Timur brought with him into Russia the code of Mecca, the art of Samarcand, the song of Ispahan. His begs were dashing, his mirzas polished. In the khanates which he left behind him on the Volga and in the Crimea, there was a courtesy, a beauty, and a splendor, not to be found in the native duchies of Nijni, Moscow, Riazan, and Tver. The native dukes and boyars of these provinces held from the Crim Tartar, known to our poets as the Great

Cham. They swore allegiance to him; they paid him annual tribute; they flattered him by adopting his clothes and arms. The humblest vassals of this Great Cham were the Moscovite dukes, who called themselves his slaves, and were his slaves. Standing before him in the streets, they held his reins, and fed his horses out of their Tartar caps. They copied his fashions and assumed his names. Their armies, raised by his consent, were dressed and mounted in the Tartar style. They fought for him against their country, crushing those free republics in the north which his cavalry could not reach.

This fawning of dukes and boyars on the Great Cham brought no good to the rustic; who might see his patch of rye trodden down, his homestead fired, and his village cross profaned by gangs of marauding horse. Even when a Tartar khan set up his flag on some river bank, as at Kazan, in some mountain gorge, as at Bakchi Serai, he was still a nomad and a rider, with his natural seat in the saddle and his natural home in the tent. A little provocation stirred his blood, and when his feet were in the stirrups, it was not easy for shepherds and villagers to turn his lance. A cloud of fire went with him; a trail of smoke and embers lay behind him. No man could be sure of reaping what he sowed; for an angry word, an insolent gesture of his duke, might bring that fiery whirlwind of the Tartar horse upon his crops. What could he do, except run away? When year by year this ruin fell upon him, he left his cabin and his field; working a little here, and begging a little there; but never striking root into the soil. Now he was a pilgrim, then a shepherd, oftener still a tramp. To pass more easily to and fro, he donned the Tartar dress; a sheep-skin robe and cap; the robe caught in at the waist by a belt, and made to turn, so that the wool could be worn outwardly by day and inwardly by night. In self-defense he picked up Tartar words, and passed, where he could pass, for one of the conquering race.

Why should he plough his land for other men to spoil? While he was watching his corn grow ripe, the khan of Crim Tartary, stung by some insult from the duke, might spur out rapidly from his luxurious camp at Bakchi Serai, and, sweeping through the plains from Perekop to Moscow, waste his fields with fire.

Like causes produce like effects. Nomadic lords produce nomadic slaves. The Russian peasant became a vagabond, just as the Syrian fellah becomes a vagabond, when from year to year his crops have been plundered by the Bedouin tribes.

When Ivan the Fourth, having learned from the Tartar Begs how to rule and fight, broke up the khanates of Kazan and Astrakhan, and ventured to defy the lord of Bakchi Serai, he found himself an independent prince at the head of a country, rich in soil, in capital, and in labor, but with fields deserted, villages destroyed, populations scattered, and public roads unsafe. The land was not unpeopled; but the peasants had lost their sense of home, and the mujiks wandered from town to town. Labor was dear in one place, worthless in another. Half the land, even in the richer provinces, lay waste; and every year some district was scourged by famine, and by the epidemics which follow in the wake of famine. How were the peasants to be "fixed" upon the land?

For seventy years this question troubled the court in the Kremlin, even more than that court was troubled by Church controversy, Tartar raid, and family strife; although within this period of seventy years St. Philip was murdered, the Great Cham burnt a portion of Moscow, Dimitri the legitimate heir was killed, and Boris Godounof usurped the throne. Ivan the Fourth tried hard to induce his people to return upon their lands; by giving up many of the crown estates; by building villages at his own expense; by coaxing, thrashing, forcing his people into order. Even if this reformer never used the term serf (krepostnoi, a man "fixed" or "fastened,)" he is not the less—for good and ill—the author of that Russian serfage which is passing away before our eyes.

CHAPTER XLVIII.

A TARTAR COURT.

In that gorgeous chamber of the Kremlin known as the treasury of Moscow, stands an armed and mounted figure, richly dight, and called a boyar of the times of Ivan the Fourth. Arms, dress, accoutrements, are those of a mirza, a Tartar noble; and an inscription on the drawn Damascus blade informs the pious Russian that there is but One God, and that Mohammed is the prophet of God! Yet the figure is really that of a boyar of the times of Ivan the Fourth.

No prince in the line of Russian rulers is so great a puzzle as this Ivan the Fourth. In spite of his many atrocious deeds, he is still regarded by many of his critics as an able reformer and a patriotic prince. Much, indeed, must be said in his favor by all fair writers. To him the Moscovites owe their deliverance from the Tartar yoke. For them he conquered the kingdom of Kazan, the empire of Siberia, the khanate of Astrakhan. On all their frontiers he subdued the crescent to the cross. With Swedes and Poles he waged an equal, sometimes a glorious war. He opened his country to foreign trade; he built ports on the Baltic, on the Caspian, on the Frozen Seas. The glories of his reign were of many kinds. He brought printers from the Rhine, and published the Acts of the Apostles in his native tongue. He sent to Frankfort for skillful physicians, to London for artificers in wood and brass. Collecting shipwrights at his river-town of Vologda, he caused them to build for him a fleet of rafts and boats, on which he could descend with his treasures to the sea. He called a parliament of his estates to consult on the public weal. He reduced the unwritten laws of his country to a code. He put down mendicancy in his empire; laid his reforming hand on the clergy; and published a uniform confession of faith.

Ivan was a savage; though he was a popular savage. Terrible he was; but terrible to the rich and great. In fact, he was a reforming Tartar khan. If he taxed the merchants, he built hamlets for peasants at his private cost. If he crushed the free cities, he settled thousands of poor on the public lands. If he destroyed the princes and boyars as a ruling caste, he put into their places the official *chins*. If he ruled by the club, he also tried to rule by the printing-press. If he sacked Novgorod and Pskoff, he built a vast number of churches, villages, and shrines. A builder by policy as well as by nature, he found an empire of logs, which he hoped to bequeath to his son as an empire of stone. Forty stone churches, sixty stone monasteries, owe their foundation to his care. He raised the quaint edifice of St. Vassili, near the Kremlin wall, which he called after his father's patron saint. He is said to have built a hundred and fifty castles, and more than three hundred communes.

Wishing to settle and civilize his people, the reformer sought his models in those Tartar provinces which he had recently subdued. Kazan and Bakchi Serai were nobler cities than Vladimir and Moscow; while the poorest mirza of the Great Cham's court was far more splendid in arms and dress than any boyar in Ivan's court.

Ivan began to tartarize his kingdom by dividing it into two parts—personal and provincial; the first of which he ruled in person; the second by deputies wielding the power of Tartar begs. He raised a regular army—then the only one in Europe—which he armed and mounted in the Tartar style. He raised a body-guard to whom he gave the Tartar tafia; a cap that no Christian in his duchy was allowed to wear. Like the Great Cham, he set apart rooms in his palace for a harem; shut up his wives and daughters from the public eye; and changed the new fashion of excluding women from his court into a binding rule. His dukes and boyars followed him, until every house had a harem, and the seclusion of females was as strict in Moscow as in Bokhara and Bagdad.

These customs kept their ground until the times of Peter the Great. The land was governed by provincial begs, called boyars and voyevods; the army was drilled and dressed like Turkish troops; and the women were kept in harems like the Sultan's odalisques. Breaking through the customs introduced by Ivan, Peter opened the imperial harem; showed his wife in public; and invited ladies to appear at court. Yet something of this Turkish fashion may still be traced in Russian family life, especially in the country towns. As every great house had its harem—a woman's quarter, into which no stranger was allowed to set his foot—so every great family had a separate cemetery for the female sex. A few of these old cemeteries still remain as convents; for example, the Novo-Devictchie, Maidens' Convent, in the suburbs of Moscow; and the Convent of the Ascension, in the Kremlin, near the Holy Gate; the burial-place of all the Tsarinas, from the time of Ivan the Terrible down to that of Peter the Great.

By subtle tricks and surprises, Ivan set his dukes and boyars quarrelling with each other, and when they were hot with speech he would get them to accuse each other, and so despoil them both. In time he procured the surrender to him of nearly all their historical rights and titles; when, like a sultan, he forced them to receive his gifts and graces, under their hands, *as slaves.* He introduced the Oriental practice of sending men, under forms of honor, into distant parts; inventing the political Siberia. His dukes were reduced in power, his boyars plundered of their wealth. The princes were too numerous to be touched, for in Ivan's time every third man in Moscow was a prince; and an English trader used to hire such a man to groom his horse or clean his boots. Not many of the ancient dukes survived this reign; but the Narichkins, the Dolgoroukis, the Golitsin, and four or five others, escaped; and these historical families look with patronizing airs on the imperial race. The Narichkins have married with Romanofs. One of this house was offered the title of imperial highness, and declined it, saying proudly to his sovereign, "No, sir, I am Narichkin." In the same spirit, Peter Dolgorouki, when he heard that the Emperor had taken away his title of prince, wrote to his majesty, "How can *you* pretend to degrade *me?* Can you rob me of my ancestors, who were grand dukes in Russia when yours were not yet counts of Holstein Gottorp?"

Moscow was governed like a Tartar camp. Ivan's bodyguards (opritchniki), roved about the streets in their Tartar caps, abusing the people of every grade, boyar and burgher, mujik and peasant, as though they had been men of a different race and faith; robbing houses, carrying off women, murdering men; so that a stranger who met a company of these fellows in the Chinese town or under the Kremlin wall, imagined that the city had been given up to the soldiery for spoil.

This effort to settle the country on Tartar principles turned the Church against the Tsar, and led to the retirement of Athanasius, the dismissal of German, and the murder of Philip. St. Philip was the martyr of Russia—slain for defending his country and his Church against this tartarizing Tsar.

Walk into the great Cathedral of the Ascension any hour of the day in any season of the year, and—on the right wing of the altar—you will find a crowd of men and women prostrate before one silver shrine. It is the tomb of St. Philip, martyr and saint. Every one comes to him, every one kisses his temples and his feet. The murder of this saint is one of those national offenses which a thousand years of penitence will not cleanse away. The penitent prays in his name; fasts in his name; burns candles in his name; and groans in spirit before the tomb, as though he were seeking forgiveness for some personal crime.

The tale of Philip's conflict with Ivan—a conflict of the Christian Church against the Tartar court—may be briefly told.

CHAPTER XLIX.

ST. PHILIP.

EARLY in the reign of Ivan the Fourth (1539), a pilgrim, poor in garb and purse, but of handsome presence, landed from a boat at the Convent of Solovetsk. He came to pray; but after resting in the island for a little while, he took the vows and became a monk. Under the name of Philip, he lived for nine or ten years in his lowly cell. The monks, his brethren, saw there was some mystery in his life; his taste, his learning, and his manner, all announcing him as one of those men who belong to the higher ranks. But the lowly brother held his peace. Nine years after his arrival, the prior of his convent died, and he was called by common assent to the vacant chair.

There was, in truth, a mystery in this monk. Among the proudest people in Moscow lived, in those days, the family of Kolicheff; to whom a son, Fedor, was born; the heir to a vast estate no less than to a glorious name. A pious mother taught the child to be good, according to her lights; to read about saints, to say long prayers, to listen for church-bells, and run with ardor to the sacrifice of mass. But being of noble birth, and having to serve his prince, Fedor was trained to ride and fence, to hunt and shoot, as well as to manage his father's forests, fisheries, and farms. At twenty-six he was introduced to Ivan, then a child of four; and as the young prince took a fancy for him, he was much at court, admired by all women, envied by many men. It seemed as though Fedor Kolicheff had only to stay at court in order to become a minister of state. But his heart was never in the life he led; the Kremlin was a nest of intrigue; the country round the city was troubled by a thousand crimes. Distressed by what he saw going on, the favorite pined for a religious life; and quitting the world in silence, giving up all he possessed, he wandered from Moscow in a pilgrim's garb. Trudging on foot, a staff in his hand, a wallet by his side, he found his way through the trackless forests of the north; now stopping in a peasant's hut, where he toiled on the land for his daily food; now dropping down the Dvina on a raft, and tugging for his passage at the oars. Crossing over to the convent, he became a monk, a priest, a prior, without betraying the secret of his noble birth and his place at court.

On coming into power, he set his heart on bringing back the convent to her ancient life. He wore the frock of Zosima, and set up an image over Savatie's tomb. Taking these worthies as his guides, he introduced the rule of assiduous work; invented forms of labor; making wax and salt; improving the fisheries and farms; building stone chapels; and teaching some of the fathers how to write and paint. Much of what is best in the convent, in the way of chapel, shrine, and picture, dates from his reign as prior. But Philip was called from his cell in the Frozen Sea to occupy a loftier and more perilous throne.

Ivan, liking the old friend of his youth, consulted him on state affairs, and called him to the Kremlin to give advice. On these occasions, Philip was startled at the change in Ivan; who, from being a paladin of the cross, had settled down in his middle age into a mixture of the gloomy monk and the savage khan. The change came on him with the death of his wife and the conquest of Kazan; after which events in his life he married two women, dressed himself in Tartar clothes, and adopted Asiatic ways. Like a chief of the Golden horde, he went about the streets of Moscow, ordering this man to be beaten, that man to be killed. The square in front of the Holy Gate was red with blood; and every house in the city was filled with sighs and groans.

Driving from their altars two aged prelates who rebuked his crimes, Ivan (in 1566) selected the Prior of Solovetsk as a man who would shed a light on his reign without disturbing him by personal reproof. Philip tried to escape this perilous post, but the Tsar insisted on his obedience; and with heavy heart he sailed from his asylum in the islands, conscious of going to meet his martyr's crown.

Ivan had judged the monk in haste. Philip was no courtier; not a man to say smooth things to princes; for under his monk's attire he carried a heart to feel, an eye to see, and a tongue to speak. In passing from Solovetsk to Moscow, he passed through Novgorod—a city disliked by Ivan on account of her wealth, her freedom, and her laws; when a crowd of burghers poured from the gates, fell on their knees before him, and implored him, as a pastor of the poor, to plead their cause before the Tsar, then threatening to ravage their district and destroy their town. On reaching Moscow, he spoke to Ivan as to a son; beseeching him to dismiss his guards, to put off his strange habits, to live a holy life, and to rule his people in the spirit of their ancient dukes.

Ivan waxed red and wroth; he wanted a priest to bless, and not to curse. The tyrant grew more violent in his moods; but the new Metropolite held out in patient and unyielding meekness for the ancient ways. Once, when Philip was performing mass, the Tsar and his guards, attired in their Tartar dress, came into his church, and took up their ranks, while Ivan himself strode up to the royal gates. As Philip went on with his service, taking no notice of the prince, a boyar cried, "It is the Tsar!" "I do not recognize the Tsar," said Philip, "in such a dress." The Tartar cap, the Tartar whip, were seen in every public place. The Tartar guards were masters of the city, and the streets were everywhere filled with the tumult of their evil deeds. They felt no reverence for holy things, and hurt the popular mind by treating the sacred images with disdain. In a procession, the Metropolite noticed one of these courtiers insolently wearing his Tartar cap. "Who is that man," asked Philip of the Tsar, "that he should profane with his Tartar costume this holy day?" Doffing his cap, the courtier denied that he was covered, and even charged the Metropolite with saying what was false. As every man in trouble went to his Metropolite for counsel, the boyars accused him of inciting the people against their prince. When Ivan married his fourth wife, a thing unlawful and unclean, the Metropolite refused to admit the marriage, and bade the Tsar absent himself from mass. Rushing from his palace into the Cathedral of the Annunciation, Ivan took his seat and scowled. Instead of pausing to bless him, Philip went on with the service, until one of the favorites strode up to the altar, looked him boldly in the face, and said, in a saucy voice, "The Tsar demands thy blessing, priest!" Paying no heed to the courtier, Philip turned round to Ivan on his throne. "Pious Tsar!" he sighed; "why art thou here? In this place we offer a bloodless sacrifice to God." Ivan threatened him, by gesture and by word. "I am a stranger and a pilgrim on earth," said Philip; "I am ready to suffer for the truth."

He was made to suffer much, and soon. Dragged from his altar, stripped of his robe, arrayed in rags, he was beaten with brooms, tossed into a sledge, driven through the streets, mocked and hooted by armed men, and thrown into a dungeon in one of the obscurest convents of the town. Poor people knelt as the sledge drove past them, every eye being wet with tears, and every throat being choked with sobs. Philip blessed them as he went, saying, "Do not grieve; it is the will of God; pray, pray!" The more patiently he bore his cross the more these people sobbed and cried. Locked in his jail and laden with chains, not only round his ankles but round his neck, he was left for seven days and nights without food and drink, in the hope that he would die. A courtier who came to see him was surprised to find him engaged in prayer. His friends and kinsmen were arrested, judged, and put to death, for no offense save that of sharing his name and blood. "Sorcerer! dost thou know this head?" was one laconic message sent to Philip from the Tsar. "Yea!" murmured the prisoner, sadly; "it is that of my nephew Ivan." Day and night a crowd of people gathered round his convent-door, until the Tsar, who feared a rising in his favor, caused him to be secretly removed to a stronger prison in the town of Tver.

One year after this removal of Philip from Moscow (1569), Ivan, setting out for Novgorod, and calling to mind the speech once made by Philip in favor of that city, sent a ruffian to kill him. "Give me thy blessing!" said the murderer, coming into his cell. "Do thy master's work," replied the holy man; and the deed was quickly done.

The martyred saint remained a few years in Tver—whence he was removed to Solovetsk, an incorruptible frame; and lay in that isle until 1660, in the reign of Alexie, father of Peter the Great, in the days of tribulation, when the country was tried by sickness, famine, and foreign wars, his body was brought to Moscow, as a solemn and penitential act, by which the ruler and his people hoped to appease the wrath of heaven. The Tsar's penitent letter of recall was read aloud before his tomb in Solovetsk, as though the saint could see and hear. The body was found entire, as on the day of sepulture—a sweet smell, as of herbs and flowers, coming out from beneath the coffin-lid. A grand procession of monks and pilgrims marched with the saint from Archangel to Moscow, where Alexie met them in the Kremlin gate, and carried the sacred dust into the cathedral, where it was laid, in the corner of glory, in a magnificent silver shrine.

On the day of his coronation, every Emperor of Russia has to kneel before his shrine and kiss his feet.

CHAPTER L.

SERFS.

BORIS GODUNOF, general, kinsman, successor of Ivan the Fourth, reduced the principle of serfage into legal form (1601). An able and patriotic man, Godunof, designed to colonize his bare river-banks and his empty steppe. He meant no harm to the rustic—on the contrary, he hoped to do him good; his project of "fixing" the rustic on his land was treated as a great reform; and after taking counsel with his boyars, he selected the festival of St. George, the patron of free cities and of the ancient Russians, for his announcement that every peasant in the empire should in future till and own forever the lands which he then tilled and held.

Down to that time, the theory of land was that of an Asiatic horde. From the Gulf of Venice to the Bay of Bengal the tenure of land might vary with race and clime; yet in every country where the Tartars reigned, the original property in the soil was everywhere said to be lodged in sultan, shah, mogul, and khan. The Russians, having lost the usage of their better time, transferred the rights which they acquired from Tartar begs and khans to their victorious prince.

This prince divided the soil according to his will; in one place founding villages for peasants, in a second place settling lands on a deserving voyavod, in a third place buying off an enemy with gifts of forests, fisheries, and lands; exactly in the fashion of Batu Khan and Timur Beg. This system of giving away crown lands was carried so far that when Godunof came to the throne (in 1598), he found his duchies and khanates consisting of a great many estates without laborers, and a great many laborers without estates. The peasants were roving hordes; and Godunof meant to fix these restless classes, by assigning to every family a personal and hereditary interest in the soil. The evil to be cured was an

Oriental evil; and he sought to cure it in the Oriental way. The khans had done the same; and Godunof only extended and defined their method, so as to bring a larger area of country under spade and plough.

There is reason to believe that this festival of St. George (in 1601) was hailed by peasant and boyar as a glorious day; that the decree which established serfage in Russia was accepted as a great and popular reform. To understand it, we must lay aside all notion of serfage in Moscow and Tamboff being the same thing as villeinage in Surrey and the Isle of France.

Serfage was a great act of colonization. Much of what was done by Godunof was politic, and even noble; for he gave up to his people millions of acres of the crown estates. The soil was given to the peasant on easy terms. He was to live on his land, to plough his field, to build his house, to pay his rates, and to serve his country in time of war. The chief concession made by the peasant, in exchange for his plot of ground, was his vagabond life.

To see that the serf—the man "fixed" on the soil—observed the terms of settlement, the prince appointed boyars and voyevods in every province as overseers; a necessary, and yet a fatal step. The overseer, a strong man dealing with a weak one, had been trained under Tartar rule; and just as the Tsar succeeded to the khan, the boyar looked upon himself as a successor to the beg. Abuses of the system soon crept in; most of all that Oriental use of the stick, which the boyar borrowed from the beg; but a serf had to endure this evil—not in his quality of serf, but in his quality of Russian. Every man struck the one below him. A Tsar boxed a boyer, a boyar beat a prince. A colonel kicked his captain, and a captain clubbed his men. This use of the stick is in every region of the East a sign of lordship; and a boyar who could flog a peasant for neglecting to till his field, to repair his cabin, and to pay his rates, would have been more than man if he had not learned to consider himself as that peasant's lord.

Yet the theory of their holding was, that the peasant held his land of the crown; even as the boyar held his land of the crown. A bargain was made between two consenting parties —peasant and noble—under the authority of law, for their mutual dealing with a certain estate—consisting (say) of land, lake, and forest, with the various rites attached to ownership—hunting, shooting, fishing, fowling, trespass, right of way, right of stoppage, right of dealing, and the like. It was a bargain binding the one above as much as it bound the one below. If a serf could not quit his homestead, neither could the lord eject him from it. If the serf was bound to serve his master, he was free to save and hold a property of his own. If local custom and lawless temper led a master to fine and flog the serf, that serf could find some comfort in the thought that the fields which he tilled belonged to himself and to his commune by a title never to be gainsaid. A peasant's rhyme, addressed to his lord, defines the series of his rights and liabilities:

"My soul is God's,
My land is mine,
My head's the Tsar's,
My back is thine!"

A likeness to the serf may be found in the East, not in the West. The closest copy of a serf is the ryot of Bengal.

Down to the reign of Peter the Great the system went on darkening in abuse. The overseer of serfs became the owner. In lonely districts who was to protect a serf? I have myself heard a rustic ordered to be flogged by his elder, on the bare request of two gentlemen, who said he was drunk and could not drive. The two gentlemen were tipsy; but the elder knew them, and he never thought of asking for their proofs. A clown accused by a gentleman must be in the wrong. "God is too high, the Tsar too distant," says the peasant's saw. In those hard times the inner spirit overcame the legal form; and serfs were beaten, starved, transported, sold; but always in defiance of the law.

Peter introduced some changes, which, in spite of his good intentions, made the evil worse. He stopped the sale of serfs, apart from the estate on which they lived—a long step forward; but he clogged the beneficial action of his edict by converting the old house-tax into a poll-tax, and levying the whole amount of tax upon the lord, to whom he gave the right of collecting his quota from the serfs. A master armed with such a power is likely to be either worse than a devil or better than a man. Peter took from the religious bodies the right, which they held in common with boyars and princes, of possessing serfs. The monks had proved themselves unfit for such a trust; and as they held their lands by a title higher than the law can give, it was hard for a convent serf to believe that any part of the fields he tilled was actually his own.

Catharine followed Peter in his war on Tartar dress, beards, manners, and traditions; but she also set her face, as Peter had done, on much that was native to the soil. She meant well by her people, and the charter of rights, which she granted to her nobles, laid the foundation in her country of a permanent, educated, middle class. She studied the question of converting the serf's occupancy into freehold. She confiscated the serfs attached to convents, placing them under a separate jurisdiction; and she published edicts tending to improve the position of the peasant towards his lord. But these imperial acts, intended to do him good, brought still worse evils on his head; for serfage, heretofore a local custom—found in one province, not in the adjoining province—found in Moscow and Voronej, not in Harkof and Kief —was now recognized, guarded and defined by general law. Catharine's yearning for an ideal order in her states induced her to "fix" the peasant of Lithuania and Little Russia on the soil, just as Godunof had "fixed" the peasant of Great Russia, giving him a homestead and a property forever on the soil. Paul, her son, took one stride forward in limiting the right of the lord to three days' labor in the seven—an edict which, though never put in force, endeared Paul's memory to the commons, many of whom regard him as a martyr in their cause. Yet Paul is one of those princes who extended the serf-empire. Paul created a new order of serfs in the appanage peasants, serfs belonging to members of the imperial house, just as the crown peasants belonged to the crown domain.

Alexander the First set an example of dealing with the question by establishing his class of free peasants; but the wars of his reign left him neither time nor means for conducting a social revolution more imposing and more perilous than a political revolution, and after a few years had passed his free peasants fell back into their former state. Nicolas was not inclined by nature to reform; the old, unchanging Tartar spirit was strong within him; and he rounded the serfage system by placing the free peasants, colonists, foresters, and miners, under a special administration of the state. Every rustic in the land who had no master of his own became a peasant of the crown.

But, from the reign of Ivan (ending in 1598) to the reign of Nicolas (ending in 1855), every patriot who dared to speak his mind inveighed against the abuse of serfage—as a thing unknown to his country in her happier times. Every false pretender, every reckless rebel, who took up arms against his sovereign, wrote on his banner, "freedom to the serf." Stenka Razin (c. 1670) proclaimed, from his camp near Astrakhan, four articles, of which the first and second ran—deposition of the reigning house and liberation of the serfs! Pugacheff, in a revolt more recent and more formidable than that of Razin (c. 1770), publicly abolished serfage in the empire, taking the peasants from their lords, and leaving them in full possession of their lands. Pestel and the conspirators of 1825 put the abolition of serfage in the front of their demands.

Catharine's wish to deal with the question was inspired by Pugacheff's letters of emancipation; and on the very eve of his triumph in St. Isaac's Square, the Emperor Nicolas named a secret committee, to report on the social condition of his empire, chiefly with the serf in view. At the end of three years, Nicolas, warned by their reports, drew up a series of acts (1828–'9), by which he founded an order of honorary citizens (not members of a guild), and set the peasants free from their lords. These acts were never printed, for as time wore on, and things kept quiet, the Emperor saw less need for change. The July days in Paris frightened him; and having already sent out orders for the masters to treat their serfs like Christian men, and to be content in exacting three days' work in seven, according to the wish of Paul, the sovereign thought he had done enough. His act of emancipation was not to see the light.

In his later years the question troubled the Emperor Nicolas day and night. In spite of his glittering array of troops, he felt that serfage left him weak, even as the great division of his people into Orthodox and Old Believers left him weak.

How weak these maladies of his country made him he only learned in the closing hours of his eventful life; and then (it is said) he told his son what he had done and left undone, enjoining him to study and complete his work.

It was well for the serf that Nicolas made him wait. The project of emancipation, drawn up under the eyes of Nicolas, was not a Russian document in either form or spirit; but a German state paper, based on the misleading western notion that serfage was but villeinage under a better name. The principle laid down by Nicolas was, that the serf should obtain his personal freedom, and the lord should take possession of his land!

CHAPTER LI.

EMANCIPATION.

ON the day when Alexander the Second came to his crown (1855), both lord and serf expected from his hands some great and healing act. The peasants trusted him, the nobles feared him. A panic seized upon the landlords. "What," they cried, "do you expect? The country is disturbed; our property will be destroyed. Look at these louts whom you talk of rendering free! They can neither read nor write; they have no capital; they have no credit; they have no enterprise. When they are not praying they are getting drunk. A change may do in the Polish provinces; in the heart of Russia, never!" The Government met this storm in the higher circles by pacific words and vigorous acts; the Emperor saying to every one whom his voice could reach that the peril lay in doing nothing, not in doing much. Slowly but surely his opinion made its way.

Addresses from the several provinces came in. Committees of advice were formed, and the Emperor sought to engage the most active and liberal spirits in his task. When the public mind was opened to new lights, a grand committee was named in St. Petersburg, consisting of the ministers of state, and a few members of the imperial council, over whom his majesty undertook to preside. A second body, called the reporting committee, was also named, under the presidency of Count Rostovtsef, one of the pardoned rebels of 1825. The grand committee studied the principles which ought to govern emancipation; the reporting committee studied and arranged the facts. A mighty heap of papers was collected; eighteen volumes of facts and figures were printed; and the net results were thrown into a draft.

The reporting committee having done their work, two bodies of delegates from the provinces, elected by the lords, were invited to meet in the capital and consider this draft. These provincial delegates raised objections, which they sent in writing to the committee; and the new articles drawn up by them were laid before the Emperor and the grand committee in an amended draft.

Up to this point the draft was in the hands of nobles and land-owners; who drew it up in their class-interests, and according to their class-ideas. If it recognized the serf's right to personal freedom, it denied him any rights in the soil. This principle of "liberty without land" was the battle-cry of all parties in the upper ranks; and many persons knew that such was the principle laid down in the late Emperor's secret and abortive act. How could a committee of landlords, trembling for their rents, do otherwise? "Emancipation, if we must," they sighed, "but emancipation without the land." The provincial delegates stoutly urged this principle; the reporting committee embodied it in their draft. Supported by these two bodies, it came before the grand committee. England, France, and Germany were cited; and as the villeins in those countries had received no grants of lands, it was resolved that the emancipated serfs should have no grants of land. The grand committee passed the amended draft.

Then, happily, the man was found. Whatever these scribes could say, the Emperor knew that forty-eight millions of his people looked to him for justice; and that every man in those forty-eight millions felt that his right in the soil was just as good as that of the Emperor in his crown. He saw that freedom without the means of living would be to the peasant a fatal gift. Unwilling to see a popular revolution turned into the movement of a class, he would not consent to make men paupers by the act which pretended to make them free.

"Liberty and land" — that was the Alexandrine principle; a golden precept which he held against the best and oldest councillors in his court.

The acts of his committees left him one course, and only one. He could appeal to a higher court. Some members of the grand committee, knowing their master's mind, had voted against the draft; and now the Emperor laid that draft before the full council, on the ground that a measure of such importance should not be settled in a lower assembly by a divided vote. Again he met with selfish views. The full council consists of princes, counts, and generals — old men mostly—who have little more to expect from the crown, and every reason to look after the estates they have acquired. They voted against the Emperor and the serfs.

When all seemed lost, however, the fight was won. Not until the full council had decided to adopt the draft, could the Emperor be persuaded to use his power and to save his country; but on the morrow of their vote, the prince, in his quality of autocrat, declared that the principle of "Liberty and land" was the principle of his emancipation act.

On the third of March, 1861 (Feb. 19, O. S.), the emancipation act was signed.

The rustic population then consisted of twenty-two millions of common serfs, three millions of appanage peasants, and twenty-three millions of crown peasants. The first class were enfranchised by that act; and a separate law has since been passed in favor of these crown peasants and appanage peasants, who are now as free in fact as they formerly were in name.

A certain portion of land, varying in different provinces according to soil and climate, was affixed to every "soul;" and government aid was promised to the peasants in buying their homesteads and allotments. The serfs were not slow to take this hint. Down to January 1, 1869, more than half the enfranchised male serfs have taken advantage of this promise; and the debt now owing from the people to the crown (that is, to the bondholders) is an enormous sum.

The Alexandrine principle of "liberty and land" being made the governing rule of the emancipation act, all reasonable fear lest the rustic, in receiving his freedom, might at once go wandering, was taken into account. Nobody knew how far the serf had been broken of those nomadic habits which led to serfage. Every one felt some doubt as to whether he could live with liberty and law; and rules were framed to prevent the return to those social anarchies which had forced the crown to "settle" the country under Boris Godunof and Peter the Great. These restrictive rules were nine in number: (1.) a peasant was not to quit his village unless he gave up, once and forever, his share of the communal lands; (2.) in case of the commune refusing to accept his portion, he was to yield his plot to the general landlord; (3.) he must have met his liabilities, if any, to the Emperor's recruiting officers; (4.) he must have paid up all arrears of local and imperial rates, and also paid in advance such taxes for the current year; (5.) he must have satisfied all private claims, fulfilled all personal contracts, under the authority of his cantonal administration; (6.) he must be free from legal judgment and pursuit; (7.) he must provide for the maintenance of all such members of his family to be left in the commune, as from either youth or age might become a burden to his village; (8.) he must make good any arrears of rent which may be due on his allotment to the lord; (9.) he must produce either a resolution passed by some other commune, admitting him as a member, or a certificate, properly signed, that he has bought the freehold of a plot of land, equal to two allotments, not above ten miles distant from the commune named. These rules—which are provisional only—are found to tie a peasant with enduring strictness to his fields.

The question, whether the serf is so far cured of his Tartar habit that he can live a settled life without being bound to his patch of ground, is still unasked. The answer to that question must come with time, province by province and town by town. Nature is slow, and habit is a growth. Reform must wait on nature, and observe her laws.

As in all such grand reforms, the parties most affected by the change were much dissatisfied at first. The serf had got too much; the lords had kept too much. In many provinces the peasants refused to hear the imperial rescript read in church. They said the priest was keeping them in the dark; for, ruled by the nobles, and playing a false part against the Emperor, he was holding back the real letters of liberation, and reading them papers forged by their lords. Fanatics and impostors took advantage of their discontent to excite sedition, and these fanatics and impostors met with some success in provinces occupied by the Poles and Malo-Russ.

Two of these risings were important. At the village of Bezdna, province of Kazan, one Anton Petrof announced himself as a prophet of God and an ambassador from the Tsar. He told the peasants that they were now free men, and that their good Emperor had given them all the land. Four thousand rustics followed him about; and when General Count Apraxine, overtaking the mob and calling upon them to give up their leader, and disperse under pain of being instantly shot down, the poor fellows cried, "We shall not give him up; we are all for the Tsar." Apraxine gave the word to fire; a hundred men dropped down with bullets in their bodies—fifty-one dead, the others badly hurt. In horror of this butchery, the people cried, "You are firing into Alexander Nicolaivitch himself!" Petrof was taken, tried by court-martial, and shot in the presence of his stupefied friends, who could not understand that a soldier was doing his duty to the crown by firing into masses of unarmed men.

A more singular and serious rising of serfs took place in the rich province of Penza, where a strange personage proclaimed himself the Grand Duke Constantine, brother of Nicolas, once a captive. Affecting radical opinions, the "grand duke" raised a red flag, collected bands of peasants, and alarmed the country far and near. A body of soldiers, sent against them by General Dreniakine, were received with clubs and stones, and forced to run away. Dreniakine marched against the rebels, and in a smart action he dispersed them through the steppe, after killing eight and seriously maiming twenty-six. The "grand duke" was suffered to get away. The country was much excited by the rising, and on Easter Sunday General Dreniakine telegraphed to St. Petersburg his duty to the minister, and asked for power to punish the revolters by martial law. The minister sent him orders to act according to his judgment; and he began to flog and shoot the villagers until order was restored within the limits of his command. The "grand duke" was denounced as one Egortsof, a Milk-Drinker; and Dreniakine soon afterwards spread a report that he was dead.

The agitation was not stilled until the Emperor himself appeared on the scene. On his way to Yalta he convoked a meeting of elders, to whom he addressed a few wise and solacing words: "I have given you all the liberties defined by the statutes; I have given you no liberties save those defined by the statutes." It was the very first time these peasants had heard of their Emperor's will being limited by law.

CHAPTER LII.

FREEDOM.

"WHAT were the first effects of emancipation in your province?" I ask a lady.

"Rather droll," replies the Princess B. "In the morning, the poor fellows could not believe their senses; in the afternoon, they got tipsy; next day, they wanted to be married."

"Doubt—drunkenness—matrimony! Yes, it was rather droll."

"You see, a serf was not suffered to drink whisky and make love as he pleased. It was a wild outburst of liberty; and perhaps the two things brought their own punishments?"

"Not the marrying, surely?"

"Ha! who knows?"

The upper ranks are much divided in opinion as to the true results of emancipation. If the liberal circles of the Winter Palace look on things in the rosiest light, the two extreme parties which stand aside as chorus and critics—the Whites and Reds, Obstructives and Socialists—regard them from two opposite points of view, as in the last degree unsound, unsafe.

When a Russian takes upon himself the office of critic, he is always gloomy, Oriental, and prophetic. He turns his face to the darker side of things; he groans in spirit, and picks up words of woe. If he has to deal as critic with the sins of his own time and country, he prepares his tongue to denounce and his soul to curse; and his self-examination, whether in respect to his private vices or his public failings, is conducted in a dark, reproachful, and inquisitorial spirit.

In one house you fall among the Whites—a charming set of men to meet in drawing-room or club; urbane, accomplished, profligate; owners who never saw their serfs, landlords who never lived on their estates; fine fellows—whether young or old—who spent their lives in roving from St. Petersburg to Paris, and were known by sight in every gaming-house, in every theatre, from the Neva to the Seine. These men will tell you, with an exquisite smile, that Russia has come to the dogs. "Free labor!" they exclaim with scorn, "the country is sinking under these free institutions year by year — sinking in morals, sinking in production, sinking in political strength. A peasant works less, drinks more than ever. While he was a serf he could be flogged into industry, if not into sobriety. Now he is master, he will please himself; and his pleasure is to dawdle in the dram-shop and to slumber on the stove. Not only is he going down himself, but he is pulling every one else down in his wake. The burgher is worse off; the merchant finds nothing to buy and sell. Less land is under plough and spade; the quantity of corn, oats, barley, and maize produced is less than in the good old times. Russia is poorer than she was, financially and physically. Famines have become more frequent; arson is increasing; while the crimes of burglary and murder are keeping pace with the strides of fire and famine. As rich and poor, we are more divided than we were as lords and serfs. The rich used to care for the poor, and the poorer classes lived on the waste of rich men's boards. They had an influence on each other, and always for their mutual good. In this new scheme we are strangers when we are not rivals, competitors when we are not foes. A rustic cares for neither lord nor priest. A landlord who desires to live on his estate must bow and smile, must bend and cringe, in order to keep his own. The rustics rob his farm, they net his lake, they beat his bailiff, they insult his wife. His time is wasted in complaining—now to the police, now to the magistrate, now again to the cantonal chief. All classes are at strife, and the seeds of revolution are broadly sown."

In a second house you fall among the Reds—a far more

dashing and excited set; many of whom have also spent much time in passing from St. Petersburg to Paris, though not with the hope of becoming known to croupiers and ballet-girls; men with pallid brows and sparkling eyes, who make a science of their social whims, and treat the emancipating acts as so many paths to that republic of rustics which they desire to see. "These circulars, reports, and edicts were necessary," they allege, "in order to open men's eyes to the tragic facts. Our miseries were hidden; our princes were so rich, our palaces so splendid, and our troops so numerous, that the world—and even we ourselves—believed the imperial government strong enough to march in any direction, to strike down every foe. The Tsar was so great that no one thought of his serfs; the sun was so brilliant that you could not see the motes. But now that reign of deceit is gone forever, and our wretchedness is exposed to every eye. You say we are free, and prospering in our freedom; but the facts are otherwise; we are neither free nor prosperous. The act of emancipation was a snare. Men fancied they were going to be freed from their lords; but when the day of deliverance came they found themselves taken from a bad master and delivered to a worse. A man who was once a serf became a slave. He had belonged to a neighbor, often to a friend, and now he became a property of the crown. Branded with the Black Eagle, he was fastened to the soil by a stronger chain. A false civilization seized him, held him in her embrace, and made him pass into the fire. What has that civilization done for him? Starved him; stripped him; ruined him. Go into our cities. Look at our burghers; watch how they lie and cheat; hear how they bear false witness; note how they buy with one yard, sell with another yard. Go into our communes. Mark the dull eye and the stupid face of the village lout, who lives alone, like a wild beast, far from his fellows—part of the forest, as a log of wood is part of the forest. Observe how he drinks and shuffles; how he says his prayers, and shirks his duty, and begets his kind, with hardly more thought in his head than a wolf and a bear. This state of things must be swept away. The poor man is the victim of all tyrants, all impostors; the minister cheats him of his freedom, and the landlord of his field; but the hour of revolution is drawing nigh; and people will greet that coming hour with their rallying cry—More liberty and more land!"

A stranger listening to every one, looking into every thing, will see that on the fringe of actual fact there are appearances which might seem to justify, according to the point of view, these opposite and extreme opinions; yet, on massing and balancing his observations of the country as a whole, a stranger must perceive that under emancipation the peasant is better dressed, better lodged, and better fed; that his wife is healthier, his children cleaner, his homestead tidier; that he and his belongings are improved by the gift which changed him from a chattel into a man.

A peasant spends much money, it is true, in drams; but he spends yet more in clothing for his wife. He builds his cabin of better wood, and in the eastern provinces, if not in all, you find improvements in the walls and roof. He paints the logs, and fills up cracks with plaster, where he formerly left them bare and stuffed with moss. He sends his boys to school, and goes himself more frequently to church. If he exports less corn and fur to other countries, it is because, being richer, he can now afford to eat white bread and wear a cat-skin cap.

The burgher class and the merchant class have been equally benefited by the change. A good many peasants have become burghers, and a good many burghers merchants. All the domestic and useful trades have been quickened into life. More shoes are worn, more carts are wanted, more cabins are built. Hats, coats, and cloaks are in higher demand; the bakeries and breweries find more to do; the teacher gets more pupils, and the banker has more customers on his books.

This movement runs along the line; for in the wake of emancipation every other liberty and right is following fast. Five years ago (1864), the Emperor called into existence two local parliaments in every province; a district assembly and a provincial assembly: in which every class, from prince to peasant, was to have his voice. The district assembly is elected by classes; nobles, clergy, merchants, husbandmen; each apart, and free; the provincial assembly consists of delegates from the several district assemblies. The district assembly settles all questions as to roads and bridges; the provincial assembly looks to building prisons, draining pools, damming rivers, and the like. The peasant interest is strong in the district assembly, the landlord interest in the provincial assembly; and they are equally useful as schools of freedom, eloquence, and public spirit. On these local boards, the cleverest men in every province are being trained for civic, and, if need be, parliamentary life.

On every side, an observer notes with pleasure a tendency of the villagers to move upon the towns and enter into the higher activities of civic life. This tendency is carrying them back beyond the Tartar times into the better days of Novgorod and Pskoff.

In his commune, a peasant may hope to pass through the dreary existence led by his mule and ox; his thoughts given up to his cabbage-soup, his buckwheat porridge, his loaf of black bread, and his darling dram. If he acquires in his village some patriarchal virtues—love of home, respect for age, delight in tales and songs, and preference for oral over written law—he also learns, without knowing why, to think and feel like a Bedouin in his tent, and a Kirghiz on his steppe. A rustic is nearly always humming old tunes. Whether you see him felling his pine, unloading his team, or sitting at his door, he is nearly always singing the same old dirge of love or war. When he breaks into a brisker stave, it is always into a song of revenge and hate. Bandits are his heroes; and the staid young fellow who dares not whisper to his partner in a dance, will roar out such a riotous squall:

"I'll toil in the fields no more!
For what can I gain by the spade?
My hands are empty, my heart is sore;
A knife! my friend's in the forest glade!"

Another youth may sing:

"I'll rob the merchant at his stall,
I'll slay the noble in his hall;
With girls and whisky I'll have my fling,
And the world will honor me like a king."

One of the most popular of these robber songs has a chorus running thus, addressed in menace to the noble and the rich:

"We have come to drink your wine,
We have come to steal your gold,
We have come to kiss your wives!
Ha! ha!"

This reckless sense of right and wrong is due to that serfage under which the peasants groaned for two hundred and sixty years. Serfage made men indifferent to life and death. The crimes of serfage have scarcely any parallel, except among savage tribes; and the liberty which some of the freed peasants enjoyed the most was the liberty of revenge.

Ivan Gorski was living in Tamboff, in very close friendship with a family of seven persons, when he conceived a grudge against them on some unknown ground, obtained a gun, and asked his friends to let him practice firing in their yard. They let him put up his target, and blaze away till he became a very fair shot, and people got used to the noise of his gun. When these two points were gained, he took off every member of the house. He could not tell the reason of his crime.

Daria Sokolof was employed as nurse in a family, and when the child grew up went back to her village, parting from her master and mistress on the best of terms. Some years passed by. On going into the town to sell her fruit and herbs, and finding a bad market, she went to her old home and asked for a lodging for the night. Her master was ill, and her mistress put her to bed. At two in the morning she got up, seized an Italian iron, crept to her master's room, and beat his brains out; then to her mistress's room, and killed her also. Afterwards she went into the servant's room, and murdered her; into the boy's room, and murdered him. A pet dog lay on the lad's coverlet, and she smashed its skull. She took a little money—not much; went home, and slept till daylight. No one suspected her, for no living creature knew she had been to the house. Twelve months elapsed before a clue was found; but as no witness of the crime was left, she could only be condemned to a dozen years in the Siberian mines. Her case excited much remark, and persons are even now petitioning the ministry of justice to let her off!

It is only by living in a wider field, by acting for himself, by gaining a higher knowledge of men and things, that the peasant can escape from the bad traditions and morbid sentiments of his former life. It will be an immense advantage for the empire of villages to become. as other nations are, an empire of both villages and towns.

CHAPTER LIII.

TSEK AND ARTEL.

THE obstacles which lie in the way of a peasant wishing to become a townsman are very great. After he has freed himself from his obligations to the commune and the crown, and arrived at the gates of Moscow, with his papers in perfect order, how is a rustic to live in that great city? By getting work. That would be the only trouble of a French paysan or an English plough-boy. In Russia it is different. The towns are not open and unwalled, so that men may come and go as they list. They are strongholds; held, in each case, by an army, in the ranks of which every man has his appointed place.

No man—not of noble birth—can live the burgher life in Moscow, save by gaining a place in one of the recognized orders of society—in a tsek, a guild, or a chin.

A tsek is an association of craftsmen and petty traders, such as the tailoring tsek, the cooking tsek, and the peddling tsek; the members of which pay a small sum of money, elect their own elders, and manage their own affairs. The elder of a tsek gives to each member a printed form, which must be countersigned by the police not less than once a year. A guild is a higher kind of tsek, the members of which pay a tax to the state for the privilege of buying and selling, and for immunity from serving in the ranks. A chin is a grade in the public service, parted somewhat sharply into fourteen stages—from that of a certified collegian up to that of an acting privy-councillor. A peasant might enter a guild if he could pay the tax; but the impost is heavy, even for the lowest guild; and a man who comes into Moscow in search of work must seek a place in some cheap and humble tsek. He need not follow the calling of his tsek—a clerk may belong to a shoemaker's tsek, and a gentleman's servant to a hawker's tsek. But in one or other of these societies a peasant must get his name inscribed and his papers signed, under penalty of being seized by the police and hustled into the ranks.

Every year he must go in person to the Office of Addresses, a vast establishment on the Tverskoi Boulevard, where the name, residence, and occupation of every man and woman living in this great city is entered on the public books. At this Office of Addresses he has to leave his regular papers, taking a receipt which serves him as a passport for a week; in the mean while the police examine his papers, verify the elder's signature, and mark them afresh with an official stamp. Every time he changes his lodging he must go in person to the Office of Addresses and record the change. A tax of three or four shillings a year is levied on his papers by the police, half of which money goes to the crown and half to the provincial hospitals. In case of poverty and sickness, his inscription in a tsek entitles a man to be received into a government hospital should there be room for him in any of the wards.

To lose his papers is a calamity for the rustic hardly less serious than to lose his leg. Without his papers he is an outlaw at the mercy of every one who hates him. He must go back at once to his village; if he has been lucky enough to get his name on the books of a tsek, he must find the elder, prove his loss, procure fresh evidence of his identity, and get this evidence countersigned by the police. Yet when a rustic comes to Moscow nothing is more likely than that his passport will be stolen. In China-town there is a rag fair, called the Hustling Market, where cheap-jacks sell every sort of ware—old sheep-skins, rusty locks and keys, felt boots (third wear), and span-new saints in brass and tin. This market is a hiring-place for servants; and lads who have no friends in Moscow flock to this market in search of work. A fellow walks up to the rustic with a town-bred air: "You want a place? Very well; let me see your passport." Taking his papers from his boot—a peasant always puts his purse and papers in his boot—he offers them gladly to the man, who dodges through the crowd in a moment, while the rustic is gaping at him with open mouth. A thief knows where he can sell these papers, just as he could sell a stolen watch.

Having got his name inscribed in a tsek, his passport signed by his elder and countersigned by the police, the peasant, now become a burgher, looks about him for an artel, which, if he have money enough, he proceeds to join.

An artel is an association of workmen following the same craft, and organized on certain lines, with the principles of which they are made familiar in their village life. An artel is a commune carried from the country into the town. The members of an artel join together for their mutual benefit and insurance. They elect an elder, and confide to him the management of their concerns. They agree to work in common at their craft, to have no private interests, to throw their earnings into a single fund, and, after paying the very light cost of their association, to divide the sum total into equal shares. In practical effect, the artel is a finer form of communism than the commune itself. In the village commune they only divide the land; in the city artel they divide the produce.

The origin of artels is involved in mist. Some writers of the Panslavonic school profess to find traces of such an association in the tenth century; but the only proof adduced is the existence of a rule making towns and villages responsible, in cases of murder, for the fines inflicted on the criminal—a rule which these writers would find in the Frankish, Saxon, and other codes. The safer view appears to be, that the artel came from Asia. No one knows the origin of this term artel—it seems to be a Tartar word, and it is nowhere found in use until the reign of those tartarized Grand Dukes of Moscow, Ivan the Third and Ivan the Fourth. In fact, the artel seems to have been planted in Russia with the commune and the serf.

The first artel of which we have any notice was a gang of thieves, who roamed about the country taking what they liked with a rude hand—inviting themselves to weddings and merry-makings, where they not only ate and drank as they pleased, but carried away the wine, the victuals, and the plate. These freebooters elected a chief, whom they called their ataman. They were bound to stand by each other in weal and woe. No rogue could go where he pleased—no thief could plunder on his personal account. The spoil was thrown into a common heap, from which every member of the artel got an equal share.

These bandit artels must have been strong and prosperous, since the principle of their association passed with little or no change into ordinary city life and trade. The burghers kept the word artel; they translated ataman into elder (starost); and in every minor detail they copied their original, rule by rule. These early artels had very few articles of association; and the principal were: that the members formed one body, bound to stand by each other; that they were to be governed by a chief, elected by general suffrage; that every man was appointed to his post by the artel; that a member could not refuse to do the thing required of him; that no one should be suffered to drink, swear, game, and quarrel; that every one should bear himself towards his comrade like a brother; that no present should be received, unless it were shared by each; that a member could not name a man to serve in his stead, except with the consent of all. In after times these simple rules were supplemented by provisions for restoring to the member's heirs the value of his rights in the common fund. In case of death, these additional rules provided that the subscriber's share should go to his son, if he had a son; if not, to his next of kin, as any other property would descend. So far the estate was held to be a joint concern as regards the question of use, and a series of personal properties as regards the actual ownership. All these city artels took the motto of "Honesty and truth."

An artel, then, was, in its origin, no other than an association of craftsmen for their mutual support against the miseries of city life, just as the commune was an association of laborers for their mutual support against the miseries of country life. Each sprang, in its turn, from a sense of the weakness of individual men in struggling with the hard necessities of time and place. One body sought protection in numbers and mutual help against occasional lack of employment; the other against occasional attacks from wolves and bears, and against the annual floods of rain and drifts of snow. An artel was a republic like a commune; with a right of meeting, a right of election, a right of fine and punishment. No one interfered with the members, save in a general way. They made their own rules, obeyed their own chiefs, and were in every sense a state within the state. Yet these societies lived and throve, because they proved, on trial, to be as beneficial to the upper as they were to the lower class; an artel offering advantages to employers of labor like those offered by a commune to the ministers of finance and war.

If an English banker wants a clerk, he must go into the open market and find a servant, whom he has to hire on the strength of his character as certified from his latest place. He takes him on trial, subject to the chance of his proving an honest man. If a Russian banker wants a clerk, he sends for the elder of an artel, looks at his list, and hires his servant from the society, in that society's name. He seeks no character, takes no guaranty. The artel is responsible for the clerk, and the banker trusts him in perfect confidence to the full extent of the artel fund. If the clerk should prove to be a rogue—a thing which sometimes happens—the banker calls in the elder, certifies the fact, and gets his money paid back at once.

These things may happen, yet they are not common. Petty thieving is the vice of every Eastern race, and Russians of the lower class are not exceptions to the rule; yet, in the artels, it is certain that this tendency to pick and steal is greatly curbed, if not wholly suppressed. "Honesty and truth," from being a phrase on the tongue, may come at length to be a habit of the mind. A decent life is strenuously enjoined, and no member is allowed to drink and game; thus many of the vices which lead to theft are held in check by the public opinion of his circle; yet the temptation sometimes grows too strong, and a confidential clerk decamps with his employer's box. Another merit of these artels then comes out.

A robbery has taken place in the bank, a clerk is missing, and the banker feels assured that the money and the man are gone together. Notice is sent to the police; but Moscow is a very big city; and Rebrof, clever as he may be in catching thieves, has no instant means of following a man who has just committed in a bank parlor his virgin crime. But the elder knows his man, and the members, who will have to suffer for his fault, are well acquainted with his haunts. Setting their eyes and tongues at work, they follow him with the energy of a pack of wolves on a trail of blood, never slackening in their race until they hunt him down and yield him up to trial, judgment, and the mines.

Bankers like Baron Stieglitz, of St. Petersburg, merchants like Mazourin and Alexief, in Moscow, have artels of their own, founded in the first instance for their own work-people. On entering an artel, a man pays a considerable sum of money—the average is a thousand rubles, one hundred and fifty pounds—though he need not always pay the whole sum down at once. That payment is the good-will; what is called the buying in. He goes to work wherever the artel may appoint him. He gets no separate wages; for the payment is made to the elder for one and all. So far this is share and share alike. But then the old rule about receiving presents has been much relaxed of late; and a good servant often receives from his master more than he receives as his share from the general fund. This innovation, it is true, destroys the old character of the artel as a society for the mutual assurance of strong and weak; but in the progress of free thought and action it is a revolution not to be withstood, and hardly to be gainsaid.

One day, when dining with a Swede, a banker in St. Petersburg, I was struck by the quick eyes and ready hands of my host's butler, and, on my dropping a word in his praise, my host broke out, "Ha, that fellow is a golden man; he is my butler, valet, clerk, cashier, and master of the household—all in one."

"Is he a peasant?"

"Yes; a peasant from the South. I get him for nothing—for the price of a common lout."

"He comes to you from an artel?"

"Yes, he and some dozen more; he is worth the other twelve."

"You pay the same wage for each and all?"

"To the artel, so; but, hist! We make up for extra care and service by a thumping New-Year's gift."

"Then the artel is beginning to fail of its original purpose—that of securing to the weak, the idle, and the stupid men as high a wage as it gave to the strong, the enterprising, and the able men?"

"Can you suppose that clever and pushing fellows will work like horses, all for nothing, now that they are free? A serf might do so; he lived in terror of the stick; he had no notion of his rights; and he had worked for others all his life. An artel is a useful thing, and no one (least of all a foreign banker) wishes to see the institution fail; but it must go with the times. If it can not find the means of drawing the best men into it by paying them fairly for what they do, it will pass away."

An artel is a vast convenience to the foreign masters, whatever it may be to the native men.

CHAPTER LIV.

MASTERS AND MEN.

NOT in one town, in one province only, but in every town, we find two nations living in presence of each other; just as we find them in Finland and Livonia; an upper race and a lower; a foreign race and a native; and in nearly all these towns and provinces the foreign race are the masters, the native race their men.

On the open plains and in the forest lands this division into masters and men is not so strongly marked as in the towns. Here and there we find a stranger in possession of the soil; but the rule is not so; and while the towns may be said to belong in a rough way to the German, the country, as a whole, is the property of the Russ. The people may be parted into these two classes; not in commercial things only, but in professional study and in official life. The trade, the art, the science, and the power of Russia have all been lodged by law in the stranger's hand—the Russ being made an underling, even when he was not made a serf; and it is only in our own time—since the close of the Crimean war—that the crown has come, as it were, to the help of nature in recovering Russia for the Russ.

The dynasty is foreign. The fact is too common to excite remark; the first and most liberal countries in the world, so far as they have kings at all, being governed by princes of alien blood. In London the dynasty is Hanoverian; in Berlin it is Swabian; in Paris it is Corsican; in Vienna it is Swiss; in Florence it is Savoyard; in Copenhagen it is Holstein; in Stockholm it is French; in Brussels it is Cobourg; at the Hague it is Rhenish; in Lisbon it is Kohary; in Athens it is Danish; in Rio it is Portuguese. No bad moral would be, therefore, drawn from the fact of a Gottorp reigning on the Neva and the Moskva, were it not a fact that the Russian peasant had some reason to regard his prince as being not less foreign in spirit than he was in blood. The two princes who are best known to him—Ivan the Terrible and Peter the Great—announced, in season and out of season, that they were not Russ. "Take care of the weight," said Ivan to an English artist, giving him some bars of gold to be worked into plate, "for the Russians are all thieves." The artist smiled. "Why are you laughing?" asked the Tsar. "I was thinking that, when you called the Russians thieves, your Majesty forgot that you were Russ yourself." "Pooh!" replied the Tsar, "I am a German, not a Russ." Peter was loud in his scorn of every thing Muscovite. He spoke the German tongue; he wore the German garb. He shaved his beard and trimmed his hair in the German style. He built a German city, which he made his capital and his home, and he called that city by a German name. He loved to smoke his German pipe, and to quicken his brain with German beer. To him the new empire which he meant to found was a German empire, with ports like Hamburg, cities like Frankfort and Berlin; and he thought little more of his faithful Russ than as a horde of savages whom it had become his duty to improve into the likeness of Dutch and German boors.

To the imperial mind, itself foreign, the stranger has always been a type of order, peace, and progress; while the native has been a type of waste, disorder, and stagnation. Hence favors without end have been heaped on Germans by the reigning house, while Russians have been left to feel the presence of their Government chiefly in the tax-collector and the sergeant of police. This difference has become a subject for proverbs and jokes. When the Emperor asked a man who had done him service how he would like to be remembered in return, he said: "If your Majesty will only make me a German, every thing else will come in time."

Ministers, ambassadors, chamberlains, have almost all been German; and when a Russian has been employed in a great command, it has been rather in war than in the more delicate affairs of state. The German, as a rule, is better taught and trained than the Russian; knowing arts and sciences, to which the Russian is supposed to be a stranger, now and forever, as if learning were a thing beyond his reach. Peter made a law by which certain arts and crafts were to remain forever in German hands. A Russian could not be a druggist, lest he should poison his neighbor; nor a chimney-sweep, lest he should set his shed on fire.

Such laws have been repealed by edicts; yet many remain in force, in virtue of a wider power than that of minister and prince. No Russian would take his dose of salts, his camomile pill, from the hands of his brother Russ. He has no confidence in native skill and care. A Russ may be a good physician, being quick, alert, and sympathetic; yet no amount of training seems to fit him for the delicate office of mixing drugs. He likes to lash out, and can not curb his fury to the minute accuracy of an eye-glass and a pair of scales. A few grains, more or less, in a potion are to him nothing at all. In Moscow, where the Panslavonic hope is strong, I heard of more than one case in which the desire to deal at a native shop had sent the patriot to an untimely grave.

"You can not teach a Russian girl," said a lady, who was speaking to me about her servants. "That girl, now, is a good sort of creature in her way; she never tires of work, never utters a complaint; she goes to mass on Saints'-days and Sundays; and she would rather die of hunger than taste eggs and milk in Lent. But I can not persuade her to wash a sheet, to sweep a room, and to rock a cradle in my English way. If I show her how to do it, she says, with a pensive look, that her people do things thus and thus; and if I insist on having my own way in my own house, she will submit to force under a sort of protest, and will then run home to tell her parents and her pope that her English lady is possessed by an evil spirit."

The strangers who hold so many offices of trust in the

country, and who form its intellectual aristocracy, are not considered in Berlin as of pure Germanic stock. They come from the Baltic provinces—from Livonia and Lithuania; but they trace their houses, not to the Letts and Wends of those regions, but to the old Teutonic knights. There can be no mistake about their energy and power.

Long before the days of Peter the Great they had a footing in the land; under Peter they became its masters; and ever since his reign they have been striving to subdue and civilize the people as their ancestors in Ost and West Preussen civilized the ancient Letts and Finns.

No love is lost between these strangers and natives, masters and men. The two races have nothing in common; neither blood, nor speech, nor faith. They differ like West and East. A German cuts his hair short, and trims his beard and mustache. He wears a hat and shoes, and wraps his limbs in soft, warm cloth. He strips himself at night, and prefers to sleep in a bed to frying his body on a stove. He washes himself once a day. He never drinks whisky, and he loves sour-krout. A German believes in science, a Russian believes in fate. One looks for his guide to experience, while the other is turning to his invisible powers. If a German child falls sick, his father sends for a doctor; if a Russian child falls sick, his father kneels to his saint.

In the North country, where wolves abound, a foreigner brings in his lambs at night; but the native says, a lamb is either born to be devoured by wolves or not, and any attempt to cross his fate is flying in the face of heaven. A German is a man of ideas and methods. He believes in details. From his wide experience of the world he knows that one man can make carts, while a second can write poems, and a third can drill troops. He loves to see things in order, and his business going on with the smoothness of a machine. He rises early, and goes to bed late. With a pipe in his mouth, a glass of beer at his side, a pair of spectacles on his nose, he can toil for sixteen hours a day, nor fancy that the labor is beyond his strength. He seldom faints at his desk, and he never forgets the respect which may be due to his chief. In offices of trust he is the soul of probity and intelligence. It is a rare thing, even in Russia, for a German to be bought with money; and his own strict dealing makes him hard with the wretch whom he has reason to suspect of yielding to a bribe. In the higher reaches cf character he is still more of a puzzle to his men. With all his love of order and routine, he is a dreamer and an idealist; and on the moral side of his nature he is capable of a tenderness, a chivalry, an enthusiasm, of which the Russian finds no traces in himself.

A Russ, on the other side, is a man of facts and of illusions; but his facts are in the region of his ideas, while his illusions rest in the region of his habits. It has been said, in irony, of course, that a Russian never dreams—except when he is wide awake!

Let us go into a Russian work-shop and a German work-shop; two flax-mills, say, at one of the great river towns.

In the first we find the master and his men of one race, with habits of life and thought essentially the same. They dine at the same table, eat the same kind of food. They wear the same long hair and beards, and dress in the same caftan and boots; they play the same games of draughts and whist; they drink the same whisky and quass; they kneel at the same village shrine; they kiss the same cross; and they confess their sins to a common priest. If one gets tipsy on Sunday night, the other is likely to have a fellow-feeling for his fault. If the master strikes the man, it is an affair between the two. The man either bears the blow with patience or returns it with the nearest cudgel. Of this family quarrel the magistrate never hears.

In the second we find a more perfect industrial order, and a master with a shaven chin. This master, though he may be kind and just, is foreign in custom and severe in drill. To him his craft is first and his workmen next. He insists on regular hours, on work that knows no pause. He keeps the men to their tasks; allows no Monday loss on account of Sunday drink; and sets his face against the singing of those brigand songs in which the Russian delights to spend his time. If his men are absent, he stops their wages—not wishing them to make up by night for what they waste by day. In case of need, he hauls them up before the nearest judge.

The races stand apart. A hundred German colonies exist on Russian soil; old colonies, new colonies, farming colonies, religious colonies. Every thing about these foreign villages is clean and bright. The roads are well kept, the cabins well built, the gardens well trimmed. The carts are better made, the teams are better groomed, the harvests are better housed than among the natives; yet no perceptible influence flows from the German colony into the Russian commune; and a hamlet lying a league from such a settlement as Strelna or Sarepta is not unlikely to be worse for the example of its smiling face.

The natives see their master in an odious light. They look on his clean face as that of a girl, and express the utmost contempt for his pipe of tobacco, his pair of spectacles, and his pot of beer. Whisky, they say, is the drink for men. Worse than all else, they regard him as a heretic, to whom Heaven may have given (as Arabs say) the power of the stick, but who is not the less disowned by the Church and cast out from God.

CHAPTER LV.

THE BIBLE.

A LEARNED father of the ancient rite made some remarks to me on the Bible in Russia, which live in my mind as parts of the picture of this great country.

I knew that our Bible Society have a branch in Petersburg, and that copies of the New Testament and the Psalms have been scattered, through their agency, from the White Sea to the Black; but, being well aware that the right to found that branch of our Society in Russia was originally urged by men of the world in London upon men of the same class in St. Petersburg, and that the ministers of Alexander the First gave their consent in a time of war, when they wanted English help in men and money against the French, I supposed that the purposes in view had been political, and that this heavenly seed was cast into ungrateful soil. I had no conception of the good which our Society has been doing in silence for so many years.

"The Scriptures which came to us from England," said

this priest, "have been the mainstay, not of our religion only, but of our national life."

"Then they have been much read?"

"In thousands, in ten thousands of pious homes. The true Russian likes his Bible—yes, even better than his dram—for the Bible tells him of a world beyond his daily field of toil, a world of angels and of spirits, in which he believes with a nearer faith than he puts in the wood and water about his feet. In every second house of Great Russia—the true, old Russia, in which we speak the same language and have the same God—you will find a copy of the Bible, and men who have the promise in their hearts."

In my journey through the country I find this true, though not so much in the letter as in the spirit. Except in New England and in Scotland, no people in the world, so far as they can read at all, are greater Bible-readers than the Russians.

In thinking of Russia we forget the time when she was free, even as she is now again growing free, and take scant heed of the fact that she possessed a popular version of Scripture, used in all her churches and chapels, long before such a treasure was obtained by England, Germany, and France.

"Love for the Bible and love for Russia," said the priest, "go with us hand in hand, as the Tsar in his palace and the monk in his convent know. A patriotic government gives us the Bible, a monastic government takes it away."

"What do you mean by a patriotic government and a monastic government, when speaking of the Bible?"

"By a patriotic government, that of Alexander the First and Alexander the Second; by a monastic government, that of Nicolas. The first Alexander gave us the Bible; Nicolas took it away; the second Alexander gave it us again. The first Alexander was a prince of gentle ways and simple thoughts—a mystic, as men of worldly training call a man who lives with God. Like all true Russians, he had a deep and quick perception of the presence of things unseen. In the midst of his earthly troubles—and they were great—he turned into himself. He was a Bible-reader. In the Holy Word he found that peace which the world could neither give nor take away; and what he found for himself he set his heart on sharing with his children everywhere. Consulting Prince Golitsin, then his minister of public worship, he found that pious and noble man—Golitsin was a Russian—of his mind. They read the Book together, and, seeing that it was good for them, they sent for Stanislaus, archbishop of Mohiloff, and asked him why people should not read the Bible, each man for himself, and in his native tongue? Up to that time our sacred books were printed only in Bulgaric; a Slavonic speech which people used to understand; but which is now an unknown dialect, even to the popes who drone it every day from the altar steps. Two English doctors—the good Patterson and the good Pinkerton—brought us the New Testament, printed in the Russian tongue; and, by help of the Tsar and his council, scattered the copies into every province and every town, from the frontiers of Poland to those of China. I am an old man now; but my veins still throb with the fervor of that day when we first received, in our native speech, the word that was to bring us eternal life. The books were instantly bought up and read; friends lent them to each other; and family meetings were held, in which the Promise was read aloud. The popes explained the text; the elders gave out chapter and verse. Even in parties which met to drink whisky and play cards, some neighbor would produce his Bible, when the company gave up their games to listen while an aged man read out the story of the passion and the cross. That story spoke to the Russian heart; for the Russ, when left alone, has something of the Galilean in his nature—a something soft and feminine, almost sacrificial; helping him to feel, with a force which he could never reach by reasoning, the patient beauty of his Redeemer's life and death.

"And what were the effects of this Bible-reading?"

"Who can tell! You plant the acorn, your descendants sit beneath the oak. One thing it did for us, which we could never have done without its help—the Bible drove the Jesuits from our midst—and if we had it now in every house it would drive away these monks."

The story of the battle of the Bible Society and the Order of Jesus may be read in Joly, and in other writers. When that Order was suppressed in Rome, and the Fathers were banished from every Catholic state in Europe, a remnant was received into Russia by the insane Emperor Paul, who took them into his favor in the hope of vexing the Roman Court, and of making them useful agents in his Catholic provinces. Well they repaid him for the shelter given—not only in the Polish cities, but in the privatest recesses of his home. Father Gruber is said to have been familiar with every secret of the palace under Paul. These exiles were a band of outlaws, living in defiance of their spiritual chief and of their temporal prince; but while they clung with unslackening grasp to the great traditions of their Society, they sought, by visible service to mankind, the means of overcoming the hostility of popes and kings. No honest writer will deny that they were useful to the Russians in a secular sense, whatever trouble they may have caused them in a religious sense. They brought into this country the light of science and the love of art then flourishing in the West; and the colleges which they opened for the education of youth were far in advance of the native schools. They built their schools at Moscow, Riga, Petersburg, Odessa, on the banks of the Volga, on the shores of the Caspian Sea. They sought to be useful in a thousand ways; in the foreign colony, at the military station, in the city prison, at the Siberian mine. They went out as doctors and as teachers. They followed the army into Astrakhan, and toiled among the Kozaks of the Don; but while they labored to do good, they labored in a foreign and offensive spirit. To the Russ people they were strangers and enemies; subjects of a foreign prince, and members of a hostile church. Some ladies of the court went over to their rite; a youth of high family followed these court ladies; then the clergy took alarm, and raised their voices against the strangers. What offended the Russians most of all was the assumption by these Jesuits of the name of missionaries, as though the people were a savage horde not yet reclaimed to God and His Holy Church. Unhappily for the fathers, this title was expressly forbidden to the Catholic clergy by Russian law, and this assumption was an act of disobedience which left them at the mercy of the crown.

But while the Emperor Paul was kind to them, these acts

were passed in silence, and Alexander seemed unlikely to withdraw his favor from his father's friends. The issue of a New Testament in the native speech brought on the conflict and insured their fate.

Following the traditions of their Order, the Jesuits heard the proposal to print the Bible in the Russian tongue, so that every man should read it for himself, with fear, and armed themselves to oppose the scheme. They spoke, they wrote, they preached against it. Calling it an error, they showed how much it was disliked in Rome. They said it was an English invasion of the country; and they stirred up the popes to attack it; saying it would be the ruin, not only of the Roman clergy, but of the Greek.

Alexander's eyes were opened to the character of his guests. The Bible was a comfort to himself, and why should others be refused the blessing he had found? Who were these men, that they should prevent his people reading the Word of Life?

A dangerous question for the Tsar to ask; for Prince Golitsin was close at hand with his reply. The worst day's work the Jesuits had ever done was to disturb this prince's family by converting his nephew to the Roman Church. Golitsin called it seduction; and seduction from the national faith is a public crime. When, therefore, Alexander came to ask who these men were, Golitsin answered that they were teachers of false doctrine; disturbers of the public peace; men who were banished by their sovereigns; a body disbanded by their popes. And then, in spite of their good deeds, they were sent away—first from Moscow and Petersburg, afterwards from every city of the empire. Their expulsion was one of the most popular acts of a long and glorious reign.

The Jesuit writers lay the blame of their expulsion on the Bible Societies.

From other sources I learn that the New Testament was free until Alexander's death, and that the copies found their way into every city and village of the land. With the death of Alexander the First came a change. After the conspiracy of 1825, the new Emperor listened to his black clergy, and the Bible was placed under close arrest.

The Russian Bible Society was called a Russian parliament. All parties in the state were represented on the board of management; Orthodox bishops sitting next to Old Believers, and Old Believers next to Dissenting priests. The Bible, in which they all believed, was a common ground, on which they could meet and exchange the words of peace. But Nicolas, ruling by the sword, had no desire to see these boards pursuing their active and independent course; and his monks had little trouble in persuading him to replace the Bible by an official Book of Saints.

CHAPTER LVI.

PARISH PRIESTS.

In this empire of villages there is a force of six hundred and ten thousand parish priests (a little more or less); each parish priest the centre of a circle, who regard him not only as a man of God, ordained to bless in His holy name, but as a father to advise them in weal and woe. These priests are not only popular, but in country villages they are themselves the people.

Father Peter, the village pope, is a countryman like the members of his flock. In his youth, he must have been at school and college—a smart lad, perhaps, alert of tongue and learned in decrees and canons; but he has long since sobered down into the dull and patient priest you see. In speech, in gait, in dress, he is exactly like the peasants in yon dram-shop and yon field. His cabin is built of logs; his wife grows girkins, which she carries in a creel to the nearest town for sale; and the reverend gentleman puts his right hand on the plough. He does not preach and teach; for he has little to say, and not a word that any of his neighbors would care to hear. Knowing that his lot in life is fixed, he has no inducement to refresh his mind with learning, and to burnish up his oratorical arms. The world slips past him, unperceived; and, with his grip on the peasant's spade, he sinks insensibly into the peasant's class. Yet Peter's life, though it may be hard and poor, is not without lines of natural grace, the more affecting from the homeliness of every thing around. His cabin is very clean; some flower-pots stand on his window-sill; a heap of books loads his presses; and his walls are picturesque with pictures of chapel and saint. A pale and comely wife is sitting near his door, knitting her children's hose, and watching the urchins at their play. Those boys are singing beneath a tree—singing with soft, sad faces one of their ritual psalms. A calm and tender influence flows from his house into the neighboring sheds. The dullest hind in the hamlet sees that the pastor's little ones are kept in order, and that his cabin is the pattern of a tidy village hut.

The pastor has his patch of land to till, his bit of garden ground to tend; but on every side you find the homely folk about him helping in his labor, each peasant in his turn, so as to make his duties light. Presents of many kinds are made to him—ducklings, fish, cucumbers, even shoes and wraps, as well as angel-day offerings and benediction-fees. A priest is so great a man in a village, that, even when he is a tipsy, idle fellow, he is treated by his parishioners with a child-like duty and respect. The pastor can do much to help his flock, not only in their spiritual wants, but in their secular affairs. In any quarrel with the police, it is of great importance to a peasant that his priest should take his part; and the pastor commonly takes his neighbor's part, not only because he himself is poor, and knows the man, but because he hates all public officers and suspects all men in power.

A great day for the parish priest is that on which a child is born in his commune.

When Dimitri (the peasant living in yon big house is called Dimitri) hears that a son has been given to him, he runs for his priest, and Father Peter comes in stately haste to welcome and bless the little one. Finding the baby swinging in his liulka, Father Peter puts on his cope, unclasps his book, turns his face to the holy icons, and begins his prayer. "Lord God," he cries, "we beg Thee to send down the light of Thy face upon this child, Thy servant Constantine; and be he signed with the cross of Thy only-begotten Son. Amen."

In two or three weeks the christening of little Constantine, "servant of God," takes place. When the rite is performed at home, the house has to be turned, as it were, into a chapel for the nonce; no difficult thing, as parlor, kitchen, hall, saloon, are decorated with the Son, the Mother, and the patron saint. A room is set apart for the office; a rug is spread before the sacred pictures; and on a table are laid three candles, a fine napkin, and a glass of water from the well. A silver-gilt basin is sent from the village church. Attended by his reader and his deacon, each carrying a bundle, Father Peter walks to the house, bearing a cross and singing a psalm, while the censer is swung before him in the street.

The rite then given is long and solemn, the ceremony consisting of many parts. First comes the act of driving out the fiends; when the pope, not yet in his perfect robes, takes up the baby, breathes on his face, crosses him three times—on temple, breast, and lips—and exorcises the devil and all his imps; ending with the words, "May every evil and unclean spirit that has taken up his abode in this infant's heart depart from hence!" Then comes the act of renouncing the Evil One and all his works, in the baby's name. "Dost thou renounce the devil?" asks the pope; on which the sponsors turn, with the child, towards the setting sun, that land of shadows in which the Prince of Darkness is supposed to dwell, and answer, each, "I have renounced him." "Spit on him!" cries the pope, who jets his own saliva into a corner, as though the devil were present in the room. The sponsors spit in turn. Here follows the confession of faith; the sponsors being asked whether they believe that Christ is King and God; and, on answering that they believe in Him as King and God, are told to fall down and worship Him as such. Next comes the rite of baptism, when the pope puts on his brightest robe, the parents are sent away, and the child is left to his godfathers and godmothers. A taper is put into each sponsor's hand; the candles near the font are lighted; incense is flung about; the reader and deacon sing; and the pope inaudibly recites a prayer. The water is blessed by the pope dipping his right hand into it three times, by breathing on it, praying over it, and signing it with the cross. He uses for that purpose a feather which has been dipped into holy oil. The child is anointed five times; first on the forehead, with this phrase: "Constantine, the servant of God, is anointed with the oil of gladness;" next on the chest, to heal his soul and body; then on the two ears, to quicken his sense of the Word; afterwards on his hands and feet, to do God's will and walk in his way. Seized by the pope, the child is now plunged into the font three times by rapid dips, the priest repeating at each dip, "Constantine, the servant of God, is now baptized in the name of the Father, and of the Son, and of the Holy Ghost." If the young Christian is not drowned in the font (as sometimes happens), he is clad in white, he receives his name, his guardian angel, and his cross.

The rite of baptism ended, the sacrament of unction opens. This sacrament, called the seal of the gift of the Holy Spirit, is said to represent the "laying on of hands" in the early Christian Church. With a small feather, dipped once more into the sacred oil, the pope again touches the baby's forehead, chest, lips, hands, and feet, saying each time, "The seal of the gift of the Holy Spirit;" on which reader, deacon, and priest all break into chants of hallelujah! After unction comes the act of sacrifice; when the child, who has nothing else of his own to give, offers up the *hair of his head*. Taking a pair of shears, the pope snips off the down in four places from the baby's head, making a cross, and saying, as he cuts each piece away, "Constantine, the servant of God, is shorn in Thy name." The hair is thrown into the font; more litany is sung; and the child is at length given back, fatigued and sleepy, into his mother's arms.

Ten or twelve days later, Constantine must be taken by his mother to mass, and receive the sacrament, as a sign of his visible acceptance in the Church. A nurse walks up the steps before the royal gates; and when the deacon comes forward with the cup in his hand, she goes to meet him. He takes a small spoon and puts a drop of wine into the infant's mouth, saying, "Constantine, the servant of God, communicates in the name of the Father, Son, and Holy Ghost." Later in the service, the pope himself takes up the child, and, pressing his nose against the icons on the screen, cries, loudly, "Constantine, the servant of God, is now received into the Church of Christ."

Not less grand a time for Father Peter is a wedding-day. The rite is longer, and the fees are more. Old Tartar customs keep their hold on these common folk, if not on the higher ranks, and courtship, as we understand it, is a thing unknown. A match is made by the proposeress and the parents, not by the youth and maiden—for in habit, if not in law, the sexes live apart, and do not see much of each other until the knot is tied.

A servant came into the parlor of a house in which I was staying as a guest—came in simpering and crying—to say that she wished to leave her place. "To leave! For what cause?"

Well, she was going to be married.

"Married, Maria!" cried her mistress; "when?" "The day after next," replied the woman, shedding tears.

"So soon, Maria! And what sort of man are you going to wed?"

The woman dropped her eyes. She could not say; she had not seen him yet. The proposeress had done it all, and sent her word to appear in church at four o'clock, the hour for marrying persons of her class.

"You really mean to take this man whom you have never seen?"

"I must," said the woman; "the prayers have been put up in church."

"Do the parish popes raise no objections to such marriages?"

"No," laughed the lady. "Why should they object? A wedding brings them fees; and in their cabins you will find more children than kopecks."

The livings held by the parish clergy are not rich. Some few city holdings may be worth three or four hundred pounds a year; these are the prizes. Few of the country pastors have an income, over and above the kitchen-garden and plough of land, exceeding forty or fifty pounds a year. The city priest, like the country priest, has neither rank nor power in the Church. The only chance for an ambitious man is, that his wife may die; in which event he can take the vows, put on cowl and frock, obtain a career, become a fellow in the corporation of monks, and rise, if he be daring, supple, and adroit, to high places in his church.

That the parish priests are not content with their position, is one of those open secrets in the Church which every day become more difficult to keep. As married men, they feel that they are needlessly depressed in public esteem, and that the higher offices in the system should lie open to them no less than to the monks. Being many in number, rich in learning, intimate with the people, they ought to be strong in favor; yet through the craft of their black rivals, they have been left, not only without the right of meeting, but without the means of making their voices heard. The peasant was never beaten down so low in the scale of life as his parish priest; for the serf had always his communal meeting, his choice of elders, his right of speech, and his faculty of appeal. The parish priests expect a change; they expect it, not from within the clerical body, but from without; not from a synod of monks, but from a married and reforming Tsar.

This change is coming on; a great and healing revolution; an act of emancipation for the working clergy, not less striking and beneficent than the act of emancipation for the toiling serfs.

CHAPTER LVII.

A CONSERVATIVE REVOLUTION.

In the great conflict between monks and parish priests, the ignorant classes side with the monks, the educated classes with the parish priests.

The Black Clergy, having no wives and children, stand apart from the world, and hold a doctrine hostile to the family spirit. Their rivals—though they have faults, from which the clergy in countries more advanced are free—are educated and social beings; and taking them man for man through all their grades, it is impossible to deny that the parish priests are vastly superior to the monks.

Yet the White Clergy occupied (until 1869) a place in every way inferior to the Black. They were an isolated caste; they held no certain rank; they could not rise in the Church; they exercised no power in her councils. Once a priest, a man was a priest forever. A monk might live to be

Rector, Archimandrite, Bishop, and Metropolite. Not so a married priest; the round of whose duty was confined to his parish work—to christening infants, to confessing women, to marrying lovers, to reading prayers for the dead, to saying mass, to collecting fees, and quarrelling with the peasants about his tithe. A monk directed his education; a monk appointed him to his cure of souls; a monk inspected his labor, and loaded him with either praise or blame. A body of monks could drive him from his parish church; throw him into prison; utterly destroy the prospects of his life.

Great changes have been made in the present year; changes of deeper moment to the nation than any thing effected in the Church since the reforms of Peter the Great.

This work of reform was started by the Emperor throwing open the clerical service to all the world, and putting an end to that customary succession of father and son as popes. Down to this year, the clergy has been a class apart, a sacred body, a Levitical order—in brief, a *caste*. Russia had her priestly families, like the Tartars and the Jews; and all the sons of a pope were bound to enter into the Church. This Oriental usage has been broken through. The clergy has been freed from a galling yoke, and the service has been opened to every one who may acquire the learning and enjoy the call. Young men, who would otherwise have been forced to take orders, will now be able to live by trade; the crowd of clerical idlers will melt away; and many a poor student with brains will be drawn into the spiritual ranks. This great reform is being carried forward less by edicts which would fret the consciences of ignorant men than by the application of general rules. To wit: a question has arisen whether, under this open system, the old rule of "once a priest, always a priest," holds good. It is a serious question, not for individuals only, but for the clerical society; and the monks have been moving heaven and earth to have their rule of "once a priest, always a priest" confirmed. But they have failed. No rule has been laid down in words, but a precedent has been laid down in fact.

Father Goumilef, a parish priest in the town of Riazan, applies for leave to give up his frock and re-enter the world. Count Tolstoi, Minister of Education, and the Emperor's personal representative in the Holy Governing Synod, persuades that body to support Goumilef's prayer. On the 12th of November (Oct. 31, O. S.) — a red-letter day henceforth in the Russian calendar—the Emperor signs his release; allowing Goumilef to return from the clerical to the secular life. All his rights as a citizen are restored, and he is free to enter the public service in any province of the empire, save only that of Riazan, in which he has served the altar as a parish priest.

Connected with the abolition of caste came the new laws regulating the standing of a parish priest's children—laws conceived in a most gracious spirit. All sons of a parish priest are in future to rank as nobles; sons of a deacon are to be accounted gentlemen; sons of readers are to rank as burghers.

In his task of raising the parish clergy to a higher level, the reforming Emperor has found a tower of strength in Innocent, the noticeable man who occupies, in Troitsa, the Archimandrite's chair, in Moscow, the Metropolite's throne.

Innocent passed his early years as a married priest in Siberia—doing, in the wild countries around the shores of Lake Baikal, genuine missionary work. A noble wife went with him to and fro; heaven blessed him with children; and the father learned how to speak with effect to sire and son. Thousands of converts blessed the devoted pair. At length the woman fainted by the way, and Innocent was left to mourn her loss; but not alone; their children remained to be his pride and stay.

When the Holy Governing Synod raised the missionary region of Irkutsk into a bishop's see, the crozier was forced upon Innocent by events. Already known as the Apostle of Siberia, the synod could do little more than note the fact, and give him official rank. Of course, a mitre implied a cowl and gown; but Innocent, though his wife was dead, refused to become a monk. In stronger words than he was wont to use, he urged that the exclusion of married popes from high office in the priesthood was a custom, not a canon, of his Church. To every call from the monks he answered that every man should be called to labor in the vineyard of the Lord according to his gifts. He yielded for the sake of peace; but though he took the vows, he held to his views on clerical celibacy, and the White Clergy had now a bishop to whom they could look up as a worthy champion of their cause.

On the death of Philaret, two years ago, this friend of the White Clergy was chosen by the Emperor to take his seat; so that now the actual Archimandrite of Troitsa, and Metropolite of Moscow, though he wears the cowl, is looked upon in Church society as a supporter of the married priests.

By happy chance, a first step had been taken towards one great reform by Philaret, in raising to the chair of Rector of the Ecclesiastical Academy of Moscow a priest who was not a monk.

Forty miles to the north of Moscow rises a table-land, on the edge of which is built a convent dedicated to the Holy Trinity, called in Russian, Troitsa. This convent is said to be the richest in the world; not only in sacred dust and miraculous images, but in cups and coffers, in wands and crosses, in lamps and crowns. The shrine of St. Sergie, wrought in the purest silver, weighs a thousand pounds; and in the same cathedral with St. Sergie's shrine there is a relievo of the Last Supper, in which all the figures, save that of Judas, are of finest gold. But these costly gauds are not the things which draw pilgrims to the Troitsa. They come to kneel before that Talking Madonna which, once upon a time, held speech with Serapion, a holy monk. They crowd round that portrait of St. Nicolas, which was struck by a shot from a Polish siege-gun, in the year of tribulation, when the Poles had made themselves masters of Moscow and the surrounding plains. They come still more to kiss the forehead of St. Sergie, the self-denying monk, who founded the convent, and blessed the banner of Dimitri, before that prince set forth on his campaign against the Tartar hordes on the Don. St. Sergie is the defense of his country, and his grave in the convent has never been polluted by the footprint of a foe. Often as Moscow fell, the Troitsa remained inviolate ground. The Tartars never reached it. Twice, if not more, the Poles advanced against it; once with a mighty power, and the will to reduce it, cost them what lives it might. They lay before it sixteen months, and had to retire from before the walls at last. The French under Napoleon wished to seize it, and a body of troops was sent to the attack; but the saintly presence which had driven off the Poles was too much for the French. The troops returned, and the virgin convent stood.

These miracles of defense have given a vast celebrity to the saint, who has come to be thought not only holy himself, but a cause of holiness in others. On the way from Moscow to Troitsa stands the hamlet of Hotkoff, in which lies the dust of Sergie's father and mother; over whose tombs a church and convent have been built. Every pilgrim on the road to Troitsa stops at this convent and adores their bones. "Have you been to Troitsa before?" we heard a pilgrim ask his fellow, as they trudged along the road. "Yes, thanks be to God." "Has Sergie given you what you came to seek?" "Well, no, not all." "Then you neglected to stop at Hotkoff and adore his parents; he was angry with you." "Perhaps; God knows. It may be so. Next time I will go to Hotkoff. Overlook my sin!" A railway has been made from Moscow to Troitsa, and the lazy herd of pilgrims go by train. The better sort still march along the dirty road, and count their beads in front of the wooden chapels and many rich crosses, as of old. St. Sergie has gained in wealth, and lost in credit, by the convenience offered to pilgrims in the railway line.

In the centre of this fortress and sanctuary the monks erected an academy, in which priests were to be trained for their future work. A young man lives in it under Troitsa rule, and leaves it with the Troitsa brand. The rector is a man of rank in the church, equal to the Master of Trinity among ourselves. Until the day when Philaret brought Father Gorski into office, his post had always been filled by an Archimandrite. Now Father Gorski was a learned man, a good writer, and a great authority on points of church antiquity and ceremonial. Great in reputation, he was also advanced in years. Some objected to him on the ground that he was not a monk; but his fame as a learned man, his noticeable piety, and his nearness with the Metropolite, carried him through. Even the monks forgave him when they found that he lived, like themselves, a secluded and cloistered life.

They hardly saw how much they were giving up in that early fight; for this man of monk-like habit had not taken vows; and in one of the strongholds of their power they were placing the education of their clergy in charge of a parish priest!

A second step in the line of march has been taken in the nomination of a married pope to the post of Rector of the Ecclesiastical Academy of St. Petersburg. Father Yanycheff is this new rector; and Father Yanycheff's wife is still alive. This call of a married man to such a chair has fired the Church with hope and fear—the White Clergy looking on it with surprise and joy, the Black Clergy with amazement and despair.

Dr. Yanycheff—in whose person the fight is raging between these benedicts and celibates—is a young priest, who was educated in the academy, until he took his degree of doctor, on which he was placed in the chair of theology at the University of St. Petersburg. In that chair he became popular; his lectures being eloquent, his manners easy, and his opinions liberal. Some of the sleepy old prelates took alarm. Yanycheff, they said, was exciting his pupils; he was telling them to read and think; and the sleepy old prelates could see no good in such exercises of the brain. Reading and thinking lead men into doubt, and doubt is the plague by which souls are lost. They moved the Holy Governing Synod to interfere, and on the synod interfering, the professor resigned his chair. Resolved on keeping his conscience free, he married, and accepted the office of pope in a city on the Rhine. His intellectual worth was widely known; and when, in process of time, a teacher was required for the young Princess Dagmar, a man skillful in languages and arts, as well as learned and liberal, Dr. Yanycheff, was chosen for the task of preparing the imperial bride. The way in which he discharged his delicate office brought him into favor with the great; and on his return to his own country with the princess, Count Tolstoi got him appointed rector of the academy—a position of highest trust in the Church, since it gives him a leading influence in the education of future popes.

The monks are all aghast; the Holy Governing Synod protests; and even the Metropolite refuses to recognize this act. But Count Tolstoi is firm, and the synod knows but too well how the enemy stands at court. Yanycheff, on his side, has been prudent; and the wonder caused by his nomination is sensibly dying down. Meantime, people are getting used to the idea of a man with wife and child conducting the education of their future parish priests.

Once launched on a career of clerical reform, the court has moved with regular, if with cautious strides. All men can see that the first work to be done is to be done in the schoolroom and the college; for in Russia, as elsewhere, the teachers make the taught; and as the rectors train the priests, ideas prevalent in the rectorial chairs will come in a few years to be the paramount views of the Church.

A law has recently been passed by the Council of State, and promulgated by the Emperor, which deals the hardest blow yet suffered by the monks; a law taking away the right of nominating rectors of seminaries and academies from the archbishops, and vesting it in a board of teachers and professors; subject only to approval—which may soon become a thing of course—by the higher spiritual powers. This law is opposed by all the convents and their chiefs; even Innocent, though friendly to the married clergy, stands, on this point, with his class.

A first election under this new law has just occurred in Moscow. When the law was published, Prof. Nicodemus, holding the chair of Rector in the Ecclesiastical Seminary of Moscow, sent in his resignation, on the ground that his position was become that of a rector on sufferance. Every one felt that by resigning his chair he was doing a noble thing; and if it had been possible for a monk to get a majority of votes in an open board, Nicodemus would, on that account, have been the popular choice. But no man wearing a cowl and gown had any chance. The contest lay between two married priests: Father Blagorazumof, a teacher in the seminary, and Father Smirnof, editor of the Orthodox Review. Innocent took some part against Father Smirnof, whose writings he did not like; and Father Blagorazumof was elected to the vacant chair.

What has been done in Moscow will probably be done in other cities; so that in twenty years from the present time the education of youths for the ministry will have fallen entirely into the hands of married men.

The same principle of election has been applied to the appointment of rural deans. These officers were formerly named by the bishop, according to his sole will and pleasure. Now, by imperial order, they are elected by deputies from the parish priests.

CHAPTER LVIII.

SECRET POLICE.

THE new principle of referring things to a popular vote is coming into play on every side; nowhere in a form more striking than in the courts of law. Some twenty years ago the administration of justice was the darkest blot on Russian life.

What the Emperor had to meet and put away, on this side of his government, was a colossal evil.

In a country over which the prince has to rule as well as reign, a good many men must have a share in the exercise of irresponsible and imperial power—more perhaps than would have to divide the beneficent authority of a constitutional king. A prince has only two eyes, two ears, and two hands. The circle which he can see, and hear, and reach, is drawn closely round his person, and in all that he would do beyond that line he must act through an intelligence other than his own; and for the blunders of this second self he has to bear the blame.

The parties who exercise this power in the imperial name are the secret police and the provincial governors, general and local.

The secret police have an authority which knows no bounds, save that of the Emperor's direct command. They have a province of their own, apart from, and above, all other provinces in the state. Their chief, Count Shouvalof, is the first functionary of the empire, the only man who has a right of audience by day and night. In Eastern nations rank is measured in no small degree by a person's right of access to the sovereign. Now, the right of audience in the winter palace is governed by the clearest rules. Ordinary ministers of the crown—home office, education, finance—can only see the

Emperor once a week. Greater ministers—war and foreign affairs—can see him once a day, but only at certain stated hours. A minister of police can walk into his cabinet any hour of the day, into his bedroom any hour of the night.

Not many years ago the power of this minister was equal to his rank at court; in home affairs he was supreme; and many a poor ruler found himself at once his tool and dupe. Much of this power has now been lodged in courts of law, over which the police have no control; but over and beyond the law, a vast reserve is left with the police, who can still revise a sentence, and, as an "administrative measure," send a man into exile who has been acquitted by the courts.

While I was staying at Archangel, an actor and actress were brought from St. Petersburg in a tarantass, set down in the grass-grown square, near the poet's pedestal, and told to shift for themselves, though they were on no account to quit the town without the governor's pass. No one could tell what they had done. Their lips were closed; the newspapers were silent; but a thousand tongues were busy with their tale; and the likelier story seemed to be, that they had been playing a part in some drama of actual life. Clandestine marriages are not so rare in Russia as they are in England and the United States. Young princes love to run away with dancers, singers, and their like. Now these exiles in the North country were said to have been concerned in a runaway match, by which the pride of a powerful family had been stung; and since it was impossible to punish the offending parties, these poor artists had been whisked off their tinsel thrones in order to appease a parent's wounded pride. The man and woman were not man and wife; but care for such loss of fame as a pretty woman might undergo by riding in a tarantass, day and night, twelve hundred versts, through a wild country, with a man who was not her spouse, seems never to have troubled the director of police. Stage heroines have no character in official eyes. There they were, in the North; and there they would have to stay, until the real offenders should be able to make their peace, whether they could manage to live in that city of trade, as honest folks should live, or not. Clever in their art, they opened a barn long closed, and the parlors of Archangel were agog with glee. What they performed could hardly be called a play. Two persons make a poor company, and these artists were of no high rank. They just contrived to keep their visitors awake by doing easy tricks in magic, and by acting short scenes from some of the naughtiest pieces in the world. It is to be hoped, on every ground, that the angry gods may be appeased, that the hero and heroine of this comedy may come back to the great city in which their talents are better known.

These actors were sent from the capital on a simple order from the police. They have not been tried; they have not been heard in defense; they have not been told the nature of their crime. An agent drove to their door in a drojki, asked to see So-and-so, and on going up, said, in tones which only the police can use: "Get ready; in three hours we start—for Archangel." Young or aged, male or female, the victim in such a case must snatch up what he can, follow his captor to the street, get into his drojki, and obey in silence the invisible powers. Not a word can be said in bar of his sentence; no court will open its doors to his appeal; no judge can hear his case.

Their case is far from being a rare one. In the same streets of Archangel you meet a lady of middle age, who has been exiled from St. Petersburg on simple suspicion of being concerned in seducing students of the university from their allegiance to the country and the Church.

Following in the wake of other changes, some reforms have been made in the universities; made, on the whole, in a liberal and pacific sense. Nicolas put the students into uniform; hung swords in their belts; and gave them a certain standing in the public eye, as officers of the crown. They were his servants; and as his servants they enjoyed some rights which they dearly prized. They ranked as nobles. They had their own police. They stood apart, as a separate corporation; and, whether they sang through the street or sat in the play-house, they appeared in public as a corporate body, and always in the front. But the reforming Emperor seeks to restore these civilian youths to the habits of civil life. Their swords have been hung up, their uniforms laid aside, their right of singing songs and damning plays in a body put away. All these distinctions are now abolished; and, like other civilians, the students have been placed under the city police and the ordinary courts.

These changes are unpopular with the students, who imagine that their dignity has been lessened by stripping them of uniform and sword; and some of these young men, professing all the while republican and communistic creeds, are clamoring for their class distinctions, and even hankering for the times when they were "servants of the Tsar."

In the month of March (1869) some noisy meetings of these young men took place. The Emperor heard of them, and sent for Trepof, his first master of police—a man of shrewd wit and generous temper, under whom the police have become all but popular. "What do these students want?" his Majesty began. "Two things," replied the master; "bread and state." "Bread?" exclaimed the Emperor. "Yes," said the master; "many of them are poor; with empty bellies, active brains, and saucy tongues."

"What can be done for them, poor fellows?"

"A few purses, sire, would keep them quiet; twenty thousand rubles now, and promise of a yearly grant in aid of poor students." "Let it be so," said the prince.

These rubles were sent at once to the rector and professors to dispense, according to their knowledge of the students' needs; but, unluckily, the rector and professors treated the imperial gift as a bit of personal patronage, and they gave the purses to each others' sons and nephews, lads who could well afford to pay their fees. The students called fresh meetings, talked much nonsense, and drew up an appeal to the people, written in a florid and offensive style.

Treating the Government as an equal power, these madcaps printed what they called an ultimatum of four articles: (1.) they demanded the right of establishing a students' club; (2.) the right of meeting and addressing the Government as a corporate body; (3.) the control of all purses and scholarships given to poor students; (4.) the abolition of university fees. Following these articles came an appeal to the people for support against the minions of the crown!

A party in the state—the enemies of reform—were said to have raised a fund for the purpose of corrupting these young men; and this party were suspected of employing the agency of clever women in carrying out their plans. It was not easy to detect these female plotters at their work, for the revolution they were trying to bring about was made with smiles and banter over cups of tea; but ladies were arrested in several streets, and the lady to be seen in Archangel was one of these victims—exiled on "suspicion" of having been concerned in printing the appeal.

When she came into exile every one was amazed; she seemed so weak and broken; she showed so little spirit; and when people talked with her they found she had none of the talents necessary for intrigue. The comedy of government by "suspicion" stood confessed. Here was a prince, the idol of his country, armed in his mail of proof, surrounded by a million bayonets, not to speak of artillery, cavalry, and ships; and there was a frail creature, fifty years old, with neither beauty, followers, nor fortune to promote her views: in such a foe, what could the Emperor be supposed to fear?

A young writer of some talent in St. Petersburg, one Dimitri Pisareff, was bathing in the sea near his summer-house, and, getting beyond his depth, was drowned. The young man was a politician, and, having caused much scandal by his writings, he had passed some years in the fortress of St. Peter and St. Paul. Freed by the Emperor, he resumed his pen. After his death, Pavlenkoff, a bookseller in the city, who admired his talents, and thought he had served his country, opened a subscription among his readers for the purpose of erecting a stone above the young author's grave. The secret police took notice of the fact, and as Dimitri Pisareff was one of the names in their black list, they understood this effort to do him honor as a public censure of their zeal. Pavlenkoff was arrested in his shop, put into a cart, and, with neither charge nor hearing, driven to the province of Viatka, twelve hundred versts from home. That poor bookseller still remains in exile.

A more curious case is that of Gierst, a young novelist of mark, who began, in the year 1868, to publish in a monthly magazine, called "Russian Notes" ("Otetchestvenniva Zapiski"), a romance which he called "Old and Young Russia." The opening chapters showed that his tale was likely to be clever; bold in thought and brilliant in style. Gierst took the part of Young Russia against Old Russia, and his chapters were devoured by youths in all the colleges and schools. Every one began to talk of the story, and to discuss the questions raised by it—men and things in the past, in contrast with the hopes and talents of the present reign. The police took part with the elders; and when the novelist who made the stir could not be answered with argument, they silenced him by a midnight call. An officer came to his lodgings with the usual order to depart at once. Away sped the horses, he knew not whither—driving on night and day, until they arrived at Totma, one of the smaller towns in the province of Vologda, nine hundred versts from St. Petersburg. There he was tossed out of his cart, and told to remain until fresh orders came from the minister of police.

None of Gierst's friends, at first, knew where he was. His rooms in St. Petersburg were empty; he had gone away; and the only trace which he had left behind was the tale of a domestic, who had seen him carried off. No one dared to ask about him. Reference to him in the journals was forbidden; and the public only learned from the non-appearance of his story in the "Notes" that the police had somehow interfered with the free exercise of his pen. The letters which he wrote to the papers were laid aside as being too dangerous for the public eye; and it was only by a ruse that he conveyed to his readers the knowledge of his whereabouts.

Gierst sent to the editor of "Notes" a letter of apology for the interruption of his tale. He merely said it would not be carried farther for the present; and the police raised no objection to the publication of this letter in the "Notes." They overlooked the date which the letter bore; and the one word "Totma" told the public all.

The world enjoyed a laugh at the police; and the irritated officials tried to vent their rage on the young wit who had proved that they were fools. Gierst remains an exile at Totma, and the public still awaits the story from his hands. But a thousand novels, rich in art and red in spirit, could not have touched the public conscience like the haunting memory of this unfinished tale.

CHAPTER LIX.

PROVINCIAL RULERS.

RUSSIA is divided into provinces, each of which is ruled by a governor and a vice-governor named by the crown.

A dozen years ago the governor and his lieutenant was each a petty Tsar—doing what he pleased in his department, and answering only now and then, like a Turkish pasha, by forfeiture of office, for the public good. Charged with the maintenance of public order, he was armed with a power as terrible as that of the imperial police—the right to suspect his neighbor of discontent, and act on this bare suspicion as though the fault were proved in a court of law. In England and the United States the word suspicion has lost its use, and well-nigh lost its sense. Our officers of police are not permitted to "suspect" a thief. They must either take him in the fact or leave him alone. From Calais to Perm, however, the word "suspicion" is still a name of fear; for in all the countries lying between the English Channel and the Ural Mountains, "ordre superieure" is a force to which rights of man and courts of law must equally give way.

The governor, or vice-governor, of a Russian province, representing his sovereign lord, might find, or fancy that he found, some reason to suspect a man of disaffection to the crown. He might be wrong, he might even be absurdly wrong. The man might be loyal as himself; might even be in a position to prove that loyalty in open court; and yet his innocence would avail him nothing. Proofs are idle when the courts are not open to appeal; and judges have no power to hear the facts. "Done by superior orders," was the answer to all cries and protests. A resistless power was about his feet, and he was swept away by a force from which there was no appeal—not even to the ruling prince; and the victim of an erring, perhaps a malicious, governor, had no resource against the wrong, except in resignation to what might seem to be the will of God.

The men who could use and abuse this terrible power were many. Russia is divided into forty-nine provinces, besides the kingdom of Poland, the Grand Duchy of Finland, the Empire of Siberia, the khanates and principalities of the Caucasus. In these forty-nine provinces the governors and vice-governors had the power to exile any body on mere suspicion of political discontent. In other regions of the empire this power was even more diffused than it was in the purely Russian districts. Taking all the Russians in one mass, there can hardly have been less than two hundred men (excluding the police) who could seize a citizen in the name of public order, and condemn him, unheard, to live in any part of the empire from the Persian frontiers to the Polar Sea.

The Princess V———, a native of Podolia, young, accomplished, wealthy, was loved by all her friends, adored by all the young men of her province. One happy youth possessed her heart, and this young man was worthy of the fortune he had won. Their days of courtship passed, and they were looking forward to the day when they would wear together their sacred crowns; but then an unseen agent crossed their path and broke their hearts. Some days before their betrothal should have taken place, an officer of police appeared at the lover's door with a peremptory order for him to quit Poltava for the distant government of Perm. Taken from his house at a moment's notice, he was hurried to the general office of police, where his papers were made out, and, being put into a common cart, he was whisked away in the company of two gendarmes. A month was occupied in his journey; two or three months elapsed before his friends in Podolia knew that he was safe. He found a friend in the mountain town, by whom his life as an exile was made a little less rugged than it might have been. An advocate was won for him at court; the senate was moved, though cautiously, in his behalf; and at the end of two years his tormentor was persuaded to relax his grip. But though he was suffered to leave his place of banishment, he was forbidden to return to his native town.

The princess kept her faith to him—staying in Podolia while he was still at Perm; living down the suspicions in which they were both involved—and joined him at St. Petersburg so soon as he got leave to enter that city. There they were married, and there I met them in society. Not a cloud is on their fame. They are free to go and come, except that they must not live in their native town. No power save that which sent the bridegroom into exile can recall them to their home. Yet down to this hour the gentleman has never been able to ascertain the nature of his offense.

In time the country will free herself from this Asiatic abuse of power. With bold but cautious hand the Emperor has felt his way. His governors of provinces have been told to act with prudence; not to think of sending men into exile unless the case is flagrant, and only then after reference of all the facts to St. Petersburg.

Some dozen years ago, before the new reforms had taken hold, and officers in the public service had come to count on the appeal being heard, a case occurred which allows one to give, in the form of an anecdote, a picture of the evils now being slowly rooted out. Count A———, a young vice-governor, fresh from college, came to live in a certain town of the Black Soil country. Fond of dogs and horses, fond of wines and dinners, the young gentleman found his official income far below his wants. He took "his own" (what Russian officials used to call vzietka) from every side; for he loved to keep his house open, his stable full, his card-room merry; and a nice house, a good stable, and a merry card-room, cost a good many rubles in the year. He was lucky with his cards — luckier, some losers said, than a perfectly honest player should be; yet the two ends of his income and his outgo never could be made to meet.

The treasurer of the town was Andrew Ivanovitch Gorr, a man of peasant birth, who had been sent to college, and, after taking a good degree, had been put into the civil service, where, by his soft ways, his patient deference to those above him, and his perfect loyalty to his trust, he had risen to the post of treasurer in this provincial town.

Count A——— called Andrew into his chamber, and bade him, with a careless gesture, pay a small debt for him. Andrew bowed, and waited for the rubles. A——— just waived him off; but seeing that he would not take the hint, the count said, "Yes, yes, pay the debt; we will arrange it in the afternoon." Then Andrew paid the money, and in less than a week he was asked to pay again. From week to week he went on paying, with due submission to his chief, but with an inward doubt as to whether this paying would come out well. Twice or thrice the count was good enough to speak of his affairs, and even to name a day when the money which he was taking from the public coffers should be replaced. In the mean time the debt was every week increasing in amount; so that the provincial chest was all but drained to pay the vice-governor's personal debts.

Andrew was in despair, for the day was fast coming round when the Imperial auditors would come to revise his books and count the money in his box. Unless the fund was restored before they came he would be lost; for the balance was in his charge, and the count could hardly cover his default. On Andrew telling his wife what he had been drawn, by his habit of obeying orders, into doing, he was urged by that sage adviser to go at once to the governor and beg him to replace the cash before the auditors arrived.

"The auditors will come next week?" asked A———. "All will be well. I will send a messenger to my estates. In five days he will come back, and the money shall be paid. Prepare a draft of the account, and bring it to my house, with the proper receipt and seal."

On the fifth day the auditors arrived, a little before their time; and being eager to push on, they named the next morning, at ten o'clock, for going into the accounts. The treasurer ran to the palace, and saw the count in his public room, surrounded by his secretaries. "It is well," he said to Andrew, with his pleasant smile; "the messenger has come back with the money; bring the paper and the receipt to my smoking-room at ten o'clock to-night, and we'll put the account to rights."

Andrew was at his door by ten o'clock with the statement of his debts, and a receipt for the money. "Yes," said the count, dropping his eye down the line of figures, "the account is just — fifteen thousand seven hundred rubles. Let me look at the receipt. Yes, that is well drawn. You deserve to be promoted, Andrew! Talents like yours are lost in a provincial town. You ought to be a minister of state! Oblige me by asking my man to come in."

A servant entered.

"Go up to the madame, and ask her if she can come down stairs for a moment," said the count. The servant slipped away, and the count, while waiting for his return, made many jokes and pleasantries, so that the time ran swiftly past. He kept the papers in his hand.

When Andrew saw that it was near eleven o'clock, he ventured to ask if the man was not long in coming. "Long," exclaimed the vice-governor, starting up, "an age. Where can the fellow be? He must have fallen asleep on the stairs."

Going out of the room in search of him, the count closed the door behind him, saying, "Wait a few minutes; I will go myself." Andrew sat still as a stone. He noticed that the count had taken with him the schedule of debts and the signed receipt. He felt uneasy in his mind. He stared about the room, and counted the beatings of the clock. His head grew hot; his heart was beating with a throb that could be heard. No other sound broke the night; and when he opened the door and put his ear to the passage, the silence seemed to him like that of a crypt.

The clock struck twelve.

Leaping up from his stupor, he banged the door and shouted up the stairs, but no one answered him; and snatching a fearful daring from his misery, he ran along several corridors until he tripped and fell over a man in a great fur cloak. "Get up, and show me to the vice-governor's room," said Andrew fiercely, on which the domestic shook his cloak and rubbed his eyes. "The vice-governor's room?" "Yes, fellow; come, be quick." The man led him back to the room he had left; which was, in fact, the private reception-room. "Stay here, and I will seek him." Shortly the man returned with news that his master was in bed. "In bed!" cried Andrew, more and more excited; "go to him again, and ask him if he has forgotten me. Tell him I am waiting his return." A minute later he came back to say the count was fast asleep, and that his valet dared not wake him for the world. "Asleep!" groaned the poor treasurer; "you must awake him. I can not leave without seeing him. It is the Emperor's service, and will not wait."

At the Emperor's name the servant said he would try

again. An hour of misery went by before he came to say the count was in bed, and would not see him. If he had business to transact, he must come another day, and at the reception hour.

In a moment Andrew was at the count's door and in his room, to which the noise brought up a dozen people. "What is this tumult all about?" frowned the count, rising sharply in his bed. "Tumult!" said Andrew, waxing hot with terror; "I want the rubles." "Rubles!" said the count, with feigned astonishment; "what rubles do you mean?" "The rubles we have taken from the provincial coffer." "That we have taken from the coffer! We? What we? What rubles? Go to bed, man, and forget your dreams."

"Then give me back my paper and receipt."

"Paper and receipt!" said the count, with affected pity; "look to him well. See him safe home; and tell his wife to look that he does not wander in his sleep. He might fall into the river in such fits. Look to him;" and the vice-governor fell back upon his pillow as the servant bowed.

Put to the door, and left to seek his way, the treasurer felt that he was lost. The count, he saw, would swear and forswear. Even if he confessed his fault to the auditors, telling them how he had been persuaded against his duty, the count could produce his receipt in proof that the funds had been repaid.

Going back to his office, he sat down on a stool, and after looking at his books and papers once again, to see that the whole night's work was not a dream, as the count had said, he took up his pen and wrote a history of his affairs.

Restless in her bed, his wife got up to seek him; and knowing that he was busy with his accounts, and would be likely to stay late with his chief, she went into his office, where the light was burning dimly on the desk—to find him hanging from a beam. Piercing the air with her cries, she brought in a crowd of people, some of whom cut down the body, while others ran for the doctor. He was dead.

Like an Oriental, he killed himself in order that, in his death, he might punish the man whom he could not touch in life.

The paper which he left on his desk was open, and as many

persons saw it in part, and still more knew of its existence, the matter could not be hushed up, even though the vice-governor had been twenty times a count. The people cried for justice on the culprit; and by orders from St. Petersburg the count was relieved of his office, arrested on the charge of abusing a public trust, and placed on his defense before a secret commission in the town over which he had lately reigned.

The Emperor, it is said, was anxious to send him to the mines, from which so many nobler men had recently come away; but the interest of his family was great at court; the secret commission was a friendly one; and he escaped with the sentence of perpetual dismissal from the public service—not a light sentence to a man who is at once a beggar and a count.

Alexander, feeling for the widow of his dead servant, ordered the pension which would have been due to her husband to be paid to her for life.

CHAPTER LX.

OPEN COURTS.

OFFENSES like those of A——— (some twelve years old), in which a great offense was proved, yet justice was defeated more than half, in spite of the imperial wishes, led the council of state into considering how far it would be well to replace the secret commissions by regular courts of law.

The public benefits of such a change were obvious. Justice would be done, with little or no respect to persons; and the Emperor would be relieved from his direct and personal action in the punishment of crime. But what the public gained the circles round the prince were not unlikely to lose; and these court circles raised a cry against this project of reform. "The obstacles," they said, "were vast. Except in Moscow and St. Petersburg, no lawyers could be found; the code was cumbrous and imperfect; and the public was unprepared for such a change. If it was difficult to find judges, it was impossible to find jurors." Listening to every one, and weighing facts, the Emperor held his own. He got reports drawn up; he won his opponents over one by one; and in 1865 the council of state was ready with a volume of legal reform, as vast and noble as his plan for emancipating serfs.

Courts of justice were to be open in every province, and all these courts of justice were to be public courts. Trained judges were to preside. The system of written evidence was abolished. A prisoner was to be charged in a formal act; he was to see the witnesses face to face; he was to have the right, in person or by his counsel, of questioning those witnesses on points of fact. A jury was to decide the question of guilt or innocence. The judges were to be paid by the crown, and were on no pretext whatever to receive a fee. A juror was to be a man of means—a trader, a well-off peasant, an officer of not less than five hundred rubles a year. A majority of jurors was to decide.

The Imperial code was brought into harmony with these new methods of procedure. Capital punishment was abolished for civil crimes; Siberia was exchanged for the club and the axe; Archangel and the Caucasus were substituted for the mines. The Tartar punishments of beating, flogging, running the ranks, were stopped at once, and every branch of criminal treatment was brought up—in theory, at least—to the level of England and the United States.

Term by term this new system of trial by judge and jury, instead of by secret commissions, is now being introduced into all the larger towns. I have watched the working of this new system in several provinces; but give an account, by preference, of a trial in a new court, in a new district, under circumstances which put the virtues of a jury to some local strain.

Dining one evening with a friend in Rostof, on the Lower Don, I find myself seated next to President Gravy, to whom I am introduced by our common host as an English barrister and justice of the peace. The Assize is sitting, and as a curious case of child-exposure is coming on next day, about the facts of which provincial feeling is much excited, President Gravy offers me a seat in his court.

This court is a new court, opened in the present year; a movable court, consisting of a president and two assistant judges; sitting in turn at Taganrog, Berdiansk, and Rostof, towns between which there is a good deal of rivalry in business, often degenerating into local strife. The female accused of exposing her infant comes from a Tartar village near Taganrog; and as no good thing was ever known to come from the district of Taganrog, the voice of Rostof has condemned this female, still untried, to a felon's doom.

Next morning we are in court by ten o'clock—a span-new chamber, on which the paint is not yet dry, with a portrait of the Imperial law-reformer hung above the judgment-seat. A long hall is parted into three portions by a dais and two silken cords. The judges, with the clerk and public prosecutor, sit on the dais, at a table; and the citizens of Rostof occupy the benches on either wing. In front of the dais sit the jurors, the short-hand writer (a young lady), the advocates, and witnesses; and near these latter stands the accused woman, attended by a civil officer of the court. Nothing in the room suggests the idea of feudal state and barbaric power. President Gravy wears no wig, no robe—nothing but a golden chain and the pattern civilian's coat. No halberts follow him, no mace and crown are borne before him. He enters by the common door. A priest in his robes of office stands beside a book and cross; he is the only man in costume, as the advocates wear neither wig nor gown. No soldier is seen; and no policeman except the officer in charge of the accused. There is no dock; the prisoner stands or sits as she is placed, her back against the wall. If violence is feared, the judges order in a couple of soldiers, who stand on either side the prisoner holding their naked swords; but this precaution is seldom used. An open gallery is filled with persons who come and go all day, without disturbing the court below.

President Gravy, the senior judge, is a man of forty-five. The son of a captain of gendarmerie in Odessa, he took by choice to the profession of advocate, and after three years' practice in the courts of St. Petersburg, he was sent to the new Azof circuit. His assistant judges are younger men.

President Gravy opens his court; the priest asks a blessing; the jurors are selected from a panel; the prisoner is told to stand forth; and the indictment is read by the clerk. A keen desire to see the culprit and to hear the details of her crime has filled the benches with a better class than commonly attends the court, and many of the Rostof ladies flutter in the gayest of morning robes. The case is one to excite the female heart.

Anna Kovalenka, eighteen years of age, and living, when at home, in a village on the Sea of Azof, is tall, elastic, dark, with ruddy complexion, and braided hair bound up in a crimson scarf. Some Tartar blood is in her veins, and the young woman is the ideal portrait of a Bokhara bandit's wife. A motherly old creature stands by her side—an aunt, her mother being long since dead. Her father is a peasant, badly off, with five girls; this Anna eldest of the five.

Her case is, that she had a lover, that she bore a child, that she concealed the birth, and that her infant died. In her defense, it is alleged, according to the manners of her country, that her lover was a man of her own village, not a stranger; one of those governing points which, on the Sea of Azof, make a young woman's amours right or wrong. So far, it is assumed, no fault is fairly to be charged. Her child was born and died; the facts are not disputed; but the defendants urge, in explanation, that she was very young in years; that her couching was very hard; that milk-fever set in, with loss of blood and wandering of the brain; that the young mother was helpless, that the infant was neglected unconsciously, and that it died.

Very few persons in the court appear inclined to take this view; but those who take it feel that the lover of this girl is far more guilty than the girl herself; and they ask each other why the seducer is not standing at her side to answer for his life. His name is known; he is even supposed to be in court. Gospodin Lebedeff, the public prosecutor, has done his best to include him in the criminal charge; but he is foiled by the woman's love and wit. By the Imperial code, the fellow can not be touched unless she names him as the father of her child; and all Lebedeff's appeals and menaces are thrown away upon her, this heroine of a Tartar village baffling the veteran lawyer's arts with a steadiness worthy of a better cause and a nobler man.

The first witness called is a peasant woman from the village in which Anna Kovalenka lives. She is not sworn in the

English way, the court having been put, as it were, under sacred obligations by the priest; but the bench instructs her as to the nature of evidence, and enjoins her to speak no word that is not true. She says, in few and simple words, she found the dead body; she carried it into Anna's cabin; the young woman admitted that the child was hers; and, on further questions, that she had concealed the birth. She gives her evidence quietly in a breathless court, her neighbor standing near her all the while, and the judge assisting her by questions now and then. The audience sighs when she stands down; her evidence being full enough to send the prisoner to Siberia for her natural life.

The second witness is a doctor—bland, and fat, and scientific—the witness on whose evidence the defense will lie. A quickened curiosity is felt as the fat and fatherly man, with big blue spectacles and kindly aspect, rises, bows to the bench, and enters into a long and delicate report on the maladies under which females suffer in and after the throes of labor, when the regular functions of mind and body have been deranged by a sudden call upon the powers reserved by nature for the sustenance of infant life. A buzz of talk on the ladies' bench is speedily put down by a tinkle of President Gravy's bell. The judges put minute and searching questions to this witness; but they make no notes of what he says in answer; the general purpose of which is to show that the first medical evidence picked up by the police was defective; that a woman in the situation of Anna, poor, neglected, inexperienced, might conceal her child without intending to do it harm, and might cause it to die of cold without being morally guilty of its death. Two or three questions are put to him by Lebedeff, and then the kindly, fat old gentleman wipes his spectacles and drops behind.

Lebedeff deals in a lenient spirit with the case. The facts, he says (in effect), are strong, and tell their own tale. This woman bears a child; she conceals the birth; this concealment is a crime. She puts her child away in a secret place; her child is found dead—dead of hunger and neglect. Who can doubt that she exposed and killed this child in order to rid herself at once of her burden and her shame? "The crime of child-murder is so common in our villages," he concludes, "that it cries to heaven against us. Let all good men combine to put it down, by a rigorous execution of the law."

Gospodin Tseborenko, a young advocate from Taganrog, sent over specially to conduct the defense, replies by a brief examination of the facts; contending that his client is a girl of good character, who has never had a lover beyond her village, and is not likely to have committed a crime against nature. He suggests that her child may have been dead at the birth—that in her pain and loneliness, not knowing what she was about, and never dreaming about the Code, she concealed the dead body from her father's eyes. Admitting that infant murder is the besetting sin of villagers in the south of Russia, he contends that the children put away are only such as the villagers consider things of shame—that is to say, the offspring of their women by strangers and men of rank.

President Gravy rings his bell—the court is all alert—and, after a brief presentment of the leading points to the jury, who on their side listen with grave attention to every word, he puts three several queries into writing:

I. Whether in their opinion Anna Kovalenka exposed her child with a view to kill it?

II. Whether, if she did not in their opinion expose it with a view to kill it, she willfully concealed the birth?

III. Whether, if she either knowingly exposed and killed her child, or willfully concealed the birth, there were any circumstances in the case which call for mitigation of the penalties provided by the penal code?

The sheet of paper on which he writes these queries is signed by the three judges, and handed over to the foreman, who takes it and retires with his brethren of the jury to find as they shall see fit.

While the trial has been proceeding, Anna Kovalenka has been looking on with patient unconcern, neither bold nor timid, but with a look of resignation singular to watch. Only once she kindled into spirit; that was when the peasant woman was describing how she found the body of her child. She smiled a little when her advocate was speaking—only a faint and vanishing smile. Lebedeff seemed to strike her as something sacred; and she listened to his not unkindly speech as she might have listened to a sermon by her village priest.

In twenty minutes the jury comes into court with their finding written by the foreman on the sheet of paper given to him by the judge. President Gravy rings his bell, and bids the foreman read his answer to the first query.

"No!" says the foreman, in a grave, loud voice. The audience starts, for this is the capital charge.

To the second query, "No!"

"That is enough," says the judge; and, turning to the woman, he tells her in a tender voice that she has been tried by her country and acquitted, that she is now a free woman, and may go and sit down among her friends and neighbors.

Now for the first time she melts a little; shrinks behind the policeman; snatches up the corner of her gown; and steadying herself in a moment, wipes her eyes, kisses her aunt, and creeps away by a private door.

Every body in this court has done his duty well, the jurors best of all; for these twelve men, who never saw an open court in their lives until the current year, have found a verdict of acquittal in accordance with the facts, but in the teeth of local prejudice, bent on sending the woman from Taganrog to the mines for life.

What schools for liberty and tolerance have been opened in these courts of law!

CHAPTER LXI.

ISLAM.

KAZAN is the point where Europe and Asia meet. The paper frontiers lie a hundred miles farther east, along the crests of the Ural Mountains and the banks of the Ural River; but the actual line on which the Tartar and the Russian stand face to face, on which mosque and church salute the eye together, is that of the Lower Volga, flowing through the Eastern Steppe, from Kazan to the Caspian Sea. This frontier line lies eastward of Bagdad.

Kazan, a colony of Bokhara, an outpost of Khiva, was not very long ago the seat of a splendid khanate; and she is still regarded by the fierce and languid Asiatics as the western frontier of their race and faith. In site and aspect this old city is extremely fine, especially when the floods run high, and the swamps beneath her walls become a glorious lake. A crest of hill—which poets have likened to a wave, a keel, and a stallion's back—runs parallel to the stream. This crest is the Kremlin, the strong place, the seat of empire; scarped, and walled, and armed; the battlements crowned with gateways, towers, and domes. Beyond the crest of hill, inland from the Volga, runs a fine plateau, on which stand remnants of rich old courts and towers — a plateau somewhat bare, though brightened here and there by garden, promenade, and chalet. Under this ridge lies Kaban Lake, a long, dark sheet of water, on the banks of which are built the business quarters, in which the craftsmen labor and the merchants buy and sell—a wonderfully busy and thriving town. Each quarter has a character of its own. The Kremlin is Christian; the High Street Germanesque. A fine old Tartar gateway, called the Tower of Soyonbeka, stands in front of the cathedral; but much of the citadel has been built since the khanate fell before the troops of Ivan the Fourth. Down in the lower city, by the Kaban Lake, dwell the children of Islam, the descendants of Batu Khan, the countrymen of the Golden horde.

The birth-place of these Tartar nations was the Eastern Steppe; their line of march was the Volga bank; and their affections turn still warmly to their ancient seats. The names of Khiva and Bokhara sound to a Tartar as the names of Shechem and Jerusalem sound to a Jew. In his poetry these countries are his ideal lands. He sings to his mistress of the groves of Bokhara; he compares her cheek to the apples of Khiva; and he tells her the fervor of his passion is like the summer heat of Balkh.

An Arab legend puts into the Prophet's mouth a saying, which is taken by his children as a promise, that in countries where the palm-trees bear fruit his followers should possess the land; but that in countries where the palm-trees bear no fruit, though they might be dwellers for a time, the land would never be their own. The promise, if it were a promise, has been kept in the spirit for a thousand years. No date-bearing country known to the Arabs defied their arms; from no date-bearing country, once overrun, have they been yet dislodged. When Islam pushed her outposts beyond the line of palms, as in Spain and Russia, she had to fall back, after her trial of strength on the colder fields, into her natural zones. As she fell back from Granada on Tangiers and Fez, so she retired from Kazan on Khiva and Bokhara — a most unwilling retreat, the grief of which she assuaged in some degree by passionate hope of her return. The Moors, expecting to reconquer Seville and Granada, keep the keys of their ancient palaces, the title-deeds of their ancient lands in Spain. The Kirghiz, also, claim the lands and houses of their countrymen, and the Kirghiz khan describes himself as lineal heir to the reigning princes of Kazan. In the East, as in the West, the children of Islam look on their present state as a correction laid upon them by a father for their faults. Some day they trust to find fresh favor in his sight. The term of their captivity may be long; but it will surely pass away, and when the Compassionate yields in his mercy, they will return in triumph to their ancient homes.

In the mean time, it is right to mark the different spirit in which the vanquished sons of Islam have been treated in the West and in the East. From Granada every Moor was driven by fire and sword; for many generations no Moor was suffered to come back into Spain, under pain of death. In Russia the Tartars were allowed to live in peace; and after forty years they were allowed to trade in the city which had formerly been their own. No doubt there have been fierce and frequent persecutions of the weaker side in these countries; for the great conflict of cross and crescent has grown into a second nature, equally with the Russian and Tartar, and the rivalries which once divided Moscow and Kazan still burn along the Kirghiz Steppe. The capitals may be farther off, but the causes of enmity are not removed by space and time. The cross is at St. Petersburg and Kief, the crescent at Bokhara and Khiva; but between these points there is a sympathy and an antipathy, like that which fights between the two magnetic poles. The Tartars have captured Nijni and Moscow many times; the Russians will some day plant their standards on the Tower of Timour Beg.

A man who walks through the Tartar town in Kazan, admiring the painted houses, the handsome figures, the Oriental garbs, the graceful minarets, can hardly help feeling that these children of Islam hold their own with a grace and dignity worthy of a prouder epoch. "Given to theft and eating horse-flesh," is the verdict of a Russian officer; "otherwise not so bad." "Your servants seem to be Tartar?" "Yes, the rascals make good servants; for, look you, they never drink, and when they are trusted they never steal." In all the great houses of St. Petersburg and Moscow, and in the large hotels everywhere, we have Tartar servants, chosen on account of their sobriety and honesty. The Begs and Mirzas fled from the country when their city was stormed, and only the craftsmen and shepherds remained behind; yet a new aristocracy of trade and learning has sprung up; and the titles of mirza and mollah are now enjoyed by men whose grandfathers held the plough. These Tartars of Kazan are better schooled than their Russian neighbors; most of them can read, write, and cipher; and their youths are in high demand as merchants, salesmen, and bankers' clerks—offices of trust in which, with care and patience, they are sure to rise. Mirza Yunasoff, Mirza Burnaief, and Mirza Apakof, three of the richest traders in the province, are self-made men. No one denies them the rank of mirza (lord, or prince). Mirza Yunasoff has built, at his private charge, a mosque and school.

It is very hard for a Christian to get any sort of clue to the feelings of these sober and industrious folk. That they value their religion more than their lives is easy to find out; but whether they share the dreams of their brethren in Khiva and Bokhara is not known. Meanwhile they work and pray, grow rich and strong. An innocent and useful body in the empire, they are wisely left alone, so far as they can be left alone.

They can not, however, be treated as of no importance in the state. They are of vast importance; not as enemies only, but as enemies camped on the soil, and drawing their supports from a foreign land. Even those among the Tartars who are least excited by events around them, feel that they are out of their natural place. They hate the cross. They are Asiatics; with their faces and affections turning day and night, not towards Moscow and St. Petersburg, but towards Khiva, Bokhara, and Samarcand. A foreign city is their holy place, a foreign ruler their anointed chief. They get their mollahs from Bokhara, and they wait for conquerors from the Kirghiz Steppes. They have not learned to be Russians, and they will not learn; so that, whether the Government wishes it or not, the conflict of race and creed will rage through the coming years, even as it has raged through the past.

Reforming the country on every side, the Emperor is not neglecting this Eastern point; and in the spirit of all his more recent changes, he is taking up a new position as regards the Tartar race and creed. Nature and policy combine to prevent him trying to convert the Mussulmans by force; but nothing prevents him from trying to draw them over by the moral agencies of education and humanity. Feeling that, where the magistrate would fail, the teacher may succeed, the Emperor is opening schools in his Eastern provinces, under the care of Professor Ilminski, a learned Russian, holding the chair of Tartar languages and literature in the university of Kazan. These schools already number twenty-four, of which the one near Kazan is the chief and model.

Professor Ilminski drives me over to these Tartar schools. We visit a school for boys and a school for girls; for the sexes are kept apart, in deference to Oriental notions about the female sex. The rooms are clean and well kept; the children neat in dress, and orderly in manner. They are taught by young priests especially trained for the office, and learn to sing, as well as to read and cipher. Books are printed for them in Russian type, and a Tartar press is working in connection with the university. This printing of books, especially of the Psalms and Gospels, in the Tartar tongue, is doing much good; for the natives of Kazan are a pushing and inquisitive people, fond of reading and singing; and the poorest people are glad to have good books brought to their doors, in a speech that every one can hear and judge for himself. In the same spirit the Emperor has ordered mass to be said in the Tartar tongue; a wise and thoughtful step; a hint, it may be, to the mollahs, who have not come to see, and never may come to see, that any other idioms than Arabic and Persian should be used in their mosques. If these clever traders and craftsmen of Kazan are ever to be converted from Islam to Christianity, they must be drawn over in these gentle ways, and not by the jailer's whip and the Kozak's brand.

The children sing a psalm, their bright eyes gleaming at the sound. They sing in time and tune; but in a fierce, marauding style, as though the anthem were a bandit's stave.

Not much fruit has yet been gathered from this field. "Have you any converts from the better classes?" "No; not yet," the professor sighs; "the citizens of Kazan are hard to win; but we get some little folk from villages on the steppe, and train them up in the fear of God. Once they are with us, the ycan never turn back."

Such is the present spirit of the law. A Moslem may become a Christian; a Christian may not become a Moslem; and a convert who has taken upon himself the cross can never legally lay it down. It is an Eastern, not a Western rule; and while it remains in force, the cross will be denied the use of her noblest arms. Not until conscience is left to work in its own way, as God shall guide it, free from all fear of what the police may rule, will the final victory lie with the faith of Christ.

Shi Abu Din, chief mollah of Kazan, receives me in Asiatic fashion; introduces me to two brother mollahs, licensed to travel as merchants; and leads me over the native colleges and schools. This mollah, born in a village near Kazan, was sent to the university of Bokhara, in which city he was trained for his labors among the Moslems living on Russian soil, just as our Puritan clergy used to seek their education in Holland, our Catholic clergy in Spain. Shi Abu Din is considered, even by the Professor of Tartar languages, as a learned and upright man. His swarthy brethren have just arrived from Bokhara, by way of the Kirghiz Steppe. They tell me the roads are dangerous, and the countries lying east of the Caspian Sea disturbed. Still the roads, though closed to the Russians, are open to caravan merchants, if they know the dialects and ways of men. No doubt they are open to mollahs travelling with caravans through friendly tribes.

The Tartars of Kazan are, of course, polygamists; so that their social life is as much unlike the Russian as their religious life.

CHAPTER LXII.

THE VOLGA.

FROM Kazan to the Caspian Sea, the Volga flows between Islam and Christendom. One small town, Samara, has been planted on the eastern bank—a landing-place for Orenburg and the Kirghiz Steppe. All other towns—Simbirsk, Volsk, Saratof, Tsaritzin—rise on the western bank, and look across the river towards the Ural Ridge. Samara is a Kirghiz, rather than a Russian town, and but for the military posts, and the traffic brought along the military roads, the place would be wholly in Moslem hands. Samara has a name in the East as a place for invalids—the cure being wrought by means of fermented mare's milk, the diet and medicine of rovers on the Tartar Steppe.

A Christian settlement of the Volga line from Kazan to the Caspian Sea must be a work of time. Three hundred and seventeen years have passed since Ivan the Terrible stormed Kazan; three hundred and twelve years since his armies captured Astrakhan and opened a passage through Russia to the Caspian Sea; yet the Volga is a frontier river to this very hour; and it is not too much to say that the noblest watercourse in Europe is less familiar to English merchants in Victoria's time than it was in Elizabeth's time.

The first boats which sailed the Volga, from her upper waters to her mouth, were laden with English goods. So soon as Challoner found a way up the Dvina, a body of merchants formed themselves into a society for discovering unknown lands, and this body of London merchants was the means of opening up Eastern Russia to the world.

The man who first struck the Volga was Anthony Jenkinson, agent of these discoverers, who brought out a cargo of cottons and kerseys, ready dyed and dressed, of lead and tin for roofing churches, and a vast assortment of pewter pots; all of which his masters in London expected him to exchange for the gums and silks, the gold and pearls, of mythical Cathay. Coming from the Frozen Sea, he noticed with a trader's eye that the land through which he passed was rich in hides, in fish, in salt, in train-oil, in furs, in pitch, and timber; while it was poor in many other things besides cotton shirts and pewter pots. Sailing up the Dvina to Vologda, he noted that town as a place for future trade; crossed the water-shed of Central Russia to Jaroslav and Moscow; dropped down the river Oka; and fell into the Volga at Nijni, the only town in which trade was being done, until he reached the Caspian Sea. The Volga banks were overrun by Tartar hordes, who took their spoil from every farm, and only spared the towns from fear. In ten weeks his rafts reached Astrakhan, where he saw, to his great surprise and joy, the riches of Persia and Bokhara lying about in the bazars in heaps; the alum, galls, and spices; the gems and filigrees, the shawls and bands, which he knew would fetch more in the London markets than their weight in gold. By hugging the northern shores of the Caspian Sea, he made the port of Mangishlak, in the Khanate of Khiva, early in autumn; and hiring from the natives a thousand camels, he loaded these patient beasts with his pots and pans, his sheetings and shirtings, and marched by the caravan road over the Tamdi Kuduk to Khiva, and thence across the range of Shiekh Djeli, and along the skirts of the great desert of Kizil Kum to Bokhara, near the gates of which he encamped on the day before Christmas-eve. There, to his grief, he learned that the caravan road farther east was stopped, in consequence of a war between tribes in the hill country of Turkestan; and after resting in the city of Bokhara for some weeks, he gave up his project, and, turning his face to the westward, returned to Moscow and London by the roads which he had found.

Three years later he was again in Moscow, chaffering with raftsmen for a voyage to the Caspian Sea. Queen Bess was now on the throne, and Jenkinson bore a letter from his sovereign to the Tsar, suggesting the benefits of trade and intercourse between his people and the society; and asking for his kingly help in opening up his towns and ports.

Ivan the Terrible was quick to perceive how much his power might be increased by the arts and arms which these strangers could bring him in their ships. Like Peter the Great in his genius for war, Ivan was only too well aware that, in comparison with the Swedes and Poles, his people were savages; and that his troops, though brave as wolves and hardy as bears, were still no match for such armies as the Baltic powers could send into the field. The glory of his early triumphs in the East and South had been dimmed by defeats inflicted upon him by his civilized enemies, the Poles; and the conquests of Kazan, Siberia, and Astrakhan, were all but forgotten in the reverses of his later years. He wanted ships, he wanted guns; the best of which, he had heard, could be bought for money in Elizabeth's ports, and brought to the Dvina in English ships. He was too great a savage to read the queen's letter in the way she wished; he cared no whit for maps, and could not bend his mind to the sale of hemp and pewter pots; but he saw in the queen's letter, which was addressed to him as Tsar, a recognition of the rank he had assumed, and the offer of a connection which he hoped to turn into a political alliance of the two powers.

While Ivan was weaving his net of policy, the English rafts were dropping down the Volga, towards Astrakhan, through hordes of Tartar horse. From Astrakhan they coasted the Caspian towards the south, landed at the port of Shabran, and, passing over the Georgian Alps, rode on camels through Shemaka and Ardabil, to Kasbin, then a residence of the Persian Shah. To him the queen had also sent a letter of friendship, and Jenkinson proposed to draw the great lines of Persian traffic by the Caspian and the Volga, to Archangel; connecting London and Kasbin by a near, a cheap, and an easy road; passing through the countries of a single prince, a natural ally of the Shah and of the Queen, instead of through the territories and waters of the Turk—the Venetian, the Almaigne, and the Dutch. The scheme was bold and new; of vast importance to the Russ, who had then no second outlet to the sea. But the Shah had just made peace with his enemy the Sultan, which compelled him to restore the ancient course of trade between the East and West.

Four years later, William Johnson, also an agent of the society, was sent from Archangel to Kasbin, with orders to make a good map of the River Volga and the Caspian Sea, and to build an English factory at Astrakhan for the Persian and Chinese trade. The Dvina was also studied and laid down, and the countries dividing her upper waters from the Volga were explored. A track had been worn by the natives from Vologda, one of the antique towns of Moscovy, famous for bells and candles, to Jaroslav, on the Volga; and along this track it was possible to transport the bales and boxes of English goods. This line was now laid down for the Persian and Oriental trade to follow, and factories were built in convenient spots along the route; the headquarters being fixed at Archangel and Astrakhan.

The Tsar sent home by Jenkinson not only a public letter to the queen, in which he asked her to send him cannon and ships, with men who could sail them; but a secret and verbal message, in which he proposed to make such a treaty of peace and alliance with her as that they should have the same friends and the same foes; and that if either of the two rulers should have need to quit his states, he might retire with safety and honor into those of the other. To the first he received no answer, and when Jenkinson returned to Russia on his trade affairs, the Tsar, who thought he had not delivered his message word for word, received him coldly, and ill-used the merchants in his empire; on which Thomas Randolph, a wily and able minister, was sent from London to pacify the tyrant, and protect our countrymen from his rage. But Randolph was treated worse than all; for on his arrival at Moscow, he was not only refused an audience, but placed in such custody that every one saw he was a prisoner. The letters sent to him by the queen were kept back, and those which he wrote to her were opened and returned. After eight months were passed in these insults, he was called to Vologda, received by the Tsar, and commanded to quit the Russian soil. So much insolence was used, that he was told by one of the boyars if he were not quick in going they would pitch his baggage out-of-doors.

Yet Randolph, patient and experienced, kept his temper, and when he left the Tsar he had a commercial charter in his trunk, and a special agent of Ivan in his train. This agent,

Andrew Gregorivitch, bore a letter to the queen (in Russ), in which he prayed her to sign a treaty of war and peace against all the world, and to grant him an asylum in her realm in case he should be driven from his own. Andrew found that the queen could make no treaty of the kind, though she was ready to promise his master an asylum in her states, where he might practise his own religion, and live at his own expense. He then gave ear to an impostor named Eli Bomel, a native of Wesel, whom he found in an English jail. This wretch, who professed to work by magic and the stars, proposed to go with Andrew to Russia and serve the Tsar. The agent asked for a pardon, and took him out to Moscow, where he soon became master in the tyrant's house. For Bomel made the Tsar believe that the queen, whom he described as a young and lovely virgin, was in love with him, and could be brought by sorcery to accept an offer of his hand and throne. The Tsar, who was past his prime, and feeble in health and power, never tired of doing honor to the man who promised him an alliance which would raise him above the proudest emperors and kings.

Horsey, following Randolph to Russia, saw the end of this wizard. When the Tsar found out that Bomel was deceiving him with lies, and that the queen would not write to him except on questions of trade, he sent for his favorite, laid him on the rack, drew his legs out of their sockets, flayed him with wire whips, roasted him before a fire, drew him on a sledge through the snow, and pitched him into a dungeon, where he was left to die.

Traders poured into Russia, through the line now opened from the Dvina to the Volga, stores of dyed cotton, copper pots and pans, sheets of lead rolled up for use, and articles in tin and iron of sundry sorts. Thomas Bannister and Geoffrey Ducket reached Jaroslav early in July, and, loading a fleet of rafts, dropped down the Volga to Astrakhan, where they staid six weeks in daily peril of their lives. The Turks, now friends with the Persians, were trying to recover that city, with the low countries of the Volga, from the Christian Russ; and the traders could not put to sea until the Moslem forces were drawn off. They put into Shabran, where they left their ship and crossed the mountains on camels to Shemaka, where they staid for the winter. Not before April could they venture to take the road. They pushed on to Ardabil, where they began to trade, while Bannister went on to Kasbin and procured a charter of commerce from the Shah. Only one objection was raised at Kasbin; Bannister wished to send horses through the Shah's dominions into India; but an article which he had inserted in his paper to this effect was left out by the Persian scribes. The successful trader sickened near Shemaka and died; leaving the command of his adventure to Ducket, who gathered up the goods for which they had exchanged their cloth and hardware, crossed the mountains to Shabran, and put to sea. Storm met them in the teeth; they rolled and tumbled through the waves; and after buffeting the winds for twenty days, they anchored in shallow water, where they were suddenly attacked by a horde of Moslem rievers, and after a gallant fight were overcome by superior strength. The Tartars pulled them from their ship, of which they made a prize, and, putting them into their own cutter, let them drift to sea. The cargo lost was worth no less than forty thousand pounds—a quarter of a million in our present coin.

At Astrakhan, which they reached in safety, they made some efforts to recover from the brigands part of what they had lost, and by the general's help some trifles were recovered from the wreck; but this salvage was lost once more in ascending the Volga, on which their boat was crushed by a ridge of ice. Every thing on board went down, and the grim old tyrant, Ivan the Terrible, sore about his failing suit for Elizabeth's hand, would render them no help.

Ten years elapsed before the traders sent another caravan across the Georgian Alps, but the road from Archangel to Astrakhan was never closed again; and for many years to come the English public heard far more about the Eastern Steppe than they hear in the present day.

This Eastern Steppe is overrun to-day, as it was overrun in the time of Ducket, by a tameless rabble of Asiatic tribes.

CHAPTER LXIII.

EASTERN STEPPE.

THE main attempt to colonize any portion of the Eastern Steppe with Christians was the planting of a line of Kozak camps in the countries lying between the Volga and the Don—a region in which the soil is less parched, the sand less deep, the herbage less scanty, than elsewhere in these sterile plains. But even in this favored region the fight for life is so hard and constant, that these Kozak colonists hail with joy the bugles that call them to arm and mount for a distant raid.

A wide and windy plain, sooty in color, level to the sight, with thin brown moss, and withered weeds; a herd of half-wild horses here and there; a Kalmuk rider dashing through a cloud of dust; a stray camel; a wagon drawn by oxen, ploughing heavily in the mud and marl; a hollow, dark and amber, in which lies a gypsy village; caravans of carts carrying hay and melons; a flock of sheep, watched by a Kozak lad attired in a fur cap, a skin capote, and enormous boots; a windmill on a lonely ridge; a mighty arch of sky overhead, shot with long lines of green and crimson light—such is an evening picture of the Eastern Steppe.

Time out of mind two hostile forces have been flowing from the deserts of Central Asia through this Eastern Steppe towards the fertile districts watered by the Don. These forces are the Turkish and Mongolian tribes. A cloud hangs over the earlier movements of these tribes; but when the invaders come under European ken, they are seen to be divided by differences of type and creed. The Turkish races rank among the handsomest on earth, the Mongolian races rank among the ugliest on earth. The Turkish tribes are children of Mohammed, the Mongolian tribes are children of Buddha. The first are a settled people, living in towns, and tilling the soil; the second a nomadic people, dwelling in tents, and roving from plain to plain with their flocks and herds.

The Moslem hordes which crossed the Ural River settled on the steppe, built cities on the Volga and the Donets, pushed their conquests up to the gates of Kief. The Buddhistic hordes which fought under Batu Khan destroyed this earlier work; but when they settled on the steppe, and married Moslem women, many of these heirs of Batu Khan embraced the religion of their wives, and helped the True Believers to erect such cities in their rear as Khiva, Bokhara, Samarcand, and Balkh, which afterwards became the strongholds of their faith. Yet most of the Mongol princes held by their ancient creed, and all the new-comers from their country added to their strength on this Eastern Steppe. These Turks and Mongols, enemies in Asia, kept up their feuds in Europe; and the early Moslem settlers in these plains were sorely pressed by their Buddhistic rulers, until the arrival of Timour Beg restored the Crescent to its old supremacy on the Eastern Steppe.

This feud between Buddha and Mohammed led in these countries to the final triumphs of the Cross.

The plains on which they fought for twenty generations are even now tented and cropped by Asiatic tribes—Kalmuks, Kirghiz, Nogays, Gypsies. The Kalmuks are Buddhists, the Kirghiz and Nogays are Moslem, the Gypsies are simply Gypsies.

The Kalmuks, a pastoral and warlike people, never yet confined in houses, are the true proprietors of the steppe. But they have given it up, at least in part; for in the reign of Empress Catharine, five hundred thousand wanderers crossed the Ural River, never to come back. The Kirghiz, Turkomans, and Nogays came in and occupied their lands.

The Kalmuks who remain in the country live in corrals (temporary camps), formed by raising a number of lodges near each other, round the tent of their high-priest. A Kalmuk lodge is a frame of poles set up in the form of a ring, tented at the top, and hung with coarse brown cloth. Inside, the ground is covered with skins and furs, on which the inmates lounge and sleep. Ten, twenty, fifty persons of all ages live under a common roof. A savage is not afraid of crowding; least of all when he lies down at night. Crowds comfort him and keep him warm. A flock of sheep, a string of camels, and a herd of horses, browse around the corral; for horses, sheep, and camels are the only wealth of tribes who plant no tree, who build no house, who sow no field. Flat in feature, bronze in color, bony in frame, the Kalmuk is one of the ugliest types of living men, though he is said to produce, by mixture with the more flexible and feminine Hindoo, the splendid face and figure of the Circassian chief.

The Kalmuk, as a Buddhist, keeping to his ancient Mongol traditions, and worshipping the Dalai-Lama, eats bull beef but slightly cooked, and drinks mare's milk in his favorite forms of kumis and spirit; the first being milk fermented only, the second milk fermented and distilled. Like all his race, he will steal a cow, a camel, or a horse, from either friend or foe, whenever he finds his chance. He owes no allegiance, he knows no law. Some formal acts of obedience are expected from him; such as paying his taxes, and supplying his tale of men for the ranks; but these payments and supplies are nominal only, save in districts where the rover has settled down under Kozak rule.

These wild men come and go as they list, roving with their sheep and camels from the wall of China to the countries watered by the Don. They come in hordes, and go in armies. In the reign of Michael Romanoff fifty thousand Kalmuks poured along the Eastern Steppe; and these unwelcome guests were afterwards strengthened by a second horde of ten thousand tents. These Kalmuks treated with Peter the Great as an independent power, and for several generations they paid no tribute to the crown except by furnishing cavalry in time of war. Another horde of ten thousand tents arrived. Their prince, Ubasha, led an army of thirty thousand horsemen towards the Danube against the Turks, whom they hated as only Asiatics hate hereditary foes. Yet, on the Empress Catharine trying to place the hordes under rule and law, the same Ubasha led his tribes—five hundred thousand souls, with countless herds of cattle, camels, and horses—back from the Eastern Steppe across the Ural River into Asia; stripping whole provinces of their wealth, producing famine in the towns, and robbing the empire of her most powerful arm. Hurt in his pride by some light word from the imperial lips, the prince proposed to carry off all his people, leaving not a soul behind; but fifteen thousand tents were left, because the winter came down late, and the Volga ice was thin. The children of these laggers are the men you meet on the plains, surprise at their religious rites, and sup with in their homely tents. Steps have been often taken to reclaim and fix these rovers, but with little or no effect. Some families have joined the Kozaks, come under law, and even embraced the cross; but the vast majority cling to their wild life, their Asiatic dress, and their Buddhistic creed.

The upper classes are called White (literally, white bones), the lower classes Black, just as in Asiatic fashion the Russian nobles are called White, while the peasants are called Black.

The Kirghiz are of Turkish origin, and speak the Uzbek idiom of their race. Divided into three branches, called the Great Horde, the Middle Horde, and the Little Horde, they roam over, if they do not own, the steppes and deserts lying between the Volga and Lake Balkash. Much of this tract is sandy waste, with dots of herbage here and there, and most of it lies beyond the Russian lines. Within these lines some order may be kept; beyond them, in what is called the Independent Steppe, the Kirghiz devilry finds an open field. These children of the desert plunder friend and foe, not only lifting cattle and robbing caravans, but stealing men and women to sell as slaves. All through these deserts, from Fort Aralsk to Daman-i-koh, the slave-trade is in vogue; the Kirghiz bandits keeping the markets of Khiva and Bokhara well supplied with boys and girls for sale. Nor is the traffic likely to decline until the flag of some civilized people floats from the Tower of Timour Beg. Fired by hereditary hate, these Kirghiz bandits look on every man of Mongolian birth and Buddhistic faith as lawful spoil. They follow him to his pastures, plunder his tent, drive off his herds, and sell him as a slave. But when this lawful prey escapes their hands they raid and rob on more friendly soil; and many of the captives whom they carry to Khiva and Bokhara come from the Persian valleys of Atrek and Meshid. Girls from these valleys fetch a higher price, and Persia has not strength enough to protect her children from their raids.

When Ubasha fled from the Volga with his Kalmuk hosts,

these Kirghiz had a year of sweet revenge. They lay in wait for their retiring foes; they broke upon their camps by night; they stole their horses; they devoured their food; they carried off their women. Hanging on the flank and rear of this moving mass, they cut off stragglers, stopped communications, hid the wells; inflicting far more miseries on the Kalmuks than these rovers suffered from all the generals sent against them by the crown.

These Kalmuks gone, the Kirghiz crossed the borders and appeared on the Volga, where they have been well received. Their khan is rich and powerful, and in coming in contact with Europe he has learned to value science; but the attempts which have been made to settle some portions of his tribe at Ryn Peski have met with no success. The Emperor has built a house for the khan, but the khan himself, preferring to live out-of-doors, has pitched his tent on the lawn! A Bedouin of the desert is not more untamable than a Kirghiz of the steppe.

The Nogays are Mongolians of a separate horde. Coming into the country with Jani Beg, they spread themselves through the southern plains, took wives of the people, and embraced the Mussulman faith. At first they were a nomadic soldiery, living in camps; and even after the war had died out, they kept to their wagons, and roamed through the country as the seasons came and went. "We live on wheels," they used to say: "one man has a house on the ground, another man has a house on wheels. It is the will of God." Yet, in the course of five hundred years, these Nogays have in some measure changed their habits of life, though they have not changed their creed. Many of them are settlers on the land, which they farm in a rough style; growing millet, grapes, and melons for their daily food. Being strict Mohammedans, they drink no wine, and marry two or three wives apiece. All wives are bought with money; and divorce, though easy to obtain, is seldom tried. The men are proud of their descent and their religion, and the crown allows their cadis and mollahs to settle most of their disputes. They pay a tax, but they are not enrolled for war.

These Mongolians occupy the Russian Steppe between the Molochnaya River and the Sea of Azof.

The Gypsies, here called Tsiganie, live a nomadic life in the Eastern Steppe, as in other countries, sleeping in wretched tents of coarse brown cloth, and grovelling like dogs and swine in the mire. They own a few carts, and ponies to match the carts, in which they carry their wives and little folk from fair to fair, stealing poultry, telling fortunes, shoeing horses, and existing only from hand to mouth. They will not labor—they will not learn. Some Gypsies show a talent for music, and many of their girls have a beauty of person which is highly prized. A few become public singers; and a splendid specimen of her race may marry—like the present Princess Sergie Golitsin of Moscow—into the highest rank; but as a race they live apart, in true Asiatic style; reiving and prowling on their neighbors' farms, begging at one house, thieving at the next; a class of outlaws, objects of fear to many, and of disgust to all. In summer they lodge on the grass, in winter they burrow in the ground; taking no more thought of the heat and dew than of the frost and snow. In color they are almost bronze, with big fierce eyes and famished looks, as though they were the embodied life of the dirt in which they wallow by day and dream by night. Some efforts have been made by Government to civilize these mysterious tribes, but hitherto without results; and the marauders are only to be kept in check on the Eastern Steppe by occasional onsets of Kozak horse.

CHAPTER LXIV.

DON KOZAKS.

SINCE the flight of their countrymen under Ubasha, the Kalmuks have been closely pressed by their Moslem foes.

Their chief tormentors came from the Caucasus; from the hills of which countries, Nogays and Turkomans, eternal enemies of their race and faith, descended on their pasture lands, drove out their sheep and camels, broke up their corrals, and insulted their religious rites. No government could prevent these raids, except by following the raiders home. But then, these Nogays and Turkomans were independent tribes; their homes were built on the heights beyond the Russian lines; and the necessities under which Russia lay—first, to protect her own plains from insult; next, to preserve the peace between these Buddhists and Moslems, gave her a better excuse for occupying the hill-countries in her front than the sympathy felt in high quarters for the Georgian Church. Pressed by these enemies, some of the Kalmuks have appealed to the crown for help, and have even quitted their camps, and sought protection within the Kozak lines.

The Kozak camps along the outer and inner frontiers—the Ural line and the Volga line—are peopled by a mixed race of Malo-Russians, Kalmuks, and Kirghiz; but the element that fuses and connects these rival forces comes from the old free Ukraine, and is thoroughly Slavonic in creed and race.

A Kozak of the Volga and the Don is not a Russian of Moscow, but of Novgorod and Kief; a man who for hundreds of years has held his own. His horse is always saddled; his lance is always sharp. By day and night his face is towards the enemy; his camp is in a state of siege. Compared with a Russian of Moscow, the Kozak is a jovial fellow, heady and ready, prompt in remark, and keen in jest; his mouth full of song, his head full of romance, and his heart full of love.

On the Ural River the Kozak has a little less of the Kalmuk, a little more of the Kirghiz, in his veins; but the Ukraine blood is dominant in both. It would be impossible for the Kalmuk and Kirghiz to live in peace, if these followers of the Grand Lama and the Arabian Prophet were not held in check by the Kozak camps.

First at St. Romanof, afterwards at Cemikarakorskoe, and other camps on the Don, I find the Kozaks in these camps; eat and drink with them, join in their festivals, watch their dances, hear their national songs, and observe them fight their fights. An aged story-teller comes into my room at St. Romanof to spin long yarns about Kozak daring and adventure in the Caucasian wars. I notice, as a peculiarity of these gallant recitals, that the old warrior's stories turn on practices and stratagems, never on open and manly fights; the tricks by which a picket was misled, a village captured, a caravan cut off, a heap of booty won. As the old man speaks of a farm-yard entered, of a herd of cows surprised, his face will gleam with a sudden joy; and then the younkers listening to his tale will clap their hands and stamp their feet, impatient to mount their stallions and ride away. When he tells of harems forced and mosques profaned, the Kalmuks who are present color and pant with Asiatic glee.

These Kozaks live in villages, composed of houses and gardens built in a kind of maze; the houses thatched with straw, the walls painted yellow, and a ring-fence running round the cluster of habitations, with an opening only at two or three points. The ins and outs are difficult; the passages guarded by savage dogs; the whole camp being a pen for the cattle as well as a fortress for the men. A church, of no great size and splendor, springs from the highest mound in the hamlet; for these Kozaks of the Eastern Steppe are nearly all attached to the ancient Slavonic rite. A flock of sheep is baa-ing on the steppe, a train of carts and oxen moving on the road. A fowler crushes through the herbage with his gun. On every side we see some evidence of life; and if the plain is still dark and bare, the Kozak love of garden, fence, and color lends a charm to the Southern country never to be seen in the North.

A thousand souls are camped at St. Romanof, in a rude hamlet, with the usual paint and fence. Each house stands by itself, with its own yard and garden, vines, and melon-beds, guarded by a savage dog. The type is Malo-Russ, the complexion yellow and Tartar-like; the teeth are very fine, the eyes are burning with hidden fire. Men and boys all ride, and every child appears to possess a horse. Yet half the men are nursing babies, while the women are doing the heavier kinds of work. A superstition of the steppe accounts for the fact of half these men carrying infants in their arms, the naked brats pressed closely beneath their coats. They think that unless a father nurses his first-born son his wife will die of the second child; and as a woman costs so many cows and horses, it is a serious thing—apart from his affections—for a man on the Eastern Steppe to lose his wife.

No smoking is allowed in a Kozak camp, for dread of fire; though my host at Cemikarakorskoe smokes himself, and invites his guests to smoke. Outside the fence the women are frying melons and making wine—a strong and curious liquor, thick as treacle, with a finer taste. It is an ancient custom, lost, except on the Don. A plain church, with a lofty belfry, adorns the camp; but a majority of the Kozaks being Old Believers, the camp may be said to absent itself from mass. These rough fellows, ready as they seem for raiding and thieving, are just now overwhelmed with sorrow on account of their church affairs!

Their bishop, Father Plato, has been seized in his house at Novo Cherkask, and sent up the Don to Kremenskoe, a convent near Kalatch. A very old man, he has now been two years a prisoner in that convent; and no one in the camp can learn the nature of his offense. The Kozaks bear his trouble with saddened hearts and flashing eyes; for these colonists look on the board of Black Clergy sitting in St. Isaac's Square, not only as a conclave going beyond its functions, but as the Chert, the Black One, the incarnate Evil Spirit.

Cemikarakorskoe is a chief camp or town on the Lower Don. "How many souls have you in camp?" I ask my host, as we stroll about. "We do not know; our folk don't relish counting; but we have always five hundred saddles ready in the stalls." The men look wild, but they are gradually taming down. Fine herds of cattle dot the plains beyond their fence, and some of the families sow fields of corn and maize. They grow abundance of purple grapes, from which they press a strong and sparkling wine. My host puts on his table a vintage as good as Asti; and some folk say the vineyards of the Don are finer than those of the Garonne and the Marne!

These Kozaks have soil enough to grow their food, and fill the markets with their surplus. No division of land has taken place for thirty-two years. A plain extends in front as far as the eye can reach; it is a common property, and every man can take what he likes. The poorest fellows have thirty acres apiece. In their home affairs, these colonists are still a state within the state. Their hetman has been abolished; their grand ataman is the crown prince; but his work is wholly nominal, and they elect their own atamans and judges for a limited term. Every one is eligible for the office of local ataman—a colonel of the camp, who commands the village in peace and war; but he must not leave his quarters for the whole of his three years. An officer is sent from St. Petersburg to drill and command the troops. Every one is eligible as judge—an officer who tries all cases under forty rubles of account, and, like an ataman, the judge may not quit his village even in time of war.

A great reform is taking place among these camps. All officers above the rank of ataman and judge are now appointed by the crown, as such men are in every branch of the public force. An ataman-general resides with an effective staff at Novo Cherkask, a town lying back from the Don, in a position to guard against surprise—a town with streets and houses, and with thoroughfares lit by lamps instead of being watched by savage dogs. But Novo Cherkask is a Russian city, not a Kozak camp; the ataman-general is a Russian soldier, not a Kozak chief; and the object kept in view at Novo Cherkask is that of safely and steadily bringing these old military colonists on the Eastern Steppe under the action of imperial law.

But such a change must be a work of time. General Potapoff, the last ruler in Novo Cherkask, a man of high talents, fell to his work so fast that a revolt seemed likely to occur along the whole line of the Don. On proof that he was not the man for such a post, this general was promoted to Vilna, as commander-in-chief in the fourth military district; while General Chertkoff, an old man of conservative views, was sent down from St. Petersburg to soothe the camps and keep things quiet in the steppe. The Emperor made a little joke on his officers' names:—"After the flood, the devil;" Potap meaning deluge, and Chert the Evil One; and when his brave Kozaks had laughed at the jest, every thing fell back for a time into the ancient ruts.

Of course, in a free Russia all men must be put on an equal footing before the law, and Kozak privilege must go the way that every other privilege is going. Yet where is the class of men that willingly gives up a special right?

A Kozak is a being slow to change; and a prince who has to keep his eye fixed day and night on these Eastern steppes, and on the cities lying beyond them, Khiva and Bokhara, out of which have come from age to age those rolling swarms of savage tribes, can hardly be expected, even in the cause of uniform law, to break his lines of defense, and drive his faithful pickets into open revolt against his rule.

CHAPTER LXV.

UNDER ARMS.

AN army is in every state, whether bond or free, a thing of privilege and tradition; and in giving a new spirit to his Government, it is essential that the Emperor should bring his army into some closer relation to the country he is making free.

The first thing is to raise the profession of arms to a higher grade, by giving to every soldier in the ranks the old privilege of a prince and boyar—his immunity from blows and stripes. A soldier can not now be flogged. Before the present reign, the army was in theory an open school of merit, and occasionally a man like General Skobeleff rose from the rank of peasant to the highest posts. But Skobeleff was a man of genius—a good writer, as well as a splendid soldier; and his nomination as commander of St. Petersburg took no one by surprise. Such cases of advancement are extremely rare; rare as in the Austrian service, and in our own. But the reforms now introduced into the army are making this opening for talent wide enough to give every one a chance. The soldiers are better taught, better clothed, and better lodged. In distant provinces they are not yet equal to the show-troops seen on a summer day at Tsarskoe Seloe; but they are lodged and treated, even in these far-off stations, with a care to which aforetime they were never used. Every man has a pair of strong boots, a good overcoat, a bashlik for his head. His rations are much improved; good beef is weighed to him; and he is not compelled to fast. The brutal punishment of running the ranks has been put down.

A man who served in the army, just before the Crimean war broke out, put the difference between the old system and the new in a luminous way.

"God bless the Emperor," he said; "he gave me life, and all that I can give him in return is his."

"You were a prisoner, then?"

"I was a soldier, young and hot. Some Kozak blood was in my veins; unlike the serfs, I could not bear a blow, and broke my duty as a soldier to escape an act of shame."

"For what were you degraded?"

"Well! I was a fool. A fool? I was in love; and staked my liberty for a pretty girl. I kissed her, and was lost."

"That is what the greatest conquerors have done. You lost yourself for a rosy lip?"

"Well—yes; and—no," said Michael. "You see, I was a youngster then. A man is not a graybeard when he counts his nineteen summers; and a pair of bright eyes, backed by a saucy tongue, is more than a lad of spirit can pass without a singe. Katinka's eyes were bright as her words were arch. You see, in those days we were all young troops on the road; going down from Yaroslav into the South, to fight for the Holy Cross and the Golden Keys. The Frank and Turk were coming up into our towns, to mock our religion and to steal our wives; and after a great festa in the Church, when the golden icon was brought round the ranks, and every man kissed it in his turn, we marched out of Yaroslav with rolling drums, and pious hymns, and blessings on our arms. The town soon dropped behind us, and with the steppe in front, we turned back more than once to look at the shining domes and towers, which few of us could hope to see again. For three days we kept well on; the fourth day some of our lads were missing; for the roads were heavy, the wells were almost dry, and the regiment was badly shod. Many were sick; but some were feigning; and the punishment for shamming is the rod. Our colonel, a tall, gaunt fellow, stiff as a pike and tight as a cord, whom no fatigue could touch, began to flog the stragglers; and as every man in the ranks had to take his turn in whipping his fellows, the temper of the whole regiment became morose and savage. In those old times—some eighteen years ago—we had a rough-and-ready sort of punishment, called running the ranks."

"Running the ranks?"

"It is done so: if a lad has either fallen asleep on his post, or vexed his officer, or stolen his comrade's pipe, or failed to answer at the roll, he is called to the parade-ground of his company, told to give up his gun, and strip himself naked to the waist. A soldier grounds the musket, to which the culprit's two hands are now tied fast near the muzzle; the bayonet is then fixed, and the butt-end lifted from the ground so as to bring the point of the bayonet close to the culprit's heart. The company is then drawn up in two long lines, in open order; and into every man's hand is given a rod newly cut and steeped for a night in water to make it hard. The offender is led between these lines; led by the butt-end of his gun, the slightest motion of which he must obey, on pain of being pricked to death; and the troops lay on his naked back, with a will or not, as their mood may chance to be. The pain is always great, and the sufferer dares not shrink before the rod; as in doing so he would fall on the bayonet-point. But the shame of running the ranks was greater than the pain. Some fellows learned to bear it; but these were men who had lost all sense of shame. For my own part, I think it was worse than death and hell."

"You have not borne it?"

"Never! I will tell you. We had marched about a thousand versts towards the South. Our companies were greatly thinned; for every second man who had left Yaroslav with beating heart and singing his joyous psalm, was left behind us, either in the sick-ward or on the steppe—most of them on the steppe. Many of the men had run away; some because they did not want to fight, and others because they had vexed their officers by petty faults. We had a fortnight yet to march before reaching those lines of Perikop, where the Tartars used to fight us; and our stiff colonel cried out daily down our squads, that if we skulked on the march the Turks would be in Moscow, not the Russians at Stamboul."

"Yes!"

"We had a fortnight yet to march; but the men were so spent and sore that we halted in a roadside village three days to mend our shoes and recruit our strength. That halt unmade me. What with her laughing eyes and her merry tricks, the girl who served out whisky and halibut to our company won my heart. Her father kept the inn and posting-house of the village; he had to find us quarters, and supply us with meat and drink. The girl was about the sheds in which we lay from early morning until late at night. I don't say she cared for me, though I was thought a handsome lad; but she was like a wild kitten, and would purr and play about you till your blood was all on fire; and into the stable or the straw-shed, screaming with laughter, and daring you to chase and capture her—with a kiss, of course. It was rare good sport; but some of the men, too broken to engage in making love, were jealous of the fun, and said it would end in trouble. Well, when the drum tapped for our companies to fall in, my cloak was missing, and I began to hunt through the shed in which we had slept the last three nights. The cloak could not be found. While running up and down, upsetting stools and scattering sheaves of straw, I caught Katinka's laughing face at the window of the shed, and at the very same instant heard the word of command to march. I had no intention to quit the ranks; but I wanted my cloak, the loss of which would have been visited upon me by the anger of my captain and by the wintry frosts. I ran after Katinka, who darted round the sheds with the cloak on her arm, crowing with delight as she slipped through the stakes and past the corners, until she bounded into the straw-yard, panting and spent. To get the cloak from her was the work of a second; but to smother her red mouth with kisses was a task which must have taken me some time; for just as I was getting free from her, two men of my company came up and took me prisoner. Graybeards of twenty-five, who had seen what they call the world, these fellows cared no more for a pretty girl than for a holy saint. They told the colonel lies; they said I meant to straggle and desert; and the colonel sentenced me to run the ranks."

"You escaped the shame?"

"By taking my chance of death. The colonel stood before me, bolt upright, his hand upon the shoulder of his horse. Too well I knew how to merit death in a time of war; and striding up to him, by a rapid motion, ere any one could pull me back, I struck that officer with my open palm across his cheek. A minute later I was pinioned, thrown into a cart, and placed under a double guard. At Perikop I was brought before commissioners and condemned to die; but the Franks were now coming up the Bosphorus in ships, and the prince commanding in the Crimea, being anxious to make the war popular, was in a tender mood; and finding that my record in the regiment was good, he changed my sentence of death into one of imprisonment in a fortress during life. My comrades thought I should be pardoned in a few weeks and placed in some other company for service; but my crime was too black to be forgiven in that iron reign."

"Iron reign?"

"The reign of Nicolas was the iron reign. I was sent to a fortress, where I lay, a prisoner, until Nicolas went to heaven."

"You lived two years in jail?"

"Lived! No; you do not live in prison, you die. But when the saints are cross you take a very long time to die."

"You wished to die?"

"Well, no; you only wish to sleep, to forget your pain, to escape from the watcher's eyes. When the rings are soldered round your ankles, and the cuffs are fastened round your wrists, you feel that you have ceased to be a man. Cold, passive, cruel in your temper, you are now a savage beast, without the savage freedom of the wolf and bear. Your legs swell out, and the bones grow gritty, and like to snap."

"Which are the worse to bear—the leg-rings or the cuffs?"

"The cuffs. When they are taken off, a man goes all but mad. He clasps and claps his hands for joy; he can lift his palms in prayer, besides being able to chase the spiders and kill the fleas. Worst of all to the prisoner are the eyelets in his door, through which the sentinel watches him from dawn to dusk. Though lonely, he is never alone. Do what he may, the passionless holes are open, and a freezing glance may be fixed upon him. In his sleeping and in his waking hour those eyes are on him, and he gladly waits for darkness to come down, that he may feel secure from that maddening watch. Sometimes a man goes boldly to the door, spits through the holes, yells like a wild beast, and forces the sentinel to retire in shame."

"You gained your freedom in the general amnesty?"

"Yes; when the young prince came to his throne he opened our prison-doors and set us free. Were you ever a prisoner? No! Then you can never know what it is to be free. You walk out of darkness into light; you wake out of misery into joy. The air you breathe makes you strong like a draught of wine. You feel that you belong to God."

Under Nicolas the soldiers were so dressed and drilled that they were always falling sick. A third of the army was in hospital the whole year round, and little more than half the men could ever be returned as fit to march. Being badly clothed and poorly fed, they flew to drink. They died in heaps, and rather like sheep than men.

The case is different now; for the soldier is better clothed and fed than persons of his class in ordinary life. The men are allowed to stand and walk in their natural way; and, having more bread to eat, they show less craving after drink. A school is opened in every barrack, and pressure is put on the men to make them learn. Many of the soldiers can read, and some can write. Gazettes and papers are taken in; libraries are being formed; and the Russian army promises to become as bright as that of Germany or France. The change is great; and every one finds the root of this reform in that abolition of the Tartar stick, which comes, like other great reforms, from the Crimean war.

CHAPTER LXVI.

ALEXANDER.

THE Crimean war restored the people to their national life. "Sebastopol!" said a general officer to me just now, "Sebastopol perished, that our country might be free." The Tartar kingdom, founded by Ivan the Terrible, reformed by Peter the Great, existed in the spirit, even where it clothed itself in Western names and forms, until the allies landed from their transports. Routed on the Alma, beaten at Balaclava, that kingdom made her final effort on the heights of Inkermann; hurling, in Tartar force and fashion, her last "great horde" across that Baidar valley, in the rocks and caves of which a remnant of the tribes of Batu Khan and Timour Beg still lingers; fighting in mist and fog, on wooded slope and stony ridge, her gallant and despairing fight. What followed Inkermann was detail only. Met and foiled that wintry day, she reeled and bled to death. A grave was made for her, as one may say, not far from the spot on which she fought and fell. Before the landing-place in Sebastopol sprang the walls and frowned the guns of an imperial fort—the strongest pile in Russia, perhaps in Europe; rising tier on tier, and armed with two hundred and sixty guns; a fort in the fire of which no ship then floating on the sea could live. It bore the builder's name—the name of Nicolas, Autocrat of all the Russians; a colossal sovereign, who for thirty years had awed and stifled men like Genghis Khan. That fort became a ruin. The guns were torn to rags, the walls were shivered into dust. No stone was left in its place to tell the tale of its former pride; and it is even now an easier task to trace the outlines of Kherson, dead for five hundred years, than to restore, from what remains of them, the features of that proud, imperial fort. The prince, the fortress, and the kingdom fell; their work on earth accomplished to the final act. This ruin is their grave.

Asiatic Russia passed away, and European Russia struggled into life.

Holding under the "Great Cham," the Duke of Moscow was in ancient times a dependent prince, like the Hospodar of Valachia, like the Pasha of Egypt in modern days. Doing homage, paying tribute to his Tartar lord, the duke ruled in his place, coined money in his name, adopted his dress and habits, fought his battles, and took into pay his officers and troops. Cities which the Tartar could not reach, his vassal crushed.

The Tartar system was a village system, as it is with every pastoral and predatory race; a village for the followers, and a camp or residence for the prince. The Russian system was a mixed system, as it was in Germany and France; a village for the husbandman, a town for the boyar, merchant, and professional man. The old Russian towns were rich and free; ruled by codes of law, by popular assemblies, and by elected dukes. Novgorod, Moscow, Pskoff, Vladimir, Nijni, were models of a hundred prosperous towns; but when the Duke of Moscow wrested his independence from the khan in the seventeenth century, he took up the Tartar policy of weakening the free cities, and centring all authority in his camp. That camp was Moscow, which Ivan put under martial law, and governed, in Asiatic fashion, by the stick. The court became a Tartar court. The dress and manners of Bakchi Serai were imitated in the Kremlin; women were put into harems; the Tartar distinction of white and black (noble and ignoble) was established. From the time when the grand dukes became Tsars they were called White, the peasants Black; and the poor of every class, whether they lived in towns or villages, were styled, in contempt, as their Moslem masters had always styled them, Christians—bearers of the cross—a name which descended to the serfs, and clung to them so long as a serf existed on Russian soil.

In leaving Moscow, Peter the Great was only acting like the Crim Tartar who had changed his camp from Eski-Crim to Bakchi Serai. The camp was his country, and where he rested for a season was his camp. In Old Russia, as in Germany and France, authority was historical; in Crim-Tartary, as in Turkey and Bokhara, it was personal. Ivan the Terrible introduced, and Peter the Great extended, the personal system. In her better days Russia had a noble class, as well as a citizen class and a peasant class; but these signs of a glorious past were gradually put away. "No man is noble in my empire, unless I make him so," said Peter. "No man is noble in my empire, except when I speak to him, and only while I speak to him," said Paul. The governors of provinces became pashas, with the right of living on the districts they were sent to rule; that is to say, of taking from the people meat, drink, house, dogs, horses, women, at their sovereign will.

Though softened from time to time, here by fine phrases, there by mystic patriotism, this Tartar system lived into the present reign. Under this system, the prince was every thing, the people nothing; the army a horde, the nobility an official mob, the Church a department of police, the commons a herd of slaves.

Nicolas prized that system, and being a man of powerful frame and daring mind, he carried it forward to a point from which it had been falling back since the reign of Peter the

Great. Unlike Peter, Nicolas saw no use in Western science and Western arts. He hated railways, he abhorred the press. He made his court a camp; he dressed his students in uniform; he turned education into drill. He was the State, the Church, the Army, all in one. Desiring to shut up his empire, as the Khans of Khiva and Bokhara close their states, he drew a cordon round his frontier, over which it was nearly as difficult for a stranger to enter as for a subject to escape; and while he occupied the throne, his country was almost as much a mystery to mankind as the realm of Prester John. With mystery came distrust, for the unknown is always feared; and Europe lay in front of this Tartar prince, exactly as in former ages Moscow lay before Timour Beg. A system such as Nicolas loved could not exist in presence of free and powerful states; and Europe had to march upon the armies of Nicolas, even as Ivan the Terrible had to march upon the troops of Yediguer Khan.

The system was Mongolian, not Slavonic; and the mighty sovereign who upheld it, and perished with it, will be regarded in future ages as the prince who was at once the last Asiatic emperor and the last European khan.

When Alexander the Second came to his sceptre, what was his estate? His empire was a wreck. The allies were upon his soil; his ports were closed; his ships were sunk; his armies were held at bay. Looking from the Neva to the Thames, he could not see one friend on whom in his trouble he could call for help. The system was perfect; the isolation was complete. But why had that system, reared at such a price, collapsed so thoroughly at the point where it seemed to be most strong?"

His armies counted a million men. Why were these hosts unable to protect their soil? They were at home; they knew the country; they were used to its windy plains, its summer heats, and its wintry snows. They were fighting, too, for every thing that men hold dear on earth. When Alexander compared his million men against the forces of his rivals actually in the field, his wonder grew into amazement. These soldiers of his foes were weak in number, far from home, and fighting only for pride and pay. How were such armies able to maintain themselves on Russian ground?

Before the Emperor Nicolas died, he read the truth—read it in the light of his burning towns, his wasting armies, and his fruitless cannonades. He found that he and his million troops were matched against a hundred millions of eager and adventurous foes. Free nations were all against him; and the serf nation which he ruled so sternly was not for him. Russia was not with him. Here he was weak, with an incurable fret and sore. The serfs, the Old Believers, and the sectaries of every name, were all against him, looking on his system as a foreign, not to say an abominable thing, and praying night and day that the hour of their deliverance from his rule might quickly come. No people stood behind the soldiery in his war against the Western Powers.

In spite of genius, valor, enterprise, success, an army fighting for itself, unwarmed by popular applause, is sure in the end to fail. The discovery that he and his troops were fighting against the world of free thought and liberal science killed him. When the blow was dealt, and his pride was gone, Nicolas is said to have confided to his son Alexander the causes of his failure as he had come to see them, and to have urged the prince to pursue another and more liberal course. Who can say whether this is true or not, for who can know the secrets of that dying bed?

Yet every man can see that the new sovereign acted as if some such warning had been given. He began his reign with acts of mercy. Hundreds of prison doors were opened, thousands of exiles were released from bonds. An honorable peace was made with the Western Powers, and the dream of marching on Stamboul was brushed aside. An empire of seventy millions was found big enough to hold her own. Alexander proved that he had none of the Tartar's lust of territory by giving up part of Bessarabia for the sake of peace.

Secured on his frontiers, Alexander turned his eyes on the people and the provinces committed to his care. A vast majority of his countrymen were serfs. Not one in ten could read; not one in fifty could sign his name. Great numbers of his people stood aloof from the Official Church. The serfs were much oppressed by the nobles; the Old Believers were bitterly persecuted by the monks; yet these two classes were the bone and sinew of the land. If strength was sought beyond the army and the official classes, where could he find it, save among these serfs in the country, these Old Believers in the towns? In no other places. How could such populations, suffering as they were from physical bondage and religious hate, be reconciled to the empire, added to the national force?

Studying the men over whom he was called to rule, the Emperor went down among his people; living on their river banks and in their rural communes; passing from the Arctic to the Caspian Sea, from the Vistula to the Ural mines; kneeling with them at Solovetsk and Troitsa; parleying with them on the roadside and by the inland lake; observing them in the forest and in the mine; until he felt that he had seen more of the Russian soil, knew more of the Russian people, than any of the ministers about his court.

In the light of knowledge thus carefully acquired, he opened the great question of the serfs; and feeling strong in his minute acquaintance with his country, had the happy courage to insist on his principle of "liberty with land," against the views of his councils and committees in favor of "liberty without land."

Before that act was carried out in every part, he began his great reform in the army. He put down flogging, beating, and striking in the ranks. He opened schools in the camp, cleared the avenues of promotion, and raised the soldier's condition on the moral, not less than on the material side.

The universities were then reformed in a pacific sense. Swords were put down, uniforms laid aside, and corporate privileges withdrawn. Education was divorced from its connection with the camp. Lay professors occupied the chairs, and the young men attending lectures stood on the same level with their fellows, subject to the same magistrate, amenable to the common code. The schools became free, and students ceased to be feared as "servants of the Tsar."

This change was followed by that immense reform in the administration of justice which transferred the trial of offenders from the police office to the courts of law; replacing an always arbitrary and often corrupted official by an impartial jury, acting in union with an educated judge.

At the same period he opened those local parliaments, the

district assemblies and the provincial assemblies, which are training men to think and speak, to listen and decide—to believe in argument, to respect opposing views, and exercise the virtues required in public life.

In the wake of these reforms came the still more delicate question of Church reform; including the relations of the Black clergy to the White; of the Orthodox clergy, whether Black or White, to the Old Believers; of the Holy Governing Synod to Dissenters; as also the influence which the Church should exercise over secular education, and the supremacy of the canon law over the civil law.

Each of these great reforms would seem, in a country like Russia, to require a lifetime; yet under this daring and beneficent ruler they are all proceeding side by side. Opposed by the three most powerful parties in the empire—the Black Clergy, who feel that power is slipping from their hands—the old military chiefs, who think their soldiers should be kept in order by the stick—the thriftless nobles, who prefer Homberg and Paris to a dull life on their estates—the Emperor not the less keeps steadily working out his ends. What wonder that he is adored by peasants, burghers, and parish priests, by all who wish to live in peace, to till their fields, to mind their shops, and to say their prayers!

A free Russia is a pacific Russia. By his genius and his occupation, a Russian is less inclined to war than either a Briton or a Gaul; and as the right of voting on public questions comes to be his habit, his voice will be more and more cast for the policy that gives him peace. In one direction only he looks with dread—across that opening of the Eastern Steppe through which he has seen so many hordes of his enemies swarm into his towns and fields. Through that opening he has pushed—is now pushing—and will push his way, until Khiva and Bokhara fall into his power, as Tashkend and Kokan have fallen into his power.

Why should we English regret his march, repine at his success? Is he not fighting, for all the world, a battle of law, of order, and of civilization? Would not Russia at Bokhara mean the English at Bokhara also? Would not roads be made, and stations built, and passes guarded through the steppe for traders and travellers of every race? Could any other people undertake this task? Why then should we cry down the Moscovite? Even in our selfish interests, it would be well for us to have a civilized neighbor on our frontier rather than a savage tribe; a neighbor bound by law and courtesy, instead of a savage khan who murders our envoy and rejects our trade!

Russia requires a hundred years of peace; but she will not find that peace until she has closed the passage of her Eastern Steppe by planting the banner of St. George on the Tower of Timour Beg.

Meantime, the reforming Emperor holds his course—a lonely man, much crossed by care, much tried by family afflictions, much enduring in his public life.

One dark December day, near dusk, two Englishmen hail a boat on the Neva brink, and push out rapidly through the bars of ice towards that grim fortress of St. Peter and St. Paul, in which lie buried under marble slab and golden cross the emperors and empresses (with one exception) since the reign of Peter the Great. As they are pushing onward, they observe the watermen drop their oars and doff their caps; and looking round, they see the imperial barge, propelled by twenty rowers, athwart their stern. The Emperor sits in that barge alone; an officer is standing by his side, and the helmsman directs the rowers how to pull. Saluting as he glides past their boat, the Emperor jumps to land, and muffling his loose gray cloak about his neck, steps hastily along the planks and up the roadway leading to the church. No one goes with him. The six or eight idlers whom he meets on the road just touch their hats, and stand aside to let him pass. Trying the front door of that sombre church, he finds it locked; and striding off quickly to a second door, he sees a man in plain clothes, and beckons to him. The door is quickly opened, and the lord of seventy millions walks into the church that is to be his final home. The English visitors are near. "Wait for an instant," says the man in plain clothes; "the Emperor is within;" but adds, "you can step into the porch; his majesty will not keep you long." The porch is parted from the church by glass doors only, and the English visitors look down upon the scene within. Long aisles and columns stretch and rise before them. Flags and trophies, won in a hundred battles, fought against the Swede and Frank, the Perse and Turk, adorn the walls, and here and there a silver lamp burns fitfully in front of a pictured saint. Between the columns stand, in white sepulchral rows, the imperial tombs—a weird and ghastly vista, gleaming in that red and sombre light.

Alone, his cap drawn tightly on his brow, and muffled in his loose gray coat, the Emperor passes from slab to slab; now pausing for an instant, as if conning an inscription on the stone, now crossing the nave absorbed and bent; here hidden for a moment in the gloom, there moving furtively along the aisle. The dead are all around him—Peter, Catharine, Paul—fierce warriors, tender women, innocent babes, and overhead the dust and glory of a hundred wars. What brings him hither in this wintry dusk? The weight of life? The love of death? He stops, unbonnets, kneels—at the foot of his mother's tomb! Once more he pauses, kneels—kneels a long time, as if in prayer; then, rising, kisses the golden cross. That slab is the tomb of his eldest son!

A moment later he is gone.

THE END.

VALUABLE STANDARD WORKS

FOR PUBLIC AND PRIVATE LIBRARIES,

PUBLISHED BY HARPER & BROTHERS, NEW YORK.

☞ *For a full List of Books suitable for Libraries, see* HARPER & BROTHERS' TRADE-LIST *and* CATALOGUE, *which may be had gratuitously on application to the Publishers personally, or by letter enclosing Five Cents.*

☞ HARPER & BROTHERS *will send any of the following works by mail, postage prepaid, to any part of the United States, on receipt of the price.*

MOTLEY'S DUTCH REPUBLIC. The Rise of the Dutch Republic. By JOHN LOTHROP MOTLEY, LL.D., D.C.L. With a Portrait of William of Orange. 3 vols., 8vo, Cloth, $10 50.

MOTLEY'S UNITED NETHERLANDS. History of the United Netherlands: from the Death of William the Silent to the Twelve Years' Truce—1609. With a full View of the English-Dutch Struggle against Spain, and of the Origin and Destruction of the Spanish Armada. By JOHN LOTHROP MOTLEY, LL.D., D.C.L. Portraits. 4 vols., 8vo, Cloth, $14 00.

NAPOLEON'S LIFE OF CÆSAR. The History of Julius Cæsar. By His Imperial Majesty NAPOLEON III. Two Volumes ready. Library Edition, 8vo, Cloth, $3 50 per vol.

Maps to Vols. I. and II. sold separately. Price $1 50 *each*, NET.

HAYDN'S DICTIONARY OF DATES, relating to all Ages and Nations. For Universal Reference. Edited by BENJAMIN VINCENT, Assistant Secretary and Keeper of the Library of the Royal Institution of Great Britain; and Revised for the Use of American Readers. 8vo, Cloth, $5 00; Sheep, $6 00.

HARTWIG'S POLAR WORLD. The Polar World: a Popular Description of Man and Nature in the Arctic and Antarctic Regions of the Globe. By Dr. G. HARTWIG, Author of "The Sea and its Living Wonders," "The Harmonies of Nature," and "The Tropical World." With Additional Chapters and 163 Illustrations. 8vo, Cloth, Beveled Edges, $3 75.

WALLACE'S MALAY ARCHIPELAGO. The Malay Archipelago: the Land of the Orang-Utan and the Bird of Paradise. A Narrative of Travel, 1854–1862. With Studies of Man and Nature. By ALFRED RUSSEL WALLACE. With Ten Maps and Fifty-one Elegant Illustrations. Crown 8vo, Cloth, $3 50.

WHYMPER'S ALASKA. Travel and Adventure in the Territory of Alaska, formerly Russian America—now Ceded to the United States—and in various other parts of the North Pacific. By FREDERICK WHYMPER. With Map and Illustrations. Crown 8vo, Cloth, $2 50.

ORTON'S ANDES AND THE AMAZON. The Andes and the Amazon; or, Across the Continent of South America. By JAMES ORTON, M.A., Professor of Natural History in Vassar College, Poughkeepsie, N. Y., and Corresponding Member of the Academy of Natural Sciences, Philadelphia. With a New Map of Equatorial America and numerous Illustrations. Crown 8vo, Cloth, $2 00.

WINCHELL'S SKETCHES OF CREATION. Sketches of Creation: a Popular View of some of the Grand Conclusions of the Sciences in reference to the History of Matter and of Life. Together with a Statement of the Intimations of Science respecting the Primordial Condition and the Ultimate Destiny of the Earth and the Solar System. By ALEXANDER WINCHELL, LL.D., Professor of Geology, Zoology, and Botany in the University of Michigan, and Director of the State Geological Survey. With Illustrations. 12mo, Cloth, $2 00.

WHITE'S MASSACRE OF ST. BARTHOLOMEW. The Massacre of St. Bartholomew: Preceded by a History of the Religious Wars in the Reign of Charles IX. By HENRY WHITE, M.A. With Illustrations. 8vo, Cloth, $1 75.

LOSSING'S FIELD-BOOK OF THE REVOLUTION. Pictorial Field-Book of the Revolution; or, Illustrations, by Pen and Pencil, of the History, Biography, Scenery, Relics, and Traditions of the War for Independence. By BENSON J. LOSSING. 2 vols., 8vo, Cloth, $14 00; Sheep, $15 00; Half Calf, $18 00; Full Turkey Morocco, $22 00.

LOSSING'S FIELD-BOOK OF THE WAR OF 1812. Pictorial Field-Book of the War of 1812; or, Illustrations, by Pen and Pencil, of the History, Biography, Scenery, Relics, and Traditions of the Last War for American Independence. By BENSON J. LOSSING. With several hundred Engravings on Wood, by Lossing and Barritt, chiefly from Original Sketches by the Author. 1088 pages, 8vo, Cloth, $7 00; Sheep, $8 50; Half Calf, $10 00.

ALFORD'S GREEK TESTAMENT. The Greek Testament: with a critically-revised Text; a Digest of Various Readings; Marginal References to Verbal and Idiomatic Usage; Prolegomena; and a Critical and Exegetical Commentary. For the Use of Theological Students and Ministers. By HENRY ALFORD, D.D., Dean of Canterbury. Vol. I., containing the Four Gospels. 944 pages, 8vo, Cloth, $6 00; Sheep, $6 50.

ABBOTT'S HISTORY OF THE FRENCH REVOLUTION. The French Revolution of 1789, as viewed in the Light of Republican Institutions. By JOHN S. C. ABBOTT. With 100 Engravings. 8vo, Cloth, $5 00.

ABBOTT'S NAPOLEON BONAPARTE. The History of Napoleon Bonaparte. By JOHN S. C. ABBOTT. With Maps, Woodcuts, and Portraits on Steel. 2 vols., 8vo, Cloth, $10 00.

ABBOTT'S NAPOLEON AT ST. HELENA; or, Interesting Anecdotes and Remarkable Conversations of the Emperor during the Five and a Half Years of his Captivity. Collected from the Memorials of Las Casas, O'Meara, Montholon, Antommarchi, and others. By JOHN S. C. ABBOTT. With Illustrations. 8vo, Cloth, $5 00.

ADDISON'S COMPLETE WORKS. The Works of Joseph Addison, embracing the whole of the "Spectator." Complete in 3 vols., 8vo, Cloth, $6 00.

ALCOCK'S JAPAN. The Capital of the Tycoon: a Narrative of a Three Years' Residence in Japan. By Sir RUTHERFORD ALCOCK, K.C.B., Her Majesty's Envoy Extraordinary and Minister Plenipotentiary in Japan. With Maps and Engravings. 2 vols., 12mo, Cloth, $3 50.

ALISON'S HISTORY OF EUROPE. FIRST SERIES: From the Commencement of the French Revolution, in 1789, to the Restoration of the Bourbons, in 1815. [In addition to the Notes on Chapter LXXVI., which correct the errors of the original work concerning the United States, a copious Analytical Index has been appended to this American edition.] SECOND SERIES: From the Fall of Napoleon, in 1815, to the Accession of Louis Napoleon, in 1852. 8 vols., 8vo, Cloth, $16 00.

BANCROFT'S MISCELLANIES. Literary and Historical Miscellanies. By GEORGE BANCROFT. 8vo, Cloth, $3 00.

BALDWIN'S PRE-HISTORIC NATIONS. Pre-Historic Nations; or, Inquiries concerning some of the Great Peoples and Civilizations of Antiquity, and their Probable Relation to a still Older Civilization of the Ethiopians or Cushites of Arabia. By JOHN D. BALDWIN, Member of the American Oriental Society. 12mo, Cloth, $1 75.

BARTH'S NORTH AND CENTRAL AFRICA. Travels and Discoveries in North and Central Africa: being a Journal of an Expedition undertaken under the Auspices of H. B. M.'s Government, in the Years 1849–1855. By HENRY BARTH, Ph.D., D.C.L. Illustrated. 3 vols., 8vo, Cloth, $12 00.

HENRY WARD BEECHER'S SERMONS. Sermons by HENRY WARD BEECHER, Plymouth Church, Brooklyn. Selected from Published and Unpublished Discourses, and Revised by their Author. With Steel Portrait. Complete in 2 vols., 8vo, Cloth, $5 00.

LYMAN BEECHER'S AUTOBIOGRAPHY, &c. Autobiography, Correspondence, &c., of Lyman Beecher, D.D. Edited by his Son, CHARLES BEECHER. With Three Steel Portraits, and Engravings on Wood. In 2 vols., 12mo, Cloth, $5 00.

BOSWELL'S JOHNSON. The Life of Samuel Johnson, LL.D. Including a Journey to the Hebrides. By JAMES BOSWELL, Esq. A New Edition, with numerous Additions and Notes. By JOHN WILSON CROKER, LL.D., F.R.S. Portrait of Boswell. 2 vols., 8vo, Cloth, $4 00.

DRAPER'S CIVIL WAR. History of the American Civil War. By JOHN W. DRAPER, M.D., LL.D., Professor of Chemistry and Physiology in the University of New York. In Three Vols. 8vo, Cloth, $3 50 per vol.

DRAPER'S INTELLECTUAL DEVELOPMENT OF EUROPE. A History of the Intellectual Development of Europe. By JOHN W. DRAPER, M.D., LL.D., Professor of Chemistry and Physiology in the University of New York. 8vo, Cloth, $5 00.

DRAPER'S AMERICAN CIVIL POLICY. Thoughts on the Future Civil Policy of America. By JOHN W. DRAPER, M.D., LL.D., Professor of Chemistry and Physiology in the University of New York. Crown 8vo, Cloth, $2 50.

DU CHAILLU'S AFRICA. Explorations and Adventures in Equatorial Africa: with Accounts of the Manners and Customs of the People, and of the Chase of the Gorilla, the Crocodile, Leopard, Elephant, Hippopotamus, and other Animals. By PAUL B. DU CHAILLU. Numerous Illustrations. 8vo, Cloth, $5 00.

DU CHAILLU'S ASHANGO LAND. A Journey to Ashango Land: and Further Penetration into Equatorial Africa. By PAUL B. DU CHAILLU. New Edition. Handsomely Illustrated. 8vo, Cloth, $5 00.

BURNS'S LIFE AND WORKS. The Life and Works of Robert Burns. Edited by ROBERT CHAMBERS. 4 vols., 12mo, Cloth, $6 00.

BELLOWS'S OLD WORLD. The Old World in its New Face: Impressions of Europe in 1867–1868. By HENRY W. BELLOWS. 2 vols., 12mo, Cloth, $3 50.

BRODHEAD'S HISTORY OF NEW YORK. History of the State of New York. By JOHN ROMEYN BRODHEAD. First Period, 1609–1664. 8vo, Cloth, $3 00.

BULWER'S PROSE WORKS. Miscellaneous Prose Works of Edward Bulwer, Lord Lytton. 2 vols., 12mo, Cloth, $3 50.

CARLYLE'S FREDERICK THE GREAT. History of Friedrich II., called Frederick the Great. By THOMAS CARLYLE. Portraits, Maps, Plans, &c. 6 vols., 12mo, Cloth, $12 00.

CARLYLE'S FRENCH REVOLUTION. History of the French Revolution. Newly Revised by the Author, with Index, &c. 2 vols., 12mo, Cloth, $3 50.

CARLYLE'S OLIVER CROMWELL. Letters and Speeches of Oliver Cromwell. With Elucidations and Connecting Narrative. 2 vols., 12mo, Cloth, $3 50.

CHALMERS'S POSTHUMOUS WORKS. The Posthumous Works of Dr. Chalmers. Edited by his Son-in-Law, Rev. WILLIAM HANNA, LL.D. Complete in 9 vols., 12mo, Cloth, $13 50.

COLERIDGE'S COMPLETE WORKS. The Complete Works of Samuel Taylor Coleridge. With an Introductory Essay upon his Philosophical and Theological Opinions. Edited by Professor SHEDD. Complete in Seven Vols. With a fine Portrait. Small 8vo, Cloth, $10 50.

CURTIS'S HISTORY OF THE CONSTITUTION. History of the Origin, Formation, and Adoption of the Constitution of the United States. By GEORGE TICKNOR CURTIS. 2 vols., 8vo, Cloth, $6 00.

DOOLITTLE'S CHINA. Social Life of the Chinese: with some Account of their Religious, Governmental, Educational, and Business Customs and Opinions. With special but not exclusive Reference to Fuhchau. By Rev. JUSTUS DOOLITTLE, Fourteen Years Member of the Fuhchau Mission of the American Board. Illustrated with more than 150 characteristic Engravings on Wood. 2 vols., 12mo, Cloth, $5 00.

DAVIS'S CARTHAGE. Carthage and her Remains: being an Account of the Excavations and Researches on the Site of the Phœnician Metropolis in Africa and other adjacent Places. Conducted under the Auspices of Her Majesty's Government. By Dr. DAVIS, F.R.G.S. Profusely Illustrated with Maps, Woodcuts, Chromo-Lithographs, &c. 8vo, Cloth, $4 00.

EDGEWORTH'S (MISS) NOVELS. With Engravings. 10 vols., 12mo, Cloth, $15 00.

GIBBON'S ROME. History of the Decline and Fall of the Roman Empire. By EDWARD GIBBON. With Notes by Rev. H. H. MILMAN and M. GUIZOT. A new cheap Edition. To which is added a complete Index of the whole Work, and a Portrait of the Author. 6 vols., 12mo, Cloth, $9 00.

HARPER'S PICTORIAL HISTORY OF THE REBELLION. Harper's Pictorial History of the Great Rebellion in the United States. With nearly 1000 Illustrations. In Two Vols., 4to. Price $6 00 per vol.

HARPER'S NEW CLASSICAL LIBRARY. Literal Translations.

The following Volumes are now ready. Portraits. 12mo, Cloth, $1 50 each.

CÆSAR.—VIRGIL.—SALLUST.—HORACE.—CICERO'S ORATIONS.—CICERO'S OFFICES, &c.—CICERO ON ORATORY AND ORATORS.—TACITUS (2 vols.).—TERENCE.—SOPHOCLES.—JUVENAL.—XENOPHON.—HOMER'S ILIAD.—HOMER'S ODYSSEY.—HERODOTUS.—DEMOSTHENES.—THUCYDIDES.—ÆSCHYLUS.—EURIPIDES (2 vols.).

HELPS'S SPANISH CONQUEST. The Spanish Conquest in America, and its Relation to the History of Slavery and to the Government of Colonies. By ARTHUR HELPS. 4 vols., 12mo, Cloth, $6 00.

HUME'S HISTORY OF ENGLAND. History of England, from the Invasion of Julius Cæsar to the Abdication of James II., 1688. By DAVID HUME. A new Edition, with the Author's last Corrections and Improvements. To which is Prefixed a short Account of his Life, written by Himself. With a Portrait of the Author. 6 vols., 12mo, Cloth, $9 00.

GROTE'S HISTORY OF GREECE. 12 vols., 12mo, Cloth, $18 00.

HALE'S (MRS.) WOMAN'S RECORD. Woman's Record; or, Biographical Sketches of all Distinguished Women, from the Creation to the Present Time. Arranged in Four Eras, with Selections from Female Writers of each Era. By Mrs. SARAH JOSEPHA HALE. Illustrated with more than 200 Portraits. 8vo, Cloth, $5 00.

HALL'S ARCTIC RESEARCHES. Arctic Researches and Life among the Esquimaux: being the Narrative of an Expedition in Search of Sir John Franklin, in the Years 1860, 1861, and 1862. By CHARLES FRANCIS HALL. With Maps and 100 Illustrations. The Illustrations are from Original Drawings by Charles Parsons, Henry L. Stephens, Solomon Eytinge, W. S. L. Jewett, and Granville Perkins, after Sketches by Captain Hall. 8vo, Cloth, $5 00.

HALLAM'S CONSTITUTIONAL HISTORY OF ENGLAND, from the Accession of Henry VII. to the Death of George II. 8vo, Cloth, $2 00.

HALLAM'S LITERATURE. Introduction to the Literature of Europe during the Fifteenth, Sixteenth, and Seventeenth Centuries. By HENRY HALLAM. 2 vols., 8vo, Cloth, $4 00.

HALLAM'S MIDDLE AGES. State of Europe during the Middle Ages. By HENRY HALLAM. 8vo, Cloth, $2 00.

HILDRETH'S HISTORY OF THE UNITED STATES. FIRST SERIES: From the First Settlement of the Country to the Adoption of the Federal Constitution. SECOND SERIES: From the Adoption of the Federal Constitution to the End of the Sixteenth Congress. 6 vols., 8vo, Cloth, $18 00.

JAY'S WORKS. Complete Works of Rev. William Jay: comprising his Sermons, Family Discourses, Morning and Evening Exercises for every Day in the Year, Family Prayers, &c. Author's enlarged Edition, revised. 3 vols., 8vo, Cloth, $6 00.

JOHNSON'S COMPLETE WORKS. The Works of Samuel Johnson, LL.D. With an Essay on his Life and Genius, by ARTHUR MURPHY, Esq. Portrait of Johnson. 2 vols., 8vo, Cloth, $4 00.

KINGLAKE'S CRIMEAN WAR. The Invasion of the Crimea, and an Account of its Progress down to the Death of Lord Raglan. By ALEXANDER WILLIAM KINGLAKE. With Maps and Plans. Two Vols. ready. 12mo, Cloth, $2 00 per vol.

KRUMMACHER'S DAVID, KING OF ISRAEL. David, the King of Israel: a Portrait drawn from Bible History and the Book of Psalms. By FREDERICK WILLIAM KRUMMACHER, D.D., Author of "Elijah the Tishbite," &c. Translated under the express Sanction of the Author by the Rev. M. G. EASTON, M.A. With a Letter from Dr. Krummacher to his American Readers, and a Portrait. 12mo, Cloth, $1 75.

LAMB'S COMPLETE WORKS. The Works of Charles Lamb. Comprising his Letters, Poems, Essays of Elia, Essays upon Shakspeare, Hogarth, &c., and a Sketch of his Life, with the Final Memorials, by T. NOON TALFOURD. Portrait. 2 vols., 12mo, Cloth, $3 00.

LIVINGSTONE'S SOUTH AFRICA. Missionary Travels and Researches in South Africa; including a Sketch of Sixteen Years' Residence in the Interior of Africa, and a Journey from the Cape of Good Hope to Loando on the West Coast; thence across the Continent, down the River Zambesi, to the Eastern Ocean. By David Livingstone, LL.D., D.C.L. With Portrait, Maps by Arrowsmith, and numerous Illustrations. 8vo, Cloth, $4 50.

LIVINGSTONES' ZAMBESI. Narrative of an Expedition to the Zambesi and its Tributaries, and of the Discovery of the Lakes Shirwa and Nyassa. 1858-1864. By David and Charles Livingstone. With Map and Illustrations. 8vo, Cloth, $5 00.

M'CLINTOCK & STRONG'S CYCLOPÆDIA. Cyclopædia of Biblical, Theological, and Ecclesiastical Literature. Prepared by the Rev. John M'Clintock, D.D., and James Strong, S.T.D. 3 *vols. now ready.* Royal 8vo. Price per vol., Cloth, $5 00; Sheep, $6 00; Half Morocco, $8 00.

MARCY'S ARMY LIFE ON THE BORDER. Thirty Years of Army Life on the Border. Comprising Descriptions of the Indian Nomads of the Plains; Explorations of New Territory; a Trip across the Rocky Mountains in the Winter; Descriptions of the Habits of Different Animals found in the West, and the Methods of Hunting them; with Incidents in the Life of Different Frontier Men, &c., &c. By Brevet Brigadier-General R. B. Marcy, U.S.A., Author of "The Prairie Traveller." With numerous Illustrations. 8vo, Cloth, Beveled Edges, $3 00.

MACAULAY'S HISTORY OF ENGLAND. The History of England from the Accession of James II. By Thomas Babington Macaulay. With an Original Portrait of the Author. 5 vols., 8vo, Cloth, $10 00; 12mo, Cloth, $7 50.

MOSHEIM'S ECCLESIASTICAL HISTORY, Ancient and Modern; in which the Rise, Progress, and Variation of Church Power are considered in their Connection with the State of Learning and Philosophy, and the Political History of Europe during that Period. Translated, with Notes, &c., by A. Maclaine, D.D. A new Edition, continued to 1826, by C. Coote, LL.D. 2 vols., 8vo, Cloth, $4 00.

NEVIUS'S CHINA. China and the Chinese: a General Description of the Country and its Inhabitants; its Civilization and Form of Government; its Religious and Social Institutions; its Intercourse with other Nations; and its Present Condition and Prospects. By the Rev. John L. Nevius, Ten Years a Missionary in China. With a Map and Illustrations. 12mo, Cloth, $1 75.

OLIN'S (Dr.) LIFE AND LETTERS. 2 vols., 12mo, Cloth, $3 00.

OLIN'S (Dr.) TRAVELS. Travels in Egypt, Arabia Petræa, and the Holy Land. Engravings. 2 vols., 8vo, Cloth, $3 00.

OLIN'S (Dr.) WORKS. The Works of Stephen Olin, D.D., late President of the Wesleyan University. 2 vols., 12mo, Cloth, $3 00.

OLIPHANT'S CHINA AND JAPAN. Narrative of the Earl of Elgin's Mission to China and Japan, in the Years 1857, '58, '59. By Laurence Oliphant, Private Secretary to Lord Elgin. Illustrations. 8vo, Cloth, $3 50.

OLIPHANT'S (Mrs.) LIFE OF EDWARD IRVING. The Life of Edward Irving, Minister of the National Scotch Church, London. Illustrated by his Journals and Correspondence. By Mrs. Oliphant. Portrait. 8vo, Cloth, $3 50.

PAGE'S LA PLATA. La Plata, the Argentine Confederation, and Paraguay. Being a Narrative of the Exploration of the Tributaries of the River La Plata and Adjacent Countries, during the Years 1853, '54, '55, and '56, under the Orders of the United States Government. New Edition, containing Farther Explorations in La Plata, during 1859 and '60. By Thomas J. Page, U.S.N., Commander of the Expeditions. With Map and numerous Engravings. 8vo, Cloth, $5 00.

PRIME'S COINS, MEDALS, AND SEALS. Coins, Medals, and Seals, Ancient and Modern. Illustrated and Described. With a Sketch of the History of Coins and Coinage, Instructions for Young Collectors, Tables of Comparative Rarity, Price-Lists of English and American Coins, Medals, and Tokens, &c., &c. Edited by W. C. Prime, Author of "Boat Life in Egypt and Nubia," "Tent Life in the Holy Land," &c., &c. 8vo, Cloth, $3 50.

SPRING'S SERMONS. Pulpit Ministrations; or, Sabbath Readings. A Series of Discourses on Christian Doctrine and Duty. By Rev. Gardiner Spring, D.D., Pastor of the Brick Presbyterian Church in the City of New York. Portrait on Steel. 2 vols., 8vo, Cloth, $6 00.

POETS OF THE NINETEENTH CENTURY. The Poets of the Nineteenth Century. Selected and Edited by the Rev. ROBERT ARIS WILLMOTT. With English and American Additions, arranged by EVERT A. DUYCKINCK, Editor of "Cyclopædia of American Literature." Comprising Selections from the Greatest Authors of the Age. Superbly Illustrated with 132 Engravings from Designs by the most Eminent Artists. In elegant small 4to form, printed on Superfine Tinted Paper, richly bound in extra Cloth, Beveled, Gilt Edges, $6 00; Half Calf, $6 00; Full Turkey Morocco, $10 00.

SHAKSPEARE. The Dramatic Works of William Shakspeare, with the Corrections and Illustrations of Dr. JOHNSON, G. STEEVENS, and others. Revised by ISAAC REED. Engravings. 6 vols., Royal 12mo, Cloth, $9 00.

SMILES'S LIFE OF THE STEPHENSONS. The Life of George Stephenson, and of his Son, Robert Stephenson; comprising, also, a History of the Invention and Introduction of the Railway Locomotive. By SAMUEL SMILES, Author of "Self-Help," &c. With Steel Portraits and numerous Illustrations. 8vo, Cloth, $3 00.

SMILES'S HISTORY OF THE HUGUENOTS. The Huguenots: their Settlements, Churches, and Industries in England and Ireland. By SAMUEL SMILES. With an Appendix relating to the Huguenots in America. Crown 8vo, Cloth, Beveled, $1 75.

SMILES'S SELF-HELP. Self-Help; with Illustrations of Character, Conduct, and Perseverance. By SAMUEL SMILES. New Edition, Revised and Enlarged. 12mo, Cloth, $1 00.

SPEKE'S AFRICA. Journal of the Discovery of the Source of the Nile. By Captain JOHN HANNING SPEKE, Captain H. M. Indian Army, Fellow and Gold Medalist of the Royal Geographical Society, Hon. Corresponding Member and Gold Medalist of the French Geographical Society, &c. With Maps and Portraits and numerous Illustrations, chiefly from Drawings by Captain GRANT. 8vo, Cloth, uniform with Livingstone, Barth, Burton, &c., $4 00.

STRICKLAND'S (MISS) QUEENS OF SCOTLAND. Lives of the Queens of Scotland and English Princesses connected with the Regal Succession of Great Britain. By AGNES STRICKLAND. 8 vols., 12mo, Cloth, $12 00.

THE STUDENT'S HISTORIES.

France. Engravings. 12mo, Cloth, $2 00.
Gibbon. Engravings. 12mo, Cloth, $2 00.
Greece. Engravings. 12mo, Cloth, $2 00.
Hume. Engravings. 12mo, Cloth, $2 00.
Rome. By Liddell. Engravings. 12mo, Cloth, $2 00.
Old Testament History. Engravings. 12mo, Cloth, $2 00.
New Testament History. Engravings. 12mo, Cloth, $2 00.
Strickland's Queens of England. Abridged. Engravings. 12mo, Cloth, $2 00.

TENNYSON'S COMPLETE POEMS. The Complete Poems of Alfred Tennyson, Poet Laureate. With numerous Illustrations by Eminent Artists, and Three Characteristic Portraits. 8vo, Paper, 50 cents; Cloth, $1 00.

THOMSON'S LAND AND THE BOOK. The Land and the Book; or, Biblical Illustrations drawn from the Manners and Customs, the Scenes and the Scenery of the Holy Land. By W. M. THOMSON, D.D., Twenty-five Years a Missionary of the A.B.C.F.M. in Syria and Palestine. With two elaborate Maps of Palestine, an accurate Plan of Jerusalem, and several hundred Engravings, representing the Scenery, Topography, and Productions of the Holy Land, and the Costumes, Manners, and Habits of the People. 2 large 12mo vols., Cloth, $5 00.

TICKNOR'S HISTORY OF SPANISH LITERATURE. With Criticisms on the particular Works, and Biographical Notices of Prominent Writers. 3 vols., 8vo, Cloth, $5 00.

VÁMBÉRY'S CENTRAL ASIA. Travels in Central Asia. Being the Account of a Journey from Teheran across the Turkoman Desert, on the Eastern Shore of the Caspian, to Khiva, Bokhara, and Samarcand, performed in the Year 1863. By ARMINIUS VÁMBÉRY, Member of the Hungarian Academy of Pesth, by whom he was sent on this Scientific Mission. With Map and Woodcuts. 8vo, Cloth, $4 50.

WOOD'S HOMES WITHOUT HANDS. Homes Without Hands: being a Description of the Habitations of Animals, classed according to their Principle of Construction. By J. G. WOOD, M.A., F.L.S., Author of "Illustrated Natural History." With about 140 Illustrations, engraved by G. Pearson, from Original Designs made by F. W. Keyl and E. A. Smith under the Author's Superintendence. 8vo, Cloth, Beveled Edges, $4 50.

www.ingramcontent.com/pod-product-compliance
Lightning Source LLC
LaVergne TN
LVHW010142110826
845151LV00002B/404

* 9 7 8 1 4 2 5 5 3 8 7 3 6 *